CONSUMER PRIVACY
AND DATA PROTECTION

Aspen Custom Publishing Series

CONSUMER PRIVACY AND DATA PROTECTION

First Edition

Daniel J. Solove
John Marshall Harlan Research Professor of Law
George Washington University Law School

Paul M. Schwartz
Jefferson E. Peyser Professor of Law
U.C. Berkeley Law School

Published by Wolters Kluwer in New York.

Wolters Kluwer serves customers worldwide with CCH, Aspen Publishers, and Kluwer Law International products. (www.wolterskluwerlb.com)

To contact Customer Care, e-mail customer.service@wolterskluwer.com, call 1-800-234-1660, fax 1-800-901-9075, or mail correspondence to:

> Wolters Kluwer
> Attn: Order Department
> PO Box 990
> Frederick, MD 21705

Printed in the United States of America.

1 2 3 4 5 6 7 8 9 0

ISBN 978-1-4548-6154-6

About Wolters Kluwer Law & Business

Wolters Kluwer Law & Business is a leading global provider of intelligent information and digital solutions for legal and business professionals in key specialty areas, and respected educational resources for professors and law students. Wolters Kluwer Law & Business connects legal and business professionals as well as those in the education market with timely, specialized authoritative content and information-enabled solutions to support success through productivity, accuracy and mobility.

Serving customers worldwide, Wolters Kluwer Law & Business products include those under the Aspen Publishers, CCH, Kluwer Law International, Loislaw, ftwilliam.com and MediRegs family of products.

CCH products have been a trusted resource since 1913, and are highly regarded resources for legal, securities, antitrust and trade regulation, government contracting, banking, pension, payroll, employment and labor, and healthcare reimbursement and compliance professionals.

Aspen Publishers products provide essential information to attorneys, business professionals and law students. Written by preeminent authorities, the product line offers analytical and practical information in a range of specialty practice areas from securities law and intellectual property to mergers and acquisitions and pension/benefits. Aspen's trusted legal education resources provide professors and students with high-quality, up-to-date and effective resources for successful instruction and study in all areas of the law.

Kluwer Law International products provide the global business community with reliable international legal information in English. Legal practitioners, corporate counsel and business executives around the world rely on Kluwer Law journals, looseleafs, books, and electronic products for comprehensive information in many areas of international legal practice.

Loislaw is a comprehensive online legal research product providing legal content to law firm practitioners of various specializations. Loislaw provides attorneys with the ability to quickly and efficiently find the necessary legal information they need, when and where they need it, by facilitating access to primary law as well as state-specific law, records, forms and treatises.

ftwilliam.com offers employee benefits professionals the highest quality plan documents (retirement, welfare and non-qualified) and government forms (5500/PBGC, 1099 and IRS) software at highly competitive prices.

MediRegs products provide integrated health care compliance content and software solutions for professionals in healthcare, higher education and life sciences, including professionals in accounting, law and consulting.

Wolters Kluwer Law & Business, a division of Wolters Kluwer, is headquartered in New York. Wolters Kluwer is a market-leading global information services company focused on professionals.

To my parents and grandparents—DJS

To Steffie, Clara, and Leo—PMS

SUMMARY OF CONTENTS

CONTENTS

PREFACE

The rapid growth of the Internet, coupled with new business practices and new efforts by government to deploy technology for law enforcement and the administration of programs, has raised far-reaching questions about the future of privacy.

Central to many of these debates is the role of law. To what extent can the law safeguard the right of privacy in an era of rapidly evolving technology? What competing interests must be considered? What is the appropriate role of the courts and the legislatures? These questions are not new, but they have acquired greater urgency as the law is asked to evaluate an increasingly complex array of privacy matters.

For lawyers, this rapid growth has raised both new challenges and new opportunities. In the private sector, attorneys now routinely advise business clients about the development of privacy policies, compliance with privacy statutes, and privacy regulations in new markets. Attorneys litigate on behalf of clients who believe that their privacy has been violated, while others defend against these allegations. State attorneys general have become leading champions of privacy rights. Policymakers in government evaluate new legislative proposals both to expand and to limit privacy claims. Legal advisors on trade policy, technology development, consumer protection, and national security all consider privacy issues in the course of their work. Clearly, information privacy has emerged as one of the critical legal subjects in the modern era.

This text aims to provide a comprehensive and accessible introduction to the legal, social, and political issues involving information privacy. The text begins with a broad introduction to the conceptual underpinnings of information privacy. It sets forth clearly and concisely the range of laws that address information privacy, and it discusses the basic policy issues that inhabit the field. The text then examines the legal and policy implications of the growing accumulation and use of financial data. The next chapters examine the regulation of consumer data and the expanding legal requirements for data security. We have included extensive notes and commentary, and have integrated cases and statutes with theoretical and policy perspectives. To facilitate discussion and debate, we have included excerpts from commentators with a wide range of viewpoints. Technical terms are clearly explained.

When selecting cases, we have included the leading cases as well as endeavoured to provide a solid historical background and a timely and fresh perspective on the major privacy issues facing lawyers in the twenty-first century. Important majority opinions are followed by equally important dissents. The text includes extensive notes and commentary, and it integrates cases and statutes with theoretical and policy perspectives. To facilitate discussion and debate, we have included excerpts from commentators with a wide range of viewpoints. Technical terms are clearly explained.

A Note on the Casebook Website. We strive to keep the book up to date between editions, and we maintain a web page for the book with downloadable updates and other useful information. We invite you to visit the website:

http://informationprivacylaw.com

A Note on New Changes to the Book. We made many changes and updates to the book but have retained its basic organizational structure and pedagogical style. Specific changes and additions to the book are documented in the Teacher's Manual.

A Note on the Editing. We have deleted many citations and footnotes from the cases to facilitate readability. The footnotes that have been retained in the cases have been renumbered. When discussing books, articles, and other materials in the notes and commentary, we have included full citations in footnotes in order to make the text easier to read. We have also included many citations to additional works in the footnotes that may be of interest to the reader.

Daniel J. Solove
Paul M. Schwartz

November 2014

ACKNOWLEDGMENTS

Daniel J. Solove: I would like to thank Carl Coleman, Scott Forbes, Susan Freiwald, Tomás Gómez-Arostegui, Stephen Gottlieb, Marcia Hofmann, Chris Hoofnagle, John Jacobi, Orin Kerr, Raymond Ku, Peter Raven-Hansen, Joel Reidenberg, Neil Richards, Michael Risinger, Lior Strahilevitz, Peter Swire, William Thompson, and Peter Winn for helpful comments and suggestions. Charlie Sullivan and Jake Barnes provided indispensable advice about how to bring this project to fruition. Special thanks to Richard Mixter at Aspen Publishers for his encouragement and faith in this project. Thanks as well to the other folks at Aspen who have contributed greatly to the editing and development of this book: John Devins, Christine Hannan, Carmen Reid, Jessica Barmack, John Burdeaux, and Sandra Doherty. I would like to thank my research assistants Peter Choy, Monica Contreras, Carly Grey, Maeve Miller, James Murphy, Poornima Ravishankar, Sheerin Shahinpoor, Vladimir Semendyai, John Spaccarotella, Tiffany Stedman, Lourdes Turrecha, Eli Weiss, and Kate Yannitte. I would also like to thank Dean Blake Morant for providing the resources I needed. And thanks to my wife Pamela Solove and son Griffin Solove, who kept me in good cheer throughout this project.

Paul M. Schwartz: For their suggestions, encouragement, and insights into information privacy law, I would like to thank Ken Bamberger, Fred Cate, Malcolm Crompton, Christopher Gulotta, Andrew Guzman, Chris Hoofnagle, Ted Janger, Ronald D. Lee, Lance Liebman, Steven McDonald, Viktor Mayer-Schönberger, Deirdre Mulligan, Karl-Nikolaus Peifer, Joel Reidenberg, Ira Rubinstein, Pam Samuelson, Lior Strahilevitz, Peter Swire, William M. Treanor, and Peter Winn. I benefited as well from the help of my talented research assistants: Cesar Alvarez, Henry Becker, Benedikt Burger, Sarah Chai, Kai-Dieter Classen, Leah Duranti, Sarah Haji, Anne Hilby, Thaddeus Houston, Jesse Koehler, Leah Mekhneche, Devon Mongeluzzi, Joseph Mornin, Alpa Patel, Karl Saddlemire, Brian St. John, Malvika Sinha, Laura Sullivan, and Sebastian Zimmeck. Many thanks to my co-author, Daniel Solove. Many thanks as well to my mother, Nancy Schwartz, and to Laura Schwartz and Ed Holden; David Schwartz and Kathy Smith; and Daniel Schwartz.

A profound debt is owed Spiros Simitis. My interest in the subject of information privacy began in 1985 with his suggestion that I visit his office of the Hessian Data Protection Commissioner in Wiesbaden and sit in on meetings there. Through his scholarship, example, and friendship, Professor Simitis has provided essential guidance during the decades since that initial trip to Wiesbaden. My portion of the book is dedicated to Steffie, Clara, and Leo, with my gratitude and love.

Finally, both of us would like to thank Marc Rotenberg, who helped us shape the book in its first two editions and provided invaluable input.

We are grateful to the following sources for their permission to reprint excerpts of their scholarship:

Anita L. Allen, *Coercing Privacy*, 40 William & Mary L. Rev. 723 (1999). Used by permission. © 1999 by William & Mary Law Review and Anita L. Allen.

William C. Banks & M.E. Bowman, *Executive Authority For National Security Surveillance,* 50 Am. U. L. Rev. 1 (2000). Reprinted with permission.

Fred H. Cate, *The Privacy Problem: A Broader View of Information Privacy and the Costs and Consequences of Protecting It*, 4 First Reports 1 (March 2003). Reprinted with permission.

Julie E. Cohen, *Examined Lives: Informational Privacy*, 52 Stan. L. Rev. 1371 (2000). © 2000. Reprinted by permission of the Stanford Law Review in the format textbook via Copyright Clearance Center and Julie Cohen.

Julie E. Cohen, *A Right to Read Anonymously: A Closer Look at "Copyright Management" in Cyberspace,* 28 Conn. L. Rev. 981 (1996). © 1996 by Connecticut Law Review and Julie E. Cohen. Reprinted with permission.

Mary DeRosa, *Data Mining and Data Analysis for Counterterrorism,* Center for Strategic and International Studies 6-8 (CSIS) (2004). Reprinted with permission.

Eric Goldman, *The Privacy Hoax,* Forbes (Oct. 14, 2002) available at http:// www.ericgoldman.org/Articles/privacyhoax.htm. Reprinted with permission. Lawrence O. Gostin, Health Information Privacy, 80 Cornell L. Rev. 451 (1995). Reprinted with permission.

Steven Hetcher, *The FTC as Internet Privacy Norm Entrepreneur*, 53 Vand. L. Rev. 2041 (2000). Reprinted with the permission of Steven Hetcher.

Edward Janger & Paul M. Schwartz, *The Gramm-Leach-Bliley Act, Information Privacy, and the Limits of Default Rules*, 86 Minn. L. Rev. 1219 (2002). Reprinted with permission.

Orin S. Kerr, *A User's Guide to the Stored Communications Act — and a Legislator's Guide to Amending It*, 72 Geo. Wash. L. Rev. 1208 (2004). Reprinted with permission.

Orin S. Kerr, *Internet Surveillance Law After the USA PATRIOT Act: The Big Brother That Isn't*, 97 Nw. U. L. Rev. 607 (2003). Reprinted with permission.

Catharine A. MacKinnon, Toward a Feminist Theory of the State 190-193 (1989). © 1989 by Harvard University Press. Reprinted with permission.

Richard A. Posner, *The Right of Privacy,* 12 Ga. L. Rev. 393 (1978). Reprinted with permission.

Marc Rotenberg, *Fair Information Practices and the Architecture of Privacy (What Larry Doesn't Get)*, 2001 Stan. Tech. L. Rev. 1, 43 (2001). Reprinted with permission.

Paul M. Schwartz, *Privacy and Democracy in Cyberspace*, 52 Vand. L. Rev. 1609 (1999). Reprinted with the permission of Paul Schwartz.

Reva B. Seigel, *The Rule of Love: Wife Beating as Prerogative of Privacy*, 105 Yale L.J. 2117 (1996). Reprinted by permission of the *Yale Law Journal* Company and the William S. Hein Company, from the *Yale Law Journal,* vol. 105, pages 2117-2207.

Spiros Simitis, *Reviewing Privacy in an Informational Society*, 135 U. Pa. L. Rev. 707, 709-710, 724-726, 732-738, 746 (1987). © 1987 by the University of Pennsylvania Law Review. Reprinted by permission of the University of Pennsylvania Law Review and Spiros Simitis.

Daniel J. Solove, *Conceptualizing Privacy,* 90 California Law Review 1087 (2002). © 2002 by the California Law Review.

Daniel J. Solove, *Reconstructing Electronic Surveillance Law*, 72 George Washington Law Review 1264 (2004). © 2004 by Daniel J. Solove.

Daniel J. Solove, *The Virtues of Knowing Less: Justifying Privacy Protections Against Disclosure*, 53 Duke Law Journal 967 (2003). © 2003 by Daniel J. Solove.

Jeff Sovern, *Opting In, Opting Out, or No Options at All: The Fight for Control of Personal Information*, 74 Wash. L. Rev. 1033 (1999). Reprinted with permission.

Michael E. Staten & Fred H. Cate, *The Impact of Opt-In Privacy Rules on Retail Markets: A Case Study of MBNA*, 52 Duke L.J. 745 (2003). Reprinted with permission.

Alan Westin, Privacy and Freedom 7, 31-38 (1967). A study sponsored by the Association of the Bar of the City of New York. Reprinted with permission.

Peter A. Winn, *Online Court Records: Balancing Judicial Accountability and Privacy in an Age of Electronic Information*, 79 Wash. L. Rev. 307 (2004). Reprinted with permission.

CONSUMER PRIVACY AND DATA PROTECTION

CHAPTER 1

INTRODUCTION

CHAPTER OUTLINE

A. INFORMATION PRIVACY, TECHNOLOGY, AND THE LAW

We live in a world shaped by technology and fueled by information. Technological devices — such as mobile phones, video and audio recording devices, computers, and the Internet — have revolutionized our ability to capture information about the world and to communicate with each other. Information is the lifeblood of today's society. Increasingly, our everyday activities involve the transfer and recording of information. The government collects vast quantities of personal information in records pertaining to an individual's birth, marriage, divorce, property, court proceedings, motor vehicles, voting activities, criminal transgressions, professional licensing, and other activities. Private sector entities also amass gigantic databases of personal information for marketing purposes or to prepare credit histories. Wherever we go, whatever we do, we could easily leave behind a trail of data that is recorded and gathered together.

These new technologies, coupled with the increasing use of personal information by business and government, pose new challenges for the protection of privacy. This book is about the law's response to new challenges to privacy. A significant amount of law regulates information privacy in the United States and around the world. Is this law responsive to the present and future dangers to privacy? Can information privacy itself endanger other important values? What duties and responsibilities must corporations, government agencies, and other private and public sector entities have with regard to personal data? What rights do individuals have to prevent and redress invasions to their privacy? When and how should privacy rights be limited? Does the war on terrorism require less privacy and more sharing of information? How should the law respond to an age of rapid technological change? Has the meaning of privacy changed in the age of social media and powerful search engines? These are some of the questions that this text will address.

This book's topic is information privacy law. Information privacy concerns the collection, use, and disclosure of personal information. Information privacy is often contrasted with "decisional privacy," which concerns the freedom to make decisions about one's body and family. Decisional privacy involves matters such as contraception, procreation, abortion, and child rearing, and is at the center of a series of Supreme Court cases often referred to as "substantive due process" or "the constitutional right to privacy." But information privacy increasingly incorporates elements of decisional privacy as the use of data both expands and limits individual autonomy.

Information privacy law is an interrelated web of tort law, federal and state constitutional law, federal and state statutory law, evidentiary privileges, property law, contract law, and criminal law. Information privacy law is relatively new, although its roots reach far back. It is developing coherence as privacy doctrines in one area are being used to inform and structure legal responses in other areas. Information privacy law raises a related set of political, policy, and philosophical questions: What is privacy? Why is privacy important? What is the impact of technology on privacy? How does privacy affect the efforts of law enforcement and national security agencies to protect the public? What is the role of the courts, the legislatures, and the law in safeguarding, or in placing limits on, privacy?

Furthermore, one might wonder: Why study information privacy law? There are a number of answers to this question. First, in today's Information Age, privacy is an issue of paramount significance for freedom, democracy, and security. One of the central issues of information privacy concerns the power of commercial and government entities over individual autonomy and decision making. Privacy also concerns the drawing of rules that may limit this autonomy and decision making by necessarily permitting commercial and government entities access to personal information. Understood broadly, information privacy plays an important role in the society we are constructing in today's Information Age.

Second, information privacy is an issue of growing public concern. Information privacy has become a priority on the legislative agenda of Congress and many state legislatures. Information privacy problems are also timely, frequently in the news, and often the subject of litigation.

Third, there are many new laws and legal developments regarding information privacy. It is a growth area in the law. Increased litigation, legislation, regulation, as well as public concern over privacy are spurring corporations in a variety of businesses to address privacy. Lawyers are drafting privacy policies, litigating privacy issues, and developing ways for dot-com companies, corporations, hospitals, insurers, and banks to conform to privacy regulations. A new position, the Chief Privacy Officer, is a mainstay at most corporations. The leading organization of these officers, the International Association of Privacy Professionals (IAPP), boasts thousands of members. Attorneys increasingly are grappling with privacy issues — either through litigation of privacy violations or through measures to comply with privacy regulations and to prevent litigation. All of these developments demand lawyers who are well-versed in the grand scheme and subtle nuances of information privacy law.

Fourth, information privacy law is an engaging and fascinating topic. The issues are controversial, complex, relevant, and current. Few areas of law are more closely intertwined with our world of rapid technological innovation. Moreover, concerns regarding information privacy play an important role in debates regarding security in post-9/11 America. The study of privacy law also helps us understand how our legal institutions respond to change and may help prepare us for other challenges ahead.

B. INFORMATION PRIVACY LAW: ORIGINS AND TYPES

Information privacy law is a wide-ranging body of law, encompassing common law, constitutional law, statutory law, and international law. This section will provide a brief introduction to the various strands of information privacy law that will be covered throughout this book. It begins by looking in detail at the most important article ever written about privacy.

1. COMMON LAW

(a) The Warren and Brandeis Article

The common law's development of tort remedies to protect privacy is one of the most significant chapters in the history of privacy law. In the late nineteenth century, considerable concerns about privacy captured the public's attention, ultimately resulting in the 1890 publication of Samuel Warren and Louis Brandeis's pathbreaking article, *The Right to Privacy*.[1] According to Roscoe Pound, the article did "nothing less than add a chapter to our law."[2] Harry Kalven

---

[1] Samuel Warren & Louis Brandeis, *The Right to Privacy*, 4 Harv. L. Rev. 193 (1890).
[2] Quoted in Alpheus Mason, *Brandeis: A Free Man's Life* 70 (1946).

even hailed it as the "most influential law review article of all."[3] The clearest indication of the article's ongoing vitality can be found in the Supreme Court's decision *Kyllo v. United States*, 533 U.S. 27 (2001). The Brandeis and Warren article is cited by the majority, those in concurrence, and even those in dissent.

Several developments in the late nineteenth century created a growing interest in privacy. First, the press became increasingly sensationalistic. Prior to the Civil War, wide-circulation newspapers were rare. However, the development of a new form of sensationalistic journalism, known as "yellow journalism," made newspapers wildly successful. In 1833, Benjamin Day began publishing a newspaper called *The Sun* patterned after the "penny presses" in London (so named because they sold for a penny). The *Sun* contained news of scandals, such as family squabbles, public drunkenness, and petty crimes. In about four months, the *Sun* had a circulation of 4,000, almost the same as the existing New York daily papers. Just two months later, the *Sun* was reaching 8,000 in circulation. Other penny press papers soon followed. In reporting on his travels in America, Charles Dickens observed that New York newspapers were "pulling off the roofs of private houses."[4] In his great novel of 1844, *The Life and Adventures of Martin Chuzzlewit*, he listed (imaginary) New York newspapers called *The Sewer, The Stabber, The Family Spy, The Private Listener, The Peeper, The Plunderer,* and *The Keyhole Reporter.*[5]

Between 1850 and 1890, newspaper circulation increased about 1,000 percent — from 100 papers with 800,000 readers to 900 papers with more than 8 million readers. Joseph Pulitzer and William Randolph Hearst became the leading rivals in the newspaper business, each amassing newspaper empires. Their highly sensationalistic journalism became the paradigm for yellow journalism.[6]

Second, technological developments caused great alarm for privacy. In their article, Warren and Brandeis pointed to the invention of "instantaneous photography" as a new challenge to privacy. Photography had been around for many years before Warren and Brandeis penned their article. However, the equipment was expensive, cumbersome, and complicated to use. In 1884, the Eastman Kodak Company introduced the "snap camera," a handheld camera that was small and cheap enough for use by the general public. The snap camera allowed people to take candid photographs in public places for the first time. In the late nineteenth century, few daily newspapers even printed drawings, let alone photographs. Warren and Brandeis, however, astutely recognized the potential for the new technology of cameras to be used by the sensationalistic press.

The question of the origin of Warren and Brandeis's article has led to considerable debate. Some scholars suggest that Warren and Brandeis were

---

[3] Harry Kalven, Jr., *Privacy in Tort Law — Were Warren and Brandeis Wrong?*, 31 Law & Contemp. Probs. 326, 327 (1966).

[4] Charles Dickens, *American Notes* (1842).

[5] Charles Dickens, *The Life and Adventures of Martin Chuzzlewit* (1844).

[6] For more information about yellow journalism, *see generally* Gini Graham Scott, *Mind Your Own Business: The Battle for Personal Privacy* 37-38 (1995); Robert Ellis Smith, *Ben Franklin's Web Site: Privacy and Curiosity from Plymouth Rock to the Internet* 102-20 (2000).

strongly influenced by an article written in 1890 by E.L. Godkin, a famous social commentator in his day.[7] In the article, Godkin observed:

> . . . Privacy is a distinctly modern product, one of the luxuries of civilization, which is not only unsought for but unknown in primitive or barbarous societies. . . .
>
> The chief enemy of privacy in modern life is that interest in other people and their affairs known as curiosity, which in the days before newspapers created personal gossip. . . . [A]s long as gossip was oral, it spread, as regarded any one individual, over a very small area, and was confined to the immediate circle of his acquaintances. It did not reach, or but rarely reached, those who knew nothing of him. It did not make his name, or his walk, or his conversation familiar to strangers. . . . [G]ossip about private individuals is now printed, and makes its victim, with all his imperfections on his head, known to hundreds or thousands miles away from his place of abode; and, what is worst of all, brings to his knowledge exactly what is said about him, with all its details. It thus inflicts what is, to many men, the great pain of believing that everybody he meets in the street is perfectly familiar with some folly, or misfortune, or indiscretion, or weakness, which he had previously supposed had never got beyond his domestic circle. . . .
>
> In truth, there is only one remedy for the violations of the right to privacy within the reach of the American public, and that is but an imperfect one. It is to be found in attaching social discredit to invasions of it on the part of conductors of the press. At present this check can hardly be said to exist. It is to a large extent nullified by the fact that the offence is often pecuniarily profitable.[8]

Warren and Brandeis referred to Godkin's essay, and their article does bear some similarities to his work. One difference is that Godkin, although recognizing the growing threats to privacy, remained cynical about the possibility of a solution, expressing only the hope that attitudes would change to be more respectful of privacy. Warren and Brandeis had a different view. In their judgment, the law could and should provide protection for privacy.

Another theory suggests that incursions by journalists into the privacy of Samuel Warren inspired the article. Warren, a wealthy and powerful attorney in Boston, practiced law with Louis Brandeis, who later went on to become a U.S. Supreme Court Justice. In 1883, Samuel Warren married Mabel Bayard, the daughter of a prominent senator from Delaware, and set up house in Boston's Back Bay. The Warrens were among the Boston elite and were frequently reported on in the *Saturday Evening Gazette*, "which specialized in 'blue blood items,' " and "reported their activities in lurid detail."[9]

According to William Prosser, Warren was motivated to write the article because reporters intruded upon his daughter's wedding. However, this certainly could not have been the reason because in 1890, Warren's oldest daughter was

---

[7] *See* Elbridge L. Adams, *The Right to Privacy and Its Relation to the Law of Libel*, 39 Am. L. Rev. 37 (1905); Dorothy J. Glancy, *The Invention of the Right to Privacy*, 21 Ariz. L. Rev. 1 (1979).

[8] E.L. Godkin, *The Rights of the Citizen: To His Own Reputation*, Scribner's Mag. (1890); *see also* E.L. Godkin, *The Right to Privacy*, The Nation (Dec. 25, 1890).

[9] Mason, *Brandeis, supra*, at 46.

not even ten years old![10] Most likely, the impetus for writing the article was Warren's displeasure about a number of stories in the *Gazette* about his dinner parties.[11]

Whatever inspired them to write, Warren and Brandeis published an article that profoundly shaped the development of the law of privacy.

(b) The Recognition of Warren and Brandeis's Privacy Torts

Warren and Brandeis's 1890 article suggested that the existing causes of action under the common law did not adequately protect privacy but that the legal concepts in the common law could be modified to achieve the task. As early as 1903, courts and legislatures responded to the Warren and Brandeis article by creating a number of privacy torts to redress the harms that Warren and Brandeis had noted. In *Roberson v. Rochester Folding Box Co.*, 64 N.E. 442 (N.Y. 1902), the New York Court of Appeals refused to recognize a common law tort action for privacy invasions. Franklin Mills Flour displayed a lithograph of Abigail Roberson (a teenager) on 25,000 advertisement flyers without her consent. The lithograph printed her photograph with the advertising pun: "Flour of the Family." Roberson claimed that the use of her image on the flyer caused her great humiliation and resulted in illness requiring medical help. The court, however, concluded:

> . . . There is no precedent for such an action to be found in the decisions of this court. . . . Mention of such a right is not to be found in Blackstone, Kent, or any other of the great commentators upon the law; nor, so far as the learning of counsel or the courts in this case have been able to discover, does its existence seem to have been asserted prior to about the year 1890. . . .
>
> The legislative body could very well interfere and arbitrarily provide that no one should be permitted for his own selfish purpose to use the picture or the name of another for advertising purposes without his general consent. In such event no embarrassment would result to the general body of law, for the law would be applicable only to cases provided for by statute. The courts, however, being without authority to legislate, are required to decide cases upon principle, and so are necessarily embarrassed by precedents created by an extreme, and therefore unjustifiable, application of an old principle. . . . [W]hile justice in a given case may be worked out by a decision of the court according to the notions of right which govern the individual judge or body of judges comprising the court, the mischief which will finally result may be almost incalculable under our system, which makes a decision in one case a precedent for decisions in all future cases which are akin to it in the essential facts. . . .

---

[10] *See* James H. Barron, *Warren and Brandeis*, The Right to Privacy, 4 Harv. L. Rev. 193 (1890): *Demystifying a Landmark Citation*, 13 Suffolk L. Rev. 875 (1979).

[11] *See* Smith, *Ben Franklin's Web Site, supra*, at 118-19. For further discussion of the circumstances surrounding the publication of the article, see Martin Burgess Green, *The Mount Vernon Street Warrens: A Boston Story, 1860–1910* (1989); Morris L. Ernst & Alan U. Schwartz, *Privacy: The Right to Be Let Alone* 45-46 (1962); Philippa Strum, *Brandeis: Beyond Progressivism* (1993); Lewis J. Paper, *Brandeis* (1983); Irwin R. Kramer, *The Birth of Privacy Law: A Century Since Warren and Brandeis*, 39 Cath. U. L. Rev. 703 (1990); Dorothy Glancy, *The Invention of the Right to Privacy*, 21 Ariz. L. Rev. 1, 25-27 (1979); Symposium, *The Right to Privacy One Hundred Years Later*, 41 Case W. Res. L. Rev. 643-928 (1991).

Shortly after the decision, a note in the *Yale Law Journal* criticized the *Roberson* decision because it enabled the press "to pry into and grossly display before the public matters of the most private and personal concern."[12] One of the judges in the majority defended the opinion in the *Columbia Law Review*.[13]

In 1903, the New York legislature responded to the explicit invitation in *Roberson* to legislate by creating a privacy tort action by statute. *See* N.Y. Civ. Rights Act § 51. This statute is still in use today. As you will see again later in this text, courts are frequently engaged in a dialogue with legislatures about the scope of privacy rights.

In the 1905 case *Pavesich v. New England Life Insurance Co.*, 50 S.E. 68 (Ga. 1905), Georgia became the first state to recognize a common law tort action for privacy invasions. There, a newspaper published a life insurance advertisement with a photograph of the plaintiff without the plaintiff's consent. The court held:

> . . . The right of privacy has its foundation in the instincts of nature. It is recognized intuitively, consciousness being the witness that can be called to establish its existence. Any person whose intellect is in a normal condition recognizes at once that as to each individual member of society there are matters private, and there are matters public so far as the individual is concerned. Each individual as instinctively resents any encroachment by the public upon his rights which are of a private nature as he does the withdrawal of those of his rights which are of a public nature. A right of privacy in matters purely private is therefore derived from natural law. . . .
>
> All will admit that the individual who desires to live a life of seclusion cannot be compelled against his consent, to exhibit his person in any public place, unless such exhibition is demanded by the law of the land. He may be required to come from his place of seclusion to perform public duties — to serve as a juror and to testify as a witness and the like; but, when the public duty is once performed, if he exercises his liberty to go again into seclusion, no one can deny him the right. One who desires to live a life of partial seclusion has a right to choose the times, places, and manner in which and at which he will submit himself to the public gaze. Subject to the limitation above referred to, the body of a person cannot be put on exhibition at any time or at any place without his consent. . . .
>
> It therefore follows from what has been said that a violation of the right of privacy is a direct invasion of a legal right of the individual. . . .

In 1960, Dean William Prosser wrote his famous article, *Privacy*, examining the over 300 privacy tort cases decided in the 70 years since the Warren and Brandeis article.

---

[12] *An Actionable Right to Privacy?*, 12 Yale L.J. 34 (1902).

[13] Denis O'Brien, *The Right to Privacy*, 2 Colum. L. Rev. 486 (1902).

WILLIAM PROSSER, *PRIVACY*

48 Cal. L. Rev. 383 (1960)

. . . The law of privacy comprises four distinct kinds of invasion of four different interests of the plaintiff, which are tied together by the common name, but otherwise have almost nothing in common except that each represents an interference with the right of the plaintiff, in the phrase coined by Judge Cooley, "to be let alone." Without any attempt at exact definition, these four torts may be described as follows:

1. Intrusion upon the plaintiff's seclusion or solitude, or into his private affairs.
2. Public disclosure of embarrassing private facts about the plaintiff.
3. Publicity which places the plaintiff in a false light in the public eye.
4. Appropriation, for the defendant's advantage, of the plaintiff's name or likeness. . . .

Judge Briggs has described the present state of the law of privacy as "still that of a haystack in a hurricane." Disarray there certainly is; but almost all of the confusion is due to a failure to separate and distinguish these four forms of invasion and to realize that they call for different things. . . .

Taking them in order — intrusion, disclosure, false light, and appropriation — the first and second require the invasion of something secret, secluded or private pertaining to the plaintiff; the third and fourth do not. The second and third depend upon publicity, while the first does not, nor does the fourth, although it usually involves it. The third requires falsity or fiction; the other three do not. The fourth involves a use for the defendant's advantage, which is not true of the rest. Obviously this is an area in which one must tread warily and be on the lookout for bogs. Nor is the difficulty decreased by the fact that quite often two or more of these forms of invasion may be found in the same case, and quite conceivably in all four.

NOTES & QUESTIONS

1. *The Restatement of Torts.* Prosser's analytical framework imposed order and clarity on the jumbled line of cases that followed the Warren and Brandeis article. The Restatement of Torts recognizes the four torts Prosser described in his article. These torts are known collectively as "invasion of privacy." The torts are: (1) intrusion upon seclusion, (2) public disclosure of private facts, (3) false light, and (4) appropriation.

2. *The Interests Protected by the Privacy Torts.* In response to Prosser's assertion that the privacy torts have almost "nothing in common," Edward Bloustein replied that "what provoked Warren and Brandeis to write their article was a fear that a rampant press feeding on the stuff of private life would destroy individual dignity and integrity and emasculate individual

freedom and independence." This underlying principle is a protection of "human dignity" and "personality."[14]

In contrast to Bloustein, Robert Post contends that the privacy torts do "not simply uphold the interests of individuals against the demands of the community, but instead safeguard[ ] rules of civility that in some significant measure constitute both individuals and community." Post argues that the torts establish boundaries between people, which when violated create strife. The privacy torts promote "forms of respect [for other people] by which we maintain a community."[15]

3. **Prosser's Privacy at 50.** In 2010, the *California Law Review* held a symposium at Berkeley Law School to celebrate the fiftieth anniversary of the publication of Prosser's *Privacy*. The verdict on the momentous article is mixed. Lior Strahilevitz advocates abandoning the Prosser categories and replacing them with a unitary tort for invasion of privacy. The key under the recast privacy tort would simply be whether "the gravity of the harm to the plaintiff's privacy interest [is] outweighed by a paramount public policy interest."[16]

Along similar negative lines, Neil Richards and Daniel Solove concluded that Prosser's view of the privacy tort has been "rigid and ossifying." Dean Prosser "stunted [privacy law's] development in ways that have limited its ability to adapt to the problems of the Information Age." The authors conclude that tort law should look beyond the narrow categories Prosser proposed in order for it to "regain the creative spirit it once possessed." One way for tort law to do so, in their view, would be to adopt the English approach to the tort of confidentiality.[17]

In contrast, Paul Schwartz and Karl-Nikolaus Peifer praised Prosser: "Prosser pragmatically assessed the kind and amount of privacy that the American legal system was willing to accommodate." In their summary, "Prosser's contribution generated useful doctrinal categories where previously had been unclassified cases and a lingering air of skepticism towards the tort."[18]

Would it be useful to extend the four privacy torts as Richards and Solove propose? Or would a better approach be to replace Prosser's four torts with pure balancing as Strahilevitz advocates? Or do Prosser's categories adequately capture the various privacy interests that should be addressed by tort law?

---

[14] Edward J. Bloustein, *Privacy as an Aspect of Human Dignity: An Answer to Dean Prosser*, 39 N.Y.U. L. Rev. 962, 974, 1000-01 (1964).

[15] Robert C. Post, *The Social Foundations of Privacy: Community and Self in the Common Law Tort*, 77 Cal. L. Rev. 957 (1989).

[16] Lior Strahilevitz, *Reunifying Privacy Law*, 98 Cal. L. Rev. 2007 (2010).

[17] Neil Richards & Daniel Solove, *Prosser's Privacy Law: A Mixed Legacy*, 98 Cal. L. Rev. 1887, 1924 (2010).

[18] Paul M. Schwartz & Karl-Nikolaus Peifer, *Prosser's Privacy and the German Right of Personality*, 98 Cal. L. Rev. 1925, 1982 (2010).

LAKE V. WAL-MART STORES, INC.

582 N.W.2d 231 (Minn. 1998)

BLATZ, C.J. . . . Elli Lake and Melissa Weber appeal from a dismissal of their complaint for failure to state a claim upon which relief may be granted. The district court and court of appeals held that Lake and Weber's complaint alleging intrusion upon seclusion, appropriation, publication of private facts, and false light publicity could not proceed because Minnesota does not recognize a common law tort action for invasion of privacy. We reverse as to the claims of intrusion upon seclusion, appropriation, and publication of private facts, but affirm as to false light publicity.

Nineteen-year-old Elli Lake and 20-year-old Melissa Weber vacationed in Mexico in March 1995 with Weber's sister. During the vacation, Weber's sister took a photograph of Lake and Weber naked in the shower together. After their vacation, Lake and Weber brought five rolls of film to the Dilworth, Minnesota Wal-Mart store and photo lab. When they received their developed photographs along with the negatives, an enclosed written notice stated that one or more of the photographs had not been printed because of their "nature."

In July 1995, an acquaintance of Lake and Weber alluded to the photograph and questioned their sexual orientation. Again, in December 1995, another friend told Lake and Weber that a Wal-Mart employee had shown her a copy of the photograph. By February 1996, Lake was informed that one or more copies of the photograph were circulating in the community.

Lake and Weber filed a complaint against Wal-Mart Stores, Inc. and one or more as-yet unidentified Wal-Mart employees on February 23, 1996, alleging the four traditional invasion of privacy torts — intrusion upon seclusion, appropriation, publication of private facts, and false light publicity. . . . The district court granted Wal-Mart's motion to dismiss, explaining that Minnesota has not recognized any of the four invasion of privacy torts. The court of appeals affirmed.

Whether Minnesota should recognize any or all of the invasion of privacy causes of action is a question of first impression in Minnesota. . . .

This court has the power to recognize and abolish common law doctrines. The common law is not composed of firmly fixed rules. Rather, as we have long recognized, the common law:

> is the embodiment of broad and comprehensive unwritten principles, inspired by natural reason, an innate sense of justice, adopted by common consent for the regulation and government of the affairs of men. It is the growth of ages, and an examination of many of its principles, as enunciated and discussed in the books, discloses a constant improvement and development in keeping with advancing civilization and new conditions of society. Its guiding star has always been the rule of right and wrong, and in this country its principles demonstrate that there is in fact, as well as in theory, a remedy for all wrongs.

As society changes over time, the common law must also evolve:

> It must be remembered that the common law is the result of growth, and that its development has been determined by the social needs of the community which it governs. It is the resultant of conflicting social forces, and those forces which

are for the time dominant leave their impress upon the law. It is of judicial origin, and seeks to establish doctrines and rules for the determination, protection, and enforcement of legal rights. Manifestly it must change as society changes and new rights are recognized. To be an efficient instrument, and not a mere abstraction, it must gradually adapt itself to changed conditions.

To determine the common law, we look to other states as well as to England.

The tort of invasion of privacy is rooted in a common law right to privacy first described in an 1890 law review article by Samuel Warren and Louis Brandeis. The article posited that the common law has always protected an individual's person and property, with the extent and nature of that protection changing over time. The fundamental right to privacy is both reflected in those protections and grows out of them:

> Thus, in the very early times, the law gave a remedy only for physical interference with life and property, for trespass vi et armis. Then the "right to life" served only to protect the subject from battery in its various forms; liberty meant freedom from actual restraint; and the right to property secured to the individual his lands and his cattle. Later, there came a recognition of a man's spiritual nature, of his feelings and his intellect. Gradually the scope of these legal rights broadened; and now the right to life has come to mean the right to enjoy life, — the right to be let alone; the right to liberty secures the exercise of extensive civil privileges; and the term "property" has grown to comprise every form of possession — intangible, as well as tangible.

Although no English cases explicitly articulated a "right to privacy," several cases decided under theories of property, contract, or breach of confidence also included invasion of privacy as a basis for protecting personal violations. The article encouraged recognition of the common law right to privacy, as the strength of our legal system lies in its elasticity, adaptability, capacity for growth, and ability "to meet the wants of an ever changing society and to apply immediate relief for every recognized wrong.". . .

Today, the vast majority of jurisdictions now recognize some form of the right to privacy. Only Minnesota, North Dakota, and Wyoming have not yet recognized any of the four privacy torts. Although New York and Nebraska courts have declined to recognize a common law basis for the right to privacy and instead provide statutory protection, we reject the proposition that only the legislature may establish new causes of action. The right to privacy is inherent in the English protections of individual property and contract rights and the "right to be let alone" is recognized as part of the common law across this country. Thus, it is within the province of the judiciary to establish privacy torts in this jurisdiction.

Today we join the majority of jurisdictions and recognize the tort of invasion of privacy. The right to privacy is an integral part of our humanity; one has a public persona, exposed and active, and a private persona, guarded and preserved. The heart of our liberty is choosing which parts of our lives shall become public and which parts we shall hold close. . . .

We decline to recognize the tort of false light publicity at this time. We are concerned that claims under false light are similar to claims of defamation, and to the extent that false light is more expansive than defamation, tension between this tort and the First Amendment is increased.

False light is the most widely criticized of the four privacy torts and has been rejected by several jurisdictions. . . .

Thus we recognize a right to privacy present in the common law of Minnesota, including causes of action in tort for intrusion upon seclusion, appropriation, and publication of private facts, but we decline to recognize the tort of false light publicity. . . .

TOMLJANOVICH, J. dissenting. I would not recognize a cause of action for intrusion upon seclusion, appropriation or publication of private facts. . . .

An action for an invasion of the right to privacy is not rooted in the Constitution. "[T]he Fourth Amendment cannot be translated into a general constitutional 'right to privacy.' " *Katz v. United States*, 389 U.S. 347, 350 (1967). Those privacy rights that have their origin in the Constitution are much more fundamental rights of privacy — marriage and reproduction. *See Griswold v. Connecticut*, 381 U.S. 479, 485 (1965) (penumbral rights of privacy and repose protect notions of privacy surrounding the marriage relationship and reproduction).

We have become a much more litigious society since 1975 when we acknowledged that we have never recognized a cause of action for invasion of privacy. We should be even more reluctant now to recognize a new tort.

In the absence of a constitutional basis, I would leave to the legislature the decision to create a new tort for invasion of privacy.

NOTES & QUESTIONS

1. *Other Remedies?* If the Minnesota Supreme Court had rejected the privacy tort, what other legal remedies might be available to Elli Lake?

2. *Postscript.* What happened in *Lake* after the Minnesota Supreme Court's decision? In response to a query from the casebook authors, the lead attorney for the *Lake* plaintiff, Keith L. Miller of Miller, Norman & Associates, Ltd., explained that his client lost at the trial that followed the remand. He writes: "The jury found that an invasion of Ms. Lake's privacy had occurred, but that it did not happen 'in the course and scope' of a Wal-Mart worker's employment." In other words, tort notions of agency were found to apply, and a privacy tort violation could be attributed to Wal-Mart only if the employee had carried out the tort in the course and scope of employment. Miller added: "Our proof was problematic because, expectedly, no employee could specifically be identified as the culprit. It was all circumstantial." Finally, he summarized his experience litigating this case: "Gratifying? Certainly. Remunerative? Not so much."

3. *Legislatures vs. Courts.* The dissent in *Lake* contends, in a similar way as *Roberson*, that it should be the legislature, not the courts, that recognizes new tort actions to protect privacy. In New York, the statute passed in response to *Roberson* remains the state's source for privacy tort remedies. Like New York, some states have recognized the privacy torts legislatively; other states,

like Georgia in *Pavesich* and Minnesota in *Lake*, have recognized them judicially. Which means of recognizing the torts do you believe to be most justifiable? Why? Does the legislature have expertise that courts lack? Are courts more or less sensitive to civil rights issues, such as privacy?

(c) Privacy Protection in Tort Law

The Privacy Torts. Prosser's classification of these torts survives to this day. The Restatement (Second) of Torts recognizes four privacy torts:

(1) *Public Disclosure of Private Facts.* This tort creates a cause of action for one who publicly discloses a private matter that is "highly offensive to a reasonable person" and "is not of legitimate concern to the public." Restatement (Second) of Torts § 652D (1977).

(2) *Intrusion upon Seclusion.* This tort provides a remedy when one intrudes "upon the solitude or seclusion of another or his private affairs or concerns" if the intrusion is "highly offensive to a reasonable person." Restatement (Second) of Torts § 652B (1977).

(3) *False Light.* This tort creates a cause of action when one publicly discloses a matter that places a person "in a false light" that is "highly offensive to a reasonable person." Restatement (Second) of Torts § 652E (1977).

(4) *Appropriation.* Under this tort, a plaintiff has a remedy against one "who appropriates to his own use or benefit the name or likeness" of the plaintiff. Restatement (Second) of Torts § 652C (1977).

Today, most states recognize some or all of these torts.

Breach of Confidentiality. The tort of breach of confidentiality provides a remedy when a professional (i.e., doctor, lawyer, banker) divulges a patient's or client's confidential information.

Defamation. The law of defamation existed long before Warren and Brandeis's article. Defamation law, consisting of the torts of libel and slander, creates liability when one makes a false statement about a person that harms the person's reputation. The Supreme Court has held that the First Amendment places certain limits on defamation law.

Infliction of Emotional Distress. The tort of intentional infliction of emotional distress can also serve as a remedy for certain privacy invasions. This tort provides a remedy when one "by extreme and outrageous conduct intentionally or recklessly causes severe emotional distress to another." Restatement (Second) of Torts § 46 (1977). Since privacy invasions can often result in severe emotional distress, this tort may provide a remedy. However, it is limited by the requirement of "extreme and outrageous conduct."

(d) Privacy Protection in Evidence Law

The law of evidence has long recognized privacy as an important goal that can override the truth-seeking function of the trial. Under the common law, certain communications are privileged, and hence cannot be inquired into during a legal proceeding. The law of evidence has recognized the importance of protecting the privacy of communications between attorney and client, priest and penitent, husband and wife, physician and patient, and psychotherapist and patient.

(e) Privacy Protection via Property Rights

Property Rights. Although there are few property laws specifically governing privacy, these laws often implicate privacy. The appropriation tort is akin to a property right, and some commentators suggest that personal information should be viewed as a form of property.[19] If personal information is understood as a form of property, the tort of conversion might apply to those who collect and use a person's private data. Recall, however, that Warren and Brandeis rejected property as an adequate protection for privacy. What kind of market structures might be needed if personal data is to be traded or sold?

Trespass. The law of trespass, which provides tort remedies and criminal penalties for the unauthorized entry onto another's land, can protect privacy. There is some overlap between the torts of intrusion and trespass, as many forms of intrusion involve a trespass as well.

(f) Privacy Protection in Contract Law

Sometimes specific contractual provisions protect against the collection, use, or disclosure of personal information. In certain contexts, courts have entertained actions for breach of implied contract or tort actions based on implicit duties once certain relationships are established, such as physician-patient relationships, which have been analogized to fiduciary relationships. Privacy policies as well as terms of service containing privacy provisions can sometimes be analogized to a contract.

Contract can also function as a way of sidestepping state and federal privacy laws. Many employers make employees consent to drug testing as well as e-mail and workplace surveillance in their employment contracts.

(g) Privacy Protection in Criminal Law

Warren and Brandeis noted that under certain circumstances, criminal law would be appropriate to protect privacy. The criminal law protects bodily invasions, such as assault, battery, and rape. The privacy of one's home is also protected by criminal sanctions for trespass. Stalking and harassing can give rise to criminal culpability. The crime of blackmail prohibits coercing an individual by threatening to expose her personal secrets. Many of the statutes protecting privacy also contain criminal penalties, such as the statutes pertaining to wiretapping and identity theft.

---

[19] *See, e.g.,* Alan Westin, *Privacy and Freedom* 324 (1967); *see also* Richard S. Murphy, *Property Rights in Personal Information: An Economic Defense of Privacy,* 84 Geo. L.J. 2381 (1996); Richard A. Posner, *The Economics of Justice* (1981); Lawrence Lessig, *Code and Other Laws of Cyberspace* 154-62 (1999); Paul M. Schwartz, *Property, Privacy, and Personal Data,* 117 Harv. L. Rev. 2055 (2004).

2. CONSTITUTIONAL LAW

Federal Constitutional Law. Although the United States Constitution does not specifically mention privacy, it has a number of provisions that protect privacy, and it has been interpreted as providing a right to privacy. In some instances the First Amendment serves to safeguard privacy. For example, the First Amendment protects the right to speak anonymously. *See McIntyre v. Ohio Election Comm'n*, 514 U.S. 334 (1995). The First Amendment's Freedom of Association Clause protects individuals from being compelled to disclose the groups to which they belong or contribute. Under the First Amendment "Congress shall make no law . . . abridging . . . the right of the people peaceably to assemble. . . ." For example, the Court has struck down the compulsory disclosure of the names and addresses of an organization's members, *see NAACP v. Alabama*, 357 U.S. 449 (1958), as well as a law requiring public teachers to list all organizations to which they belong or contribute. *See Shelton v. Tucker*, 364 U.S. 479 (1960).

The Third Amendment protects the privacy of the home by preventing the government from requiring soldiers to reside in people's homes: "No Soldier shall, in time of peace be quartered in any house, without the consent of the Owner, nor in time of war, but in a manner to be prescribed by law."

The Fourth Amendment provides that people have the right "to be secure in their persons, houses, papers, and effects, against unreasonable searches and seizures. . . ." Almost 40 years after writing *The Right to Privacy*, Brandeis, then a Supreme Court Justice, wrote a dissent that has had a significant influence on Fourth Amendment law. The case was *Olmstead v. United States*, 277 U.S. 438 (1928), where the Court held that wiretapping was not an invasion of privacy under the Fourth Amendment because it was not a physical trespass into the home. Justice Brandeis dissented, contending that the central interest protected by the Fourth Amendment was not property but the "right to be let alone":

> The protection guaranteed by the amendments is much broader in scope. The makers of our Constitution undertook to secure conditions favorable to the pursuit of happiness. They recognized the significance of man's spiritual nature, of his feelings and of his intellect. They knew that only a part of the pain, pleasure and satisfactions of life are to be found in material things. They sought to protect Americans in their beliefs, their thoughts, their emotions and their sensations. They conferred, as against the government, the right to be let alone — the most comprehensive of rights and the right most valued by civilized men. To protect that right, every unjustifiable intrusion by the government upon the privacy of the individual, whatever the means employed, must be deemed a violation of the Fourth Amendment.

Brandeis's dissent demonstrated that the "right to be let alone" did not merely have common law roots (as he had argued in *The Right to Privacy*) but also had constitutional roots as well in the Fourth Amendment.

Modern Fourth Amendment law incorporates much of Brandeis's view. In *Katz v. United States*, 389 U.S. 347 (1967), the Court held that the Fourth Amendment "protects people, not places" and said that the police must obtain a warrant when a search takes place in a public pay phone on a public street. The

Court currently determines a person's right to privacy by the "reasonable expectations of privacy" test, a standard articulated in Justice Harlan's concurrence to *Katz*. First, a person must "have exhibited an actual (subjective) expectation of privacy" and, second, "the expectation [must] be one that society is prepared to recognize as 'reasonable.' "

The Fifth Amendment guarantees that: "No person . . . shall be compelled in any criminal case to be a witness against himself. . . ." This right, commonly referred to as the "privilege against self-incrimination," protects privacy by restricting the ability of the government to force individuals to divulge certain information about themselves.

In the landmark 1965 case *Griswold v. Connecticut*, 318 U.S. 479 (1965), the Court declared that an individual has a constitutional right to privacy. The Court located this right within the "penumbras" or "zones" of freedom created by an expansive interpretation of the Bill of Rights. Subsequently, the Court has handed down a line of cases protecting certain fundamental life choices such as abortion and aspects of one's intimate sexual life.

In *Whalen v. Roe*, 429 U.S. 589 (1977), the Court extended its substantive due process privacy protection to information privacy, holding that the "zone of privacy" protected by the Constitution encompasses the "individual interest in avoiding disclosure of personal matters." This offshoot of the right to privacy has become known as the "constitutional right to information privacy."

State Constitutional Law. A number of states have directly provided for the protection of privacy in their constitutions. For example, the Alaska Constitution provides: "The right of the people to privacy is recognized and shall not be infringed." Alaska Const. art. I, § 22. According to the California Constitution: "All people are by their nature free and independent and have inalienable rights. Among these are enjoying and defending life and liberty, acquiring, possessing, and protecting property, and pursuing and obtaining safety, happiness, and privacy." Cal. Const. art. I, § 1. Unlike most state constitutional provisions, the California constitutional right to privacy applies not only to state actors but also to private parties. *See, e.g., Hill v. NCAA*, 865 P.2d 638 (Cal. 1994). The Florida Constitution provides: "Every natural person has the right to be let alone and free from governmental intrusion into his private life except as otherwise provided herein." Fla. Const. art. I, § 23.[20]

3. STATUTORY LAW

Federal Statutory Law. From the mid-1960s to the mid-1970s, privacy emerged as a central political and social concern. In tune with the heightened attention to privacy, philosophers, legal scholars, and others turned their focus on

---

[20] For more examples, see Ariz. Const. art. II, § 8; Mont. Const. art. II, § 10; Haw. Const. art. I, § 6; Ill. Const. art. I, §§ 6, 12; La. Const. art. I, § 5; S.C. Const. art. I, § 10; Wash. Const. art. I, § 7. For a further discussion of state constitutional protections of privacy, see Timothy O. Lenz, *"Rights Talk" About Privacy in State Courts*, 60 Alb. L. Rev. 1613 (1997); Mark Silverstein, Note, *Privacy Rights in State Constitutions: Models for Illinois?*, 1989 U. Ill. L. Rev. 215.

privacy, raising public awareness about the growing threats to privacy from technology.[21]

In the mid-1960s, electronic eavesdropping erupted into a substantial public issue, spawning numerous television news documentaries as well as receiving significant attention in major newspapers. A proposal for a National Data Center in 1965 triggered public protest and congressional hearings. At this time, the computer was a new and unexplored technological tool that raised risks of unprecedented data collection about individuals, with potentially devastating effects on privacy. Indeed, toward the end of the 1960s, the issue of the collection of personal information in databases had become one of the defining social issues of American society.

During this time the Supreme Court announced landmark decisions regarding the right to privacy, including *Griswold v. Connecticut* in 1965 and *Roe v. Wade* in 1973, which were landmark decisions regarding the right to decisional/reproductive privacy and autonomy. The famous reasonable expectations of privacy test in Fourth Amendment jurisprudence emerged in 1967 with *Katz v. United States*.

Due to growing fears about the ability of computers to store and search personal information, Congress devoted increasing attention to the issue of privacy. As Priscilla Regan observes:

> In 1965, a new problem was placed on the congressional agenda by subcommittee chairs in both the House and the Senate. The problem was defined as the invasion of privacy by computers and evoked images of *1984*, the "Computerized Man," and a dossier society. Press interest was high, public concern was generated and resulted in numerous letters being sent to members of Congress, and almost thirty days of congressional hearings were held in the late 1960s and early 1970s.[22]

In 1973, in a highly influential report, the United States Department of Health, Education, and Welfare (HEW) undertook an extensive review of data processing in the United States. Among many recommendations, the HEW report proposed that a Code of Fair Information Practices be established. The Fair Information Practices consist of a number of basic information privacy principles that allocate rights and responsibilities in the collection and use of personal information:

- There must be no personal-data record-keeping systems whose very existence is secret.

---

[21] *See, e.g.,* Vance Packard, *The Naked Society* (1964); Myron Brenton, *The Privacy Invaders* (1964); Alan Westin, *Privacy and Freedom* (1967); Arthur Miller, *The Assault on Privacy* (1971); *Nomos XII: Privacy* (J. Ronald Pennock & J.W. Chapman eds., 1971); Alan Westin & Michael A. Baker, *Databanks in a Free Society: Computers, Record-Keeping and Privacy* (1972); Aryeh Neier, *The Secret Files They Keep on You* (1975); Kenneth L. Karst, *"The Files": Legal Controls over the Accuracy and Accessibility of Stored Personal Data*, 31 Law & Contemp. Probs. 342 (1966); Symposium, *Computers, Data Banks, and Individual Privacy*, 53 Minn. L. Rev. 211-45 (1968); Symposium, *Privacy*, 31 Law & Contemp. Probs. 251-435 (1966).

[22] Priscilla M. Regan, *Legislating Privacy: Technology, Social Values, and Public Policy* 82 (1995).

- There must be a way for an individual to find out what information about him is in a record and how it is used.

- There must be a way for an individual to prevent information about him obtained for one purpose from being used or made available for other purposes without his consent.

- There must be a way for an individual to correct or amend a record of identifiable information about him.

- Any organization creating, maintaining, using, or disseminating records of identifiable personal data must ensure the reliability of the data for their intended use and must take reasonable precautions to prevent misuse of the data.[23]

As Marc Rotenberg observes, the Fair Information Practices have "played a significant role in framing privacy laws in the United States."[24]

Beginning in the 1970s, Congress has passed a number of laws protecting privacy in various sectors of the information economy:

- Fair Credit Reporting Act of 1970, Pub. L. No. 90-32, 15 U.S.C. §§ 1681 et seq. — provides citizens with rights regarding the use and disclosure of their personal information by credit reporting agencies.

- Privacy Act of 1974, Pub. L. No. 93-579, 5 U.S.C. § 552a — provides individuals with a number of rights concerning their personal information maintained in government record systems, such as the right to see one's records and to ensure that the information in them is accurate.

- Family Educational Rights and Privacy Act of 1974, Pub. L. No. 93-380, 20 U.S.C. §§ 1221 note, 1232g — protects the privacy of school records.

- Right to Financial Privacy Act of 1978, Pub. L. No. 95-630, 12 U.S.C. §§ 3401–3422 — requires a subpoena or search warrant for law enforcement officials to obtain financial records.

- Foreign Intelligence Surveillance Act of 1978, Pub. L. No. 95-511, 15 U.S.C. §§ 1801-1811 — regulates foreign intelligence gathering within the U.S.

- Privacy Protection Act of 1980, Pub. L. No. 96-440, 42 U.S.C. § 2000aa — restricts the government's ability to search and seize the work product of the press and the media.

- Cable Communications Policy Act of 1984, Pub. L. No. 98-549, 47 U.S.C. § 551 — mandates privacy protection for records maintained by cable companies.

- Electronic Communications Privacy Act of 1986, Pub. L. No. 99-508 and Pub. L. No. 103-414, 18 U.S.C §§ 2510–2522, 2701–2709 — updates federal electronic surveillance law to respond to the new developments in technology.

---

[23] *See* U.S. Dep't of Health, Education, and Welfare, *Secretary's Advisory Committee on Automated Personal Data Systems, Records, Computers, and Rights of Citizens* viii (1973).

[24] Marc Rotenberg, *Fair Information Practices and the Architecture of Privacy (What Larry Doesn't Get)*, Stan. Tech. L. Rev. 1, 44 (2001).

- Computer Matching and Privacy Protection Act of 1988, Pub. L. No. 100-503, 5 U.S.C. §§ 552a — regulates automated investigations conducted by government agencies comparing computer files.

- Employee Polygraph Protection Act of 1988, Pub. L. No. 100-347, 29 U.S.C. §§ 2001–2009 — governs the use of polygraphs by employers.

- Video Privacy Protection Act of 1988, Pub. L. No. 100-618, 18 U.S.C. §§ 2710–2711 — protects the privacy of videotape rental information.

- Telephone Consumer Protection Act of 1991, Pub. L. No. 102-243, 47 U.S.C. § 227 — provides certain remedies from repeat telephone calls by telemarketers.

- Driver's Privacy Protection Act of 1994, Pub. L. No. 103-322, 18 U.S.C. §§ 2721–2725 — restricts the states from disclosing or selling personal information in their motor vehicle records.

- Health Insurance Portability and Accountability Act of 1996, Pub. L. No. 104-191 — gives the Department of Health and Human Services (HHS) the authority to promulgate regulations governing the privacy of medical records.

- Identity Theft and Assumption Deterrence Act of 1998, Pub. L. No. 105-318, 18 U.S.C. § 1028 — criminalizes the transfer or use of fraudulent identification with the intent to commit unlawful activity.

- Children's Online Privacy Protection Act of 1998, Pub. L. No. 106-170, 15 U.S.C. §§ 6501–6506 — restricts the use of information gathered from children under age 13 by Internet websites.

- Gramm-Leach-Bliley Act of 1999, Pub. L. No. 106-102, 15 U.S.C. §§ 6801–6809 — requires privacy notices and provides opt-out rights when financial institutions seek to disclose personal data to other companies.

- CAN-SPAM Act of 2003, Pub. L. No. 108-187 — provides penalties for the transmission of unsolicited e-mail.

- Fair and Accurate Credit Transactions Act of 2003, Pub. L. No. 108-159 — amends and updates the Fair Credit Reporting Act, providing (among other things) additional protections against identity theft.

- Video Voyeurism Prevention Act of 2004, Pub. L. No. 108-495, 18 U.S.C. § 1801 — criminalizes the capturing of nude images of people (when on federal property) under circumstances where they have a reasonable expectation of privacy.

- Health Information Technology for Economic and Clinical Health Act (HITECH Act) of 2009, Pub. L. No. 111-5 — expands HIPAA's coverage, strengthens penalties for HIPAA violations, and provides for data breach notification under HIPAA.

Not all of Congress's legislation regarding privacy has been protective of privacy. A number of statutes have mandated the government collection of sensitive personal data or facilitated government investigation techniques:

- Bank Secrecy Act of 1970, Pub. L. No. 91-508 — requires banks to maintain reports of people's financial transactions to assist in government white collar investigations.

- Communications Assistance for Law Enforcement Act of 1994, Pub. L. No. 103-414 — requires telecommunication providers to help facilitate government interceptions of communications and surveillance.

- Personal Responsibility and Work Opportunity Reconciliation Act of 1996, Pub. L. No. 104-193 — requires the collection of personal information (including Social Security numbers, addresses, and wages) of all people who obtain a new job anywhere in the nation, which will be placed into a national database to help track down deadbeat parents.

- USA-PATRIOT Act of 2001, Pub. L. No. 107-56 — amends a number of electronic surveillance statutes and other statutes to facilitate law enforcement investigations and access to information.

State Statutory Law. The states have passed statutes protecting privacy in many contexts, regulating both the public and private sectors. These laws cover a wide range of subjects, from employment records and medical records to library records and student records.

States have led the way in the area of breach notification. Following California's enactment of such a statute, more than 90 percent of the states have now enacted statutes that require organizations to let the affected party know when there is a data leak involving personal data. Many states also have enacted data disposal statutes, and an increasing number of state statutes are setting substantive requirements for data security.

4. INTERNATIONAL LAW

Privacy is a global concern. International law and, more precisely, the privacy laws of other countries and international privacy norms, implicate privacy interests in the United States. For example, commercial firms in the United States must comply with the various standards for global commerce. The Organization of Economic Cooperation and Development (OECD) developed an extensive series of privacy guidelines in 1980 that formed the basis for privacy laws in North America, Europe, and East Asia.

In 1995, the European Union issued the *European Community Directive on Data Protection*, which outlines the basic principles for privacy legislation for European Union member countries.[25] The Directive became effective on October 25, 1998. Currently, the European Union is in the process of debating a sweeping Data Protection Regulation. Once enacting, this Data Protection Regulation will be immediately binding as law in all EU Member States.[26]

---

[25] *See* Directive of the European Parliament and the Council of Europe on the Protection of Individuals with Regard to the Processing of Personal Data and on the Free Movement of Such Data (1996).

[26] Proposal for a Regulation of the European Parliament and the Council on the Protection of Individuals with Regard to the Processing of Personal Data and on the Free Movement of Such Data (2012).

In November 2004, an Asian-Pacific Economic Cooperative (APEC) Privacy Framework was endorsed by the ministers of the APEC countries. The APEC countries are more than 20 nations, mostly in Asia, but also including the United States.

CHAPTER 2

PERSPECTIVES ON PRIVACY

CHAPTER OUTLINE

A. THE PHILOSOPHICAL DISCOURSE ABOUT PRIVACY

1. THE CONCEPT OF PRIVACY AND THE RIGHT TO PRIVACY

At the outset, it is important to distinguish between the concept of privacy and the right of privacy. As Hyman Gross observed, "[t]he law does not determine what privacy is, but only what situations of privacy will be afforded legal protection."[1] Privacy as a concept involves what privacy entails and how it is to be valued. Privacy as a right involves the extent to which privacy is (and should be) legally protected.

While instructive and illuminative, law cannot be the exclusive material for constructing a concept of privacy. Law is the product of the weighing of competing values, and it sometimes embodies difficult trade-offs. In order to determine what the law *should* protect, we cannot merely look to what the law *does* protect.

---

[1] Hyman Gross, *The Concept of Privacy*, 42 N.Y.U. L. Rev. 34, 36 (1967).

2. THE PUBLIC AND PRIVATE SPHERES

A long-standing distinction in philosophical discourse is between the public and private spheres. Some form of boundary between public and private has been maintained throughout the history of Western civilization.[2]

Generally, the public sphere is the realm of life experienced in the open, in the community, and in the world of politics. The private sphere is the realm of life where one retreats to isolation or to one's family. At its core is the world of the home. The private sphere, observes Edward Shils, is a realm where the individual "is not bound by the rules that govern public life. . . . The 'private life' is a secluded life, a life separated from the compelling burdens of public authority."[3]

According to Hannah Arendt, both spheres are essential dimensions of human life:

> . . . In ancient feeling, the privative trait of privacy, indicated in the word itself, was all-important; it meant literally a state of being deprived of something, and even of the highest and most human of man's capacities. A man who lived only a private life, who like the slave was not permitted to enter the public realm, or like the barbarian had chosen not to establish such a realm, was not fully human. We no longer think primarily of deprivation when we use the word "privacy," and this is partly due to the enormous enrichment of the private sphere through modern individualism. . . .
>
> To live an entirely private life means above all to be deprived of things essential to a truly human life: to be deprived of the reality that comes from being seen and heard by others, to be deprived of an "objective" relationship with them that comes from being related to and separated from them through the intermediary of a common world of things, to be deprived of the possibility of achieving something more permanent than life itself. . . .
>
> . . . [T]he four walls of one's private property offer the only reliable hiding place from the common public world, not only from everything that goes on in it but also from its very publicity, from being seen and being heard. A life spent entirely in public, in the presence of others, becomes, as we would say, shallow. While it retains visibility, it loses the quality of rising into sight from some darker ground which must remain hidden if it is not to lose its depth in a very real, non-subjective sense. . . . [4]

John Stuart Mill relied upon a notion of the public/private dichotomy to determine when society should regulate individual conduct. Mill contended that there was a realm where people had social responsibilities and where society could properly restrain people from acting or punish them for their deeds. This realm consisted in acts that were hurtful to others or to which people "may rightfully be compelled to perform; such as to give evidence in a court of justice; to bear his fair share in the common defence, or in any other joint work necessary to the interest of the society of which he enjoys the protection." However, "there

---

[2] *See* Georges Duby, *Foreword*, in *A History of the Private Life I: From Pagan Rome to Byzantium* viii (Paul Veyne ed. & Arthur Goldhammer trans., 1987); *see also* Jürgen Habermas, *The Structural Transformation of the Public Sphere* (Thomas Burger trans., 1991).

[3] Edward Shils, *Privacy: Its Constitution and Vicissitudes*, 31 Law & Contemp. Probs. 281, 283 (1966).

[4] Hannah Arendt, *The Human Condition* (1958).

is a sphere of action in which society, as distinguished from the individual, has, if any, only an indirect interest; comprehending all that portion of a person's life and conduct which affects only himself, or if it also affects others, only with their free, voluntary, and undeceived consent and participation." Conduct within this sphere consists of "self-regarding" acts, and society should not interfere with such acts. As Mill further elaborated:

> . . . I fully admit that the mischief which a person does to himself may seriously affect, both through their sympathies and their interests, those nearly connected with him and, in a minor degree, society at large. When, by conduct of this sort, a person is led to violate a distinct and assignable obligation to any other person or persons, the case is taken out of the self-regarding class, and becomes amenable to moral disapprobation in the proper sense of the term. . . . Whenever, in short, there is a definite damage, or a definite risk of damage, either to an individual or to the public, the case is taken out of the province of liberty, and placed in that of morality or law.
>
> But with regard to the merely contingent, or, as it may be called, constructive injury which a person causes to society, by conduct which neither violates any specific duty to the public, nor occasions perceptible hurt to any assignable individual except himself; the inconvenience is one which society can afford to bear, for the sake of the greater good of human freedom. . . . [5]

B. THE DEFINITION AND THE VALUE OF PRIVACY

The following excerpts explore the definition and value of privacy. Those who attempt to define privacy seek to describe what privacy constitutes. Over the past four decades, academics have defined privacy as a right of personhood, intimacy, secrecy, limited access to the self, and control over information. However, defining privacy has proven to be quite complicated, and many commentators have expressed great difficulty in defining precisely what privacy is. In the words of one commentator, "even the most strenuous advocate of a right to privacy must confess that there are serious problems of defining the essence and scope of this right."[6] According to Robert Post, "[p]rivacy is a value so complex, so entangled in competing and contradictory dimensions, so engorged with various and distinct meanings, that I sometimes despair whether it can be usefully addressed at all."[7]

Conceptualizing privacy not only involves defining privacy but articulating the value of privacy. The value of privacy concerns its importance — how privacy is to be weighed relative to other interests and values. The excerpts that follow attempt to grapple with the complicated task of defining privacy and explaining why privacy is worth protecting.

---

[5] John Stuart Mill, *On Liberty* 12, 13, 74-75 (1859).

[6] William M. Beaney, *The Right to Privacy and American Law*, 31 Law & Contemp. Probs. 253, 255 (1966).

[7] Robert C. Post, *Three Concepts of Privacy*, 89 Geo. L.J. 2087, 2087 (2001).

ALAN WESTIN, *PRIVACY AND FREEDOM*
(1967)

. . . Privacy is the claim of individuals, groups, or institutions to determine for themselves when, how, and to what extent information about them is communicated to others. Viewed in terms of the relation of the individual to social participation, privacy is the voluntary and temporary withdrawal of a person from the general society through physical or psychological means, either in a state of solitude or small-group intimacy or, when among larger groups, in a condition of anonymity or reserve. The individual's desire for privacy is never absolute, since participation in society is an equally powerful desire. Thus each individual is continually engaged in a personal adjustment process in which he balances the desire for privacy with the desire for disclosure and communication of himself to others, in light of the environmental conditions and social norms set by the society in which he lives. The individual does so in the face of pressures from the curiosity of others and from the processes of surveillance that every society sets in order to enforce its social norms. . . .

Recognizing the differences that political and sensory cultures make in setting norms of privacy among modern societies, it is still possible to describe the general functions that privacy performs for individuals and groups in Western democratic nations. Before describing these, it is helpful to explain in somewhat greater detail the four basic states of individual privacy[, which are solitude, intimacy, anonymity, and reserve.] . . .

The first state of privacy is solitude; here the individual is separated from the group and freed from the observation of other persons. He may be subjected to jarring physical stimuli, such as noise, odors, and vibrations. His peace of mind may continue to be disturbed by physical sensations of heat, cold, itching, and pain. He may believe that he is being observed by God or some supernatural force, or fear that some authority is secretly watching him. Finally, in solitude he will be especially subject to that familiar dialogue with the mind or conscience. But, despite all these physical or psychological intrusions, solitude is the most complete state of privacy that individuals can achieve.

In the second state of privacy, the individual is acting as part of a small unit that claims and is allowed to exercise corporate seclusion so that it may achieve a close, relaxed, and frank relationship between two or more individuals. Typical units of intimacy are husband and wife, the family, a friendship circle, or a work clique. Whether close contact brings relaxed relations or abrasive hostility depends on the personal interaction of the members, but without intimacy a basic need of human contact would not be met.

The third state of privacy, anonymity, occurs when the individual is in public places or performing public acts but still seeks, and finds, freedom from identification and surveillance. He may be riding a subway, attending a ball game, or walking the streets; he is among people and knows that he is being observed; but unless he is a well-known celebrity, he does not expect to be personally identified and held to the full rules of behavior and role that would operate if he were known to those observing him. In this state the individual is able to merge into the "situational landscape." Knowledge or fear that one is under systematic observation in public places destroys the sense of relaxation and freedom that men seek in open spaces and public arenas. . . .

Still another kind of anonymity is the publication of ideas anonymously. Here the individual wants to present some idea publicly to the community or to a segment of it, but does not want to be universally identified at once as the author — especially not by the authorities, who may be forced to take action if they "know" the perpetrator. The core of each of these types of anonymous action is the desire of individuals for times of "public privacy."

Reserve, the fourth and most subtle state of privacy, is the creation of a psychological barrier against unwanted intrusion; this occurs when the individual's need to limit communication about himself is protected by the willing discretion of those surrounding him. Most of our lives are spent not in solitude or anonymity but in situations of intimacy and in group settings where we are known to others. Even in the most intimate relations, communication of self to others is always incomplete and is based on the need to hold back some parts of one's self as either too personal and sacred or too shameful and profane to express. This circumstance gives rise to what Simmel called "reciprocal reserve and indifference," the relation that creates "mental distance" to protect the personality. This creation of mental distance — a variant of the concept of "social distance" — takes place in every sort of relationship under rules of social etiquette; it expresses the individual's choice to withhold or disclose information — the choice that is the dynamic aspect of privacy in daily interpersonal relations. . . .

This analysis of the various states of privacy is useful in discussing the basic question of the functions privacy performs for individuals in democratic societies. These can also be grouped conveniently under four headings — personal autonomy, emotional release, self-evaluation, and limited and protected communication. . . .

Personal Autonomy. . . . Each person is aware of the gap between what he wants to be and what he actually is, between what the world sees of him and what he knows to be his much more complex reality. In addition, there are aspects of himself that the individual does not fully understand but is slowly exploring and shaping as he develops. Every individual lives behind a mask in this manner; indeed, the first etymological meaning of the word "person" was "mask," indicating both the conscious and expressive presentation of the self to a social audience. If this mask is torn off and the individual's real self bared to a world in which everyone else still wears his mask and believes in masked performances, the individual can be seared by the hot light of selective, forced exposure. . . .

The autonomy that privacy protects is also vital to the development of individuality and consciousness of individual choice in life. . . . This development of individuality is particularly important in democratic societies, since qualities of independent thought, diversity of views, and non-conformity are considered desirable traits for individuals. Such independence requires time for sheltered experimentation and testing of ideas, for preparation and practice in thought and conduct, without fear of ridicule or penalty, and for the opportunity to alter opinions before making them public. The individual's sense that it is he who decides when to "go public" is a crucial aspect of his feeling of autonomy.

Without such time for incubation and growth, through privacy, many ideas and positions would be launched into the world with dangerous prematurity. . . .

Emotional Release. Life in society generates such tensions for the individual that both physical and psychological health demand periods of privacy for various types of emotional release. At one level, such relaxation is required from the pressure of playing social roles. Social scientists agree that each person constantly plays a series of varied and multiple roles, depending on his audience and behavioral situation. On any given day a man may move through the roles of stern father, loving husband, car-pool comedian, skilled lathe operator, union steward, water-cooler flirt, and American Legion committee chairman — all psychologically different roles that he adopts as he moves from scene to scene on the social stage. Like actors on the dramatic stage, Goffman has noted, individuals can sustain roles only for reasonable periods of time, and no individual can play indefinitely, without relief, the variety of roles that life demands. There have to be moments "off stage" when the individual can be "himself": tender, angry, irritable, lustful, or dream-filled. . . .

Another form of emotional release is provided by the protection privacy gives to minor non-compliance with social norms. Some norms are formally adopted — perhaps as law — which society really expects many persons to break. This ambivalence produces a situation in which almost everyone does break some social or institutional norms — for example, violating traffic laws, breaking sexual mores, cheating on expense accounts, overstating income-tax deductions, or smoking in rest rooms when this is prohibited. Although society will usually punish the most flagrant abuses, it tolerates the great bulk of the violations as "permissible" deviations. If there were no privacy to permit society to ignore these deviations — if all transgressions were known — most persons in society would be under organizational discipline or in jail, or could be manipulated by threats of such action. The firm expectation of having privacy for permissible deviations is a distinguishing characteristic of life in a free society. At a lesser but still important level, privacy also allows individuals to deviate temporarily from social etiquette when alone or among intimates, as by putting feet on desks, cursing, letting one's face go slack, or scratching wherever one itches.

Another aspect of release is the "safety-valve" function afforded by privacy. Most persons need to give vent to their anger at "the system," "city hall," "the boss," and various others who exercise authority over them, and to do this in the intimacy of family or friendship circles, or in private papers, without fear of being held responsible for such comments. . . . Without the aid of such release in accommodating the daily abrasions with authorities, most people would experience serious emotional pressure. . . .

Limited and Protected Communication. The greatest threat to civilized social life would be a situation in which each individual was utterly candid in his communications with others, saying exactly what he knew or felt at all times. The havoc done to interpersonal relations by children, saints, mental patients, and adult "innocents" is legendary. . . .

Privacy for limited and protected communication has two general aspects. First, it provides the individual with the opportunities he needs for sharing confidences and intimacies with those he trusts — spouse, "the family," personal friends, and close associates at work. The individual discloses because he knows that his confidences will be held, and because he knows that breach of confidence violates social norms in a civilized society. "A friend," said Emerson, "is someone before . . . [whom] I can think aloud." In addition, the individual often wants to secure counsel from persons with whom he does not have to live daily after disclosing his confidences. He seeks professionally objective advice from persons whose status in society promises that they will not later use his distress to take advantage of him. To protect freedom of limited communication, such relationships — with doctors, lawyers, ministers, psychiatrists, psychologists, and others — are given varying but important degrees of legal privilege against forced disclosure. . . .

NOTES & QUESTIONS

1. *Privacy as Control over Information.* A number of theorists, including Westin, conceive of privacy as a form of control over personal information.[8] Consider Charles Fried's definition of privacy:

> At first approximation, privacy seems to be related to secrecy, to limiting the knowledge of others about oneself. This notion must be refined. It is not true, for instance, that the less that is known about us the more privacy we have. Privacy is not simply an absence of information about what is in the minds of others; rather it is the *control* we have over information about ourselves.
>
> To refer for instance to the privacy of a lonely man on a desert island would be to engage in irony. The person who enjoys privacy is able to grant or deny access to others. . . .
>
> Privacy, thus, is control over knowledge about oneself. But it is not simply control over the quantity of information abroad; there are modulations in the quality of the knowledge as well. We may not mind that a person knows a general fact about us, and yet feel our privacy invaded if he knows the details.[9]

Is this a compelling definition of privacy?

In contrast to privacy-as-control, Christena Nippert-Eng, a sociologist, talks about the managerial dimension of privacy. Based on her wide-reaching field interviews, Nippert-Eng concludes that "participants find it incumbent upon themselves to create their own pockets of uninterruptible time and space, or take make decisions without letting anyone else unduly pressure them into a particular choice."[10] She adds that "a need to *manage* one's privacy" runs through all the definitions of privacy offered by her interview participants.

2. *Privacy as Limited Access to the Self.* Another group of theorists view privacy as a form of limited access to the self. Consider Ruth Gavison:

---

[8] *See* Adam Carlyle Breckenridge, *The Right to Privacy* 1 (1970); Randall P. Bezanson, *The Right to Privacy Revisited: Privacy, News, and Social Change, 1810–1990*, 80 Cal. L. Rev. 1133 (1992). For a critique of privacy as control, see Anita L. Allen, *Privacy as Data Control: Conceptual, Practical, and Moral Limits of the Paradigm*, 32 Conn. L. Rev. 861 (2000).

[9] Charles Fried, *Privacy*, 77 Yale L.J. 475 (1968).

[10] Christena Nippert-Eng, *Islands of Privacy* 7 (2010).

. . . Our interest in privacy . . . is related to our concern over our accessibility to others: the extent to which we are known to others, the extent to which others have physical access to us, and the extent to which we are the subject of others' attention. This concept of privacy as concern for limited accessibility enables us to identify when losses of privacy occur. Furthermore, the reasons for which we claim privacy in different situations are similar. They are related to the functions privacy has in our lives: the promotion of liberty, autonomy, selfhood, and human relations, and furthering the existence of a free society. . . .

The concept of privacy suggested here is a complex of these three independent and irreducible elements: secrecy, anonymity, and solitude. Each is independent in the sense that a loss of privacy may occur through a change in any one of the three, without a necessary loss in either of the other two. The concept is nevertheless coherent because the three elements are all part of the same notion of accessibility, and are related in many important ways.[11]

How does this theory of privacy differ from the notion of privacy as "the right to be let alone"? How does it differ from privacy as control over information? How much control should individuals have over access to themselves? Should the decision depend upon each particular person's desires? Or should there be an objective standard — a reasonable degree of control over access?

3. *Privacy as Intimacy.* A number of theorists argue that "intimacy" appropriately defines what information or matters are private. For example, Julie Inness argues that "intimacy" is the common denominator in all the matters that people claim to be private. Privacy is "the state of the agent having control over decisions concerning matters that draw their meaning and value from the agent's love, caring, or liking. These decisions cover choices on the agent's part about access to herself, the dissemination of information about herself, and her actions."[12]

Jeffrey Rosen adopts a similar view when he writes:

. . . Privacy protects us from being misdefined and judged out of context in a world of short attention spans, a world in which information can easily be confused with knowledge. True knowledge of another person is the culmination of a slow process of mutual revelation. It requires the gradual setting aside of social masks, the incremental building of trust, which leads to the exchange of personal disclosures. It cannot be rushed; this is why, after intemperate self-revelation in the heat of passion, one may feel something

---

[11] Ruth Gavison, *Privacy and the Limits of Law,* 89 Yale L.J. 421 (1980); *see also* Edward Shils, *Privacy: Its Constitution and Vicissitudes,* 31 Law & Contemp. Probs. 281, 281 (1996); Sissela Bok, *Secrets: On the Ethics of Concealment and Revelation* 10-11 (1982); Ernest Van Den Haag, *On Privacy,* in *Nomos XII: Privacy* 149 (J. Ronald Pennock & J.W. Chapman eds., 1971); Sidney M. Jourard, *Some Psychological Aspects of Privacy,* 31 L. & Contemp. Probs. 307, 307 (1966); David O'Brien, *Privacy, Law, and Public Policy* 16 (1979); Hyman Gross, *The Concept of Privacy,* 42 N.Y.U. L. Rev. 34 (1967).

[12] Julie C. Inness, *Privacy, Intimacy, and Isolation* 56, 58, 63, 64, 67 (1992). For other proponents of privacy as intimacy, see Robert S. Gerstein, *Intimacy and Privacy,* in *Philosophical Dimensions of Privacy: An Anthology* 265, 265 (Ferdinand David Schoeman ed., 1984); James Rachels, *Why Privacy Is Important,* in *Philosophical Dimensions of Privacy: An Anthology* 290, 292 (Ferdinand David Schoeman ed., 1984); Tom Gerety, *Redefining Privacy,* 12 Harv. C.R.-C.L. L. Rev. 233 (1977).

close to self-betrayal. True knowledge of another person, in all of his or her complexity, can be achieved only with a handful of friends, lovers, or family members. In order to flourish, the intimate relationships on which true knowledge of another person depends need space as well as time: sanctuaries from the gaze of the crowd in which slow mutual self-disclosure is possible.

When intimate personal information circulates among a small group of people who know us well, its significance can be weighed against other aspects of our personality and character. By contrast, when intimate information is removed from its original context and revealed to strangers, we are vulnerable to being misjudged on the basis of our most embarrassing, and therefore most memorable, tastes and preferences. . . . In a world in which citizens are bombarded with information, people form impressions quickly, based on sound bites, and these impressions are likely to oversimplify and misrepresent our complicated and often contradictory characters.[13]

Does "intimacy" adequately separate private matters from public ones? Can something be private but not intimate? Can something be intimate but not private?

In reaction to Rosen's views on privacy, Lawrence Lessig restates the problem of short attention spans in this fashion: "Privacy, the argument goes, would remedy such a problem by concealing those things that would not be understood with the given attention span. Privacy's function . . . is not to protect the presumptively innocent from true but damaging information, but rather to protect the actually innocent from damaging conclusions drawn from misunderstood information."[14] Lessig notes his skepticism regarding this approach: privacy will not alone solve the problem with the information market. Moreover, there "are possible solutions to this problem of attention span. But what should be clear is that there is no guarantee that a particular problem of attention span will have any solution at all."

JULIE E. COHEN, *EXAMINED LIVES: INFORMATIONAL PRIVACY AND THE SUBJECT AS OBJECT*

52 Stan. L. Rev. 1373 (2000)

Prevailing market-based approaches to data privacy policy — including "solutions" in the form of tradable privacy rights or heightened disclosure requirements before consent — treat preferences for informational privacy as a matter of individual taste, entitled to no more (and often much less) weight than preferences for black shoes over brown or red wine over white. But the values of informational privacy are far more fundamental. A degree of freedom from scrutiny and categorization by others promotes important noninstrumental values, and serves vital individual and collective ends.

First, informational autonomy comports with important values concerning the fair and just treatment of individuals within society. From Kant to Rawls, a central strand of Western philosophical tradition emphasizes respect for the fundamental dignity of persons, and a concomitant commitment to egalitarianism

---

[13] Jeffrey Rosen, *The Unwanted Gaze: The Destruction of Privacy in America* 8-9 (2000).

[14] Lawrence Lessig, *Privacy and Attention Span*, 89 Geo. L.J. 2063, 2065 (2001).

in both principle and practice. Advocates of strong data privacy protection argue that these principles have clear and very specific implications for the treatment of personally-identified data: They require that we forbid data-processing practices that treat individuals as mere conglomerations of transactional data, or that rank people as prospective customers, tenants, neighbors, employees, or insureds based on their financial or genetic desirability. . . .

Autonomous individuals do not spring full-blown from the womb. We must learn to process information and to draw our own conclusions about the world around us. We must learn to choose, and must learn something before we can choose anything. Here, though, information theory suggests a paradox: "Autonomy" connotes an essential independence of critical faculty and an imperviousness to influence. But to the extent that information shapes behavior, autonomy is radically contingent upon environment and circumstance. . . . Autonomy in a contingent world requires a zone of relative insulation from outside scrutiny and interference — a field of operation within which to engage in the conscious construction of self. The solution to the paradox of contingent autonomy, in other words, lies in a second paradox: To exist in fact as well as in theory, autonomy must be nurtured.

A realm of autonomous, unmonitored choice, in turn, promotes a vital diversity of speech and behavior. The recognition that anonymity shelters constitutionally-protected decisions about speech, belief, and political and intellectual association — decisions that otherwise might be chilled by unpopularity or simple difference — is part of our constitutional tradition. . . .

The benefits of informational privacy are related to, but distinct from, those afforded by seclusion from visual monitoring. It is well-recognized that respite from visual scrutiny affords individuals an important measure of psychological repose. Within our society, at least, we are accustomed to physical spaces within which we can be unobserved, and intrusion into those spaces is experienced as violating the boundaries of self. But the scrutiny, and the repose, can be informational as well as visual, and this does not depend entirely on whether the behavior takes place "in private." The injury, here, does not lie in the exposure of formerly private behaviors to public view, but in the dissolution of the boundaries that insulate different spheres of behavior from one another. The universe of all information about all record-generating behaviors generates a "picture" that, in some respects, is more detailed and intimate than that produced by visual observation, and that picture is accessible, in theory and often in reality, to just about anyone who wants to see it. In such a world, we all may be more cautious.

The point is not that people will not learn under conditions of no-privacy, but that they will learn differently, and that the experience of being watched will constrain, ex ante, the acceptable spectrum of belief and behavior. Pervasive monitoring of every first move or false start will, at the margin, incline choices toward the bland and the mainstream. The result will be a subtle yet fundamental shift in the content of our character, a blunting and blurring of rough edges and sharp lines. . . . The condition of no-privacy threatens not only to chill the expression of eccentric individuality, but also, gradually, to dampen the force of our aspirations to it. . . .

. . . [T]he insulation provided by informational privacy also plays a subtler, more conservative role in reinforcing the existing social fabric. Sociologist Erving Goffman demonstrated that the construction of social facades to mediate between self and community is both instinctive and expected. Alan Westin describes this social dimension of privacy as "reserve." This characterization, though, seems incomplete. On Goffman's account, the construction of social personae isn't just about withholding information that we don't want others to have. It is about defining the parameters of social interaction in ways that maximize social ease, and thus is about collective as well as individual comfort. We do not need, or even want, to know each other that well. Less information makes routine interactions easier; we are then free to choose, consensually and without embarrassment, the interactions that we wish to treat as less routine. Informational privacy, in short, is a constitutive element of a civil society in the broadest sense of that term. . . .

NOTES & QUESTIONS

1. *Privacy and Respect for Persons.* Julie Cohen's theory locates the purpose of privacy as promoting the development of autonomous individuals and, more broadly, civil society. Compare her theory to the following theory by Stanley Benn:

   > Finding oneself an object of scrutiny, as the focus of another's attention, brings one to a new consciousness of oneself, as something seen through another's eyes. According to [Jean-Paul] Sartre, indeed, it is a necessary condition for knowing oneself as anything at all that one should conceive oneself as an object of scrutiny. It is only through the regard of the other that the observed becomes aware of himself as an object, knowable, having a determinate character, in principle predictable. His consciousness of pure freedom as subject, as originator and chooser, is at once assailed by it; he is fixed as *something* — with limited probabilities rather than infinite, indeterminate possibilities. . . .
   >
   > The underpinning of a claim not to be watched without leave will be more general if it can be grounded in this way on the principle of respect for persons than on a utilitarian duty to avoid inflicting suffering. . . . But respect for persons will sustain an objection even to secret watching, which may do no actual harm at all. Covert observation — spying — is objectionable because it deliberately deceives a person about his world, thwarting, for reasons that *cannot* be his reasons, his attempts to make a rational choice. One cannot be said to respect a man as engaged on an enterprise worthy of consideration if one knowingly and deliberately alters his conditions of action, concealing the fact from him. . . .[15]

   How is Cohen's theory similar to and/or different from Benn's?

   Benn argues that privacy is a form of respect for persons. By being watched, Benn contends, the observed becomes "fixed as *something* — with limited probabilities rather than infinite indeterminate possibilities." Does Benn adequately capture why surveillance is harmful? Is Benn really

---

[15] Stanley I. Benn, *Privacy, Freedom, and Respect for Persons*, from *Nomos XIII: Privacy* (J. Ronald Pennock & J.W. Chapman eds., 1971).

concerned about the negative consequences of surveillance on a person's behavior? Or is Benn more concerned about the violation of respect for another?

2. ***Privacy as an Individual Right and as a Social Value.*** Consider the following argument from Priscilla Regan:

> . . . [The] emphasis of privacy as an individual right or an individual interest provides a weak basis for formulating policy to protect privacy. When privacy is defined as an individual right, policy formulation entails a balancing of the individual right to privacy against a competing interest or right. In general, the competing interest is recognized as a social interest. . . . It is also assumed that the individual has a stake in these societal interests. As a result, privacy has been on the defensive, with those alleging a privacy invasion bearing the burden of proving that a certain activity does indeed invade privacy and that the "social" benefit to be gained from the privacy invasion is less important than the individual harm incurred. . . .
>
> Privacy is a *common value* in that all individuals value some degree of privacy and have some common perceptions about privacy. Privacy is also a *public value* in that it has value not just to the individual as an individual or to all individuals in common but also to the democratic political system. . . .
>
> A public value of privacy derives not only from its protection of the individual as an individual but also from its usefulness as a restraint on the government or on the use of power. . . .[16]

DANIEL J. SOLOVE, *CONCEPTUALIZING PRIVACY*

90 Cal. L. Rev. 1087 (2002)

Despite what appears to be a welter of different conceptions of privacy, I argue that they can be dealt with under six general headings, which capture the recurrent ideas in the discourse. These headings include: (1) the right to be let alone — Samuel Warren and Louis Brandeis's famous formulation for the right to privacy; (2) limited access to the self — the ability to shield oneself from unwanted access by others; (3) secrecy — the concealment of certain matters from others; (4) control over personal information — the ability to exercise control over information about oneself; (5) personhood — the protection of one's personality, individuality, and dignity; and (6) intimacy — control over, or limited access to, one's intimate relationships or aspects of life. Some of the conceptions concentrate on means to achieve privacy; others focus on the ends or goals of privacy. Further, there is overlap between conceptions, and the conceptions discussed under different headings are by no means independent from each other. For example, control over personal information can be seen as a subset of limited access to the self, which in turn bears significant similarities to the right to be let alone. . . .

The most prevalent problem with the conceptions is that they are either too narrow or too broad. The conceptions are often too narrow because they fail to include the aspects of life that we typically view as private, and are often too

---

[16] Priscilla M. Regan, *Legislating Privacy: Technology, Social Values, and Public Policy* 213, 225 (1995).

broad because they fail to exclude matters that we do not deem private. Often, the same conceptions can suffer from being both too narrow and too broad. I contend that these problems stem from the way that the discourse goes about the task of conceptualizing privacy. . . .

Most attempts to conceptualize privacy thus far have followed the traditional method of conceptualizing. The majority of theorists conceptualize privacy by defining it *per genus et differentiam*. In other words, theorists look for a common set of necessary and sufficient elements that single out privacy as unique from other conceptions. . . .

[Philosopher Ludwig] Wittgenstein suggests that certain concepts might not share one common characteristic; rather they draw from a common pool of similar characteristics, "a complicated network of similarities overlapping and crisscrossing: sometimes overall similarities, sometimes similarities of detail." . . . Wittgenstein uses the term "family resemblances," analogizing to the overlapping and crisscrossing characteristics that exist between members of a family, such as "build, features, colour of eyes, gait, temperament, etc." For example, in a family, each child has certain features similar to each parent; and the children share similar features with each other; but they may not all resemble each other in the same way. Nevertheless, they all bear a resemblance to each other. . . .

When we state that we are protecting "privacy," we are claiming to guard against disruptions to certain practices. Privacy invasions disrupt and sometimes completely annihilate certain practices. Practices can be disrupted in certain ways, such as interference with peace of mind and tranquility, invasion of solitude, breach of confidentiality, loss of control over facts about oneself, searches of one's person and property, threats to or violations of personal security, destruction of reputation, surveillance, and so on.

There are certain similarities in particular types of disruptions as well as in the practices that they disrupt; but there are differences as well. We should conceptualize privacy by focusing on the specific types of disruption and the specific practices disrupted rather than looking for the common denominator that links all of them. If privacy is conceptualized as a web of interconnected types of disruption of specific practices, then the act of conceptualizing privacy should consist of mapping the typography of the web. . . .

It is reductive to carve the world of social practices into two spheres, public and private, and then attempt to determine what matters belong in each sphere. First, the matters we consider private change over time. While some form of dichotomy between public and private has been maintained throughout the history of Western civilization, the matters that have been considered public and private have metamorphosed throughout history due to changing attitudes, institutions, living conditions, and technology. The matters we consider to be private are shaped by culture and history, and have differed across cultures and historical epochs.

Second, although certain matters have moved from being public to being private and vice versa, the change often has been more subtle than a complete transformation from public to private. Particular matters have long remained private but in different ways; they have been understood as private but because of different attributes; or they have been regarded as private for some people or groups but not for others. In other words, to say simply that something is public or private is to make a rather general claim; what it means for something to be private is the central question. We consider our Social Security number, our sexual behavior, our diary, and our home private, but we do not consider them private in the same way. A number of aspects of life have commonly been viewed as private: the family, body, and home to name a few. To say simply that these things are private is imprecise because what it means for them to be private is different today than it was in the past. . . .

. . . [P]rivacy is not simply an empirical and historical question that measures the collective sense in any given society of what is and has long been considered to be private. Without a normative component, a conception of privacy can only provide a status report on existing privacy norms rather than guide us toward shaping privacy law and policy in the future. If we focus simply on people's current expectations of privacy, our conception of privacy would continually shrink given the increasing surveillance in the modern world. Similarly, the government could gradually condition people to accept wiretapping or other privacy incursions, thus altering society's expectations of privacy. On the other hand, if we merely seek to preserve those activities and matters that have historically been considered private, then we fail to adapt to the changing realities of the modern world. . . .

NOTES & QUESTIONS

1. *Core Characteristics vs. Family Resemblances.* Is there a core characteristic common in all the things we understand as being "private"? If so, what do you think it is? Can privacy be more adequately conceptualized by shifting away from the quest to find the common core characteristics of privacy?

2. *Context.* Solove contends that the meaning of privacy depends upon context, that there is no common denominator to all things we refer to as "privacy." Does this make privacy too amorphous a concept?

   Consider Helen Nissenbaum:

   Specifically, whether a particular action is determined a violation of privacy is a function of several variables, including the nature of the situation, or context; the nature of the information in relation to that context; the roles of agents receiving information; their relationships to information subjects; on what terms the information is shared by the subject; and the terms of further dissemination. . . .

   [N]orms of privacy in fact vary considerably from place to place, culture to culture, period to period; this theory not only incorporates this reality but systematically pinpoints the sources of variation. A second consequence is that, because questions about whether particular restrictions on flow are acceptable call for investigation into the relevant contextual details, protecting privacy will be a messy task, requiring a grasp of concepts and social institutions as well as knowledge of facts of the matter.[17]

---

[17] Helen Nissenbaum, *Privacy as Contextual Integrity,* 79 Wash. L. Rev. 119, 155-56 (2004). For a more complete account of Nissenbaum's theory, see Helen Nissenbaum, *Privacy in Context: Technology, Policy, and the Integrity of Social Life* (2010).

3. *Revising the Prosser Taxonomy.* Daniel Solove contends that the taxonomy of four privacy interests identified by William Prosser, *supra,* must be revised as well as expanded beyond tort law. Solove identifies 16 different kinds of activity that create privacy harms or problems:

> The first group of activities that affect privacy involve information collection. *Surveillance* is the watching, listening to, or recording of an individual's activities. *Interrogation* consists of various forms of questioning or probing for information.
>
> A second group of activities involves the way information is stored, manipulated, and used — what I refer to collectively as "information processing." *Aggregation* involves the combination of various pieces of data about a person. *Identification* is linking information to particular individuals. *Insecurity* involves carelessness in protecting stored information from being leaked or improperly accessed. *Secondary use* is the use of information collected for one purpose for a different purpose without a person's consent. *Exclusion* concerns the failure to allow people to know about the data that others have about them and participate in its handling and use. These activities do not involve the gathering of data, since it has already been collected. Instead, these activities involve the way data is maintained and used.
>
> The third group of activities involves the dissemination of information. *Breach of confidentiality* is breaking the promise to keep a person's information confidential. *Disclosure* involves the revelation of truthful information about a person which impacts the way others judge that person's character. *Exposure* involves revealing another's nudity, grief, or bodily functions. *Increased accessibility* is amplifying the accessibility of information. *Blackmail* is the threat to disclose personal information. *Appropriation* involves the use of another's identity to serve the aims and interests of another. *Distortion* consists of the dissemination of false or misleading information about individuals. Information dissemination activities all involve the spreading or transfer of personal data — or the threat to do so.
>
> The fourth and final group of activities involves invasions into people's private affairs. Invasion, unlike the other groupings, need not involve personal information (although in numerous instances, it does). *Intrusion* concerns invasive acts that disturb one's tranquility or solitude. *Decisional interference* involves the government's incursion into people's decisions regarding their private affairs.[18]

4. *Reductionists.* Some theorists, referred to as "reductionists," assert that privacy can be reduced to other concepts and rights. For example, Judith Jarvis Thomson contends that there is nothing particularly distinctive about privacy and to talk about things as violating the "right to privacy" is not all that useful. Privacy is really a cluster of other rights, such as the right to liberty, property rights, and the right not to be injured: "[T]he right to privacy is everywhere overlapped by other rights."[19] Is there something distinctive about privacy? Or can privacy be explained in terms of other, more primary

---

[18] Daniel J. Solove, *A Taxonomy of Privacy,* 154 U. Pa. L. Rev. 477 (2006). For a more complete account of Solove's theory, see Daniel J. Solove, *Understanding Privacy* (2008).

[19] Judith Jarvis Thomson, *The Right to Privacy,* 4 Phil. & Pub. Aff. 295 (1975).

rights and interests? What does privacy capture that these other rights and interests (autonomy, property, liberty, etc.) do not?

ANITA L. ALLEN, *COERCING PRIVACY*

40 Wm. & Mary L. Rev. 723 (1999)

. . . The final decades of the twentieth century could be remembered for the rapid erosion of expectations of personal privacy and of the taste for personal privacy in the United States. . . . I sense that people expect increasingly little physical, informational, and proprietary privacy, and that people seem to prefer less of these types of privacy relative to other goods. . . .

One way to address the erosion would be to stop the avalanche of technology and commercial opportunity responsible for the erosion. We could stop the avalanche of technology, but we will not, if the past is any indication. . . . In the United States, with a few exceptions like government-funded human cloning and fetal tissue research, the rule is that technology marches on.

We could stop the avalanche of commercial opportunity by intervening in the market for privacy; that is, we could (some way or another) increase the costs of consuming other people's privacy and lower the profits of voluntarily giving up one's own privacy. The problem with this suggested strategy is that, even without the details of implementation, it raises the specter of censorship, repression, paternalism, and bureaucracy. Privacy is something we think people are supposed to want; if it turns out that they do not, perhaps third parties should not force it on them, decreasing both their utility and that of those who enjoy disclosure, revelation, and exposure.

Of course, we force privacy on people all the time. Our elected officials criminalize public nudity, even to the point of discouraging breastfeeding. . . . It is one thing, the argument might go, to force privacy on someone by criminalizing nude sun-bathing and topless dancing. These activities have pernicious third-party effects and attract vice. It would be wrong, the argument might continue, to force privacy on someone, in the absence of harm to others, solely on the grounds that one ought not say too much about one's thoughts, feelings, and experiences; one ought not reveal in detail how one spends one's time at home; and one ought not live constantly on display. Paternalistic laws against extremes of factual and physical self-revelation seem utterly inconsistent with liberal self-expression, and yet such laws are suggested by the strong claims liberal theorists make about the value of privacy. Liberal theorists claim that we need privacy to be persons, independent thinkers, free political actors, and citizens of a tolerant democracy. . . .

For people under forty-five who understand that they do not, and cannot, expect to have many secrets, informational privacy may now seem less important. As a culture, we seem to be learning how to be happy and productive — even spiritual — knowing that we are like open books, our houses made of glass. Our parents may appear on the television shows of Oprah Winfrey or Jerry Springer to discuss incest, homosexuality, miscegenation, adultery, transvestitism, and cruelty in the family. Our adopted children may go on television to be reunited with their birth parents. Our law students may compete with their peers for a spot on the MTV program The Real World, and a chance to live with television cameras for months on end and be viewed by mass audiences. Our ten-year-olds may aspire to have their summer camp experiences — snits, fights, fun, and all — chronicled by camera crews and broadcast as entertainment for others on the Disney Channel.

Should we worry about any of this? What values are at stake? Scholars and other commentators associate privacy with several important clusters of value. Privacy has value relative to normative conceptions of spiritual personality, political freedom, health and welfare, human dignity, and autonomy. . . .

To speak of "coercing" privacy is to call attention to privacy as a foundation, a precondition of a liberal egalitarian society. Privacy is not an optional good, like a second home or an investment account. . . .

A hard task seems to lay before us — namely, deciding which forms of privacy are so critical that they should become matters of coercion. . . .

As liberals, we should not want people to sell all their freedom, and, as liberals, we should not want people to sell all their privacy and capacities for private choices. This is, in part, because the liberal conceptions of private choice as freedom from governmental and other outside interference with decision-making closely link privacy and freedom. The liberal conception of privacy as freedom from unwanted disclosures, publicity, and loss of control of personality also closely links privacy to freedom. . . .

Government will have to intervene in private lives for the sake of privacy and values associated with it. . . . The threat to liberalism is not that individuals sometimes expose their naked bodies in public places, display affection with same-sex partners in public, or broadcast personal information on national television. The threat to liberalism is that in an increasing variety of ways our lives are being emptied of privacy on a daily basis, especially physical and informational privacy. . . .

NOTES & QUESTIONS

1. *Should Privacy Be an Inalienable Right?* Allen argues that people regularly surrender their privacy and that we should "coerce" privacy. In other words, privacy must be seen as an inalienable right, one that people cannot give away. What if a person wants to live in the spotlight or to give away her personal information? Why shouldn't she be allowed to do so? Recall those who defined privacy as control over information. One aspect of control is that an individual can decide for herself how much privacy she desires. What would Allen say about such a definition of privacy?

2. *Privacy and Publicity.* Consider also whether a desire for publicity and a desire for privacy can coexist. Does the person who "tells it all" on the Jerry Springer talk show have any less expectation of privacy when she returns home to be with her family and friends or picks up the telephone to make a private call?

3. *Eroding Expectations of Privacy and Privacy Paternalism.* Allen contends that our society is changing by becoming more exhibitionistic and voyeuristic. The result is that expectations of privacy are eroding. In 2011, Allen further

develops these themes in a book, *Unpopular Privacy*. She argues that "privacy is so important and so neglected in contemporary life that democratic states, though liberal and feminist, could be justified in undertaking a rescue mission that includes enacting paternalistic privacy laws for the benefit of uneager beneficiaries."[20]

If people no longer expect privacy in many situations, then why should the law continue to protect it? If people no longer desire privacy, should the law force privacy upon them? Under what circumstances?

PAUL M. SCHWARTZ, *PRIVACY AND DEMOCRACY IN CYBERSPACE*

52 Vand. L. Rev. 1609 (1999)

. . . Self-determination is a capacity that is embodied and developed through social forms and practices. The threat to this quality arises when private or government action interferes with a person's control of her reasoning process. . . . [P]erfected surveillance of naked thought's digital expression short-circuits the individual's own process of decisionmaking. . . .

The maintenance of a democratic order requires both deliberative democracy and an individual capacity for self-determination. . . . [T]he emerging pattern of information use in cyberspace poses a risk to these two essential values. Our task now is to develop privacy standards that are capable of structuring the right kind of information use. . . .

Most scholars, and much of the law in this area, work around a liberal paradigm that we can term "privacy-control." From the age of computer mainframes in the 1960s to the current reign of the Internet's decentralized networks, academics and the law have gravitated towards the idea of privacy as a personal right to control the use of one's data. . . .

. . . [One flaw with the "privacy-control" paradigm is the "autonomy trap."] [T]he organization of information privacy through individual control of personal data rests on a view of autonomy as a given, preexisting quality. . . .

As a policy cornerstone, however, the idea of privacy-control falls straight into the "autonomy trap." The difficulty with privacy-control in the Information Age is that individual self-determination is itself shaped by the processing of personal data. . . .

To give an example of an autonomy trap in cyberspace, the act of clicking through a "consent" screen on a Web site may be considered by some observers to be an exercise of self-reliant choice. Yet, this screen can contain boilerplate language that permits all further processing and transmission of one's personal data. Even without a consent screen, some Web sites place consent boilerplate within a "privacy statement" on their home page or elsewhere on their site. For example, the online version of one New York newspaper states, "By using this site, you agree to the Privacy Policy of the New York Post." This language presents the conditions for data processing on a take-it-or-leave-it basis. It seeks to create the legal fiction that all who visit this Web site have expressed informed

---

[20] Anita L. Allen, *Unpopular Privacy* (2011).

consent to its data processing practices. An even more extreme manifestation of the "consent trap" is a belief that an initial decision to surf the Web itself is a self-reliant choice to accept all further use of one's personal data generated by this activity. . . .

The liberal ideal views autonomous individuals as able to interact freely and equally so long as the government or public does not interfere. The reality is, however, that individuals can be trapped when such glorification of freedom of action neglects the actual conditions of choice. Here, another problem arises with self-governance through information-control: the "data seclusion deception." The idea of privacy as data seclusion is easy to explain: unless the individual wishes to surrender her personal information, she is to be free to use her privacy right as a trump to keep it confidential or to subject its release to conditions that she alone wishes to set. The individual is to be at the center of shaping data anonymity. Yet, this right to keep data isolated quickly proves illusory because of the demands of the Information Age. . . .

NOTES & QUESTIONS

1. ***Privacy and Personhood.*** Like Schwartz, a number of theorists argue that privacy is essential for self-development. According to Jeffrey Reiman, privacy "protects the individual's interest in becoming, being, and remaining a person."[21] The notion that privacy protects personhood or identity is captured in Warren and Brandeis's notion of "inviolate personality." How does privacy promote self-development?

   Consider the following: "Every acceptance of a public role entails the repression, channelizing, and deflection of 'private' or personal attention, motives, and demands upon the self in order to address oneself to the expectations of others."[22] Can we really be ourselves in the public sphere? Is our "public self" any less part of our persona than our "private self"?

2. ***Privacy and Democracy.*** Schwartz views privacy as essential for a democratic society. Why is privacy important for political participation?

3. ***Privacy and Role Playing.*** Recall Westin's view of selfhood:

   Each person is aware of the gap between what he wants to be and what he actually is, between what the world sees of him and what he knows to be his much more complex reality. In addition, there are aspects of himself that the individual does not fully understand but is slowly exploring and shaping as he develops. Every individual lives behind a mask in this manner; indeed, the first etymological meaning of the word "person" was "mask," indicating both the conscious and expressive presentation of the self to a social audience. If this mask is torn off and the individual's real self bared to a world in which everyone else still wears his mask and believes in masked performances, the individual can be seared by the hot light of selective, forced exposure.

---

[21] Jeffrey H. Reiman, *Privacy, Intimacy, and Personhood*, in *Philosophical Dimensions of Privacy: An Anthology* 300, 308 (Ferdinand David Schoeman ed., 1984).

[22] Joseph Bensman & Robert Lilienfeld, *Between Public and Private: Lost Boundaries of the Self* 174 (1979).

Is there a "true" or "core" or "authentic" self? Or do we perform many roles and perhaps have multiple selves? Is there a self beneath the roles that we play?

Daniel Solove contends that "[s]ociety accepts that public reputations will be groomed to some degree. . . . Society protects privacy because it wants to provide individuals with some degree of influence over how they are judged in the public arena."[23] To what extent should the law allow people to promote a polished public image and hide the dirt in private?

4. ***Individual Autonomy, Democratic Order, and Data Trade.*** In a later article, Schwartz argues from the premise that "[p]ersonal information is an important currency in the new millennium."[24] He rejects arguments that opposed propertization of personal data, and developed a model to permit data trade consistent with individual autonomy and the maintenance of a democratic order. A key concept in this model is that of the "privacy commons," where privacy is viewed "as a social and not merely an individual good." As a result, Schwartz states, "If sound rules for the use of personal data are not established and enforced, society as a whole will suffer because people will decline to engage in a range of different social interactions due to concerns about use of personal information. A public good — the privacy commons — will be degraded." Do you think that property is a sound concept for building a public goods approach to information privacy?

SPIROS SIMITIS, *REVIEWING PRIVACY IN AN INFORMATION SOCIETY*

135 U. Pa. L. Rev. 707 (1987)

. . . The increased access to personal information resulting from modern, sophisticated techniques of automated processing has sharpened the need to abandon the search for a "neutral" concept in favor of an understanding free of abstractions and fully aware of the political and societal background of all privacy debates. Modern forms of data collection have altered the privacy discussion in three principal ways. First, privacy considerations no longer arise out of particular individual problems; rather, they express conflicts affecting everyone. The course of the privacy debate is neither determined by the caricature of a prominent golfer with a chocolate packet protruding out of his pocket, nor by the hints at the use of a sexual stimulant by a respected university professor, but by the intensive retrieval of personal data of virtually every employee, taxpayer, patient, bank customer, welfare recipient, or car driver. Second, smart cards and videotex make it possible to record and reconstruct individual activities in minute detail.[25] Surveillance has thereby lost its

---

[23] Daniel J. Solove, *The Virtues of Knowing Less: Justifying Privacy Protections Against Disclosure,* 53 Duke L.J. 957 (2003).

[24] Paul M. Schwartz, *Property, Privacy, and Personal Data,* 117 Harv. L. Rev. 2055 (2004).

[25] Editors' Note: Smart cards are also known as "chip cards" or "integrated circuit cards." These devices, generally the size of a credit card, feature an embedded circuit for the processing of data. A precursor of the Internet, Videotex enjoyed its heyday from the late 1970s to mid-1980s.

exceptional character and has become a more and more routine practice. Finally, personal information is increasingly used to enforce standards of behavior. Information processing is developing, therefore, into an essential element of long-term strategies of manipulation intended to mold and adjust individual conduct. . . .

. . . [B]ecause of both the broad availability of personal data and the elaborate matching procedures, individual activities can be accurately reconstructed through automated processing. Surveillance becomes the order of the day. Significantly enough, security agencies were among the first to discover the advantages of automated retrieval. They not only quickly computerized their own data collections but also sought and obtained access to state and private data banks. Entirely new investigation techniques, such as computer profiling, were developed, enabling the agencies to trace wanted persons by matching a presumptive pattern of consumption habits against, for instance, the records of utility companies. The successful attempts at computer-based voice and picture identification will probably influence the work of security agencies even more. . . .

Both the quest for greater transparency and the defense of free speech are legitimated by the goal of allowing the individual to understand social reality better and thus to form a personal opinion on its decisive factors as well as on possible changes. The citizen's right to be "a participator in the government of affairs," to use Jefferson's terms, reflects a profoundly rational process. It presupposes individuals who not only disperse the necessary information but also have the capacity to transform the accessible data into policy expectations. Transparency is, in other words, a basic element of competent communicative action and consequently remains indispensable as long as social discourse is to be promoted, not inhibited.

Inhibition, however, tends to be the rule once automated processing of personal data becomes a normal tool of both government and private enterprises. The price for an undoubted improvement in transparency is a no less evident loss in competence of communication. Habits, activities, and preferences are compiled, registered, and retrieved to facilitate better adjustment, not to improve the individual's capacity to act and to decide. Whatever the original incentive for computerization may have been, processing increasingly appears as the ideal means to adapt an individual to a predetermined, standardized behavior that aims at the highest possible degree of compliance with the model patient, consumer, taxpayer, employee, or citizen. Furthermore, interactive systems do not, despite all contrary assertions, restore a long lost individuality by correcting the effects of mass production in a mass society. On the contrary, the telematic integration forces the individual once more into a preset scheme. The media supplier dictates the conditions under which communication takes place, fixes the possible subjects of the dialogue, and, due to the personal data collected, is in an increasingly better position to influence the subscriber's behavior. Interactive systems, therefore, suggest individual activity where in fact no more than stereotyped reactions occur.

Videotex was typically deployed through a centralized system with one provider of information and involved the display of text on a television screen or dedicated terminal. France Telecom's Minitel was the most successful videotext system in the world.

In short, the transparency achieved through automated processing creates possibly the best conditions for colonization of the individual's lifeworld.[26] Accurate, constantly updated knowledge of her personal history is systematically incorporated into policies that deliberately structure her behavior. The more routinized automated processing augments the transparency, however, the more privacy proves to be a prerequisite to the capacity to participate in social discourse. Where privacy is dismantled, both the chance for personal assessment of the political and societal process and the opportunity to develop and maintain a particular style of life fade. . . .

The processing of personal data is not unique to a particular society. On the contrary, the attractiveness of information technology transcends political boundaries, particularly because of the opportunity to guide the individual's behavior. For a democratic society, however, the risks are high: labeling of individuals, manipulative tendencies, magnification of errors, and strengthening of social control threaten the very fabric of democracy. Yet, despite the incontestable importance of its technical aspects, informatization, like industrialization, is primarily a political and social challenge. When the relationship between information processing and democracy is understood, it becomes clear that the protection of privacy is the price necessary to secure the individual's ability to communicate and participate. Regulations that create precisely specified conditions for personal data processing are the decisive test for discerning whether society is aware of this price and willing to pay it. If the signs of experience are correct, this payment can be delayed no further. There is, in fact, no alternative to the advice of Horace: Seize the day, put not trust in the morrow. . . .

NOTES & QUESTIONS

1. *Privacy and Democracy.* As Simitis and other authors in this section observe, privacy is an issue about social structure. What is the relationship between privacy and democracy according to Simitis?

2. *Privacy Law and Information Flow.* Generally, one would assume that greater information flow facilitates democracy — it enables more expression, more political discourse, more information about the workings of government. Simitis, however, contends that privacy is "necessary to secure the individual's ability to communicate and participate." How are these two notions about information flow to be reconciled? Consider Joel Reidenberg:

   Data privacy rules are often cast as a balance between two basic liberties: fundamental human rights on one side and the free flow of information on the other side. Yet, because societies differ on how and when personal information should be available for private and public sector needs, the treatment and

---

[26] For both the colonization process and the impact of the individual's lifeworld on communicative action, see Jürgen Habermas, 1 *The Theory of Communicative Action* 70-71 (1983) (defining "lifeworld" as shared understandings about what will be treated as a fact, valid norms, and subjective experience). . . .

interaction of these liberties will express a specific delineation between the state, civil society, and the citizen.[27]

Privacy, according to Reidenberg, involves establishing a balance between protecting the rights of individuals and enabling information flow. Do you think these interests always exist in opposition? Consider financial services, communications networks, and medical care. Does privacy impair or enable information flow?[28]

C. CRITICS OF PRIVACY

RICHARD A. POSNER, *THE RIGHT OF PRIVACY*

12 Ga. L. Rev. 393 (1978)

People invariably possess information, including facts about themselves and contents of communications, that they will incur costs to conceal. Sometimes such information is of value to others: that is, others will incur costs to discover it. Thus we have two economic goods, "privacy" and "prying." . . .

[M]uch of the casual prying (a term used here without any pejorative connotation) into the private lives of friends and colleagues that is so common a feature of social life is also motivated, to a greater extent than we may realize, by rational considerations of self-interest. Prying enables one to form a more accurate picture of a friend or colleague, and the knowledge gained is useful in one's social or professional dealings with him. For example, in choosing a friend one legitimately wants to know whether he will be discreet or indiscreet, selfish or generous, and these qualities are not always apparent on initial acquaintance. Even a pure altruist needs to know the (approximate) wealth of any prospective beneficiary of his altruism in order to be able to gauge the value of a transfer to him.

The other side of the coin is that social, like business, dealings present opportunities for exploitation through misrepresentation. Psychologists and sociologists have pointed out that even in every day life people try to manipulate by misrepresentation other people's opinion of them. As one psychologist has written, the "wish for privacy expresses a desire . . . to control others' perceptions and beliefs vis-à-vis the self-concealing person." Even the strongest defenders of privacy describe the individual's right to privacy as the right to "control the flow of information about him." A seldom remarked corollary to a right to misrepresent one's character is that others have a legitimate interest in unmasking the deception.

---

[27] Joel R. Reidenberg, *Resolving Conflicting International Data Privacy Rules in Cyberspace*, 52 Stan. L. Rev. 1315 (2000).

[28] For additional reading about philosophical theories of privacy, see Judith W. DeCew, *In Pursuit of Privacy: Law, Ethics, and the Rise of Technology* (1997) (surveying and critiquing various theories of privacy); Anita L. Allen, *Uneasy Access: Privacy for Women in a Free Society* (1988) (same); Ferdinand David Schoeman, ed., *Philosophical Dimensions of Privacy* (1984) (anthology of articles about the concept of privacy).

Yet some of the demand for private information about other people is not self-protection in the foregoing sense but seems mysteriously disinterested — for example, that of the readers of newspaper gossip columns, whose "idle curiosity" Warren and Brandeis deplored, groundlessly in my opinion. Gossip columns recount the personal lives of wealthy and successful people whose tastes and habits offer models — that is, yield information — to the ordinary person in making consumption, career, and other decisions. . . . Gossip columns open people's eyes to opportunities and dangers; they are genuinely informational. . . .

Warren and Brandeis attributed the rise of curiosity about people's lives to the excesses of the press. The economist does not believe, however, that supply creates demand. A more persuasive explanation for the rise of the gossip column is the secular increase in personal incomes. There is apparently very little privacy in poor societies, where, consequently, people can easily observe at first hand the intimate lives of others. Personal surveillance is costlier in wealthier societies both because people live in conditions that give them greater privacy from such observation and because the value (and hence opportunity cost) of time is greater—too great to make a generous allotment of time to watching neighbors worthwhile. People in wealthier societies sought an alternative method of informing themselves about how others live and the press provided it. A legitimate and important function of the press is to provide specialization in prying in societies where the costs of obtaining information have become too great for the Nosey Parker. . . .

Transaction-cost considerations may also militate against the assignment of a property right to the possessor of a secret. . . . Consider, for example, . . . whether the law should allow a magazine to sell its subscriber list to another magazine without obtaining the subscribers' consent. . . . [T]he costs of obtaining subscriber approval would be high relative to the value of the list. If, therefore, we believe that these lists are generally worth more to the purchasers than being shielded from possible unwanted solicitations is worth to the subscribers, we should assign the property right to the magazine; and the law does this. . . .

Much of the demand for privacy . . . concerns discreditable information, often information concerning past or present criminal activity or moral conduct at variance with a person's professed moral standards. And often the motive for concealment is, as suggested earlier, to mislead those with whom he transacts. Other private information that people wish to conceal, while not strictly discreditable, would if revealed correct misapprehensions that the individual is trying to exploit, as when a worker conceals a serious health problem from his employer or a prospective husband conceals his sterility from his fiancée. It is not clear why society should assign the property right in such information to the individual to whom it pertains; and the common law, as we shall see, generally does not. . . .

We think it wrong (and inefficient) that the law should permit a seller in hawking his wares to make false or incomplete representations as to their quality. But people "sell" themselves as well as their goods. They profess high standards of behavior in order to induce others to engage in social or business dealings with them from which they derive an advantage but at the same time they conceal some of the facts that these acquaintances would find useful in forming an accurate picture of their character. There are practical reasons for not imposing a general legal duty of full and frank disclosure of one's material. . . .

. . . [E]veryone should be allowed to protect himself from disadvantageous transactions by ferreting out concealed facts about individuals which are material to the representations (implicit or explicit) that those individuals make concerning their moral qualities.

It is no answer that such individuals have "the right to be let alone." Very few people want to be let alone. They want to manipulate the world around them by selective disclosure of facts about themselves. Why should others be asked to take their self-serving claims at face value and be prevented from obtaining the information necessary to verify or disprove these claims?

NOTES & QUESTIONS

1. ***Posner's Conception of Privacy.*** What is Posner's definition of privacy? How does Posner determine the value of privacy (i.e., how it should be weighed relative to other interests and values)? In what circumstances is Posner likely to defend a privacy claim?

2. ***Irrational Judgments.*** One economic argument for privacy is that sometimes people form irrational judgments based upon learning certain information about others. For example, an employer may not hire certain people based on their political views or associations, sexual orientation, mental illness, and prior criminal convictions — even though these facts may have no relevance to a potential employee's abilities to do the job. These judgments decrease efficiency. In *The Economics of Justice*, Posner offers a response:

   > This objection overlooks the opportunity costs of shunning people for stupid reasons, or, stated otherwise, the gains from dealing with someone whom others shun irrationally. If ex-convicts are good workers but most employers do not know this, employers who do know will be able to hire them at a below-average wage because of their depressed job opportunities and will thereby obtain a competitive advantage over the bigots. In a diverse, decentralized, and competitive society, irrational shunning will be weeded out over time. . .[29]

   Will the market be able to eradicate irrational judgments?

3. ***The Dangers of the "Masquerade Ball."*** Consider Dennis Bailey:

   > . . . [I]t is interesting to consider the ways in which the world has become like a giant masquerade ball. Far removed from the tight knit social fabric of the village of the past, we've lost the ability to recognize the people we pass on the street. People might as well be wearing masks because we are likely to know very little about them. In other words, these strangers are anonymous to us, anonymous in the sense that not only their names, but their entire identities, are unknown to us — the intimate details of who they are, where they have come from, and how they have lived their lives.[30]

---

[29] Richard A. Posner, *The Economics of Justice* (1981). Posner further develops his theories about privacy in Richard A. Posner, *Overcoming Law* 531-51 (1995). Posner first set out his views on privacy in Richard A. Posner, *An Economic Theory of Privacy*, Regulations (May/June 1978).

[30] Dennis Bailey, *The Open Society Paradox* 26-27 (2004).

Are we living in a "masquerade ball"? Businesses and the government have unprecedented new technologies to engage in surveillance and gather information. Should the law facilitate or restrict anonymity?

Also consider Steven Nock:

> Any method of social control depends, immediately, on information about individuals. . . . There can be no social control without such information. . . .
>
> Modern Americans enjoy vastly more privacy than did their forebears because ever and ever larger numbers of strangers in our lives are legitimately denied access to our personal affairs. . . . Privacy, however, makes it difficult to form reliable opinions of one another. Legitimately shielded from other's regular scrutiny, we are thereby more immune to the routine monitoring that once formed the basis of our individual reputations.[31]

Does too much privacy erode trust and lessen social control in detrimental ways?

4. *Information Dissemination and Economic Efficiency.* Does economic theory necessarily lead to the conclusion that more personal information is generally preferable? Consider the following critique of Posner by Edward Bloustein:

> We must remember that Posner stated in *Economic Analysis of Law* that economics "cannot prescribe social change"; it can only tell us about the economic costs of managing it one way or another. . . . [Posner's] characterization of the privacy of personal information as a species of commercial fraud . . . [is an] extension[ ] of a social value judgment rather than implications or conclusions of economic theory. . . .Our society, in fact, places a very high value on maintaining individual privacy, even to the extent of concealing "discreditable" information. . . .[32]

Also consider Richard Murphy's critique of Posner:

> [D]emarcating a relatively large sphere for the private self creates an opportunity for discovery or actualization of a "true" nature, which may have a value beyond the utility of satisfying preferences. . . . As Roger Rosenblatt put it, "Out of our private gropings and self-inspections grow our imaginative values — private language, imagery, memory. In the caves of the mind one bats about to discover a light entirely of one's own which, though it should turn out to be dim, is still worth a life." Unless a person can investigate without risk of reproach what his own preferences are, he will not be able to maximize his own happiness.[33]

When can the circulation of less personal information be more economically efficient than greater information flow?

5. *Why Don't Individuals Protect Their Privacy?* Empirical studies frequently report on growing privacy concerns across the United States. Yet, individuals

---

[31] Steven L. Nock, *The Costs of Privacy: Surveillance and Reputation in America* (1993).

[32] Edward J. Bloustein, *Privacy Is Dear at Any Price: A Response to Professor Posner's Economic Theory*, 12 Ga. L. Rev. 429, 441 (1978). For another critique of Posner's approach, see Kim Lane Scheppele, *Legal Secrets: Equality and Efficiency in the Common Law* (1988).

[33] Richard S. Murphy, *Property Rights in Personal Information: An Economic Defense of Privacy*, 84 Geo. L.J. 2381 (1996).

seem willing to exchange privacy for services or small rewards and generally fail to adopt technologies and techniques that would protect their privacy. If people are willing to sell their privacy for very little in return, isn't this evidence that they do not really value privacy as much as they say they do?

Alessandro Acqusiti and Jens Grossklags have pointed to a number of reasons for this divergence between stated privacy preferences and actual behavior:

First, incomplete information affects privacy decision making because of externalities (when third parties share personal information about an individual, they might affect that individual without his being part of the transaction between those parties), information asymmetries (information relevant to the privacy decision process — for example, how personal information will be used — might be known only to a subset of the parties making decisions), risk (most privacy related payoffs are not deterministic), and uncertainties (payoffs might not only be stochastic, but dependent on unknown random distributions). Benefits and costs associated with privacy intrusions and protection are complex, multifaceted, and context-specific. They are frequently bundled with other products and services (for example, a search engine query can prompt the desired result but can also give observers information about the searcher's interests), and they are often recognized only after privacy violations have taken place. They can be monetary but also immaterial and, thus, difficult to quantify.

Second, even if individuals had access to complete information, they would be unable to process and act optimally on vast amounts of data. Especially in the presence of complex, ramified consequences associated with the protection or release of personal information, our innate bounded rationality limits our ability to acquire, memorize and process all relevant information, and it makes us rely on simplified mental models, approximate strategies, and heuristics. . . .

Third, even if individuals had access to complete information and could successfully calculate optimization strategies for their privacy sensitive decisions, they might still deviate from the rational strategy. A vast body of economic and psychological literature has revealed several forms of systematic psychological deviations from rationality that affect individual decision making. . . . Research in psychology . . . documents how individuals mispredict their own future preferences or draw inaccurate conclusions from past choices. In addition, individuals often suffer from self-control problems — in particular, the tendency to trade off costs and benefits in ways that damage their future utility in favor of immediate gratification. Individuals' behavior can also be guided by social preferences or norms, such as fairness or altruism. Many of these deviations apply naturally to privacy-sensitive scenarios.[34]

---

[34] Alessandro Acquisti & Jens Grossklags, *Privacy and Rationality in Decision Making*, IEEE, Security and Privacy 24 (2005).

FRED H. CATE, *PRINCIPLES OF INTERNET PRIVACY*

32 Conn. L. Rev. 877 (2000)

Perhaps the most important consideration when balancing restrictions on information is the historical importance of the free flow of information. The free flow concept is one that is not only enshrined in the First Amendment, but frankly in any form of democratic or market economy. In the United States, we have placed extraordinary importance on the open flow of information. As the Federal Reserve Board noted in its report to Congress on data protection in financial institutions, "it is the freedom to speak, supported by the availability of information and the free-flow of data, that is the cornerstone of a democratic society and market economy."

The significance of open data flows is reflected in the constitutional provisions not only for freedom of expression, but for copyrights — to promote the creation and dissemination of expression, and for a post office — to deliver the mail and the news. Federal regulations demonstrate a sweeping preference for openness, reflected in the Freedom of Information Act, Government in the Sunshine Act, and dozens of other laws applicable to the government. There are even more laws requiring disclosure by private industry, such as the regulatory disclosures required by securities and commodities laws, banking and insurance laws, and many others. This is a very basic tenet of the society in which we live. Laws that restrict that free flow almost always conflict with this basic principle. That does not mean that such laws are never upheld, but merely that they face a considerable constitutional hurdle.

This is done with good reason. Open information flows are not only essential to self-governance; they have also generated significant, practical benefits. The ready availability of personal information helps businesses "deliver the right products and services to the right customers, at the right time, more effectively and at lower cost," Fred Smith, founder and President of the Competitive Enterprise Institute, has written. Federal Reserve Board Governor Edward Gramlich testified before Congress in July 1999 that "[i]nformation about individuals' needs and preferences is the cornerstone of any system that allocates goods and services within an economy." The more such information is available, he continued, "the more accurately and efficiently will the economy meet those needs and preferences."

Federal Reserve Board Chairman Alan Greenspan has been perhaps the most articulate spokesperson for the extraordinary value of accessible personal information. In 1998, he wrote to Congressman Ed Markey (D-Mass.):

> A critical component of our ever more finely hewn competitive market system has been the plethora of information on the characteristics of customers both businesses and individuals. Such information has enabled producers and marketers to fine tune production schedules to the ever greater demands of our consuming public for diversity and individuality of products and services. Newly devised derivative products, for example, have enabled financial institutions to unbundle risk in a manner that enables those desirous of taking on that risk (and potential reward) to do so, and those that chose otherwise, to be

risk averse. It has enabled financial institutions to offer a wide variety of customized insurance and other products.

Detailed data obtained from consumers as they seek credit or make product choices help engender the whole set of sensitive price signals that are so essential to the functioning of an advanced information based economy such as ours. . . .

In a recent report on public record information, Richard Varn, Chief Information Officer of the State of Iowa, and I examined the critical roles played by public record information in our economy and society. We concluded that such information constitutes part of this nation's "essential infrastructure," the benefits of which are "so numerous and diverse that they impact virtually every facet of American life. . . ." The ready availability of public record data "facilitates a vibrant economy, improves efficiency, reduces costs, creates jobs, and provides valuable products and services that people want."

Perhaps most importantly, widely accessible personal information has helped to create a democratization of opportunity in the United States. Anyone can go almost anywhere, make purchases from vendors they will never see, maintain accounts with banks they will never visit, and obtain credit far from home all because of open information flows. Americans can take advantage of opportunities based on their records, on what they have done rather than who they know, because access to consumer information makes it possible for distant companies and creditors to make rational decisions about doing business with individuals. The open flow of information gives consumers real choice. This is what the open flow of information principle reflects, not just the constitutional importance of information flows, but their significant economic and social benefits as well.

NOTES & QUESTIONS

1. ***The Pros and Cons of the Free Flow of Information.*** In a striking passage, Cate points out that free flows of information create a "democratization of opportunity in the United States." With this phrase, he reminds us that part of the equality at the basis of American life concerns economic opportunity, and that, in his view, a certain kind of flow of personal information will contribute to this goal. While privacy can be problematic, can open access to information also raise difficulties? How should one establish a baseline for open access or restricted access to personal information?

2. ***The Costs of Privacy.*** Can you think of some of the other important values with which privacy might conflict and the costs that privacy can impose? What should be the baseline in measuring costs?

3. ***The Business of Data Trade.*** The trade in personal information is now a valuable part of the U.S. economy. As a single example, Google reached an agreement on April 14, 2007, to purchase DoubleClick, an online advertising company, for $3.1 billion. The deal was driven by Google's interest in behavioral advertising, in which companies use digital data collection techniques to track individuals around the Internet and serve them targeted

ads. Should consumers be allowed to sign up for a National Do Not Track List?

4. *The Benefits of Information Collection and Use.* Consider Kent Walker:

> Having some information about yourself out there in the world offers real convenience that goes beyond dollars and cents. Many people benefit from warehousing information — billing and shipping addresses, credit card numbers, individual preferences, and the like — with trustworthy third parties. Such storage of information can dramatically simplify the purchasing experience, ensure that you get a nonsmoking room, or automate the task of ordering a kiddie meal every time your child boards a plane. Likewise, most people prefer to use a credit card rather than a debit card, trading confidentiality of purchases for the convenience of deferred payment. . . .
>
> While there's often little individual incentive to participate in the aggregation of information about people, a great collective good results from the default participation of most people. The aggregation of information often requires a critical mass to be worth doing, or for the results to be worth using. (A phone book with only one out of ten numbers would hardly be worth using, let alone printing.) . . .
>
> Another example is Caller ID, which pits different privacy claims against one another. Many people like the notion of an electronic peephole, letting them know who's at the electronic door before they decide whether to pick up the phone. Yet many people block transmission of their own numbers, valuing protection of their privacy. Neither choice is necessarily right, but it's worth recognizing that the assertion of the privacy claim affects the contending desires of others. The classic Tragedy of the Commons aspects are clear. From my selfish perspective, I want access to information about everyone else — the identity of who's calling me, their listed phone number, etc. I want to be able to intrude on others without their knowing who I am (which I can accomplish by blocking Caller ID), and don't want others to be able to intrude on me unbidden (which I can accomplish by unlisting my phone number). The gain in privacy makes it harder to find the people you want to reach, and harder to know who's calling you.[35]

---

[35] Kent Walker, *Where Everybody Knows Your Name: A Pragmatic Look at the Costs of Privacy and the Benefits of Information Exchange,* 2000 Stan. Tech. L. Rev. 2, 39, 46, 48 (2000).

CHAPTER 3

FINANCIAL DATA

CHAPTER OUTLINE

A. THE FAIR CREDIT REPORTING ACT

Increasingly, companies in the United States make sales based on credit. Since 1980, almost all homes and most new cars are purchased on credit. Well over half of retail items are purchased on credit as well.[1]

As a result of the centrality of different forms of consumer borrowing, consumer reporting agencies play an increasingly significant role in economic transactions. Consumer reporting agencies prepare credit reports about people's credit history for use by creditors seeking to loan people money. Credit reports contain financial information such as bankruptcy filings, judgments and liens, mortgage foreclosures, and checking account data. Some companies also prepare

---

[1] *See generally* Robert Ellis Smith, *Ben Franklin's Web Site: Privacy and Curiosity from Plymouth Rock to the Internet* 313-25 (2000); Steven L. Nock, *The Costs of Privacy: Surveillance and Reputation in America* (1993).

investigative consumer reports, which supplement the credit report with information about an individual's character and lifestyle. Creditors depend upon credit reports to determine whether or not to offer a person a loan as well as what interest rate to charge that person. Credit reports are also reviewed by some landlords before renting out an apartment.

Credit reports contain a "credit score" that is used to assess a person's credit risk. In many cases, a low score will not necessarily mean the denial of a loan, mortgage, or credit card; rather, it means that a higher rate of interest will be charged. As Evan Hendricks notes:

> According to the Fair Isaac Corporation, a leading developer of credit scoring models, one delinquent account can lower a credit score from 70 to 120 points. A consumer with excellent credit (credit score of 720-850) would pay about 7.85% interest rate for a home equity loan, while a consumer with marginal credit (640-659) would pay 9.2% and one with poor credit (500-559) would pay a 12.1% rate. The rate swings for a new car loan are even greater, with good credit risks paying a 5.2% rate, moderate risks paying 11.4% and poor risks paying 17.2%.[2]

Credit reports are not only used in connection with granting credit. Employers use credit reports to make hiring and promotion decisions. The issuance of professional licenses, such as admittance to the bar, also can require the examination of one's credit report.

There are three major national consumer reporting agencies: Experian, Equifax, and Trans Union. Each of these three companies has information on virtually every adult American citizen, and they routinely prepare credit reports about individuals.

According to Peter Swire, our financial system has been shifting toward more traceable payment transactions: "The shift from cash to checks to credit and debit cards shows an evolution toward creating records, placing the records automatically in databases, and potentially linking the databases to reveal extremely detailed information about an individual's purchasing history."[3] This evolution is generating new problems for the protection of privacy.

In 1970, Congress passed the Fair Credit Reporting Act (FCRA), Pub. L. No. 90-321, to regulate consumer reporting agencies. The Act was inspired by allegations of abuse and lack of responsiveness of credit agencies to consumer complaints. In its statement of purpose, the FCRA states: "There is a need to insure that consumer reporting agencies exercise their grave responsibilities with fairness, impartiality, and a respect for the consumer's right to privacy." 15 U.S.C. § 1681. The FCRA requires credit reporting companies to provide an individual access to her records, establishes procedures for correcting information, and sets limitations on disclosure.

In 2003, Congress passed the Fair and Accurate Credit Transactions Act (FACTA), which amended FCRA. Evan Hendricks explains the impetus for passing the FACTA:

---

[2] Evan Hendricks, *Credit Scores and Credit Reports: How the System Really Works, What You Can Do* 3-4 (2004).

[3] Peter P. Swire, *Financial Privacy and the Theory of High-Tech Government Surveillance*, 77 Wash. U. L.Q. 461 (1999).

[K]ey provisions of the FCRA that preempted State law were set to expire on December 31, 2003. These provisions dealt with issues affecting billions of dollars in commerce: pre-approved credit card offers, duties on creditors (furnishers) to report accurately and to reinvestigate, and the sharing of personal data among corporate affiliates. Industry expressed fears that if legislation was not passed and the preemption expired, state legislatures would begin passing conflicting laws that would raise compliance costs, and worse, interfere with profits.

To consumer and privacy groups, legislation was long overdue because the 1996 FCRA Amendments were not getting the job done. All of the long-standing problems related to privacy and fair information practices persisted: inaccuracy, faulty reinvestigations, reinsertion, non-responsiveness, and lax security. More dramatically, identity theft had been crowned the nation's "fastest growing crime," and the biggest harm from identity theft, everyone knew, was to the privacy of credit reports. . . .

Both sides wanted legislation, but not the same legislation. Industry wanted a simple, straightforward bill that would do nothing more than make FCRA preemption permanent.

Consumer privacy groups called for a detailed reform bill that would set a "floor" of new protections, but which would leave the states free to go further.[4]

1. FCRA'S SCOPE AND STRUCTURE

Scope. FCRA applies to "any consumer reporting agency" that furnishes a "consumer report." 15 U.S.C. § 1681b. As a consequence, the scope of the FCRA turns on the definitions of "consumer report" and "consumer reporting agencies."

Consumer Report. A "consumer report" is any type of communication by a consumer reporting agency "bearing on a consumer's credit worthiness, credit standing, credit capacity, character, general reputation, personal characteristics, or mode of living." This communication must be used or expected to be used in part to establish a consumer's eligibility for credit, insurance, employment, or other permissible uses of credit reports as defined in FCRA. 15 U.S.C. § 1681a.

Consumer Reporting Agency. A "consumer reporting agency" is defined as "[a]ny person which, for monetary fees, dues, or on a cooperative nonprofit basis, regularly engages in whole or in part in the practice of assembling or evaluating consumer credit information or other information on consumers for the purpose of furnishing consumer reports to third parties." § 1681b(f).

Courts have held that "even if a report is used or expected to be used for a non-consumer purpose, it may still fall within the definition of a consumer report if it contains information that was originally collected by a consumer reporting agency with the expectation that it would be used for a consumer purpose." *Ippolito v. WNS, Inc.*, 864 F.2d 440 (7th Cir. 1988); *Bakker v. McKinnon*, 152 F.3d 1007 (8th Cir. 1998).

---

[4] Hendricks, *Credit Scores, supra*, at 307-08.

FTC and CFBP Enforcement. For the first 40 years after the passage of FCRA, the Federal Trade Commission (FTC) was the agency mainly responsible for rulemaking and enforcement under FCRA.

In 2010, the Dodd-Frank Act created a new federal agency called the Consumer Financial Protection Bureau (CFPB) and assigned it primary enforcement and rulemaking authority for FCRA. However, the FTC still retains some FCRA enforcement power and shares this with the CFPB.

In 2012, the FTC and CFPB signed a memorandum of understanding regarding coordinating their enforcement of FCRA.[5]

Private Right of Action. Additionally, people who are harmed by violations of FCRA can sue for negligent or willful failure to comply with FCRA's requirements.

Preemption. FCRA preempts state law relatively broadly and does so by reserving a large number of subjects for federal law. These include the pre-screening of consumer reports, procedures and requirements relating to the duties of a person who takes any adverse action with respect to a consumer, and procedures and requirements regarding the information contained in consumer reports. §§ 1681c-1, 1681t(b)(5). These are examples of subject matter preemption; the federal law occupies the regulatory area.

In 2003, FACTA amended FCRA by adding narrower restrictions targeted to mandated behavior. As an example, FACTA requires consumer reporting agencies to place fraud alerts on consumer credit files under certain circumstances. In so doing, it streamlines an area of industry procedures while, at the same time, permitting states to engage in further regulation regarding the larger subject area, which is identity theft.[6] As an example of "required conduct" preemption, FCRA requires consumer agencies to place fraud alerts on consumer credit files under certain circumstances. At the same time, it permits states to engage in further regulation regarding the larger subject area, which is identity theft.

UNITED STATES V. SPOKEO, INC.

No. CV12-05001MMM(JHx) (C.D. Cal., June 7, 2012)

COMPLAINT

Plaintiff, the United States of America, acting upon notification and authorization to the Attorney General by the Federal Trade Commission ("FTC" or "Commission"), for its Complaint alleges that:

1. Plaintiff brings this action under sections 5(a), 13(b), and 16(a) of the Federal Trade Commission Act ("FTC Act"), 15 U.S.C. §§ 45(a), 53(b), and

---

[5] Memorandum of Understanding Between the Consumer Financial Protection Bureau and the Federal Trade Commission (Jan. 20, 2012) http://files.consumerfinance.gov/f/2012/01/FTC.MOUwSig.1.20.pdf

[6] For a discussion, see Paul M. Schwartz, *Preemption and Privacy*, 118 Yale L.J. 902, 943-44 (2009).

56(a); and section 621(a) of the Fair Credit Reporting Act ("FCRA"), 15 U.S.C. § 1681 s(a), to obtain monetary civil penalties, and injunctive or other relief from Defendant for engaging in violations of the FTC Act. . . .

5. Defendant Spokeo, Inc. ("Spokeo") is a privately-held Delaware C-type corporation doing business in California. . . .

9. Spokeo assembles consumer information from "hundreds of online and offline sources," such as social networking sites, data brokers, and other sources to create consumer profiles, which Defendant promotes as "coherent people profiles" and "powerful intelligence." These consumer profiles identify specific individuals and display such information as the individual's physical address, phone number, marital status, age range, or email address. Spokeo profiles are further organized by descriptive headers denoting, among other things, a person's hobbies, ethnicity, religion, or participation on social networking sites, and may contain photos or other information, such as economic health graphics, that Spokeo attributes to a particular individual. Among other things, Spokeo sells the profiles through paid subscriptions, which provide a set number of searches based on subscription level, as well as through Application Program Interfaces ("API") that provide customized and/or higher volume access.

10. Since at least 2008, Spokeo has provided its consumer profiles to businesses, including entities operating in the human resources ("HR"), background screening, and recruiting industries, to serve as a factor in deciding whether to interview a job candidate or whether to hire a candidate after a job interview. . . .

11. In 2010, Spokeo changed its website Terms of Service to state that it was not a consumer reporting agency and that consumers may not use the company's website or information for FCRA-covered purposes. However, Spokeo failed to revoke access to or otherwise ensure that existing users, including subscribers who may have joined Spokeo through its Spokeo.com/HR page, or those who had previously purchased access to profiles through API user agreements, did not use the company's website or information for FCRA-covered purposes.

12. The consumer profiles Spokeo provides to third parties are "consumer reports" as defined in section 603(d) of the FCRA, 15 U.S.C. § 1681a(d). . . .

Spokeo profiles are consumer reports because they bear on a consumer's character, general reputation, personal characteristics, or mode of living and/or other attributes listed in section 603(d), and are "used or expected to be used ...in whole or in part" as a factor in determining the consumer's eligibility for employment or other purposes specified in section 604.

13. In providing "consumer reports" Spokeo is now and has been a "consumer reporting agency" ("CRA") as that term is defined in section 603(f) of the FCRA, 15 U.S.C. § 1681a(f). . . .

18. Section 607(a) of the FCRA, 15 U.S.C. § 1681e(a), requires that every consumer reporting agency maintain reasonable procedures to limit the furnishing of consumer reports for enumerated "permissible purposes." These reasonable procedures include making reasonable efforts to verify the identity of each prospective user of consumer report information and the uses certified by each prospective user prior to furnishing such user with a consumer report.

19. . . . Spokeo has failed to maintain such reasonable procedures. For example, Spokeo has failed to require that prospective users of the profiles

identify themselves, certify the purposes for which the information is sought, and certify that the information will be used for no other purpose.

22. Section 607(b) of the FCRA, 15 U.S.C. § 1681e(b), requires consumer reporting agencies to follow reasonable procedures to assure maximum possible accuracy of the information concerning the individual about whom the report relates.

23. . . . Defendant has failed to use reasonable procedures to assure maximum possible accuracy of consumer report information. . . .

26. Section 607(d) of the FCRA, 15 U.S.C. § 1681e(d), requires that a consumer reporting agency provide, to any person to whom it provides a consumer report ("users"), a User Notice.

27. . . . Defendant has failed to provide User Notices to users and thereby has violated section 607(d) of the FCRA, 15 U.S.C. § 1681e(d). . . .

30. Section 604 of the FCRA, 15 U.S.C. § 1681b prohibits CRAs from furnishing consumer reports to persons that it did not have reason to believe had a permissible purpose to obtain a consumer report.

31. . . . Spokeo has furnished consumer reports to persons that it did not have reason to believe had a permissible purpose to obtain a consumer report. . . .

39. Section 621(a)(2)(A) of the FCRA, 15 U.S.C. § 1681s(a)(2)(A), authorizes the Court to award monetary civil penalties in the event of a knowing violation of the FCRA, which constitutes a pattern or practice. Spokeo's violations of the FCRA, as alleged in this Complaint, have been knowing and have constituted a pattern or practice of violations. As specified by the Federal Civil Penalty Inflation Adjustment Act of 1990, 28 U.S.C. § 2461, as amended by the Debt Collection Improvements Act of 1996, Pub. L. 104-134, § 31001(s)(1), 110 Stat. 1321-373, the Court is authorized to award a penalty of not more than $2,500 per violation for violations occurring before February 10, 2009, and $3,500 per violation for violations occurring on or after that date.

40. Each instance in which Spokeo has failed to comply with the FCRA constitutes a separate violation of the FCRA for the purpose of assessing monetary civil penalties under section 621 of the FCRA, 15 U.S.C. § 1681s. Plaintiff seeks monetary civil penalties for every separate violation of the FCRA.

41. Under section 621(a) of the FCRA, 15 U.S.C. § 1681s(a), and section 13(b) of the FTC Act, 15 U.S.C. § 53(b), this Court is authorized to issue a permanent injunction prohibiting Defendant from violating the FTC Act and the FCRA. . . .

CONSENT DECREE AND ORDER FOR CIVIL PENALTIES,
INJUNCTION AND OTHER RELIEF

. . . The parties have agreed to entry of this Stipulated Final Judgment and Order for Civil Penalties, Permanent Injunction, and Other Equitable Relief ("Order") to resolve all matters in dispute in this action without trial or adjudication of any issue of law or fact herein and without Defendant admitting the truth of, or liability for, any of the matters alleged in the Complaint. Defendant has waived service of the Summons and Complaint.

THEREFORE, IT IS HEREBY ORDERED, ADJUDGED, AND DECREED as follows: . . . .

4. Defendant makes no admissions to the allegations in the Complaint, other than the jurisdictional facts. . . .

IT IS ORDERED that:

1. Judgment in the amount of eight hundred thousand dollars ($800,000) is hereby entered against Defendant, as a civil penalty for violations of the FCRA. . . .

IT IS FURTHER ORDERED that Defendant, and all other persons or entities within the scope of Fed. R. Civ. P. 65, whether acting directly or through any sole proprietorship, partnership, limited liability company, corporation, subsidiary, branch, division, device, or other business entity who receive actual notice of this Order by personal service or otherwise, are hereby permanently restrained and enjoined from violating the Fair Credit Reporting Act, 15 U.S.C. §§1681-1681x. . . .

IT IS FURTHER ORDERED that Defendant make timely submissions to the Commission: . . . .

2. For 20 years following entry of this Order, Defendant must submit a compliance notice, sworn under penalty of perjury, within 14 days of any change in the following: (a) any designated point of contact; or (b) the structure of any entity that Defendant has any ownership interest in or directly or indirectly controls that may affect compliance obligations arising under this Order, including: creation, merger, sale, or dissolution of the entity or any subsidiary, parent, or affiliate that engages in any acts or practices subject to this Order.

IT IS FURTHER ORDERED that Defendant must create certain records for 20 years after entry of the Order, and retain each such record for five (5) years. Specifically, Defendant must maintain the following records [including accounting records, personnel records, training materials, compliance documents, a copy of each advertisement and marketing material, and others.]

IT IS FURTHER ORDERED that, for the purpose of monitoring Defendant's compliance with this Order, including any failure to transfer any assets as required by this Order:

1. Within 14 days of receipt of a written request from a representative of the Commission or Plaintiff, Defendant must: submit additional compliance reports or other requested information, which must be sworn under penalty of perjury; appear for depositions; and produce documents, for inspection and copying. . . .

NOTES & QUESTIONS

1. *Unwittingly Falling Under FCRA.* According to Spokeo's founder, he did not realize Spokeo was regulated under FCRA:

> Six years ago, my Stanford roommates and I built Spokeo to help us keep in touch with friends across a dizzying array of social networks. We are honored today to be at the helm of a principal destination for millions of Americans searching for and looking to connect with others. . . .
>
> A few years ago, we were eager to share our social network search tool with anyone who could find good use for it. Focusing on a prior version of our

website, the U.S. Federal Trade Commission (FTC) believes that our targeted marketing (at that time) implicated the Fair Credit Reporting Act (FCRA), which regulates the collection, dissemination and use of consumer information, including credit information provided by consumer reporting agencies. It has never been our intention to act as a consumer reporting agency. We have made changes to our site and our internal business practices in order to ensure we don't infringe upon the FCRA's important consumer protections, and to ensure an honest and transparent service that will continue to be easy for our customers to use. We are a technology company organizing people-related data in innovative ways. We do not create our own content, we do not possess or have access to private financial information, and we do not offer consumer reports.[7]

Is it fair to charge Spokeo with violating FCRA when it did not even realize that it had to follow FCRA? Should small start-up companies be required to know when they trigger FCRA?

2. ***The Digital Frontier of Credit Services.*** An online frontier of credit services exists beyond traditional consumer reporting agencies, namely, Equifax, Experian, and Transunion (the traditional "Big Three" of the industry). Like Spokeo, a variety of new entities draw on digital information in innovative ways to estimate credit worthiness and offer credit services. This information can then be combined with up-to-date signals about whether a customer is looking for a financial product or service. As Ed Mierzwinski and Jeff Chester note, "A new data market has emerged, selling access to a consumer's intent to be 'in-market' for a product or service."[8] Online data warehouse companies, such as BlueKai, offer online marketers access to such "intent information" gathered from databrokers, such as Acxiom. For Mierzwinski and Chester, the law should view these "online scoring databases" as "equivalent to prescreened lists, which are consumer reports." These authors call on the FTC to determine whether companies that sell this information should fall under the FCRA's restrictions due to their "establishing the consumer's eligibility for personal, family, or household purposes; employment purposes; or any other purpose authorized under section 1681b [citing FCRA, 15 U.S.C. §1681a(d)(1)(A)-(C)]."

2. PERMISSIBLE USES OF CONSUMER REPORTS

Permissible Uses of Consumer Reports. Pursuant to 15 U.S.C. § 1681b, a consumer reporting agency can furnish a consumer report only under certain circumstances or for certain uses: (1) in response to a court order or grand jury subpoena; (2) to the person to whom the report pertains; (3) to a "person which [the agency] has reason to believe" intends to use the information in connection with (a) the extension of credit to a consumer; (b) employment purposes; (c) insurance

---

[7] Harrison Tang, Empowering Spokeo's Users, June 12, 2012, http://blog.spokeo.com/2012/06/empowering-spokeos-users-2.

[8] Ed Mierzwinski & Jeff Chester, *Selling Consumers Not Lists*, 46 Suffolk U. L. Rev. 845, 875 (2013).

underwriting; (d) licensing or the conferral of government benefits; (e) assessment of credit risks associated with an existing credit obligation; (f) "legitimate business need" when engaging in "a business transaction involving the consumer"; (4) to establish a person's capacity to pay child support.

A Private Right of Action and Restrictions on "[A]ny Person." FCRA does not merely place restrictions on consumer reporting agencies. More broadly, it creates a private right of action for "any consumer" regarding "[a]ny person" who under false pretenses gains a consumer report, or who willfully or knowingly fails to comply with certain of its requirements. §1681n(a). It also provides for punitive damages, reasonable attorney's fees, and statutory damages of $1,000 or actual damages. This section provides the basis for the litigation in *Smith v. Bob Smith Chevrolet*, excerpted below.

Consumer Reports for Employment Purposes. When an employer or potential employer seeks a consumer report for employment purposes, she must first disclose in writing to the consumer that a consumer report may be obtained, and the consumer must authorize in writing that the report can be obtained. The person seeking the report from a consumer reporting agency must certify that she obtained the consent of the individual and that she will not use the information in violation of any equal employment opportunity law or regulation. § 1681b(b). If the person who obtained the report takes adverse action based in any way on the report, she must provide the consumer a copy of the report and a description of the consumer's rights under the FCRA. § 1681b(b).

Pursuant to § 1681b(g):

> A consumer reporting agency shall not furnish for employment purposes, or in connection with a credit or insurance transaction or a direct marketing transaction, a consumer report that contains medical information about a consumer, unless the consumer consents to the furnishing of the report.

Law Enforcement Access. Pursuant to FCRA, "a consumer reporting agency may furnish identifying information respecting any customer, limited to his name, address, former addresses, places of employment, or former places of employment, to a governmental agency." § 1681f. The FBI can obtain "the names and addresses of all financial institutions . . . at which a consumer maintains or has maintained an account" by presenting a written request to a consumer reporting agency. § 1681u(a). Additionally, pursuant to a written request by the FBI, a consumer reporting agency must disclose "identifying information respecting a consumer, limited to name, address, former addresses, places of employment, or former places of employment." The FBI, however, must certify that the information is sought in an investigation to protect against "international terrorism or clandestine intelligence activities" and that the investigation "is not conducted solely upon the basis of activities protected by the first amendment to the Constitution of the United States." § 1681u(b). To obtain additional information from a consumer report, the FBI must obtain a court order and meet the same standard as above. § 1681u(c).

Moreover, § 1681v provides a broad release exemption "to a government agency authorized to conduct investigations of, or intelligence or counterintelligence activities or analysis related to, international terrorism." These entities can obtain a consumer report on an individual when the government agency provides "a written certification" to a consumer reporting agency that the information is "necessary" for an agency investigation or other agency activity.

Unauthorized Disclosures of Consumer Reports: Prescreening. A typical American receives a flood of credit cards offers each year. These offers follow due to the practice of "prescreening" consumers for such offers, which FCRA permits. A consumer reporting agency can furnish a consumer report, without the consumer's authorization, if

(i) the transaction consists of a firm offer of credit or insurance;

(ii) the consumer reporting agency has complied with subsection (e); and

(iii) there is not in effect the election by the consumer, made in accordance with subsection (e), to have the consumer's name and address excluded from lists of names provided by the agency pursuant to this paragraph. § 1681b(c).

Subsection (e) of § 1681b provides the consumer with a right to opt out of such unauthorized disclosures. If the consumer notifies the consumer reporting agency by phone, the opt out shall last for two years and then expire. If the consumer notifies the consumer reporting agency by submitting a signed opt-out form, then the opt out remains effective until the consumer notifies the agency otherwise. § 1681b(e).

Limitations on Information Contained in Consumer Reports. Consumer reporting agencies are excluded from providing certain information in consumer reports, such as bankruptcy proceedings more than ten years old; suits and judgments more than seven years old; paid tax liens more than seven years old; and records of arrest, indictment, or conviction of a crime more than seven years old. § 1681c(a). These limitations do not apply, however, when a company is preparing a consumer report used in connection with a credit transaction more than $150,000; underwriting a life insurance policy more than $150,000; or employing an individual with an annual salary more than $75,000. § 1681c(b).

Investigative Consumer Reports. An "investigative consumer report" is "a consumer report or portion thereof in which information on a consumer's character, general reputation, personal characteristics, or mode of living is obtained through personal interviews, with neighbors, friends, or associates." § 1681a(f). The FCRA provides limitations on investigative consumer reports. These reports cannot be prepared unless "it is clearly and accurately disclosed to the consumer that an investigative consumer report including information as to his character, general reputation, personal characteristics and mode of living, whichever are applicable, may be made." § 1681d(a)(1). The consumer, if she requests, can require disclosure "of the nature and scope of the investigation requested." § 1681d(b). Further, if the report contains any adverse information about a person gleaned from interviews with neighbors, friends, or associates, the agency must take reasonable steps to corroborate that information "from an additional source that has independent and direct knowledge of the information" or ensure that "the person interviewed is the best possible source of the information." § 1681d(d).

SMITH V. BOB SMITH CHEVROLET, INC.

275 F. Supp. 2d 808 (W.D. Ky. 2003)

HEYBURN, J. Christopher Smith ("Plaintiff") alleges that Defendant Bob Smith Chevrolet, Inc. violated the Fair Credit Reporting Act, 15 U.S.C. § 1681 *et seq.,* and invaded his privacy in violation of Kentucky common law. . . . [B]oth parties have moved for summary judgment on the issue of whether Smith Chevrolet lacked a permissible purpose when it accessed Plaintiff's credit report; Smith Chevrolet moved to dismiss the Kentucky invasion of privacy claim. . . .

The underlying facts concern the disputed sale of a 2001 GMC Suburban. Having decided that he wanted to purchase a car, on December 13, 2000, Plaintiff completed a GMAC credit application to determine his eligibility for financing. On December 23, 2000, Plaintiff went to Smith Chevrolet with the intention of purchasing the Suburban to use on a family Christmas vacation.

After arriving at the dealership, Plaintiff met with a company employee to discuss the terms of the sale. Two factors complicated the sale. First, Plaintiff wanted to trade in his 1997 Mercury Villager. Second, as an employee of General Electric — a General Motors ("GM") supplier — he was entitled to a standard discount upon proof of employment. Although Plaintiff did have the 1997 Mercury Villager to trade-in on December 23, 2000, he did not have the proper documentation needed to secure the discount. Notwithstanding this fact, a Smith Chevrolet representative agreed to sell Plaintiff the Suburban at the GM discounted price provided he proved his entitlement to the full discount at a later date. After calculating the Villager's trade-in value and the GM discount, the two sides agreed on a price and set forth the terms of the sale in a handwritten purchase order. . . .

On January 10, 2001, Plaintiff faxed and mailed proof of his eligibility for the GM discount. Shortly thereafter, Plaintiff's bank issued Smith Chevrolet a check in the amount of the balance due.

About a week or ten days later, another dispute arose which gives rise to the current litigation. At that point Smith Chevrolet claims it realized the employee who generated the typewritten Purchase Agreement inadvertently doubled the amount of Plaintiff's discount. Smith Chevrolet contacted Plaintiff, explained the calculation error and told Plaintiff that he owed the dealership more money. Furthermore, Smith Chevrolet told Plaintiff that, until he paid the difference, it refused to transfer the Suburban's title and pay off the outstanding loan attached on the Villager trade-in. These were both actions Smith Chevrolet had promised Plaintiff it would take when Plaintiff left the lot on December 23, 2000.

Following from this dispute, on February 21, 2000, Smith Chevrolet accessed Plaintiff's consumer report. The decision to access Plaintiff's report was made by Drew Smith, Smith Chevrolet's chief executive officer and part-owner. Smith Chevrolet says it accessed Plaintiff's report to determine whether Plaintiff was

(1) continuing to make payments on the Villager's loan and (2) maintaining insurance on the Villager. Plaintiff disputes Smith Chevrolet's motivations in this regard and claims that it simply wanted to invade Plaintiff's privacy.

When the parties could not agree on the amount due, Plaintiff sued Smith Chevrolet in Jefferson Circuit Court for breach of the sale contract. He demanded specific performance so that he could receive the Suburban's title and transfer the Villager loan obligations to Smith Chevrolet. About a year later, a state court jury found in Plaintiff's favor. One day earlier, on May 13, 2002, Plaintiff filed this suit in federal court. . . .

The heart of [Plaintiff's] case is the contention that Smith Chevrolet violated the FCRA when it accessed Plaintiff's credit report on February 21, 2001. Specifically, Plaintiff contends Smith Chevrolet is liable for negligently and willfully violating the responsibilities imposed by the FCRA. *See* 15 U.S.C. § 1681o (creating a private cause of action for negligent violations of the FCRA); 15 U.S.C. § 1681n (creating a private cause of action for willful violations). Both sides have filed motions for summary judgment addressing whether Smith Chevrolet had a "permissible purpose" for accessing Plaintiff's credit report. The facts central to this claim are not in dispute. Smith Chevrolet may access Plaintiff's credit report only if, as a matter of law, its actions are consistent with one of the permissible purposes set forth in 15 U.S.C. § 1681b(a)(3).

The FCRA identifies a limited set of "permissible purposes" for obtaining and using a consumer report. *See* 15 U.S.C. § 1681b(a)(3); *see also* 15 U.S.C. § 1681b(f). Those permissible purposes provide that a person may only access a consumer report if he:

> (A) intends to use the information in connection with a credit transaction involving the consumer on whom the information is to be furnished and involving the extension of credit to, or review or collection of an account of, the consumer; or
>
> (B) intends to use the information for employment purposes; or
>
> (C) intends to use the information in connection with the underwriting of insurance involving the consumer; or
>
> (D) intends to use the information in connection with a determination of the consumer's eligibility for a license or other benefit granted by a governmental instrumentality required by law to consider an applicant's financial responsibility or status; or
>
> (E) intends to use the information, as a potential investor or servicer, or current insurer, in connection with a valuation of, or an assessment of the credit or prepayment risks associated with, an existing credit obligation; or
>
> (F) otherwise has a legitimate business need for the information—
>
>> (i) in connection with a business transaction that is initiated by the consumer; or
>>
>> (ii) to review an account to determine whether the consumer continues to meet the terms of the account.

15 U.S.C. § 1681b(a)(3).

In its summary judgment motion, Smith Chevrolet contends it had three bases for accessing Plaintiff's credit report. The Court now addresses each of these arguments.

First and most persuasively, Smith Chevrolet contends its actions complied with § 1681b(a)(3)(f)(i). That section provides that one may obtain a consumer report if it "has a legitimate business need for the information . . . in connection with a business transaction that is initiated by the consumer. . ." Smith Chevrolet argues that because the transaction was in dispute, it needed to ascertain the value of its collateral. If it appeared that Plaintiff was not current on his payments for the Mercury Villager, then his indebtedness would have increased over and above the amount owed Smith Chevrolet.

As a starting point, the Court begins with the FCRA's text. The applicability of this permissible purpose boils down to whether Smith Chevrolet's use of the credit report was "in connection with a transaction initiated by the consumer," as the statute uses those terms. That restriction to the actual statutory usage is important here because, in the abstract, it is true Smith Chevrolet accessed Plaintiff's credit report in connection with a transaction Plaintiff at one point initiated. The Court concludes, however, that the statute uses the terms "in connection with a transaction initiated by the consumer" more restrictively.

Turning to the text at issue, when Congress defined the term "consumer report," it stated:

> The term "consumer report" means any written, oral, or other communication of any information by a consumer reporting agency bearing on a consumer's credit worthiness, credit standing, credit capacity, character, general reputation, personal characteristics, or mode of living which is used or expected to be used or collected in whole or in part for the purpose of serving as a factor in establishing the consumer's eligibility for—
>> (A) credit or insurance to be used primarily for personal, family, or household purposes;
>> (B) employment purposes; or
>> (C) any other purpose authorized under section 604 [15 U.S.C. § 1681b].

15 U.S.C. § 1681a(d).

This definition suggests that Congress primarily envisioned consumer reports being disseminated for the purposes of assessing "eligibility." Then, in § 1681b(a)(3), Congress listed additional specific permissible purposes pertaining to the extension of credit, collection of an account, employment purposes, the underwriting of insurance for a consumer, determining a consumer's eligibility for a governmental benefit, and the valuation of a consumer's credit risk. The rule of *ejusdem generis* provides that when general words follow an enumeration of specific terms, the general words are construed to embrace only objects similar in nature to those objects enumerated by the preceding specific words. The definition of "consumer report" therefore includes those reports needed to assess a consumer's eligibility for a benefit, as well as other predictable needs — such as collecting money owed under an agreement and assessing a particular consumer's credit or insurance risk — that arise in the midst of a typical business transaction. In fact, in every one of these situations, the consumer report is obtained either to provide a benefit to a consumer or to collect a pre-existing debt.

Tellingly, the two permissible purposes stated in § 1681b(a)(3)(F) can also be read to effectuate these same ends. That is, § 1681b(a)(3)(F)(i) suggests the retention of a credit report for the purpose of furthering a business transaction initiated by a consumer and § 1681b(a)(3)(F)(ii) permits the use of a credit report to determine whether a consumer continues to be eligible for a benefit. It is a basic principle of statutory construction that a statute should be read and construed as a whole. Like the definition of "consumer report" and consistent with the other five specific permissible purposes, these two permissible purposes also suggest that Congress intended to allow access to a consumer report either when that access would benefit a consumer or would facilitate the collection of pre-existing debt.

To be precise, Smith Chevrolet's stated reason for accessing the credit report was not in connection with a standard business transaction that Plaintiff initiated. Instead, and quite significantly in this Court's view, Smith Chevrolet accessed the credit report to determine how much additional money it could collect, apart from what the two parties agreed upon in a standard business transaction. Almost certainly, it did not access Plaintiff's credit report for a reason beneficial to the consumer. Nor did it access the credit report to collect on a pre-existing debt. Rather, it accessed the report for its own business purposes and as part of a new event: the recovery of the duplicative discount. Although this is a fine distinction, it may be an important one. Smith Chevrolet's interpretation of the phrase "in connection with" is limitless. Under its reading, so long as any company had a reason to question any part of a transaction, it could access a consumer's credit report "in connection with a business transaction" that at some point was "initiated by the consumer." That is, five weeks, five months, or five years down the line, Smith Chevrolet could access Plaintiff's credit report if some dispute ever arose about the contracted price. In the Court's view, such an interpretation would give commercial entities an unlimited blank check to access and *reaccess* a consumer credit report long after the typical issues of eligibility, price, and financing were determined. Neither the specific language nor the overall scope of the FCRA can be said to support such an interpretation. . . .

Moreover, nearly every federal court addressing this issue has similarly held that the "legitimate business need" permissible purpose should be narrowly construed in the context of the other five enumerated purposes. . . .

The Court concludes, therefore, that when Smith Chevrolet accessed Plaintiff's credit report it was not, as a practical matter, part of the transaction which Plaintiff initiated. That transaction, in so far as Plaintiff's eligibility and debt was concerned, ended when the parties created a contract for the car's price and Plaintiff paid that price in full. Under any conceivable interpretation of the facts in this case, Smith Chevrolet cannot be said to have a "legitimate business need" for Plaintiff's credit report "in connection with a transaction initiated by the consumer." § 604(a)(3)(F)(i).

Smith Chevrolet also argues that its actions were protected both by §§ 1681b(3)(A) and 1681b(a)(1)(F)(ii) which provide that:

> Any consumer reporting agency may furnish a consumer report under the following circumstances and no other: . . .
>> (A) to a person which it has reason to believe intends to use the information in connection with a credit transaction involving the consumer on

whom the information is to be furnished and involving the extension of credit to, or review or collection of an account of the consumer; or . . .

(F) otherwise has a legitimate business need for the information . . . (ii) to review an account to determine whether the consumer continues to meet the terms of the account.

Smith Chevrolet claims that it had a permissible purpose under both of these provisions because, due to its own error, Plaintiff received twice the discount he was entitled to and so a debt remained. Therefore, Smith Chevrolet says that it was reviewing whether Plaintiff owed any additional debt. And, because reviewing the size of the debt Plaintiff owed is synonymous with "collection of an account" and with determining "whether [Chris Smith] continue[d] to meet the terms of the account," Smith Chevrolet contends it therefore clearly had a permissible purpose.

The problem with this argument is that there was no outstanding debt and, consequently, there was no "account" to collect on. To be sure, Smith Chevrolet thought there *should be* an outstanding debt. Thinking there *should be* a debt, Smith Chevrolet contacted Plaintiff and ordered him to pay. At that point, Plaintiff refused to pay. Only then did Smith Chevrolet access Plaintiff's credit report.

Whether a debt or existing account exists simply cannot be a function of whether Smith Chevrolet alleges the existence of a debt. To do so would allow Smith Chevrolet infinite opportunities to access Plaintiff's credit report, so long as he could come up with a reason for thinking the account should continue in existence. As this Court has explained elsewhere, the FCRA intended to strike a balance between protecting the needs of commerce and the consumer's privacy interest. The Court finds that Smith Chevrolet must have a reasonable belief that the debt existed. Here, Smith Chevrolet's decision to investigate Plaintiff's credit report was not based on a reasonable belief that debt was owed; it was based on a belief that the original transaction was mistaken. Plaintiff had no reason to suspect that any new debt would arise after the initial transaction was completed. For all practical purposes that transaction was closed when the vehicle was delivered and Plaintiff made his payment. To find these permissible purposes applicable in this instance would extend the FCRA's language well beyond its intended purpose. . . .

Both sides have also moved for summary judgment on Plaintiff's claim of willful non-compliance. Section 1681n provides for civil liability in cases where the defendant willfully fails to comply with FCRA. In such a case, punitive damages may be awarded. 15 U.S.C. § 1681n(a)(2). This Court has recently explained the standard for liability under § 1681n, stating that, "[t]o show willful noncompliance with the FCRA, [the Plaintiff] must show that [defendant] knowingly and intentionally committed an act in conscious disregard for the rights of others, but need not show malice or evil motive."

Questions involving a party's state of mind are generally appropriately resolved by a jury rather than on summary judgment. From what the Court can ascertain at this point, the following facts are undisputed. Carol Hodges, a former Finance and Insurance Manager for Smith Chevrolet, has testified that the company did not have "written polices" regarding the acquisition of credit reports. She said that salespeople could freely access consumer credit reports. Hodges also said that the company had some unwritten rules for accessing customer credit reports, but these rules were not strictly followed. In fact, Smith Chevrolet's practices were "haphazard" and "very sloppy." Hodges had no part in the February 21, 2001, events and has no idea if Smith Chevrolet acted responsibly the day it accessed Plaintiff's credit report.

Based on these disputed facts, the Court cannot enter summary judgment on the issue of Smith Chevrolet's state of mind and will therefore deny the parties cross motions for summary judgment as they pertain to § 1681n.

Last, Smith Chevrolet has moved for summary judgment on Plaintiff's invasion of privacy claim. The Supreme Court of Kentucky adopted the principles for invasion of privacy as enunciated in the Restatement (Second) of Torts (1976) in *McCall v. Courier-Journal and Louisville Times Co.*, 623 S.W.2d 882, 887 (Ky. 1981). . . .

NOTES & QUESTIONS

1. ***Legitimate Business Need.*** A critical element in the court's decision in *Smith Chevrolet* is its finding that the auto dealership must have a "reasonable belief" that the debt existed to access the credit report. But the decision to investigate the credit report was based, in fact, on a belief that the Plaintiff should owe the car dealer more than he did (due to the mistaken double discount). How does the court interpret the FCRA's statutory provision that allows businesses access to consumer credit reports when there is "a legitimate business need for the information"?

2. ***Permissible Uses of Consumer Reports.*** The FCRA contains a provision that provides for civil liability for "obtaining a consumer report under false pretenses or knowingly without a permissible purpose." 15 U.S.C. § 1681n(a)(1)(B). But what, exactly, is a "consumer report"? A consumer report is defined based on the purposes for which it is used. These purposes include credit, insurance, and employment background checks, among others. 15 U.S.C. § 1681b.

   In *Phillips v. Grendahl*, 312 F.3d 357 (8th Cir. 2002), Mary Grendahl became suspicious of her daughter Sarah's fiancé, Lavon Phillips. She believed he was lying about being an attorney as well as his ex-wives and girlfriends. Grendahl contacted Kevin Fitzgerald, a friend who worked for a detective agency. By searching computer databases, Fitzgerald obtained Phillips's Social Security number and previous addresses. He then submitted the data to Econ Control to obtain a report called a "Finder's Report." A Finder's Report includes a person's "address, aliases, birthdate, employer addresses, and the identity of firms with which the consumer had credit accounts and firms that had made inquiries about the consumer."

   When Phillips discovered the investigation, he sued Grendahl, the detective agency Fitzgerald worked for, and Econ Control. The court concluded that the Finder's Report was a "consumer report" under FCRA. It also concluded that the defendants did not have a valid purpose under FCRA for obtaining the report:

The only purpose for obtaining the report was to obtain information on Mary Grendahl's prospective son-in-law. Investigating a person because he wants to marry one's daughter is not a statutory consumer purpose under section 1681b(a). Even if getting married can be characterized as a consumer transaction under section 1681b(a)(3), it was not Mary Grendahl, but her daughter, whom Phillips was engaged to marry. He had no business transaction pending with Mary Grendahl. There was no permissible purpose for obtaining or using a consumer report.

3. CONSUMER RIGHTS AND AGENCY RESPONSIBILITIES

Accuracy. "Whenever a consumer reporting agency prepares a consumer report it shall follow reasonable procedures to assure maximum possible accuracy of the information concerning the individual about whom the report relates." § 1681e(b).

Disclosures to the Consumer. The FCRA requires that consumer reporting agencies, upon request of the consumer, disclose, among other things:

(1) All information in the consumer's file at the time of the request, except . . . any information concerning credit scores or any other risk scores or predictors relating to the consumer.
(2) The sources of the information. . . .
(3) Identification of each person . . . that procured a consumer report [within two years for employment purposes; within one year for all other purposes] . . . .
(4) The dates, original payees, and amounts of any checks upon which is based any adverse characterization of the consumer, included in the file at the time of disclosure. . . . § 1681g.

Responsiveness to Consumer Complaints. National consumer reporting agencies must provide consumers who request disclosures under the FCRA with a toll-free telephone number at which personnel are accessible to respond to consumer inquiries during normal business hours. § 1681g(c).

Procedures in Case of Disputed Accuracy. Pursuant to § 1681i(a)(1):

If the completeness or accuracy of any item of information contained in a consumer's file at a consumer reporting agency is disputed by the consumer and the consumer notifies the agency directly of such dispute, the agency shall reinvestigate free of charge and record the current status of the disputed information or delete the item from the file. . . .

The consumer reporting agency must provide written notice to a consumer of the results of a reinvestigation within five business days after completing the investigation. § 1681i.

If the information is found to be inaccurate or incomplete or cannot be verified, the consumer reporting agency must promptly delete it from the file. § 1681i. At the request of the consumer, the consumer reporting agency must furnish notification that the item has been deleted to "any person specifically designated by the consumer who has within two years prior thereto received a consumer report for employment purposes, or within six months prior thereto received a consumer report for any other purpose." § 1681i(d).

"If the reinvestigation does not resolve the dispute, the consumer may file a brief statement setting forth the nature of the dispute." § 1681i(b).

In any subsequent consumer report, the agency must clearly note that the information in question is disputed by the consumer and provide the consumer's statement. § 1681i(c).

Public Record Information for Employment Purposes. If a consumer reporting agency furnishes a consumer report for employment purposes containing information obtained in public records that is likely to have an adverse effect on the consumer, it must either notify the consumer of the fact that public record information is being reported along with the name and address of the person to whom the information is being reported or "maintain strict procedures designed to insure that whenever public record information which is likely to have an adverse effect on a consumer's ability to obtain employment is reported it is complete and up to date." § 1681k.

Requirements on Users of Consumer Reports. If a user of a consumer report takes any adverse action on a consumer based in any way on the report, the user shall provide notice of the adverse action to the consumer, information for the consumer to contact the consumer reporting agency that prepared the report, and notice of the consumer's right to obtain a free copy of the report and to dispute the accuracy of the report. § 1681m(a). Whenever credit is denied based on information obtained through sources other than a consumer report, upon the consumer's written request, the person or entity denying credit shall disclose the nature of that information. § 1681m(b).

4. CIVIL LIABILITY AND QUALIFIED IMMUNITY

Civil Liability. As noted above, any person who "willfully fails to comply with any requirement" of the FCRA is liable to the consumer for actual damages or statutory damages between $100 and $1,000, as well as punitive damages and attorneys' fees and costs. § 1681n. Willful means that one intentionally commits an act "in conscious disregard for the rights of others." In *Safeco Insurance Co. v. Burr,* 551 U.S. 47 (2007), the Supreme Court held that acting in "reckless disregard" of a consumer's rights under FCRA was sufficient to establish willfulness.

Negligent failure to comply with any requirement of the FCRA results in liability to the consumer for actual damages as well as attorneys' fees and costs. § 1681.

Liability for Furnishing Data to a Consumer Reporting Agency. Businesses and financial institutions "furnish" the information about consumers to the consumer reporting agencies. For example, a bank that issues a consumer a credit card will furnish information about the timeliness and consistency of the consumer's payments. This is how consumer reporting agencies learn about a consumer's reliability. What if one of these entities furnishes false data to a consumer reporting agency? The data adversely affects a consumer's credit score and results in harm to the consumer. The consumer can sue not just the consumer reporting agency but also the entity that furnished the false data. However, as discussed below, FCRA's qualified immunity will apply.

Qualified Immunity from State Tort Law. Consumer reporting agencies — as well as those that furnish data to consumer reporting agencies — could potentially face extensive liability under state tort law. Under defamation law, a person or entity can be liable for disseminating false information about a person that injures the person's reputation. Disseminating false information might also give rise to a false light action. And disclosing true information could give rise to liability for public disclosure of private facts.

However, FCRA provides qualified immunity to credit reporting agencies and to the furnishers of information to credit reporting agencies:

> Except as provided in sections 1681n and 1681o of this title, no consumer may bring any action or proceeding in the nature of defamation, invasion of privacy, or negligence with respect to the reporting of information against any consumer reporting agency, or any user of information, or any person who furnishes information to a consumer reporting agency, based on information disclosed pursuant to section 1681g, 1681h, or 1681m of this title, or based on information disclosed by a user of a consumer report to or for a consumer against whom the user has taken adverse action, based in whole or in part on the report except as to false information furnished with malice or willful intent to injure such consumer. § 1681h(e).

Plaintiffs can only state tort actions when "defendants acted with malice or willful intent to injure plaintiff." § 1681h.

In *Lema v. Citibank,* 935 F. Supp. 695 (D. Md. 1996), Citibank issued the plaintiff a credit card. When the plaintiff's account became delinquent, Citibank reported the information to consumer reporting agencies. The plaintiff sued Citibank under FCRA, claiming that the information it supplied to the consumer reporting agencies was inaccurate. The court dismissed the claim:

> The FCRA imposes civil liability only on consumer reporting agencies and users of consumer information. Thus, plaintiff must show that defendants are either of those entities in order to withstand defendants' summary judgment motion. . . .
>
> Plaintiff alleges only that defendants reported to third parties information regarding transactions between defendants and plaintiff. Defendants did not therefore furnish a consumer report regarding plaintiff, nor did they act as a consumer reporting agency with respect to him.

Statute of Limitations. FCRA's statute of limitation extends to two years after the date when the plaintiff discovers the violation or five years after the date of the violation, whichever occurs earlier.

SARVER V. EXPERIAN INFORMATION SOLUTIONS

390 F.3d 969 (7th Cir. 2004)

EVANS, J. Lloyd Sarver appeals from an order granting summary judgment to Experian Information Solutions, Inc., a credit reporting company, on his claim under the Fair Credit Reporting Act (FCRA), 15 U.S.C. §§ 1681 *et seq.*

Experian reported inaccurate information on Sarver's credit report, which on August 2, 2002, caused the Monogram Bank of Georgia to deny him credit. Monogram cited the Experian credit report and particularly a reference to a bankruptcy which appeared on the report. Both before and after Monogram denied him credit, Sarver asked for a copy of his credit report. He received copies both times and both reports showed that accounts with Cross Country Bank were listed as having been "involved in bankruptcy." No other accounts had that notation, although other accounts had significant problems. A Bank One installment account had a balance past due 180 days, and another company, Providian, had written off $3,099 on a revolving account.

On August 29, 2002, Sarver wrote Experian informing it that the bankruptcy notation was inaccurate and asking that it be removed from his report. Sarver provided his full name and address but no other identifying information. On September 11, Experian sent Sarver a letter requesting further information, including his Social Security number, before it could begin an investigation. Sarver did not provide the information, but instead filed the present lawsuit, which resulted in summary judgment for Experian. It was later confirmed that the notation on the Cross Country Bank account was inaccurate and, as it turned out, another Lloyd Sarver was the culprit on that account.

In this appeal from the judgment dismissing his case, Sarver claims summary judgment was improper because issues of fact exist as to whether Experian violated FCRA, §§ 1681i and 1681e(b). . . .

Section 1681i requires a credit reporting agency to reinvestigate items on a credit report when a consumer disputes the validity of those items. An agency can terminate a reinvestigation if it determines the complaint is frivolous, "including by reason of a failure by a consumer to provide sufficient information to investigate the disputed information." § 1681i(a)(3). We do not need to decide whether Sarver's failure to provide the information Experian requested rendered his complaint frivolous; his claim under § 1681i(a) fails for another reason, a lack of evidence of damages. In order to prevail on his claims, Sarver must show that he suffered damages as a result of the inaccurate information. As we have said in *Crabill v. Trans Union, L.L.C.,* 259 F.3d 662, 664 (7th Cir. 2001):

> Without a causal relation between the violation of the statute and the loss of credit, or some other harm, a plaintiff cannot obtain an award of "actual damages."

On this point, the district court concluded that there were no damages. Our review of the record leads us to agree.

Sarver, however, disagrees and claims that he suffered damages when he was denied credit from Monogram Bank of Georgia on August 2, 2002. This letter cannot be a basis for his damage claim, however, because as of August 2,

Experian had no notice of any inaccuracies in the report. Even though Sarver asked for a copy of his report on July 18, he did not notify Experian of a problem until a month and a half later. Experian must be notified of an error before it is required to reinvestigate. As we have made clear, the FCRA is not a strict liability statute. *Henson v. CSC Credit Servs.*, 29 F.3d 280 (7th Cir. 1994).

Sarver also does not show that he suffered pecuniary damages between August 29 (when he notified Experian of the error) and February 20, 2003 (when the Cross Country account was removed from his file). He does not claim that he applied for credit during that time period or that a third party looked at his report. In addition, his claim for emotional distress fails. We have maintained a strict standard for a finding of emotional damage "because they are so easy to manufacture." *Aiello v. Providian Fin. Corp.*, 239 F.3d 876, 880 (7th Cir. 2001). We have required that when "the injured party's own testimony is the only proof of emotional damages, he must explain the circumstances of his injury in reasonable detail; he cannot rely on mere conclusory statements." *Denius v. Dunlap*, 330 F.3d 919, 929 (7th Cir. 2003). Finally, to obtain statutory damages under FCRA § 1681n(a), Sarver must show that Experian willfully violated the Act. There is similarly no evidence of willfulness. Summary judgment was properly granted on this claim.

We turn to Sarver's claim under § 1681e(b), which requires that a credit reporting agency follow "reasonable procedures to assure maximum possible accuracy" when it prepares a credit report. The reasonableness of a reporting agency's procedures is normally a question for trial unless the reasonableness or unreasonableness of the procedures is beyond question. *Crabill*, 259 F.3d at 663. However, to state a claim under the statute,

> a consumer must sufficiently allege "that a credit reporting agency prepared a report containing 'inaccurate' information." However, the credit reporting agency is not automatically liable even if the consumer proves that it prepared an inaccurate credit report because the FCRA "does not make reporting agencies strictly liable for all inaccuracies." A credit reporting agency is not liable under the FCRA if it followed "reasonable procedures to assure maximum possible accuracy," but nonetheless reported inaccurate information in the consumer's credit report.

Henson, 29 F.3d at 284. The Commentary of the Federal Trade Commission to the FCRA, 16 C.F.R. pt. 600, app., section 607 at 3.A, states that the section does not hold a reporting agency responsible where an item of information, received from a source that it reasonably believes is reputable, turns out to be inaccurate unless the agency receives notice of systemic problems with its procedures.

Experian has provided an account of its procedures. The affidavit of David Browne, Experian's compliance manager, explains that the company gathers credit information originated by approximately 40,000 sources. The information is stored in a complex system of national databases, containing approximately 200 million names and addresses and some 2.6 billion trade lines, which include information about consumer accounts, judgments, etc. The company processes over 50 million updates to trade information each day. Lenders report millions of accounts to Experian daily; they provide identifying information, including address, social security number, and date of birth. The identifying information is used to link the credit items to the appropriate consumer. Mr. Browne also notes that Experian's computer system does not store complete credit reports, but rather stores the individual items of credit information linked to identifying information. The credit report is generated at the time an inquiry for it is received.

One can easily see how, even with safeguards in place, mistakes can happen. But given the complexity of the system and the volume of information involved, a mistake does not render the procedures unreasonable. In his attempt to show that Experian's procedures are unreasonable, Sarver argues that someone should have noticed that only the Cross Country accounts were shown to have been involved in bankruptcy. That anomaly should have alerted Experian, Sarver says, to the fact that the report was inaccurate. What Sarver is asking, then, is that each computer-generated report be examined for anomalous information and, if it is found, an investigation be launched. In the absence of notice of prevalent unreliable information from a reporting lender, which would put Experian on notice that problems exist, we cannot find that such a requirement to investigate would be reasonable given the enormous volume of information Experian processes daily.

We found in *Henson* that a consumer reporting agency was not liable, as a matter of law, for reporting information from a judgment docket unless there was prior notice from the consumer that the information might be inaccurate. We said that a

> contrary rule of law would require credit reporting agencies to go beyond the face of numerous court records to determine whether they correctly report the outcome of the underlying action. Such a rule would also require credit reporting agencies to engage in background research which would substantially increase the cost of their services. In turn, they would be forced to pass on the increased costs to their customers and ultimately to the individual consumer.

Henson, 29 F.3d at 285. The same could be said for records from financial institutions. As we said, in his affidavit Mr. Browne proclaims, and there is nothing in the record to make us doubt his statement, that lenders report many millions of accounts to Experian daily. Sarver's report, dated August 26, 2002, contains entries from six different lenders. The increased cost to Experian to examine each of these entries individually would be enormous. We find that as a matter of law there is nothing in this record to show that Experian's procedures are unreasonable.

NOTES & QUESTIONS

1. *A Critical Perspective on* **Sarver.** Consider Elizabeth De Armond:

> In justifying the agency's failure to resolve the anomalies within the records attributed to the plaintiff, the court emphasized the 200 million names and addresses, the 2.6 billion trade lines, and the complexity of the system. This reasoning overlooks that the very complexity of the system reveals the ability of the agency to control the high volume of individuals and records, and that ability should alert the agency to the high risk of misattributing information. The court ruled that the agency's failure to investigate the inconsistency was

not unreasonable because the agency had no notice that the specific lender who had provided information about the impaired accounts was unreliable. However, the question, in order to protect individuals from reckless attribution, should not be whether any single provider is unreliable. The question should have been whether reporting it as the plaintiff's without checking it, given the obvious inconsistency, was reckless. Where the agency was aware of the risk of misattribution from fuzzy matching, and that matching produced a record that was unlike the others, a jury should decide whether the failure to take any steps to verify the anomalous data breached the FCRA's accuracy standard.

The *Sarver* court also reasoned that to require an agency to further investigate the accuracy of a consumer's records when an anomaly appeared would impose "enormous" increased costs. However, the court did not refer to any estimate of the costs or explain why an already complex system capable of making many comparisons among different records could not inexpensively adjust to cross-checking data when reliability was at issue. Furthermore, when an anomaly appears that would work to the consumer's detriment, an agency could simply decline to attribute the negative data should it not want to take the extra effort of verifying it. The decision allows the agency all of the benefits of its database technology with none of the responsibilities.[9]

This criticism raises a baseline issue: who should bear the costs of relative degrees of inaccuracy and accuracy in the credit system? If credit agencies need investigate more kinds of inconsistencies in credit reports, will consumers as a group bear the additional costs?

2. *Is FCRA Too Deferential to Industry Interests?* Consider De Armond on the flaws of FCRA:

[FCRA] inadequately protects individuals from the consequential and emotional damages caused by misattributed acts for several reasons. . . .

The Act's most significant flaw is that it imposes meaningful accuracy requirements only after a false and negative item has been reported, has already been put into the data sea. However, given that digitized data is far more available, accessible, duplicable, and transmittable than old paper records, once a false record has been put into the data sea, it is very hard to ever completely cull it out. . . .

The Act is designed to impose meaningful accuracy standards only after inaccurate information has already been provided by a data provider and reported by a data aggregator. The Act permits the original data provider, called a furnisher under the Act, to furnish nearly any item in a consumer's name without first verifying that it belongs to that consumer. But the Act only prohibits the furnisher from furnishing information that the furnisher either "knows or has reasonable cause to believe" to be inaccurate. A furnisher only has "'reasonable cause to believe that an item of information is inaccurate'" if the furnisher has "specific knowledge, other than solely allegations by the consumer, that would cause a reasonable person to have substantial doubts about the accuracy of the information." . . .

Thus, the agency acquires information that likely has not been subjected to any scrutiny, let alone verified. The agency acquires the information, either

---

[9] Elizabeth D. De Armond, *Frothy Chaos: Modern Data Warehousing and Old-Fashioned Defamation*, 41 Val. U. L. Rev. 1061, 1099-1102, 1108 (2007).

electronically or via magnetic tape from the provider, and stores it electronically, where it sits until needed for a report. Just as the Act imposes a relatively weak accuracy requirement on data providers at the point of initial provision, the Act places only loose limits on aggregators that then report the information. When a subscriber requests a report on a particular consumer, the aggregator, the consumer reporting agency, must only follow "reasonable procedures to assure maximum possible accuracy" of the information that it returns to the subscriber. The provision does not in fact require agencies to ensure the maximum possible accuracy of every item of information, or to do much if anything to match, verify, or cross-check the information. . . .

It is only after an individual has learned that an agency has falsely charged him or her with negative data that the individual can require an aggregator to examine the data. . . .

As *Sarver* also points out, the Experian computer system does not store computer credit reports, but only generates them when an inquiry is received. Individual items of credit information are stored linked to identifying information, which allows their retrieval and compilation into a credit report. Should individual items of information be reviewed for accuracy at the initial time that the credit agency collects them?

3. *Is Negligence the Best Standard?* Jeff Sovern notes that the FCRA's fault standard for liability — negligence — is inadequate to allow many victims to pursue relief because victims "are not normally aware of the procedures a credit bureau uses when issuing an erroneous credit report or what constitutes reasonable procedures." Because each individual consumer's losses will not be very high, consumers may not bring valid cases because of high litigation costs. Therefore, Sovern argues, credit reports should "be made strictly liable for attributing the transactions of identity thieves to innocent customers." Sovern also recommends liquidated damages for identity theft cases in order to reduce litigation costs.[10]

4. *What Constitutes Negligence in Investigating Errors in Consumer Reports?* In *Dennis v. BEH-1, LLC*, 520 F.3d 1066 (9th Cir. 2007), Jason Dennis was sued by his landlord, but the parties agreed to drop the lawsuit after reaching a settlement. The parties filed a "Request for Dismissal" with the court clerk, and the court register properly registered the dismissal. Later on, Experian Information Solutions, Inc. stated on Dennis's credit report that a civil claim judgment had been entered against him for $1,959. Dennis contacted Experian to complain about the error. Experian had Hogan Information Services, a third-party contractor, verify Dennis's claims. Hogan replied that Experian's information was correct and sent along a copy of the stipulation of settlement between Dennis and his landlord. Experian told Dennis that it would not correct his report. Dennis sued under FCRA, contending that Experian failed to maintain "reasonable procedures" under § 1681e(b) to ensure the accuracy of credit reports and that it failed to adequately reinvestigate the disputed

---

[10] Jeff Sovern, *The Jewel of Their Souls: Preventing Identity Theft Through Loss Allocation Rules*, 64 U. Pitt. L. Rev. 343, 393, 406-07 (2003).

information under § 1681i. The district court dismissed Dennis's case on summary judgment. The court of appeals, however, concluded:

> The district court erred insofar as it held that Dennis couldn't make the prima facie showing of inaccurate reporting required by sections 1681e and 1681i. Experian's credit report on Dennis *is* inaccurate. Because the case against Dennis was dismissed, there could have been no "Civil claim judgment" against him: "A dismissal without prejudice . . . has the effect of a final judgment *in favor* of the defendant." Dennis has made the prima facie showing of inaccuracy required by sections 1681e and 1681i.
>
> The district court also seems to have awarded summary judgment to Experian because Dennis didn't offer evidence of "actual damages" as required by section 1681*o*(a)(1). Here, too, the district court erred. Dennis testified that he hoped to start a business and that he diligently paid his bills on time for years so that he would have a clean credit history when he sought financing for the venture. The only blemish on his credit report in April 2003 was the erroneously reported judgment. According to Dennis, that was enough to cause several lenders to decline his applications for credit, dashing his hopes of starting a new business. Dennis also claims that Experian's error caused his next landlord to demand that Dennis pay a greater security deposit. In addition to those tangible harms, Dennis claims that Experian's inaccurate report caused him emotional distress, which we've held to be "actual damages."

The court of appeals reasoned that Hogan failed to understand the meaning of the Request for Dismissal document and that Experian could readily have detected this mistake:

> Experian could have caught Hogan's error if it had consulted the Civil Register in Dennis's case, which can be viewed free of charge on the Los Angeles Superior Court's excellent website. As described above, the Register clearly indicates that the case against Dennis was dismissed. Experian apparently never looked at the Register.
>
> Experian also could have detected Hogan's mistake by examining the document Hogan retrieved from Dennis's court file. Hogan mistakenly believed that this document proved that judgment had been entered against Dennis; in fact, the document confirms Dennis's account of what happened. The document is a written stipulation between Dennis and his landlord that no judgment would be entered against Dennis so long as Dennis complied with the payment schedule. The parties couldn't have been clearer on this point: "If paid, case dismissed. If not paid, judgment to enter upon [landlord's] declaration of non-payment. . . ."

The court of appeals further concluded that it had no need to remand the case for a jury trial regarding Experian's negligence:

> Even accepting as true everything Experian has claimed, no rational jury could find that the company wasn't negligent. The stipulation Hogan retrieved from Dennis's court file may be unusual, but it's also unambiguous, and Experian was negligent in mis-interpreting it as an entry of judgment. Experian is also responsible for the negligence of Hogan, the investigation service it hired to review Dennis's court file. . . .

When conducting a reinvestigation pursuant to 15 U.S.C. § 1681i, a credit reporting agency must exercise reasonable diligence in examining the court file to determine whether an adverse judgment has, in fact, been entered against the consumer. A reinvestigation that overlooks documents in the court file expressly stating that *no* adverse judgment was entered falls far short of this standard. On our own motion, therefore, we grant summary judgment to Dennis on his claim that Experian negligently failed to conduct a reasonable reinvestigation in violation of section 1681i. Whether Experian's failure was also willful, in violation of section 1681n, is a question for the jury on remand.

This case illustrates how important it is for Experian, a company that traffics in the reputations of ordinary people, to train its employees to understand the legal significance of the documents they rely on. Because Experian negligently failed to conduct a reasonable reinvestigation, we grant summary judgment to Dennis on this claim. We remand only so that the district court may calculate damages and award attorney's fees. As to all other claims under the Fair Credit Reporting Act, we reverse summary judgment for Experian and remand for trial. Dennis is also entitled to attorney's fees for an entirely successful appeal. 15 U.S.C. § 1681o(a)(2). . . .

5. IDENTITY THEFT AND CONSUMER REPORTING

Identity theft is one of the most rapidly growing forms of crime. Identity theft occurs when a criminal obtains an individual's personal information and uses it to open new bank accounts, acquire credit cards, and obtain loans in that individual's name. Consider the following example from journalist Bob Sullivan:

Starting in August 1998, Anthony Lemar Taylor spent a year successfully pretending to be the golf superstar [Tiger Woods]. Taylor's $50,000 spending spree included a big-screen television, stereo speakers, a living room set, even a U-Haul to move all the stolen goods. Taylor, who looks nothing like the golf legend, simply obtained a driver's license using Tiger's real name, Eldrick Woods; then, he used Wood's Social Security number to get credit in his name. . . .

When Tiger himself testified during the case in 2001, Taylor, a 30-year-old career criminal, didn't stand a chance. Wood's star power helped the state throw the book at Taylor. . . . The firm, swift justice might have made other potential identity thieves think twice, but for this: Precious few identity thefts are even investigated, let alone prosecuted to the full extent of the law. The average victim has enough trouble getting the police to bother filling out an incident report. . . .

The real world of identity theft . . . is . . . a haunting, paperwork nightmare, one often compared to financial rape, littered with small and large tragedies. . . . Couples can't buy homes because their credit is damaged. Identity theft victims are often denied access to the lowest interest rates and can pay as much as 50 percent more to borrow money. . . . And thousands of people face hundreds of hours of electronic trials against their erroneous credit reports and eventually end with fraudulent debts and endless nightly threatening calls from collection agencies.[11]

---

[11] Bob Sullivan, *Your Evil Twin: Behind the Identity Theft Epidemic* 35-36 (2004).

According to a 2007 report to the FTC, "approximately 8.3 million U.S. adults discovered that they were victims of some form of ID theft in 2005."[12] According to this report's estimates, the total losses from ID theft in that year were $15.6 billion. Moreover, "victims of all types of ID theft spent hours of their time resolving the various problems that result from ID theft. The median value for the number of hours spent resolving problems by all victims was four. However, 10 percent of all victims spent at least 55 hours resolving their problems."

In an important caveat, however, this report also notes that it may not capture all types of identity theft. In particular, it does not measure "synthetic ID theft." This activity involves a criminal creating a fictitious identity by combining information from one or more consumers. Affected consumers face considerable obstacles in detecting synthetic ID theft; therefore, any survey of identity theft, which depends on consumer self-reporting, is likely to underreport it.

A significant amount of identity theft involves the consumer reporting system. When an identity thief starts creating delinquent debts in a person's name, creditors report the delinquencies to the consumer reporting agencies, and the delinquencies begin to appear on the person's credit report. This can severely affect the person's credit score and make it impossible for the person to secure credit. What are the responsibilities of consumer reporting agencies in ensuring that the data it reports about individuals really pertains to them rather than to the identity thief who impersonated them?

In addition to protections already in FCRA, the FACTA added a few additional measures to address identity theft.

One-Call Fraud Alerts. The FACTA amends FCRA to enable consumers to alert only one consumer reporting agency of potential fraud rather than all of them. That agency must notify the other consumer reporting agencies. 15 U.S.C. § 1681c-1.

Business Transaction Data. The FACTA gives victims of identity theft the right to require certain disclosures from the creditors used by the identity thief; these disclosures concern information about the fraudulent transactions carried out in the victim's name. 15 U.S.C. § 1681g(e)(1). To obtain this information from the creditors, however, the victim must provide one form of identification from a list (that the business gets to pick) as well as proof of the claim of identity theft (police report, affidavit). The victim's request must be in writing and must specify the date of the transaction and other transaction data. Business entities can decline this request if they believe in good faith that there is not "a high degree of confidence in knowing the true identity of the individual requesting the information." § 1681g(e)(2). Further, business entities cannot be sued if they make a disclosure in good faith under these provisions. § 1681g(e)(7). Business entities are not required to alter their record-keeping practices to provide the information required by these provisions. § 1681g(e)(8).

---

[12] Synovate, Federal Trade Commission — 2006 Identity Theft Survey Report (Nov. 2007).

Block of Identity Theft Information. The FACTA amends the FCRA to provide:

> (a) *Block.* Except as otherwise provided in this section, a consumer reporting agency shall block the reporting of any information in the file of a consumer that the consumer identifies as information that resulted from an alleged identity theft, not later than 4 business days after the date of receipt by such agency of —

>> (1) appropriate proof of the identity of the consumer;
>> (2) a copy of an identity theft report;
>> (3) the identification of such information by the consumer; and
>> (4) a statement by the consumer that the information is not information relating to any transaction by the consumer.

> (b) *Notification.* A consumer reporting agency shall promptly notify the furnisher of information identified by the consumer under subsection (a) —

>> (1) that the information may be a result of identity theft;
>> (2) that an identity theft report has been filed;
>> (3) that a block has been requested under this section; and
>> (4) of the effective dates of the block. § 1681c-2.

Social Security Number Truncation. If a consumer requests it, consumer reporting agencies must not disclose the first five digits of the consumer's Social Security Number. § 1681g(a)(1)(A).

Free Consumer reports. FACTA requires consumer reporting agencies to provide a free consumer report once a year at the request of a consumer. § 1681j.

Disclosure of Credit Scores. FACTA requires consumer reporting agencies to disclose to a consumer her credit score. Many consumer reporting agencies previously would not divulge a person's credit score. § 1681g.

SLOANE V. EQUIFAX INFORMATION SERVICES, LLC

510 F.3d 495 (4th Cir. 2007)

DIANA GRIBBON MOTZ, J. After Suzanne Sloane discovered that a thief had stolen her identity and ruined her credit, she notified the police and sought to have Equifax Information Services, LLC, a credit reporting service, correct the resulting errors in her credit report. The police promptly arrested and jailed the thief. But twenty-one months later, Equifax still had not corrected the errors in Suzanne's credit report. Accordingly, Suzanne brought this action against Equifax for violations of the Fair Credit Reporting Act (FCRA), 15 U.S.C.A. §§ 1681 *et seq.* A jury found that Equifax had violated the Act in numerous respects and awarded Suzanne $351,000 in actual damages ($106,000 for economic losses and $245,000 for mental anguish, humiliation, and emotional distress). The district court entered judgment in the amount of $351,000. In addition, without permitting Equifax to file a written opposition, the court also awarded Suzanne attorney's fees in the amount of $181,083. On appeal, Equifax challenges the award of damages and attorney's fees. We affirm in part and reverse and remand in part.

On June 25, 2003, Suzanne Sloane entered Prince William Hospital to deliver a baby. She left the hospital not only a new mother, but also the victim of identity theft. A recently hired hospital employee named Shovana Sloan noticed similarity in the women's names and birth dates and, in November and December 2003, began using Suzanne's social security number to obtain credit cards, loans, cash advances, and other goods and services totaling more than $30,000. At the end of January 2004, Suzanne discovered these fraudulent transactions when Citibank notified her that it had cancelled her credit card and told her to contact Equifax if she had any concerns.

Unable to reach Equifax by telephone on a Friday evening, Suzanne went instead to the Equifax website, where she was able to access her credit report and discovered Shovana Sloan's name and evidence of the financial crimes Shovana had committed. Suzanne promptly notified the police, and contacted Equifax, which assertedly placed a fraud alert on her credit file. Equifax told Suzanne to "roll up her sleeves" and start calling all of her "20-some" creditors to notify them of the identity theft. Suzanne took the next two days off from work to contact each of her creditors, and, at their direction, she submitted numerous notarized forms to correct her credit history.

Suzanne, however, continued to experience problems with Equifax. On March 31, 2004, almost two months after reporting the identity theft to Equifax and despite her efforts to work with individual creditors as Equifax had advised, Suzanne and her husband, Tracey, tried to secure a pre-qualification letter to buy a vacation home, but were turned down. The loan officer told them that Suzanne's credit score was "terrible" — in fact, the "worst" the loan officer had ever seen — and that no loan would be possible until the numerous problems in Suzanne's Equifax credit report had been corrected. The loan officer also told Suzanne not to apply for additional credit in the meantime, because each credit inquiry would appear on her credit report and further lower her score.

Chagrined that Equifax had not yet corrected these errors in her credit report, Suzanne refrained from applying for any type of consumer credit for seven months. But, in October 2004, after the repeated breakdown of their family car, Suzanne and Tracey attempted to rely on Suzanne's credit to purchase a used car at a local dealership. Following a credit check, the car salesman pulled Tracey aside and informed him that it would be impossible to approve the financing so long as Suzanne's name appeared on the loan. Similarly, when the Sloanes returned to the mortgage company to obtain a home loan in January 2005, eight months after their initial visit, they were offered only an adjustable rate loan instead of a less expensive 30-year fixed rate loan in part because of Equifax's still inaccurate credit report.

In frustration, on March 9, 2005, more than thirteen months after first reporting the identity theft to Equifax, Suzanne sent a formal letter to the credit reporting agency, disputing twenty-four specific items in her credit report and requesting their deletion. Equifax agreed to delete the majority of these items, but after assertedly verifying two accounts with Citifinancial, Inc., Equifax notified Suzanne that it would not remove these two items. At trial, Equifax admitted that under its "verified victim policy," it should have automatically removed these

Citifinancial items at Suzanne's request, but it failed to do so in violation of its own written procedures.

Two months later, on May 9, 2005, Suzanne again wrote to Equifax, still disputing the two Citifinancial accounts, and now also contesting two Washington Mutual accounts that Equifax had previously deleted but had mistakenly restored to Suzanne's report. When Equifax attempted to correct these mistakes, it exacerbated matters further by generating a second credit file bearing Shovana Sloan's name but containing Suzanne's social security number. Compounding this mistake, on May 23, 2005, Equifax sent a letter to Suzanne's house addressed to Shovana Sloan, warning Shovana that *she* was possibly the victim of identity theft and offering to sell her a service to monitor her credit file. Then, on June 7, 2005, Equifax sent copies of *both* credit reports to Suzanne; notably, both credit reports still contained the disputed Citifinancial accounts.

The stress of these problems weighed on Suzanne and significantly contributed to the deterioration of her marriage to Tracey. . . . In May 2005, the credit situation forced Tracey, a high school teacher, to abandon his plans to take a sabbatical during which he had hoped to develop land for modular homes with his father. The Sloanes frequently fought during the day and slept in separate rooms at night. . . . Also, during this period, Suzanne was frequently unable to sleep at night, and as her insomnia worsened, she found herself nodding off while driving home from work in the evening. Even after the couple took a vacation to reconcile in August 2005, when they returned home, they were greeted with the denial of a line of credit from Wachovia Bank. . . .

On November 4, 2005 — following twenty-one months of struggle to correct her credit report — Suzanne filed this action against Equifax, Trans Union, LLC, Experian Information Solutions, Inc., and Citifinancial, alleging violations of the FCRA. After settling a separate suit against Prince William Hospital and the personnel company that placed Shovana Sloan in the hospital's accounting department, Suzanne settled her claims in this action against Experian, Trans Union, and Citifinancial. Equifax, however, refused to settle. Thus, the case proceeded to trial with Equifax the sole remaining defendant. The jury returned a verdict against Equifax, awarding Suzanne $106,000 for economic loss and $245,000 for mental anguish, humiliation, and emotional distress.

Equifax moved for judgment as a matter of law and for a new trial or remittitur on the jury's award of damages for emotional distress. The district court denied Equifax's post-trial motions and then, without permitting Equifax to submit an opposition to Suzanne's request for attorney's fees, ordered Equifax to pay $181,083 in attorney's fees. This appeal followed. . . .

In this case, the jury specifically found, via a special verdict, that Suzanne proved by a preponderance of the evidence that Equifax violated the FCRA by negligently: (1) failing to follow reasonable procedures designed to assure maximum accuracy on her consumer credit report; (2) failing to conduct a reasonable investigation to determine whether disputed information in her credit report was inaccurate; (3) failing to delete information from the report that it found after reinvestigation to be inaccurate, incomplete, or unverified; and (4) reinserting information into her credit file that it had previously deleted. On appeal, Equifax does not challenge the jury's findings that Suzanne proved that it violated the FCRA in all of these respects.

The FCRA provides a private cause of action for those damaged by violations of the statute. *See* 15 U.S.C.A. §§ 1681n, 1681o. A successful plaintiff can recover both actual and punitive damages for willful violations of the FCRA, *id.* § 1681n(a), and actual damages for negligent violations, *id.* § 1681o(a). Actual damages may include not only economic damages, but also damages for humiliation and mental distress. The statute also provides that a successful plaintiff suing under the FCRA may recover reasonable attorney's fees. 15 U.S.C.A. §§ 1681n(a)(3), 1681o(a)(2). . . .

Equifax first argues that because Suzanne assertedly suffered a single, indivisible injury, she should not recover any damages from Equifax or, alternatively, her recovery should be reduced to take account of her prior settlements with other defendants. According to Equifax, the prior settlements have fully, or almost fully, compensated Suzanne for all of her injuries.

Equifax relies on the "one satisfaction rule" to support its argument. *See Chisholm v. UHP Projects, Inc.,* 205 F.3d 731, 737 (4th Cir. 2000) ("[T]his equitable doctrine operates to reduce a plaintiff's recovery from the nonsettling defendant to prevent the plaintiff from recovering twice from the same assessment of liability."). But, in the case at hand, we cannot find, as a matter of law, that Suzanne has suffered from a "single, indivisible harm" that has already been redressed by other parties. . . .

To the contrary, Suzanne provided credible evidence that her emotional and economic damages resulted from separate acts by separate parties. She did not attempt to hold any of the credit reporting agencies responsible for damages arising from either the identity theft itself or the initial inaccuracies that the theft generated in her credit reports. Moreover, although some of Suzanne's interactions with Equifax overlapped with exchanges with other credit reporting agencies, her encounters with Equifax both predate and postdate these other exchanges. . . .

Further, during the period when Suzanne attempted to correct the mistakes made by all three agencies, each agency produced reports with different inaccuracies, and each agency either corrected or exacerbated these mistakes independently of the others. Thus, even during this period, the inaccuracies in Equifax's credit reports caused Suzanne discrete injuries independent of those caused by the other credit reporting agencies.

For all of these reasons, we reject Equifax's argument that Suzanne has suffered from a single, indivisible injury or has been doubly compensated as a consequence of her prior settlements.

Equifax next argues that the evidence does not support any award for economic losses. Equifax claims that only speculation and conjecture support such an award, and so the district court erred in denying Equifax's motion for judgment as to this award.

We disagree. The evidence at trial in this case clearly demonstrates that on numerous occasions Suzanne attempted to secure lines of credit from a variety of financial institutions, only to be either denied outright or offered credit on less advantageous terms that she might have received absent Equifax's improper conduct. At times, these financial institutions consulted credit reports from other agencies, but at other times these institutions relied exclusively on the erroneous credit information provided by Equifax. Based on these incidents, we find that there is a legally sufficient evidentiary basis for a reasonable jury to have found that Equifax's conduct resulted in economic losses for Suzanne. Therefore, the district court did not err in denying Equifax's motion regarding this award.

Additionally, Equifax asserts that the district court erred in refusing to order remittitur of the mental anguish, humiliation, and emotional distress damages award to no more than $25,000. Equifax contends that the jury's award of $245,000 is inconsistent with awards in similar cases and is disproportionate to any actual injury proved at trial. Suzanne, by contrast, contends that the evidence provides more than adequate support for the jury's award. To resolve this question, we set forth the relevant governing principles, apply these principles to the evidence before the jury, and compare the evidence and emotional distress award in Suzanne's case with the evidence and award in all assertedly relevant cases. . . .

We begin with Federal Rule of Civil Procedure 59(a), which provides that if a court concludes that a jury award of compensatory damages is excessive, it may order a new trial nisi remittitur. . . . A district court abuses its discretion only by upholding an award of damages when "the jury's verdict is against the weight of the evidence or based on evidence which is false."

In this case, the district court found that the jury's emotional distress award was "not an unreasonable conclusion from this evidence." The court noted that the jury could base its award on Equifax's specific actions, as distinct from those of the other credit reporting agencies, and that Equifax's actions directly led to the mounting frustration and distress that Suzanne felt for almost two years. As one example of Equifax's specific actions, the court recalled the letter that Equifax sent to Suzanne, many months after she had notified Equifax of the identity theft, bearing the name of the identity thief and warning the thief, not Suzanne, that the thief's personal information was in peril. . . .

Moreover, Equifax does not deny that Suzanne suffered emotional distress. Nor does Equifax contend that Suzanne failed to produce sufficient evidence to sustain some award for this injury. Rather, Equifax simply proposes replacing the jury's number with one of its own invention — offering $25,000 in place of $245,000. Yet when asked at oral argument to explain the basis for the proposed remittitur, Equifax's counsel could offer no legal or factual basis for this amount, conceding that the number had been taken "out of the air." Not only is such an unprincipled approach intrinsically unsound, but it also directly contravenes the Seventh Amendment, which precludes an appellate court from replacing an award of compensatory damages with one of the court's own choosing. In short, the issue before us is neither whether Suzanne offered sufficient evidence at trial to sustain an award for emotional distress nor whether we believe that Equifax's "out of the air" $25,000 represents a fair estimate of those damages, but whether the jury's award is *excessive* in light of evidence presented at trial.

Our previous cases establish the type of evidence required to support an award for emotional damages. We have warned that "[n]ot only is emotional distress fraught with vagueness and speculation, it is easily susceptible to fictitious and trivial claims." *Price v. City of Charlotte*, 93 F.3d 1241, 1250 (4th Cir. 1996). For this reason, although specifically recognizing that a plaintiff's testimony can provide sufficient evidence to support an emotional distress award, we have required a plaintiff to "reasonably and sufficiently explain the circumstances of [the] injury and not resort to mere conclusory statements." Thus, we have distinguished between plaintiff testimony that amounts only to "conclusory statements" and plaintiff testimony that "sufficiently articulate[s]" true "demonstrable emotional distress."

In *Knussman v. Maryland,* 272 F.3d 625 (4th Cir. 2001), we summarized the factors properly considered in determinating the potential excessiveness of an award for emotional distress. They include the factual context in which the emotional distress arose; evidence corroborating the testimony of the plaintiff; the nexus between the conduct of the defendant and the emotional distress; the degree of such mental distress; mitigating circumstances, if any; physical injuries suffered due to the emotional distress; medical attention resulting from the emotional duress; psychiatric or psychological treatment; and the loss of income, if any.

In the present case, Suzanne offered considerable objective verification of her emotional distress, chronic anxiety, and frustration during the twenty-one months that she attempted to correct Equifax's errors. First, her repeated denials of credit and continuous problems with Equifax furnish an objective and inherently reasonable "factual context" for her resulting claims of emotional distress. Suzanne also corroborated her account in two ways. She offered "sufficiently articulated" descriptions of her protracted anxiety through detailed testimony of specific events and the humiliation and anger she experienced as a result of each occurrence. She also provided evidence that the distress was apparent to others, particularly her family; Tracey, for instance, described in detail his wife's ongoing struggles with Equifax and the emotional toll these events took upon her. In addition, substantial trial evidence attested to the direct "nexus" between Equifax's violations of the FCRA and Suzanne's emotional distress. Furthermore, Suzanne's emotional distress manifested itself in terms of physical symptoms, particularly insomnia. . . .

Reviewing this evidence in light of the appropriate factors already set forth, we conclude that substantial, if not overwhelming, objective evidence supports an emotional distress award. Equifax ignores much of this evidence, however, and insists that an award of $245,000 is "inconsistent with awards in other similar cases." But Equifax relies on cases which are in fact not very "similar" to the case at hand and so provide little assistance in assessing the amount of the emotional distress award here. . . .

As Equifax's authorities indicate, finding helpful precedent for comparison here is not a simple task. The recent emergence of identity theft and the rapid growth of the credit-reporting industry present a unique dilemma without clear precedent. When Congress enacted the FCRA in 1970, it recognized the vital role that credit-reporting agencies had assumed within the burgeoning culture of American consumerism. Since the mid-1980s, the introduction of computerized information technology and data-warehousing has led to the national consolidation of the credit-reporting industry into the "Big Three" — Equifax, Experian, and Trans Union — and rendered credit reporting an integral part of our most ordinary consumer transactions. According to recent data, each of these national credit-reporting agencies has perhaps 1.5 billion credit accounts held by approximately 190 million individuals. Each receives more than two billion items of information every month, and together these three agencies issue approximately two million consumer credit reports each day.

Against this backdrop, identity theft has emerged over the last decade as one of the fastest growing white-collar crimes in the United States. . . . Given the rapid emergence of identity theft in the last decade, it comes as no surprise that past precedent fails to fully reflect the unfortunate current reality. . . .

A survey of the other, more recent FCRA cases that involve requests for remittitur of emotional distress awards suggests that approved awards more typically range between $20,000 and $75,000.

This handful of cases, while helpful, differs from the case at hand. For, unlike the plaintiffs in those cases, Suzanne did not suffer from isolated or accidental reporting errors. Rather, as a victim of identity theft, she suffered the systematic manipulation of her personal information, which, despite her best efforts, Equifax failed to correct over a protracted period of time. Of course, Equifax bore no responsibility for the initial theft, but the FCRA makes the company responsible for taking reasonable steps to correct Suzanne's credit report once she brought the theft to the company's attention; this Equifax utterly failed to do. A reasonable jury could conclude that Equifax's repeated errors engendered more emotional distress than that found in these other FCRA cases.

We also believe that some guidance can be gained from case law concerning defamation. Prior to the enactment of the FCRA, defamation was one of several common-law actions used by plaintiffs in response to the dissemination of inaccurate credit information.[13] These common-law causes of action parallel those offered under the FCRA in that they typically involve a defendant found liable for propagating inaccurate information about the plaintiff, and the effects, while unquestionably harmful, are difficult to translate into monetary terms. . . . [C]ourts frequently sustain emotional distress awards in the range of $250,000 in defamation cases.

We do not believe the evidence presented here permits an award of this magnitude because, after all, this case does not involve actual defamation. Moreover, Suzanne presented almost no evidence at trial to suggest that Equifax's violations of the FCRA resulted in harm to her reputation, and it appears that few people beyond Suzanne's family and potential creditors knew of her disastrous credit file. We therefore believe that the maximum award supported by the evidence here must be significantly less than these defamation awards. But, considering the extensive corroboration offered at trial concerning the many months of emotional distress, mental anguish, and humiliation suffered by Suzanne, we believe that the evidence does support an award in the maximum amount of $150,000. We recognize that even this amount is appreciably more than that awarded for emotional distress in most other FCRA cases. But, as explained earlier, the case at hand differs significantly from those cases. A $150,000 award reflects those differences—the repeated violations of the FCRA found by the jury in its special verdict, the number of errors contained in Equifax's credit reports, and the protracted length of time during which Equifax

---

[13] A provision of the FCRA bars consumers from bringing actions "in the nature of defamation, invasion of privacy, or negligence" in certain specified contexts, except as those causes of action arise under sections 1681n and 1681o of the FCRA. 15 U.S.C.A. § 1681h(e).

failed to correct Suzanne's credit file. Accordingly, we reduce the emotional distress award to $150,000 and grant a new trial nisi remittitur at Suzanne's option. . . .

[The court vacated the district court's grant of attorney's fees in the amount of $181,083 because the district court failed to allow Equifax to submit a written opposition to Sloane's motion for attorney's fees. The case was remanded to allow Equifax to file its opposition.]

NOTES & QUESTIONS

1. *Damages.* Was the remittitur to $150,000 appropriate? Why should damage awards be limited based on the damage awards in other cases? As the court noted, they involve very different facts than the case at bar.

   Also recall the court's statement that "this case does not involve actual defamation. . . . Suzanne presented almost no evidence at trial to suggest that Equifax's violations of the FCRA resulted in harm to her reputation, and it appears that few people beyond Suzanne's family and potential creditors knew of her disastrous credit file." Why doesn't this case involve "harm to her reputation"? Don't reports on people's creditworthiness affect their financial reputations, that is, their ability to pay back their debts, their trustworthiness, and dependability?

2. *The Harm of Identity Theft.* When assessing the damages Sloane suffered from her identity theft ordeal, how much of the harm was caused by Equifax's actions? Purportedly, the entire incident of identity theft caused her marital discord, insomnia, and emotional distress. Yet, the identity theft did involve, after all, not only Equifax, but the identity thief, creditors, and other credit reporting agencies. Are the damages assessed to Equifax proportionate to Equifax's contribution to Sloane's ordeal? Or should Equifax be viewed as the "least cost avoider," the party who can internalize the costs of preventing this harm at the least overall cost?

3. *Transparency.* Chris Hoofnagle proposes that policy responses to identity theft are hobbled by a lack of information about the dimensions of the problem.[14] He argues: "We are asking the wrong people about the crime. . . . Victims often do not know how their personal data were stolen or who stole the information." Hoofnagle's solution is to create a reporting requirement on financial institutions, including all lenders and organizations that control access to accounts (such as PayPal and Western Union). There would be three disclosure requirements for these entities: "(1) the number of identity theft incidents suffered or avoided; (2) the forms of identity theft attempted and the financial products targeted (e.g., mortgage loan or credit card); and (3) the amount of loss suffered or avoided."

   Do you think that consumers would respond to such market information and actually switch accounts from one organization to another? Personal information might be stolen from nonfinancial institutions, such as a college,

---

[14] Chris Jay Hoofnagle, *Identity Theft: Making the Known Unknowns Known*, 21 Harv. J. L. & Tech. 97 (2007).

and then used by a criminal for fraud at a bank. How can incentives be provided for nonfinancial institutions to have adequate security?

B. THE GRAMM-LEACH-BLILEY ACT

In 1999, Congress passed the Financial Services Modernization Act, more commonly known as the Gramm-Leach-Bliley Act (GLBA), Pub. L. No. 106-102, codified at 15 U.S.C. §§ 6801–6809. The GLBA was designed to restructure the financial services industries, which had long been regulated under the Glass-Steagall Act of 1933. The Glass-Steagall Act, passed in response to the Great Depression, prevented different types of financial institutions (e.g., banks, brokerage houses, insurers) from affiliating with each other. The GLBA enables the creation of financial conglomerates that provide a host of different forms of financial services.

The law authorizes widespread sharing of personal information by financial institutions such as banks, insurers, and investment companies. The law permits sharing of personal information between companies that are joined together or affiliated with each other as well as sharing of information between unaffiliated companies. To protect privacy, the Act requires a variety of agencies (FTC, Comptroller of Currency, SEC, and a number of others) to establish "appropriate standards for the financial institutions subject to their jurisdiction" to "insure security and confidentiality of customer records and information" and "protect against unauthorized access" to the records. 15 U.S.C. § 6801.

Nonpublic Personal Information. The privacy provisions of the GLBA only apply to "nonpublic personal information" that consists of "personally identifiable financial information." § 6809(4). Thus, the law only protects *financial* information that is *not public*.

Sharing of Information with Affiliated Companies. The GLBA permits financial institutions that are joined together to share the "nonpublic personal information" that each affiliate possesses. For example, suppose an affiliate has access to a person's medical information. This information could be shared with an affiliate bank that could then turn down a person for a loan. Affiliates must tell customers that they are sharing such information. § 6802(a). The disclosure can be in the form of a general disclosure in a privacy policy. § 6803(a). There is no way for individuals to block this sharing of information.

Sharing of Information with Nonaffiliated Companies. Financial institutions can share personal information with nonaffiliated companies only if they first provide individuals with the ability to opt out of the disclosure. § 6802(b). However, people cannot opt out if the financial institution provides personal data to nonaffiliated third parties "to perform services for or functions on behalf of the financial institution, including marketing of the financial institution's own products and services, or financial products or services offered pursuant to joint agreements between two or more financial institutions." § 6802(b)(2). The financial institution must disclose the information sharing and must have a contract with the third party requiring the third party to maintain the confidentiality of the information. § 6802(b)(2). Third parties receiving personal data from a financial institution cannot reuse that information. § 6802(c). These provisions do not apply to disclosures to credit reporting agencies.

Limits on Disclosure. Financial institutions cannot disclose (other than to credit reporting agencies) account numbers or credit card numbers for use in direct marketing (telemarketing, e-mail, or mail). § 6802(d).

Privacy Notices. The GLBA requires that financial institutions inform customers of their privacy policies. In particular, customers must be informed about policies concerning the disclosure of personal information to affiliates and other companies and categories of information that are disclosed and the security of personal data. § 6803(a).

The Safeguards Rule. The GLBA requires the FTC and other agencies to establish security standards for nonpublic personal information. *See* 15 U.S.C. §§ 6801(b), 6805(b)(2). The FTC issued its final regulations on May 23, 2002. According to the regulations, financial institutions "shall develop, implement, and maintain a comprehensive information security program" that is appropriate to the "size and complexity" of the institution, the "nature and scope" of the institution's activities, and the "sensitivity of any customer information at issue." 16 C.F.R. § 314.3(a). An "information security program" is defined as "the administrative, technical, or physical safeguards [an institution uses] to access, collect, distribute, process, store, use, transmit, dispose of, or otherwise handle customer information." § 314.2(b).

Preemption. The GLBA does not preempt state laws that provide greater protection to privacy. § 6807(b). As will be discussed below, Vermont has made use of this provision and requires opt in, or affirmative consumer consent, before a financial institution can share nonpublic personal financial information pertaining to a consumer to a nonaffiliated third party.

Critics and Supporters. Consider the following critique by Ted Janger and Paul Schwartz:

> The GLB Act has managed to disappoint both industry leaders and privacy advocates alike. Why are so many observers frustrated with the GLB Act? We have already noted the complaint of financial services companies regarding the expense of privacy notices. These organizations also argue that there have been scant pay-off from the costly mailings — and strong evidence backs up this claim. For example, a survey from the American Banker's Association found that 22% of banking customers said that they received a privacy notice but did not read it, and 41% could not even recall receiving a notice. The survey also found only 0.5% of banking customers had exercised their opt-out rights. . . .
>
> Not only are privacy notices difficult to understand, but they are written in a fashion that makes it hard to exercise the opt-out rights that GLB Act mandates. For example, opt-out provisions are sometimes buried in privacy notices. As the

Public Citizen Litigation Group has found, "Explanations of how to opt-out invariably appear at the end of the notices. Thus, before they learn how to opt-out, consumers must trudge through up to ten pages of fine print. . . ." Public Citizen also identified many passages regarding opt-out that "are obviously designed to discourage consumers from exercising their rights under the statute." For example, some financial institutions include an opt-out box only "in a thicket of misleading statements." . . . A final tactic of GLB Act privacy notices is to state that consumers who opt-out may fail to receive "valuable offers." . . .

The GLB Act merely contains an opt-out requirement; as a result, information can be disclosed to non-affiliated entities unless individuals take affirmative action, namely, informing the financial entity that they refuse this sharing of their personal data. By setting its default as an opt-out, the GLB Act fails to create any penalty on the party with superior knowledge, the financial entity, should negotiations fail to occur. In other words, the GLB leaves the burden of bargaining on the less informed party, the individual consumer. These doubts about the efficacy of opt-out are supported, at least indirectly, by the evidence concerning sometimes confusing, sometimes misleading privacy notices. . . . An opt-out default creates incentives for privacy notices that lead to *inaction* by the consumer.[15]

Marcy Peek argues that the GLBA has actually done more to facilitate information sharing than to protect privacy. Enabling greater information uses so long as customers have a right to opt out has resulted in much more information sharing since "the opt-out right is meaningless in practice; the right to opt out of the trafficking of one's personal information is explained in lengthy, legalistic privacy policies that most people throw away as just more junk mail." More broadly, Peek argues, several laws purporting to protect privacy often "represent a façade of protection for consumers, keeping them complacent in the purported knowledge that someone is protecting their privacy interests." In the end, Peek argues, "corporate power drives information privacy law."[16]

In contrast, Peter Swire argues that the GLBA "works surprisingly well as privacy legislation":

Recognizing the criticisms to date, and the limits of the available evidence, I would like to make the case for a decidedly more optimistic view of the effect of the GLB notices. Even in their current flawed form and even if not a single consumer exercised the opt-out right, I contend that a principal effect of the notices has been to require financial institutions to inspect their own practices. In this respect, the detail and complexity of the GLB notices is actually a virtue. In order to draft the notice, many financial institutions undertook an extensive process, often for the first time, to learn just how data is and is not shared between different parts of the organization and with third parties. Based on my extensive discussions with people in the industry, I believe that many institutions discovered practices that they decided, upon deliberation, to change. One public example of this was the decision of Bank of America no longer to share its customers' data with third parties, even subject to opt-out. The detailed

---

[15] Ted Janger & Paul M. Schwartz, *The Gramm-Leach-Bliley Act, Information Privacy, and the Limits of Default Rules*, 86 Minn. L. Rev. 1219, 1230-32, 1241 (2002).

[16] Marcy E. Peek, Information *Privacy and Corporate Power: Towards a Re-Imagination of Information Privacy Law*, 37 Seton Hall L. Rev. 127, 147-49, 137 (2006).

and complex notice, in short, created a more detailed roadmap for privacy compliance.[17]

The critics of the GLBA and Swire appear to be looking at the statute from two different perspectives. The critics are looking at it from a consumer-centric view; Swire sees the positive effect that the statute has on practices within institutions. Is there a way for a statute to have a positive impact in both areas?

C. FEDERAL AND STATE FINANCIAL PRIVACY LAWS

1. STATE FINANCIAL LAWS

The Vermont Opt-In Approach. In contrast to the GLBA approach, Vermont permits sharing of personal data by financial institutions with nonaffiliated companies only if companies obtain an individual's consent. This requirement of a positive response before information can be shared is termed an "opt in." State of Vermont, Department, Insurance, Securities & Health Care Administration, Banking Division, Regulation B-2001-01, Privacy of Consumer Financial and Health Information Regulation. This regulation also carefully defines the acceptable form of and process for opt-in notice. For example, when consumers want to revoke their opting in to information sharing, financial institutions cannot force "the consumer to write his or her own letter." Financial institutions also cannot make consumers "use a check-off box that was provided with the initial notice but [that] is not included with subsequent notices."

California's SB1. California's Financial Information Privacy Act, known as "SB1," Cal. Fin. Code §§ 4050–4060, was enacted "to afford persons greater privacy protections that those provided in . . . the federal Gramm-Leach-Bliley Act." § 4051. Specifically, the California legislature found that the Gramm-Leach-Bliley Act "increases the likelihood that the personal financial information of California residents will be widely shared among, between, and within companies" and that "the policies intended to protect financial privacy imposed by the Gramm-Leach-Bliley Act are inadequate to meet the privacy concerns of California residents." § 4051.5.

In contrast to the Gramm-Leach-Bliley Act, which provides people with an opt-out right, SB1, like the Vermont regulation, requires opt in:

> [A] financial institution shall not sell, share, transfer, or otherwise disclose nonpublic personal information to or with any nonaffiliated third parties without the explicit prior consent of the consumer to whom the nonpublic personal information relates. § 4052.5.

SB1 permits financial institutions to offer incentives or discounts for people to opt in. § 4053.

---

[17] Peter P. Swire, *The Surprising Virtues of the New Financial Privacy Law*, 86 Minn. L. Rev. 1263, 1315-16 (2002).

Financial institutions challenged SB1, arguing that it was preempted by the FCRA. In *American Bankers Ass'n v. Lockyer*, 541 F.3d 1214 (9th Cir. 2008), the Ninth Circuit found that § 4053(b)(1) of SB1 had applications that federal law did not preempt. In particular, it ruled that the affiliate-sharing provisions of SB1 could be narrowed to "exclude the regulation of consumer report information as defined by the FCRA, 15 U.S.C. 1681a(d)(1)." This ruling means that the opt-in provided for Californian residents by SB1 survives for nonpublic personal information that does not fall within the definition of a "consumer report" in FCRA.

The North Dakota Opt-In Referendum and Other States. In June 2002, North Dakotans overwhelmingly rejected, by a 73 percent vote, a 2001 state law that had established an opt-out rather than opt-in standard for financial institutions in North Dakota. The Privacy Rights Clearinghouse noted: "The referendum in North Dakota was the first time this issue has been taken directly to voters."[18] New Mexico has also provided an opt-in requirement for financial institutions before sharing of personal consumer data is permitted with nonaffiliated companies.

2. LAWS REGULATING GOVERNMENT ACCESS TO FINANCIAL DATA

Access to financial data is a key tool for law enforcement to investigate criminal activity. Although this material is covered in more depth in Chapter 5, this section will briefly describe some of the key laws and cases that regulate government access to financial data.

The Bank Secrecy Act. The Bank Secrecy Act of 1970, 31 U.S.C. § 1081, requires the retention of bank records and creation of reports that would be useful in criminal, tax, or regulatory investigations or proceedings. The Act requires that federally insured banks record the identities of account holders as well as copies of each check, draft, or other financial instrument. Regulations promulgated under the Act by the Secretary of the Treasury require reporting to the government of financial transactions exceeding $10,000 if made within the United States and exceeding $5,000 if into or out of the United States. *See* 31 C.F.R. § 103.

A group of bankers challenged the law as violating the Fourth Amendment, but the U.S. Supreme Court held that the bankers did not possess Fourth Amendment rights in the information because "corporations can claim no equality with individuals in the enjoyment of a right to privacy." *California Bankers Association v. Shultz,* 416 U.S. 21 (1974). Depositors who were also involved in the case lacked standing because they failed to allege that they "were engaged in the type of $10,000 domestic currency transaction which would necessitate that their bank report it to the Government."

---

[18] Privacy Rights Clearinghouse, *North Dakota Votes for "Opt-In" Financial Privacy*, June 21, 2002, at www.privacyrights.org/ar/nd_optin.htm.

The Fourth Amendment. In *United States v. Miller*, 425 U.S. 435 (1976), the U.S. Supreme Court held that people lack a reasonable expectation of privacy in their bank records because they "contain only information voluntarily conveyed to the banks and exposed to their employees in the ordinary course of business." The Court followed the doctrine that has become known as the third party doctrine, which holds that when data is maintained by third parties, there is no reasonable expectation of privacy — and no Fourth Amendment protection.

The Right to Financial Privacy Act. In response to *Miller*, in 1978, Congress passed the Right to Financial Privacy Act (RFPA), Pub. L. No. 95-630. The RFPA prevents banks and other financial institutions from disclosing a person's financial information to the government unless the records are disclosed pursuant to subpoena or search warrant. *See* 29 U.S.C. §§ 3401–3422.

3. IDENTITY THEFT STATUTES

The Identity Theft Assumption and Deterrence Act. Congress responded to the growth of identity theft by passing the Identity Theft and Assumption Deterrence Act in 1998. The Act makes it a federal crime to "knowingly transfer or use, without lawful authority, a means of identification of another person with the intent to commit, or to aid or abet, any unlawful activity that constitutes a violation of Federal law, or that constitutes a felony under any applicable State or local law." 18 U.S.C. § 1028.

State Legislative Responses. The vast majority of states now have statutes concerning identity theft. Before 1998, only three states had enacted statutes dealing explicitly with identity theft.[19] Arizona was one of these states; it punishes identity theft as a low-grade felony, but its statute does not address victims' rights and remedies. Ariz. Rev. Stat. Ann. § 13-2008(D). The passage of the federal Identity Theft Assumption and Deterrence Act in 1998 sparked most states to pass their own identity theft legislation — more than 40 states now have identity theft statutes on the books.[20]

Many identity theft statutes focus on defining criminal penalties for the crime. Penalties are tied to the amount of money the thief steals. For example, in Florida, identity theft is a second-degree felony if it results in an injury of $75,000 or more, Fla. Stat. Ann. § 817.568(2)(b), but is only a first-degree misdemeanor if the individual is harassed without having reached the $75,000 threshold. Fla. Stat. Ann. § 817.568(3). New Jersey likewise penalizes identity thefts resulting in injury over $75,000 as a second-degree crime; injuries between $500 and $75,000 constitute a third-degree crime; injuries between $200 and $500 constitute a fourth-degree crime; and injuries less than $200 constitute a disorderly persons offense. N.J.S.A. §§ 2C:21-17(c)(1)–(2). Pennsylvania

---

[19] U.S. General Accountability Office, *Report to the Honorable Sam Johnson House of Representatives, Identity Theft: Greater Awareness and Use of Existing Data Are Needed* 7 (June 2002).

[20] *Id.* at 6.

punishes identity thefts in a similar manner. *See* Pa. Stat. Ann. tit. 18, § 4120(c)(1).

Should penalties be tied to the dollar value of the things the thief wrongfully took or to the mental distress and harm caused to the victims, which might not be correlated to such a dollar value?

California, in contrast to most other states, has some of the most comprehensive and powerful identity theft laws. For example, California permits victims to obtain the fraudulent applications that the identity thief made as well as a record of the thief's transactions in the victim's name. Cal. Penal Code § 530.8; Cal. Civil Code § 1748.95. California also assists victims in stopping debt collectors from continuing to try to collect debts that the thief created. Cal. Civ. Code § 1788.18. The central difference between California's approach and that of other states is that California grants powerful rights to victims to assist them in fixing the damage of an identity theft. California also requires companies to notify consumers of data security breaches where personal information about consumers is compromised. Cal. Civ. Code § 1798.82(a).

Assessing Identity Theft Statutes. Daniel Solove contends that many statutes addressing identity theft focus mainly on enhancing criminal penalties and ignore the real roots of the problem:

> [T]he prevailing approach toward dealing with identity theft — by relying on increasing criminal penalties and by depending upon individuals to take great lengths to try to protect themselves against their vulnerabilities to identity theft — has the wrong focus. . . . The underlying cause of identity theft is an architecture that makes us vulnerable to such crimes and unable to adequately repair the damage. . . .
>
> This architecture is not created by identity thieves; rather, it is exploited by them. It is an architecture of vulnerability, one where personal information is not protected with adequate security, where identity thieves have easy access to data and the ability to use it in detrimental ways. We are increasingly living with what I call "digital dossiers" about our lives, and these dossiers are not controlled by us but by various entities, such as private-sector companies and the government. These dossiers play a profound role in our lives in modern society. The identity thief taps into these dossiers and uses them, manipulates them, and pollutes them. The identity thief's ability to so easily access and use our personal data stems from an architecture that does not provide adequate security to our personal information and that does not afford us with a sufficient degree of participation in the collection, dissemination, and use of that information. Consequently, it is difficult for the victim to figure out what is going on and how she can remedy the situation. . . .
>
> Private sector entities lack adequate ways of controlling access to records and accounts in a person's name, and numerous companies engage in the common practice of using SSNs, mother's maiden names, and addresses for access to account information. Additionally, creditors give out credit and establish new accounts if the applicant supplies a name, SSN, and address.[21]

---

[21] Daniel J. Solove, *Identity Theft, Privacy, and the Architecture of Vulnerability,* 54 Hastings L.J. 1227 (2003). For a response to Solove's proposals for solutions and a defense of his own proposed solution, see Lynn M. LoPucki, *Did Privacy Cause Identity Theft?*, 54 Hastings L.J. 1277 (2003).

Lynn LoPucki and Solove agree that the problem of identity theft is caused by the frequent use of Social Security numbers as identifiers. According to LoPucki:

> The problem is not that thieves have access to personal information, but that creditors and credit-reporting agencies often lack both the means and the incentives to correctly identify the persons who seek credit from them or on whom they report.[22]

LoPucki suggests that the problem is caused by the lack of a reliable means for identification. He proposes a system where the government maintains a database of identification information that people submit, such as biometric data, photographs, and other personal information. Solove argues that more sophisticated identification systems come with other problems, such as an increase in data gathering about people and an inability of people who are the victims of abusive spouses or stalkers to hide. However, both Solove and LoPucki agree that identity theft is, in large part, a problem caused by the system in which credit is granted in the United States.

4. TORT LAW

WOLFE V. MBNA AMERICA BANK

485 F. Supp. 2d 874 (W.D. Tenn. 2007)

DONALD, J. Before the Court is Defendant MBNA America Bank's ("Defendant") Motion to Dismiss Plaintiff's Fourth Amended Complaint made pursuant to Rule 12(b)(6) of the Federal Rules of Civil Procedure. Plaintiff Mark Wolfe ("Plaintiff") filed his Fourth Amended Complaint on September 15, 2006, alleging a claim under the Tennessee Consumer Protection Act of 1977 ("TCPA"), Tenn. Code Ann. § 47-18-104(a)-(b), as well as claims for negligence, gross negligence, and defamation.

Plaintiff, now a twenty-seven year old male, is a resident of the State of Tennessee. In or about April 2000, Defendant received a credit account application in Plaintiff's name from a telemarketing company. The application listed Plaintiff's address as 3557 Frankie Carolyn Drive, Apartment 4, Memphis, Tennessee 38118. Plaintiff did not reside and had never resided at this address.

Upon receipt of the application, Defendant issued a credit card bearing Plaintiff's name to an unknown and unauthorized individual residing at the address listed on the application. Plaintiff alleges that Defendant, prior to issuing the card, did not attempt to verify whether the information contained in the credit account application was authentic and accurate. After receiving the card, the unknown and unauthorized individual charged $864.00 to the credit account, exceeding the account's $500.00 credit limit. When no payments were made on the account, Defendant, without investigating whether the account was obtained using a stolen identity, declared the account delinquent and transferred the

---

[22] Lynn M. LoPucki, *Human Identification Theory and the Identity Theft Problem*, 80 Tex. L. Rev. 89, 94 (2001).

account to NCO Financial Systems, Inc. ("NCO"), a debt collection agency. Defendant also notified various credit reporting agencies that the account was delinquent.

In order to collect the debt on the delinquent account, NCO hired an attorney, who discovered Plaintiff's actual address. The attorney, in a letter dated November 29, 2004, notified Plaintiff of the delinquent account and requested payment. Upon receipt of this letter, Plaintiff contacted the attorney to inquire about the account, but was told that he would receive information about the account in thirty (30) days. Plaintiff never received any further information.

In January 2005, Plaintiff applied for a job with a bank, but Plaintiff was not hired due to his poor credit score. Following this denial, Plaintiff contacted Defendant numerous times to dispute the delinquent account but was unable to obtain any "adequate or real explanation" from Defendant. At some point in time, Defendant mailed a notice of arbitration proceedings to the address listed on the credit account application, which subsequently resulted in an arbitration award against Plaintiff. Despite Plaintiff notifying Defendant that his identity was stolen, Defendant continues to list the credit account bearing Plaintiff's name as delinquent and has not corrected the information provided to credit reporting agencies regarding the account. . . .

A motion to dismiss for failure to state a claim only tests whether the plaintiff has pleaded a cognizable claim. . . .

Plaintiff alleges that Defendant had a *duty to verify* "the accuracy and authenticity of a credit application completed in Plaintiff's name before issuing a credit card." . . . Plaintiff alleges that Defendant failed to comply with [its duty to verify], and thus, is negligent and/or grossly negligent.

In Tennessee, negligence is established if a plaintiff demonstrates: "(1) a duty of care owed by the defendant to the plaintiff; (2) conduct falling below the applicable standard of care amounts to a breach of that duty; (3) an injury or loss; (4) causation in fact; and (5) proximate, or legal cause." To establish gross negligence, a plaintiff "must demonstrate ordinary negligence and must then prove that the defendant acted 'with utter unconcern for the safety of others, or . . . with such reckless disregard for the rights of others that a conscious indifference to consequences is implied in law' ". . . .

Addressing the first context or duty, Defendant asserts that Plaintiff's negligence and gross negligence claims should be dismissed because Tennessee negligence law does not impose a duty on Defendant to verify the authenticity and accuracy of a credit account application prior to issuing a credit card. Defendant, characterizing Plaintiff's claim as one for the "negligent enablement of identity theft," argues that a duty to verify essentially constitutes a duty to prevent third-party criminal activity. Defendant argues that Tennessee courts have never held that commercial banks have a common law duty to prevent the theft of a non-customer's identity. Defendant further argues that it, like Plaintiff, is a victim of identity theft.

Under Tennessee negligence law, a duty is defined as "the legal obligation a defendant owes to a plaintiff to conform to the reasonable person standard of care in order to protect against unreasonable risks of harm." "Whether a defendant owes a duty to a plaintiff in any given situation is a question of law for the court." The "existence and scope of the duty of the defendant in a particular case rests on all the relevant circumstances, including the foreseeability of harm to the plaintiff and other similarly situated persons." A harm is foreseeable "if a reasonable person could foresee the probability of its occurrence or if the person was on notice that the likelihood of danger to the party to whom is owed a duty is probable."

Because Tennessee courts have not specifically addressed whether Tennessee negligence law imposes a duty to verify on commercial banks, Defendant cites in support of its argument the Supreme Court of South Carolina's decision in *Huggins v. Citibank, N.A.,* 585 S.E.2d 275 (S.C. 2003). In *Huggins,* the plaintiff alleged, among other things, that the defendant bank was negligent for issuing a credit card in the plaintiff's name to an unknown and unauthorized person "without any investigation, verification, or corroboration" of the authenticity and accuracy of the credit account application. The defendant argued that under South Carolina negligence law, it had no duty to verify the accuracy and authenticity of the credit account application because plaintiff was technically a non-customer. The South Carolina Supreme Court, despite finding that "it is foreseeable that injury may arise by the negligent issuance of a credit card," ultimately found that no duty to verify existed because "[t]he relationship, if any, between credit card issuers and potential victims of identity theft is far too attenuated to rise to the level of a duty between them." Noting the similarity between negligence law in Tennessee and South Carolina, Defendant argues that its relationship with Plaintiff, like the parties in *Huggins,* was and is too attenuated to warrant the imposition of a duty to verify.

Upon review, the Court finds the South Carolina Supreme Court's conclusion in *Huggins* to be flawed. In reaching its conclusion, the *Huggins* court relied heavily on the fact that there was no prior business relationship between the parties, that is, the plaintiff was not a customer of the defendant bank. The Court believes that the court's reliance on this fact is misplaced. While the existence of a prior business relationship might have some meaning in the context of a contractual dispute, a prior business relationship has little meaning in the context of negligence law. Instead, to determine whether a duty exists between parties, the Court must examine all relevant circumstances, with emphasis on the foreseeability of the alleged harm. As to the issue of foreseeability, the South Carolina Supreme Court found that "it is foreseeable that injury may arise by the negligent issuance of a credit card" and that such injury "could be prevented if credit card issuers carefully scrutinized credit card applications." The Court agrees with and adopts these findings.

With the alarming increase in identity theft in recent years, commercial banks and credit card issuers have become the first, and often last, line of defense in preventing the devastating damage that identity theft inflicts. Because the injury resulting from the negligent issuance of a credit card is foreseeable and preventable, the Court finds that under Tennessee negligence law, Defendant has a duty to verify the authenticity and accuracy of a credit account application before issuing a credit card. The Court, however, emphasizes that this duty to verify does not impose upon Defendant a duty to prevent all identity theft. The Court recognizes that despite banks utilizing the most reasonable and vigilant verification methods, some criminals will still be able to obtain enough personal information to secure a credit card with a stolen identity. Rather, this duty to verify merely requires Defendant to implement reasonable and cost-effective verification methods that can prevent criminals, in some instances, from obtaining a credit card with a stolen identity. Whether Defendant complied with this duty before issuing a credit card in Plaintiff's name is an issue for the trier of fact. Accordingly, Defendant's motion to dismiss Plaintiff's negligence and gross negligence claims in the first factual context is DENIED.

NOTES & QUESTIONS

1. *Tort Law to the Rescue?* In *Wolfe*, the district court located a duty in tort law that required a bank to take steps to verify identity before issuing a credit card in the plaintiff's name to a person. The court operated under a negligence theory: the bank need not prevent all identity theft (strict liability), but merely use reasonable verification methods. What kind of practical steps might a bank take to make sure that the person to whom it issues a credit card is, in fact, the intended person? In light of the LoPucki-Solove debate (excerpted above) about the flawed system for checking and otherwise verifying identity, how successful are any "reasonable" means likely to be?

2. *The Breach of Confidentiality Tort and Financial Institutions.* Recall the breach of confidentiality tort from Chapter 6. Under the common law, a doctor can be liable to a patient if she discloses the patient's personal information. A number of jurisdictions extend the tort of breach of confidentiality to disclosures by banks and financial institutions of their customers' financial information. In *Peterson v. Idaho First Nat'l Bank*, 367 P.2d 284 (Idaho 1961), the court held that a bank could be sued for breach of confidentiality for disclosing customer information:

> It is generally stated that the relation between a bank and its general depositor is that of debtor and creditor. . . . But it is also said that in discharging its obligation to a depositor a bank must do so subject to the rules of agency. . . .
>
> All agree that a bank should protect its business records from the prying eyes of the public, moved by curiosity or malice. No one questions its right to protect its fiduciary relationship with its customers, which, in sound banking practice, as a matter of common knowledge, is done everywhere. . . .
>
> To give such information to third persons or to the public at the instance of the customer or depositor is certainly not beyond the scope of banking powers. It is a different matter, however, when such information is sought from the bank without the consent of the depositor or customer of the bank. Indeed, it is an implied term of the contract between the banker and his customer that the banker will not divulge to third persons, without the consent of the customer, express or implied, either the state of the customer's account or any of his transactions with the bank, or any information relating to the customer acquired through the keeping of his account. . . .
>
> It is inconceivable that a bank would at any time consider itself at liberty to disclose the intimate details of its depositors' accounts. Inviolate secrecy is one of the inherent and fundamental precepts of the relationship of the bank and its customers or depositors.

Several other jurisdictions have held likewise. *See, e.g., Barnett Bank of West Florida v. Hooper*, 498 So. 2d 923 (Fla. 1986); *Indiana Nat'l Bank v. Chapman*, 482 N.E.2d 474 (Ind. App. 1985); *Suburban Trust Co. v. Waller*, 408 A.2d 758 (Md. App. 1979); *Richfield Bank & Trust Co. v. Sjogren*, 244 N.W.2d 648 (Minn. 1976); *McGuire v. Shubert*, 722 A.2d 1087 (Pa. Super. 1998).

CONSUMER DATA

CHAPTER OUTLINE

We live in a world where commercial entities collect and maintain extensive databases of personal information about individuals. These businesses amass this information for myriad purposes. One of their chief reasons for their interest in personal data is to enhance their ability to market products and services to people.

A burgeoning form of marketing today consists of behavioral marketing—examining the behavior patterns of consumers to target advertisements to them. Today's marketer can draw on a wealth of knowledge and insights about human behavior to maximize the effectiveness of advertising. Interactions on the Internet and with other digital platforms permit the creation of an immense trail of personal data, as almost everything that people do online can be tracked. Individuals can now be followed across different websites or digital media. Advertisements can be tailored to specific individuals.

Consumer data can be used for other purposes too. It can be used to make inferences about a person's trustworthiness or aptitude for a job. It can be used for background checks or to determine whether a person will be an easy or difficult customer to deal with. The government can access consumer data for use in criminal investigations, general profiling, or a broad-scale amassing of data.

This chapter explores how the law regulates the collection and use of consumer data.

A. THE U.S. SYSTEM OF CONSUMER DATA PRIVACY REGULATION

In the United States, myriad types of law, which form a complicated patchwork of regulation, regulate consumer data privacy. In some contexts, the law provides strong protections of privacy. In other contexts, the law provides minimal protections. And in a number of contexts, there is hardly any legal protection.

1. STRUCTURE

The Sectoral Approach. Consumer privacy in the United States is regulated by "sectoral" laws that focus on various sectors of the economy. Different laws regulate different industries. In contrast to the United States, Europe and many other countries have an "omnibus" approach toward regulating privacy. Under an omnibus approach, one overarching statute regulates personal information use irrespective of the entities or industry that wishes to process the information. These general laws are frequently then supplemented in European countries and elsewhere outside of the United States by more targeted, sectoral laws. The "omnibus" law provides a general safety-net in these countries for areas or regulatory issues that a sectoral statute may not address.

The sectoral approach in the United States can sometimes draw even finer distinctions for similar kinds of information. For example, cable TV records are regulated differently from video rental or sale records. There are no industry-specific federal statutes directed towards the personal information contained in records of most merchants (bookstores, supermarkets, clothing stores, electronics stories, etc.).

Self-Regulation. Self-regulation has formed a key foundation for U.S. consumer privacy law. As businesses began offering their products and services on the Internet in the 1990s, they operated in a realm that was largely unregulated. To ease concerns of consumers and to demonstrate that they could regulate themselves, businesses began to post privacy policies on their websites. These policies describe the information that is collected, how it will be used and shared, and how it will be safeguarded. Consumers are sometimes offered a choice to opt-out of some uses of their data.

Although privacy regulation has proliferated, some industries still lack a sectoral law. Privacy regulation also tends to allow businesses great flexibility in how they collect, use, or disclose personal data. Most companies use an approach called "notice and choice." They provide a privacy policy (sometimes called a "privacy notice") that describes the ways in which personal data will be collected, used, or disclosed. Consumers are then considered to have a choice. They can accept these terms and do business with the company, or they can refrain from doing business with the company. Sometimes companies offer choices to consumers regarding specific uses or disclosures of their information. Consumers may be given the ability to "opt out" of certain uses or disclosures. An "opt out" means that a consumer's information will be processed unless she takes action to contact the data processing entity and indicate her contrary wishes.

Since the late 1990s, the Federal Trade Commission (FTC) has deemed violations of privacy policies to be an "unfair or deceptive" practice under the FTC Act. The FTC has the power to enforce the FTC Act. The result of the FTC's involvement has been to create a system of quasi-self-regulation, where companies define the substantive terms of how they will collect, use, and disclose personal data, but they are then held accountable to these terms by the FTC. Over time, however, the FTC has interpreted the FTC Act as requiring more of companies than merely following promises.

The Chief Privacy Officer. Over the last two decades, there has been a significant rise of "privacy professionals." The association for such individuals — the International Association of Privacy Professionals (IAPP) — has grown at rates from 30 percent to 40 percent. Beyond the large membership of this organization, a further indication of the ongoing development and specialization of privacy work is provided by the three certification titles that the IAPP grants. By taking examinations, an applicant can become a Certified Information Privacy Professional (CIPP), a Certified Information Privacy Manager (CIPM), or a Certified Information Privacy Technologist (CIPT).

Many companies have a chief privacy officer (CPO) who handles a number of tasks. Overall, CPOs develop a "privacy program" within an institution.[1] A

---

[1] For two practitioner-oriented guides to the role of a CPO, see Michelle Finneran Dennedy et al., *The Privacy Engineer's Manifesto* (2014); *Building a Privacy Program* (Kirk M. Herath ed., 2011).

privacy program typically has both elements involving compliance and strategy. Compliance means developing safeguards, including training the workface, to make sure that the company follows all privacy and security laws and regulations. Strategic thinking means assessing privacy risks, training the workforce about privacy awareness, helping to shape products and services so that they minimize any potential privacy concerns, and stopping or limiting a company's actions that consumers might find too privacy-invasive. The CPO often not only helps manage the information companies have about consumers but also the data maintained about the workforce.

In some industries, laws or regulations require that companies have a designated employee to handle privacy and security responsibilities. An example would be the FTC's Safeguards Rule, issued pursuant to the Gramm-Leach-Bliley Act, which requires the designation of one employee at the covered entity to manage the company's responsibilities pursuant to the Rule. In other industries, businesses voluntarily have CPOs. In such companies, the rise of the CPO is tied to an increase of privacy and security obligations, whether through statutes, regulations, or contracts. As a consequence, it is efficient for the company to have a specialized employee to do this work. CPOs are now common in most large and medium-sized businesses.

As Kenneth Bamberger and Deirdre Mulligan note, "[C]orporate privacy management in the United States has undergone a profound transformation."[2] Based on a series of interviews with leading CPOs, Bamberger and Mulligan present an account of "privacy on the ground." In their view, these firms, driven by the leadership of CPOs, have adopted a dynamic approach to privacy issues. The approach "stressed the importance of integrating practices into corporate decisionmaking that would prevent the violation of consumer expectations." The respondent CPOs also emphasized the importance of developing "company law," by which they meant "consistent and coordinated firm-specific global privacy policies intended to ensure that a firm both complies with the requirements of all relevant jurisdictions and acts concordantly when dealing with additional business issues not governed by any particular regulation."

2. TYPES OF LAW

Tort Law. Tort law has been used by plaintiffs in response to various forms of data collection, use, or disclosure. Plaintiffs have attempted to use the Warren and Brandeis privacy torts, which were originally developed to address issues involving privacy and the media, as well as other torts, such as negligence. Later in this chapter we will explore how these attempts have fared.

Contract Law. In many instances, companies have a privacy policy that specifies how that information is to be collected, used, or disclosed. Later in this chapter we will explore whether these policies can be enforced as contracts or via promissory estoppel.

---

[2] Kenneth A. Bamberger & Deirdre K. Mulligan, *Privacy on the Books and on the Ground*, 63 Stan. L. Rev. 247, 251 (2011).

Property Law. Some commentators argue that personal data should be treated as akin to property. If businesses want to collect or use it in certain ways, they must buy it from the individual, or otherwise trade for it. Later in this chapter we will explore whether treating personal data this way will result in the appropriate forms of data protection.

FTC Section 5 Enforcement. Since the mid-1990s, the Federal Trade Commission (FTC) has used Section 5 of the FTC Act to regulate consumer privacy. Section 5 prohibits "unfair or deceptive acts or practices in or affecting commerce." 15 U.S.C. § 45. The FTC views violations of privacy policies as a "deceptive" practice. It views a number of other practices as "unfair." The FTC's Section 5 jurisdiction is quite broad and encompasses most industries (except for a few carve outs). As a result, it has become the dominant agency regulating privacy in the United States. We will explore the FTC's enforcement of Section 5 later in this chapter.

Federal Statutory Regulation. There are numerous federal statutes pertaining to consumer privacy. As discussed above, the United States follows a sectoral approach to privacy regulation, so statutes differ in different industries and some industries lack their own law. The federal statutes will be discussed later in this chapter.

State Statutory Regulation. Many states have passed sectoral legislation regulating business records and databases. These state statutes sometimes have stronger protections of privacy than federal statutes. There are thousands of state statutes involving privacy, and because there are so many, this chapter focuses primarily on the federal statutes.

State statutes play a key role in the protection of privacy — even beyond the borders of a particular state. For example, California has passed a series of strong privacy protections, and, as a general matter, California can be said to have the strongest privacy law in the United States.[3] These statutes typically protect the personal data of California residents regardless of where the data processing occurs. Many companies have a segment of their business involving customers from California, which is not surprising because this state would be the world's eighth largest economy if it were a stand-alone country. Thus, these companies must comply with California's privacy laws for their customers based in this economically important state. Some companies carve out different policies and procedures to deal with California law, but others just follow California law for all customers because it is easier to follow just one set of rules, and California's laws are often the strictest.

The list of California privacy laws is extensive. California passed the first data breach notification law in 2002, and 46 states have now followed suit. One of California's more unique consumer privacy protections is its "Shine the Light" law. Passed in 2003, SB27, Cal. Civ. Code § 1798.83, allows consumers to obtain from businesses information about the personal data that the businesses

---

[3] The California Office of Privacy Protection maintains a comprehensive summary of California's privacy statutes: http://www.privacy.ca.gov/lawenforcement/laws.htm.

disclosed to third parties for direct marketing purposes. People can find out the kinds of personal information that a company provided to third parties for direct marketing purposes as well as the "names and addresses of all of the third parties that received personal information from the business." § 1798.83(1). The law applies to businesses with 20 or more employees. § 1798(c)(1). Companies with privacy policies that allow people to opt out of the sharing of their data with third parties are exempt. § 1798(c)(2).

Other California privacy laws include an obligation placed on rental car companies to inform customers if they have a "black box" in their vehicles; the Confidentiality of Medical Information Act (CMIA), which is a general health information privacy law for the state; and the Song-Beverly Credit Card Act, discussed below, which limits the kinds of personal information collected by companies that accept credit cards.

NOTES & QUESTIONS

1. *The Case for Less Privacy Regulation.* Several commentators argue that self-regulation is preferable to creating more state and federal privacy laws. Fred Cate points out that self-regulation is "more flexible and more sensitive to specific contexts and therefore allow[s] individuals to determine a more tailored balance between information uses and privacy than privacy laws do."[4] Eric Goldman argues:

> Relatively few consumers have bought privacy management tools, such as software to browse anonymously and manage Internet cookies and e-mail. Many vendors are now migrating away from consumer-centric business models. So, although consumers can take technological control over their own situation, few consumers do.
>
> Plus, as most online marketers know, people will "sell" their personal data incredibly cheaply. As Internet pundit Esther Dyson has said: "You do a survey, and consumers say they are very concerned about their privacy. Then you offer them a discount on a book, and they'll tell you everything." Indeed, a recent Jupiter report said that 82% of respondents would give personal information to new shopping sites to enter a $100 sweepstakes.
>
> Clearly consumers' stated privacy concerns diverge from what consumers do. Two theories might explain the divergence.
>
> First, asking consumers what they care about reveals only whether they value privacy. That's half the equation. Of more interest is how much consumers will pay — in time or money — for the corresponding benefits. For now the cost-benefit ratio is tilted too high for consumers to spend much time or money on privacy.
>
> Second, consumers don't have uniform interests. Regarding online privacy, consumers can be segmented into two groups: activists, who actively protect their online privacy, and apathetics, who do little or nothing to protect themselves. The activists are very vocal but appear to be a tiny market segment.
>
> Using consumer segmentation, the analytical defect of broad-based online privacy regulations becomes apparent. The activists, by definition, take care of

---

[4] Fred H. Cate, *Privacy in Perspective* 26 (2001); *see also* Fred H. Cate, *Privacy in the Information Age* (1997).

themselves. They demand privacy protections from businesses and, if they don't get it, use technology to protect themselves or take their business elsewhere.

In contrast, mainstream consumers don't change their behavior based on online privacy concerns. If these people won't take even minimal steps to protect themselves, why should government regulation do it for them?

Further, online businesses will invest in privacy when it's profitable. . . . When companies believed that few consumers would change their behavior if they were offered greater privacy, those companies did nothing or put into place privacy policies that disabused consumers of privacy expectations. Of course, if companies later discovered that they were losing business because customers wanted more privacy, they would increase their privacy initiatives.

Consumer behavior will tell companies what level of privacy to provide. Let the market continue unimpeded rather than chase phantom consumer fears through unnecessary regulation.[5]

In contrast, Peter Swire contends that privacy legislation need not be antithetical to business interests. According to Swire, privacy legislation should be viewed as similar to the "trustwrap" that Johnson & Johnson placed around bottles of Tylenol after a scare involving cyanide poisoning of the pain reliever.[6] Swire believes that "privacy legislation targeted at online practices" would provide the kind of safety to allow consumers to engage in cyberspace activities with confidence.

2. *Flexible Regulation.* Some commentators contend that a middle ground can be found between traditional legal regulation and self-regulation. Dennis Hirsch argues that environmental law suggests ways to regulate privacy that are flexible and that mix legal regulation with self-regulation:

Over the past forty years, environmental law has been at the epicenter of an intense and productive debate about the most effective way to regulate. Initial environmental laws took the form of prescriptive, uniform standards that have come to be known as "command-and-control" regulation. These methods, while effective in some settings, proved costly and controversial. In the decades that followed, governments, academics, environmental and business groups, and others poured tremendous resources into figuring out how to improve upon these methods. This work has produced a "second generation" of environmental regulation. . . .

Second generation initiatives encourage the regulated parties themselves to choose the means by which they will achieve environmental performance goals. That is what defines them and distinguishes them from first generation regulations under which the agency has the primary decisionmaking power over pollution control methods. This difference tends to make second generation strategies more cost-effective and adaptable than command-and-control rules. The proliferation of second generation strategies has led some to identify the environmental field as having "some of the most innovative regulatory instruments in all of American law."

Privacy regulation today finds itself in a debate similar to the one that the environmental field has been engaged in for years. On the one hand, there is a

---

[5] Eric Goldman, *The Privacy Hoax,* Forbes (Oct. 14, 2002), available at http://www.ericgoldman.org/Articles/privacyhoax.htm.

[6] Peter P. Swire, *Trustwrap: the Importance of Legal Rules to Electronic Commerce and Internet Privacy,* 54 Hastings L.J. 847 (2003).

growing sense that the digital age is causing unprecedented damage to privacy and that action must be taken immediately to mitigate these injuries. On the other, a chorus of voices warns against the dangers of imposing intrusive and costly regulation on the emerging business sectors of the information economy. Missing thus far from the dialogue is any significant discussion of the more flexible "second generation" regulatory strategies that might be able to bridge this gap. It took environmental law decades to arrive at these alternatives. The privacy field could capitalize on this experience by looking to these environmental policies as models for privacy regulation.[7]

Is the analogy of privacy law to environmental law an apt one? To what extent are the privacy statutes discussed in this book thus far command-and-control rules versus flexible rules? Is Hirsch calling less for self-regulation than for industry input into the form and content of rules?

3. ***Is Privacy Still Possible?*** Is privacy still possible in an Information Age? Scott McNealy, CEO of Sun Microsystems, Inc., once remarked: "You already have zero privacy. Get over it." Should we eulogize the death of privacy and move on? Or is it possible to protect privacy in modern times? Consider David Brin:

> . . . [I]t is already far too late to prevent the invasion of cameras and databases. The *djinn* cannot be crammed back into its bottle. No matter how many laws are passed, it will prove quite impossible to legislate away the new surveillance tools and databases. They are here to stay.
>
> Light *is* going to shine into nearly every corner of our lives. . . .
>
> If neo-Western civilization has one great trick in its repertoire, a technique more responsible than any other for its success, that trick is *accountability*. Especially the knack — which no other culture ever mastered — of making accountability apply to the mighty. . . .
>
> Kevin Kelly, executive editor of *Wired* magazine, expressed the same idea with the gritty clarity of information-age journalism: "The answer to the whole privacy question is more knowledge. More knowledge about who's watching you. More knowledge about the information that flows between us — particularly the meta-information about who knows what and where it's going."
>
> In other words, we may not be able to eliminate the intrusive glare shining on citizens of the next century, but the glare just might be rendered harmless through the application of more light aimed in the other direction.[8]

Is greater transparency the solution to the increasing threats to privacy?

4. ***Privacy Enhancing Technologies and Privacy by Design.*** As part of the self-governance, technology can assist companies as well as consumers in making privacy choices. Privacy on the Internet can be protected by another form of regulatory mechanism — technology. According to Joel Reidenberg, "law and government regulation are not the only source of rule-making. Technological capabilities and system design choices impose rules on participants."[9]

---

[7] Dennis D. Hirsch, *Protecting the Inner Environment: What Privacy Regulation Can Learn from Environmental Law*, 41 Ga. L. Rev. 1, 8-10 (2006).

[8] David Brin, *The Transparent Society* 8-23 (1998).

[9] Joel Reidenberg, *Lex Informatica: The Formulation of Information Policy Rules Through Technology*, 76 Tex. L. Rev. 553 (1998).

Reidenberg calls such forms of technological governance "Lex Informatica." In *Code*, Lawrence Lessig developed similar ideas, as expressed in his famous adage: code is law.[10] By that he means that a central fashion in which regulation takes place in cyberspace is through technological configurations and system design choice.[11]

In the privacy context, Privacy Enhancing Technologies (PETs) have received much attention from scholars and the privacy policy community. Herbert Burkert describes PETs as "technical and organizational concepts that aim at protecting personal identity. These concepts usually involve encryption in the form digital signatures, blind signature or digital pseudonyms."[12]

Ann Cavoukian, the Information and Privacy Commissioner of Ontario, Canada, has coined the term "privacy by design," a related concept to PETs. According to Cavoukian, "*Privacy by Design* refers to the philosophy and approach of embedding privacy into the design, operation and management of information technologies and systems, across the entire information life cycle."[13]

Ira Rubinstein has developed a useful taxonomy of PETs as either "substitute PETs" or "complementary PETs."[14] In his definition, "[s]ubstitute PETs seek to protect privacy by ensuring that little or no personal data is collected in the first place, thereby making legal protections superfluous." As an example, Rubinstein points to client-centric architecture, such as the Tor network, that prevents or minimizes the collection of personal data by permitting anonymous browsing. He also notes that in "practice, many substitute PETs are more theoretical than practical" with few being widely deployed.

In contrast, complementary PETs are designed to implement legislative privacy principles or related legal requirements. Here, Rubinstein draws a further distinction and identifies two types of complementary PETs. First, there are "privacy-friendly PETs," which give people more control over their personal data through improved notice and consent mechanisms, browser management tools, and dashboard interfaces. Second, "privacy-preserving PETs" resemble substitute PETs in that they rely on technology to limit data collection while also complementing legal requirements. Rubinstein's examples of this final category are privacy-preserving data mining and privacy-preserving targeted advertising. He concludes by arguing that "the market incentives for substitute PETs are feeble" and that "regulatory incentives may still be necessary to overcome the reluctance of private firms to increase their investments in PETs, especially in the face of limited consumer demand, competing business needs, and a weak economy."

---

[10] Larry Lessig, Code and Other Laws of Cyberspace (1999).

[11] For an analysis of Lessig's suggestions for privacy, see Paul M. Schwartz, *Beyond Lessig's Code for Internet Privacy*, 2000 Wisc. L. Rev. 743.

[12] Herbert Burkert, Privacy-Enhancing Technologies: Typology, Critique, Vision, in Technology and Privacy: The New Landscape 123, 125, 128 (Philip E. Agre & Marc Rotenberg, eds., 1997).

[13] Ann Cavoukian, Privacy by Design Resolution (2010), http://www.ipc.on.ca/site_documents/pbd-resolution.pdf.

[14] Ira S. Rubinstein, *Regulating Privacy by Design*, 26 Berkeley Tech. L.J. 1409 (2012).

Additionally, Rubinstein contrasts PETs with privacy by design. Whereas most PETs are "added-on to existing systems, sometimes as an afterthought by designers and sometimes by privacy-sensitive end-users," privacy by design is a systematic approach to developing any product or service "that embeds privacy into the underlying specifications or architecture." Although this approach has great potential, Rubinstein suggests that in order for privacy by design to achieve greater success than PETs, governments will have to clarify what it means for companies to "build in" privacy from the outset rather than "bolt it on" at the end and create regulatory incentives that will spur broader adoption.

3. PERSONALLY IDENTIFIABLE INFORMATION (PII)

PII is one of the most central concepts in privacy regulation. It defines the scope and boundaries of a large range of privacy statutes and regulations. Federal statutes that turn on this distinction include the Children's Online Privacy Protection Act, the Gramm-Leach-Bliley Act, the HITECH Act, and the Video Privacy Protection Act. Moreover, state statutes that rely on PII as a jurisdictional trigger include California's Song-Beverly Credit Card Act and the many data security breach notification laws. These laws all share the same basic assumption—that in the absence of PII, there is no privacy harm. Thus, privacy regulation focuses on the collection, use, and disclosure of PII and leaves non-PII unregulated.

Given PII's importance, it is surprising that information privacy law in the United States lacks a uniform definition of the term. Computer science has also shown that the very concept of PII is far from straightforward. Increasingly, technologists can take information that appears on its face to be non-identifiable and turn it into identifiable data. Instead of defining PII in a coherent and consistent manner, privacy law offers multiple competing definitions, each with some significant problems and limitations.

Approaches to PII. There are three predominant approaches to defining PII in various laws and regulations: (1) the "tautological" approach, (2) the "non-public" approach, and (3) the "specific-types" approach.[15] These approaches are also made either as a rule or standard. A standard is an open-ended decision-making yardstick, and a rule, its counterpart, is a harder-edged decision-making tool.

The tautological approach defines PII as any information that identifies a person. The Video Privacy Protection Act (VPPA) demonstrates this model. The VPPA, which safeguards the privacy of video sales and rentals, simply defines "personally identifiable information" as "information which identifies a person." One problem with this approach is that it simply states that PII is PII without providing guidance about how to identify PII.

---

[15] Paul M. Schwartz & Daniel J. Solove, *The PII Problem: Privacy and a New Concept of Personally Identifiable Information,* 86 N.Y.U. L. Rev. 1815 (2011). For an analysis of concepts of personal information in the European Union, see Paul M. Schwartz & Daniel J. Solove, *Reconciling Personal Information in the U.S. and EU,* 102 Cal. L. Rev. 877 (2014).

A second approach toward defining PII focuses on non-public information. The Gramm-Leach-Bliley Act (GLB Act) epitomizes this approach by defining "personally identifiable financial information" as "nonpublic personal information." The statute fails to define "nonpublic," but presumably this term means information not found within the public domain. The non-public approach, however, does not map onto whether the information is in fact identifiable.

The third approach is to list specific types of data that constitute PII. In the context of the specific-types approach, if the information falls into an enumerated group, it becomes a kind of statutory "per se" PII. The federal Children's Online Privacy Protection Act (COPPA) of 1998 illustrates this approach. COPPA states that personal information is "individually identifiable information about an individual collected online" that includes a number of elements beginning with "first and last name," and continuing through a physical address, Social Security number, telephone number, and e-mail address. Its definition of PII also includes "any other identifier that the [Federal Trade Commission (FTC)] determines permits the physical or online contacting of a specific individual." A limitation with the specific-types approach is that it can fail to respond to new technology, which is capable of transforming the kinds of data that are PII.

State privacy laws also define personal information. One of the most important of these laws is the Song-Beverly Credit Card Act, which prevents business from requesting "personal identification information" during credit card transactions. This statute has been the object of considerable litigation. In *Pineda v. Williams-Sonoma Stores* (2011), the California Supreme Court evaluated whether a ZIP code was protection personal information under the Song-Beverly Act. In *Apple v. Krescent* (2013), the same court considered whether this law's prohibitions extended to online merchants offering products that were downloadable.

PINEDA V. WILLIAMS-SONOMA STORES

246 P.3d 162 (Cal. 2011)

MORENO, J. The Song-Beverly Credit Card Act of 1971 (Credit Card Act) (Civ. Code, § 1747 *et seq.*) is "designed to promote consumer protection." *Florez v. Linens 'N Things, Inc.*, 108 Cal. App. 4th 447, 450, (2003). One of its provisions, section 1747.08, prohibits businesses from requesting that cardholders provide "personal identification information" during credit card transactions, and then recording that information.

Plaintiff sued defendant retailer, asserting a violation of the Credit Card Act. Plaintiff alleges that while she was paying for a purchase with her credit card in one of defendant's stores, the cashier asked plaintiff for her ZIP code. Believing it necessary to complete the transaction, plaintiff provided the requested information and the cashier recorded it. Plaintiff further alleges that defendant subsequently used her name and ZIP code to locate her home address.

We are now asked to resolve whether section 1747.08 is violated when a business requests and records a customer's ZIP code during a credit card transaction. In light of the statute's plain language, protective purpose, and legislative history, we conclude a ZIP code constitutes "personal identification information" as that phrase is used in section 1747.08. Thus, requesting and recording a cardholder's ZIP code, without more, violates the Credit Card Act. We therefore reverse the contrary judgment of the Court of Appeal and remand for further proceedings consistent with our decision. . . .

Plaintiff visited one of [defendant Williams-Sonoma's] California stores and selected an item for purchase. She then went to the cashier to pay for the item with her credit card. The cashier asked plaintiff for her ZIP code and, believing she was required to provide the requested information to complete the transaction, plaintiff provided it. The cashier entered plaintiff's ZIP code into the electronic cash register and then completed the transaction. At the end of the transaction, defendant had plaintiff's credit card number, name, and ZIP code recorded in its database.

Defendant subsequently used customized computer software to perform reverse searches from databases that contain millions of names, e-mail addresses, telephone numbers, and street addresses, and that are indexed in a manner resembling a reverse telephone book. The software matched plaintiff's name and ZIP code with plaintiff's previously undisclosed address, giving defendant the information, which it now maintains in its own database. Defendant uses its database to market products to customers and may also sell the information it has compiled to other businesses. . . .

Section 1747.08, subdivision (a) provides, in pertinent part, "[N]o person, firm, partnership, association, or corporation that accepts credit cards for the transaction of business shall . . . : (2) Request, or require as a condition to accepting the credit card as payment in full or in part for goods or services, the cardholder to provide *personal identification information,* which the person, firm, partnership, association, or corporation accepting the credit card writes, causes to be written, or otherwise records upon the credit card transaction form or otherwise. Subdivision (b) defines personal identification information as "information concerning the cardholder, other than information set forth on the credit card, and including, but not limited to, the cardholder's address and telephone number." Because we must accept as true plaintiff's allegation that defendant requested and then recorded her ZIP code, the outcome of this case hinges on whether a cardholder's ZIP code, without more, constitutes personal identification information within the meaning of section 1747.08. We hold that it does.

Subdivision (b) defines personal identification information as "information *concerning* the cardholder . . . including, but not limited to, the cardholder's address and telephone number" (italics added). "Concerning" is a broad term meaning "pertaining to; regarding; having relation to; [or] respecting. . . ." (Webster's New Internat. Dict. (2d ed. 1941) p. 552.) A cardholder's ZIP code, which refers to the area where a cardholder works or lives is certainly information that pertains to or regards the cardholder.

In nonetheless concluding the Legislature did not intend for a ZIP code, without more, to constitute personal identification information, the Court of Appeal pointed to the enumerated examples of such information in subdivision (b), i.e., "the cardholder's address and telephone number." . . . [T]he Court of Appeal reasoned that an address and telephone number are "specific in nature regarding an individual." By contrast, the court continued, a ZIP code pertains to the *group* of individuals who live within the ZIP code. Thus, the Court of Appeal concluded, a ZIP code, without more, is unlike the other terms specifically identified in subdivision (b).

There are several problems with this reasoning. First, a ZIP code is readily understood to be part of an address; when one addresses a letter to another person, a ZIP code is always included. The question then is whether the Legislature, by providing that "personal identification information" includes "the cardholder's address" intended to include components of the address. The answer must be yes. Otherwise, a business could ask not just for a cardholder's ZIP code, but also for the cardholder's street and city in addition to the ZIP code, so long as it did not also ask for the house number. Such a construction would render the statute's protections hollow. Thus, the word "address" in the statute should be construed as encompassing not only a complete address, but also its components.

Second, the court's conclusion rests upon the assumption that a complete address and telephone number, unlike a ZIP code, are specific to an individual. That this assumption holds true in all, or even most, instances is doubtful. In the case of a cardholder's home address, for example, the information may pertain to a group of individuals living in the same household. Similarly, a home telephone number might well refer to more than one individual. The problem is even more evident in the case of a cardholder's *work* address or telephone number—such information could easily pertain to tens, hundreds, or even thousands of individuals. Of course, section 1747.08 explicitly provides that a cardholder's address and telephone number constitute personal identification information; that such information *might also* pertain to individuals other than the cardholder is immaterial. Similarly, that a cardholder's ZIP code pertains to individuals in addition to the cardholder does not render it dissimilar to an address or telephone number.

More significantly, the Court of Appeal ignores another reasonable interpretation of what the enumerated terms in section 1747.08, subdivision (b) have in common, that is, they both constitute information unnecessary to the sales transaction that, alone or together with other data such as a cardholder's name or credit card number, can be used for the retailer's business purposes. Under this reading, a cardholder's ZIP code is similar to his or her address or telephone number, in that a ZIP code is both unnecessary to the transaction and can be used, together with the cardholder's name, to locate his or her full address. The retailer can then, as plaintiff alleges defendant has done here, use the accumulated information for its own purposes or sell the information to other businesses.

There are several reasons to prefer this latter, broader interpretation over the one adopted by the Court of Appeal. The Court of Appeal's interpretation, by contrast, would permit retailers to obtain indirectly what they are clearly prohibited from obtaining directly, "end-running" the statute's clear purpose. This is so because information that can be permissibly obtained under the Court of Appeal's construction could easily be used to locate the cardholder's complete address or telephone number. Such an interpretation would vitiate the statute's effectiveness. . . .

[T]he legislative history of section 1747.08 offers additional evidence that plaintiff's construction is the correct one. . . .

Thus, in light of the statutory language, as well as the legislative history and evident purpose of the statute, we hold that personal identification information, as that term is used in section 1747.08, includes a cardholder's ZIP code.

APPLE V. KRESCENT

292 P.3d 883 (Cal. 2013)

LIU, J. The Song-Beverly Credit Card Act of 1971 (Credit Card Act) governs the issuance and use of credit cards. ([Cal.] Civ. Code, § 1747 *et seq.*). One of its provisions, section 1747.08, prohibits retailers from "[r]equest[ing], or requir[ing] as a condition to accepting the credit card as payment . . ., the cardholder to write any personal identification information upon the credit card transaction form or otherwise". . . . It also prohibits retailers from requesting or requiring the cardholder "to provide personal identification information, which the [retailer] . . . writes, causes to be written, or otherwise records upon the credit card transaction form or otherwise," and from "[u]tiliz[ing] . . . a credit card form which contains preprinted spaces specifically designed for filling in any personal identification information of the cardholder." . . . .

We must resolve whether section 1747.08 prohibits an online retailer from requesting or requiring personal identification information from a customer as a condition to accepting a credit card as payment for an electronically downloadable product. Upon careful consideration of the statute's text, structure, and purpose, we hold that section 1747.08 does not apply to online purchases in which the product is downloaded electronically. . . .

Petitioner Apple Inc. (Apple), defendant below, operates an Internet Web site and an online iTunes store through which it sells digital media such as downloadable audio and video files. In June 2011, plaintiff below, David Krescent, sued Apple on behalf of himself and a putative class of similarly situated individuals for alleged violations of section 1747.08. Specifically, Krescent alleged that he purchased media downloads from Apple on various occasions and that, as a condition of receiving these downloads, he was required to provide his telephone number and address in order to complete his credit card purchase. He further alleged that Apple records each customer's personal information, is not contractually or legally obligated to collect a customer's telephone number or address in order to complete the credit card transaction, and does not require a customer's telephone number or address for any special purpose incidental but related to the individual credit card transaction, such as shipping or delivery. Although he alleged that "the credit card transaction would be permitted to proceed" without any personal identification information, Krescent also contended that "even if the credit card processing company or companies required a valid billing address and [credit card identification number], under no circumstance would [plaintiff's] telephone number be required to complete his transaction, that is, under no circumstance does [Apple] need [plaintiff's] phone number in order to complete a [media] download transaction.". . .

We review de novo questions of statutory construction. In doing so, "our fundamental task is to ascertain the intent of the lawmakers so as to effectuate the purpose of the statute." As always, we start with the language of the statute, "giv[ing] the words their usual and ordinary meaning . . . while construing them in light of the statute as a whole and the statute's purpose." *Pineda v. Williams Sonoma*, 246 P.3d 612 (Cal. 2011). . . .

We begin with the text of the statute. Section 1747.08(a) provides: "Except as provided in subdivision (c), no person, firm, partnership, association, or corporation that accepts credit cards for the transaction of business shall do any of the following: (1) Request, or require as a condition to accepting the credit card as payment in full or in part for goods or services, the cardholder to write any personal identification information upon the credit card transaction form or otherwise. (2) Request, or require as a condition to accepting the credit card as payment in full or in part for goods or services, the cardholder to provide personal identification information, which the person, firm, partnership, association, or corporation accepting the credit card writes, causes to be written, or otherwise records upon the credit card transaction form or otherwise. (3) Utilize, in any credit card transaction, a credit card form which contains preprinted spaces specifically designated for filling in any personal identification information of the cardholder." Section 1747.08, subdivision (b) (hereafter section 1747.08(b)) defines "personal identification information" as "information concerning the cardholder, other than information set forth on the credit card, and including, but not limited to, the cardholder's address and telephone number." . . .

Although section 1747.08 does not explicitly reference online transactions, both parties maintain that the Legislature's intent is apparent from the plain meaning of the statute's terms. Krescent contends that the language of section 1747.08(a) "must be read as an all-inclusive prohibition on every businesses [sic] regardless of the form of the transaction." According to Krescent, in directing the statutory prohibition at any "person, firm, partnership, association, or corporation that accepts credit cards for the transaction of business" (§ 1747.08(a)), the Legislature intended to include all retailers without exception. If the Legislature intended to exempt online retailers, he contends, it could have done so.

Apple, on the other hand, argues that the first sentence of section 1747.08(a) must be construed in light of other language in the statute indicating that the Legislature had in mind only in-person business transactions. For example, section 1747.08(a)(1) prohibits a retailer from requesting or requiring a "cardholder to *write* any personal identification information *upon the credit card transaction form* or otherwise." (Italics added.) Section 1747.08(a)(2) prohibits a retailer from requesting or requiring the cardholder to provide such information, which the retailer "*writes, causes to be written, or otherwise records upon the credit card transaction form* or otherwise." (Italics added.) And section 1747.08(a)(3) prohibits the retailer from utilizing "a *credit card form which contains preprinted spaces.*" (Italics added.) Apple says the terms "write" and "forms" imply, by their physicality, that section 1747.08 applies only to in-person transactions. Apple further argues that the definition of "credit card" in section 1747.02—"any card, plate, coupon book, or other single credit device existing for the purpose of being used from time to time *upon presentation* to obtain money, property, labor, or services on credit"—indicates that the Legislature contemplated only those transactions in which the card is physically presented or displayed to the retailer. (§ 1747.02, subd. (a), italics added.)

We think the text of section 1747.08(a) alone is not decisive on the question before us. The statutory language suggests that the Legislature, at the time it enacted former section 1747.8, did not contemplate commercial transactions conducted on the Internet. But it does not seem awkward or improper to describe the act of typing characters into a digital display as "writing" on a computerized "form." In construing statutes that predate their possible applicability to new technology, courts have not relied on wooden construction of their terms. Fidelity to legislative intent does not "make it impossible to apply a legal text to technologies that did not exist when the text was created. . . . Drafters of every era know that technological advances will proceed apace and that the rules they create will one day apply to all sorts of circumstances they could not possibly envision." (Scalia & Garner, *Reading Law: The Interpretation of Legal Texts* (2012). . . .

In this case . . . the plain meaning of the statutes text is not decisive. An examination of the statutory scheme as a whole is necessary to determine whether it is applicable to a transaction made possible by technology that the Legislature did not envision. . . .

We recently considered the history and purpose of the [Song-Beverly Act and determined that] "[t]he statute's overriding purpose was to "protect the personal privacy of consumers who pay for transactions with credit cards." (*Pineda*, 246 P.3d at 636). . . . Specifically, the Legislature "sought to address the misuse of personal identification information for, *inter alia*, marketing purposes, and found that there would be no legitimate need to obtain such information from credit card customers if it was not necessary to the completion of the credit card transaction." . . .

While it is clear that the Legislature enacted the Credit Card Act to protect consumer privacy, it is also clear that the Legislature did not intend to achieve privacy protection without regard to exposing consumers and retailers to undue risk of fraud. The legislative history shows that the Legislature enacted the statute's prohibitions only after carefully considering and rejecting the possibility that the collection of personal identification information by brick-and-mortar retailers could serve a legitimate purpose such as fraud prevention. In particular, the Senate Judiciary Committee considered the standard procedure followed by brick-and-mortar retailers in the 1990s to verify the identity of credit card users—which included "verify[ing] the identification of the cardholder by comparing the signature on the credit card transaction form with the signature on the back of the card" and "contact [ing] the credit card issuer's authorization center [to] obtain approval" for sales above a specified "floor limit"—and concluded that the collection of personal identification information was not a necessary step in that procedure. (Sen. Judiciary Com., Analysis of Assem. Bill No. 2920 (1989–1990 Reg. Sess.) as amended June 27, 1990, p. 3.) This finding supported the Legislature's judgment that brick-and-mortar retailers in the 1990s had no genuine need to collect personal identification information and would instead use such information primarily for unsolicited marketing. (See *id.* at pp. 3-4 [noting that the "problem" the bill was designed to address was retailers' practice of leading consumers "to mistakenly believe that [personal identification information] is a necessary condition to complete the credit card transaction, when, in fact, it is not" and "acquir[ing] this additional personal information for their own business purposes—for example, to build mailing or telephone lists which they can subsequently use for their own in-house marketing efforts, or sell to direct-mail or tele-marketing specialists, or to others"]; *id.* at pp. 5-7 [explaining that retailers had no genuine need for personal identification information to address problems such as billing errors, lost credit cards, and product problems].) We cannot assume that the Legislature, had it confronted a type of transaction in which the standard mechanisms for verifying a cardholder's identity were not available, would have made the same policy choice as it did with respect to transactions in which it found no tension between privacy protection and fraud prevention. . . .

The safeguards against fraud that are provided in section 1747.08(d) are not available to the online retailer selling an electronically downloadable product. Unlike a brick-and-mortar retailer, an online retailer cannot visually inspect the credit card, the signature on the back of the card, or the customer's photo identification. Thus, section 1747.08(d)—the key antifraud mechanism in the statutory scheme—has no practical application to online transactions involving electronically downloadable products. We cannot conclude that if the Legislature in 1990 had been prescient enough to anticipate online transactions involving electronically downloadable products, it would have intended section 1747.08(a)'s prohibitions to apply to such transactions despite the unavailability of section 1747.08 (d)'s safeguards.

Krescent's complaint reinforces our conclusion insofar as it failed to allege that Apple does not require any personal identification information to verify the identity of the credit card user. His complaint merely alleged that "the credit card transaction would be permitted to proceed without any further information" and that Apple "is not contractually obligated to provide a consumer's telephone number and/or address in order to complete the credit card transaction," thereby rendering inapplicable the exception set forth in section 1747.08(c)(3)(A). Even if credit card transactions may proceed without any personal identification information under the contractual terms that bind retailers and credit card companies, the fact remains that the Legislature saw fit to include section 1747.08(d)'s safeguards against fraud in the statutory scheme. The inclusion of section 1747.08(d), separate and apart from the exception in section 1747.08(c)(3)(A), reflects the Legislature's judgment that consumers and retailers have an interest in combating fraud that is independent of whatever security measures are (or are not) required by contracts between retailers and credit card issuers. Consistent with this legislative judgment, both parties acknowledged at oral argument that retailers often bear the risk of loss from fraudulent credit card charges. . . .

KENNARD, J. DISSENTING. . . . To protect consumer privacy, California statutory law prohibits retail sellers from recording the personal identification information, such as home addresses and telephone numbers, of their credit-card-using customers. Cal. Civ. Code § 1747.08, Subdiv. (a). The statute does not exempt online sales of downloadable products from this prohibition, and on its face the statute applies to sales conducted over the Internet just as it does to sales conducted face-to-face or by mail or telephone. Yet the majority holds that online sales of downloadable products are not covered by the statute, thus leaving Internet retailers free to demand personal identification information from their credit-card-using customers and to resell that information to others. The majority's decision is a major win for these sellers, but a major loss for consumers, who in their online activities already face an ever-increasing encroachment upon their privacy.

Unlike the majority, I conclude that the statute means just what it says and contains no exemption, express or implied, for online sales of downloadable products. The majority's expressed concern that this plain-meaning construction of the statute leaves online sellers with no way to detect and prevent fraudulent purchases is unjustified. . . .

BAXTER, J. DISSENTING. . . . Section 1747.08 of the [Cal.] Civil Code was enacted to prevent any retailer such as defendant Apple Inc. from collecting and exploiting the personal identification information of consumers who use credit cards to make their purchases. Plaintiff's complaint sufficiently states a cause of action under this statute: it alleges that defendant required and recorded plaintiff's address and telephone number as a condition to his online purchases of electronically downloadable products, and that defendant's actions were not otherwise permitted by the statute. In holding to the contrary, the majority relies on speculation and debatable factual assumptions to carve out an expansive exception to section 1747.08 that leaves online retailers free to collect and use the personal identification information of credit card users as they wish. . . .

The majority implicitly agrees that defendant's conduct falls within the plain terms of section 1747.08(a). . . . The majority holds, however, that plaintiff was not entitled to protection of his personal identification information because online credit card purchases of electronically downloadable products are categorically exempt from the statute's application. . . . Although recognizing this is a question of statutory construction, the majority reaches a result that is contrary to the terms, purpose, and legislative history of section 1747.08. . . .

NOTES & QUESTIONS

1. **Pineda *and the "Specific Types" Approach to PII.*** The California Supreme Court reversed the lower courts in *Pineda*, but did so on the narrowest possible grounds. It analyzed the statutory language and legislative history, and found that both supported a legislative intent to include a ZIP code as part of the "cardholder's address." In other words, that statutory category included "not only a complete address, but its components."

   In a sense, the California Supreme Court in *Pineda* only tweaked a subcategory within the specific-types approach to defining PII. It did not reach the broader conclusion that the Song-Beverly Act reflected a policy to prevent retailers from collecting "identification" indices that would permit a definitive linkage between a customer and her address. In fact, the law can be read simply as a prohibition on merchants collecting information that is specific enough to allow the unique identification of a person. Although as many as tens of thousands of people might share a ZIP code, it was precisely the piece of information, when added to a person's name, which permitted linkage of the customer to a wealth of PII about her.

2. **Krescent *and Antifraud Considerations.*** Two years after *Pineda*, the California Supreme Court in *Krescent* decided that the overall statutory scheme of the Song-Beverly Act indicated a legislative desire to balance privacy protection and fraud protection. In particular, for electronically downloadable products, merchants faced limitations on their anti-fraud activities, which brick-and-mortar retailers did not. Ultimately, the California Supreme Court found that the legislature did not intend to have the relevant prohibitions in the Act extend to online merchants. How do you think the legislature should respond to this decision? Should online merchants be prevented from collecting telephone numbers and addresses from customers?

3. ***E-mailed Receipts, ZIP Codes, and Deposits.*** The Song-Beverly Act has led to litigation beyond *Pineda* and *Krescent*. For example, a federal court found that Nordstrom violated the act by requesting an e-mail address to mail a customer a receipt and then also using the e-mail to send the customer promotional communications and materials. Capp v. Nordstrom, 2013 WL 5739102 (E.D. Cal. 2013). The court found that an e-mail address was "personal identification information" under the Song-Beverly Act. It declared that a credit cardholder's e-mail address was an even "more specific and personal" reference to the person than the ZIP code at stake in *Pineda*. It stated, "Instead of referring to the general area in which a cardholder lives or works, a cardholder's email address permits direct contact and implicates the privacy interests of a cardholder."

The Ninth Circuit has also considered whether the Song-Beverly Act prevented RedBox, a self-service kiosk used to rent movies and video games, from collecting ZIP codes. Sinibaldi v. Redbox Automated Retail, 754 F.3d 703 (9th Cir. 2014). The Ninth Circuit noted that the Song-Beverly Act contained a specific exemption where "the credit card is being used as a deposit to secure payment in the event of default, loss, damage, or similar occurrence." Cal. Civ. Code 1747.08(c)(1). While Redbox's request for the ZIP code was one for "personal identification information" under the Song-Beverly Act, it was collecting this information along with the credit card number as a deposit to secure payment should the customer not return the DVD after the first day. Hence, Redbox did not violate the Song-Beverly Act by requesting this personal data.

4. ***Behavioral Marketing and PII.*** The burgeoning practice of behavioral marketing, which is also sometimes termed "targeted marketing," involves examining the behavioral patterns of consumers to target advertisements to them. In this technique, companies generally do not track individuals through use of their names. Instead they utilize software to build personal profiles that exclude this item but that contain a wealth of details about the individual. Typically, these firms associate these personal profiles with a single alphanumerical code placed on an individual's computer. These codes are

used to decide which advertisements people see as well as the kinds of products that are offered to them.

While advertising networks may not know a person's name, identification of individuals is nonetheless possible in many cases. For example, enough pieces of information linked to a single person, even in the absence of a name, Social Security number, or financial information, will permit identification of the individual. Nonetheless, online companies have attempted to short-circuit the discussion of privacy harms and necessary legal reforms by simply asserting that they do not collect PII.

5. ***Ohm on the PII Problem.*** In the view of Paul Ohm, privacy law must abandon its reliance on PII and find a new regulatory paradigm.[16] He argues that the concept of PII is unworkable and unfixable. He points to new re-identification research that has demonstrated that de-identified records can be re-identified "with astonishing ease." This occurs because there is already so much data available about individuals that is linked to their identity. To re-identify records, one can simply try to match the information in the records to other available data about an identified person. For example, Netflix, a popular online movie rental service, made a supposedly de-identified database of ratings publicly available as part of a contest to improve the predictive capabilities of its movie recommending software. Two researchers, Arvind Narayanan and Vitaly Shmatikov, found a way to link this data with the movie ratings that some participating individuals gave to films in the Internet Movie Database (IMDb), a popular website with information and ratings about movies.[17] They did this by matching the data to individuals' public movie ratings on IMDb.[18]

Because data can be so readily linked to a person's identity, Ohm contends that the "list of potential PII will never stop growing until it includes everything." Ohm proposes that regulators abandon PII and instead "prevent privacy harm by squeezing and reducing the flow of information in society, even though in doing so they may need to sacrifice, at least a little, important counter values like innovation, free speech, and security." He would replace the current reliance on PII as a gatekeeper for privacy law with a cost-benefit analysis for *all* data processing and data collection of any kind. Ohm proposes that privacy regulation "should weigh the benefits of unfettered information flow against the cost of privacy harms." He proposes a minimum floor of safe handling of data for every data processor in the United States plus even stricter practices to be imposed on the entities that he terms "large entropy reducers." Ohm writes:

---

[16] Paul Ohm, *Broken Promises of Privacy*, 57 UCLA L. Rev. 1701 (2010).

[17] Arvind Narayanan & Vitaly Shmatikov, *Robust De-Anonymization of Large Sparse Datasets*, 2008 IEEE Symp. on Security and Privacy 111 (Feb. 5, 2008), available at http://arxiv.org/PS_cache/cs/pdf/0610/0610105v2.pdf.

[18] Narayanan & Shmatikov concede that the results did not "imply anything about the percentage of IMDb users who can be identified in the Netflix Prize dataset." *Id.* For an insightful technical analysis of the limits of the Netflix study and how it is has been misunderstood, see Jane Yakowitz, *Tragedy of the Data Commons*, 25 Harv. J.L. & Tech. 1 (2011).

Large entropy reducers are entities that amass massive databases containing so many links between so many disparate kinds of information that they represent a significant part of the database of ruin, even if they delete from their databases all particularly sensitive and directly linkable information. We can justify treating these entities differently using the language of duty and fault. Because large entropy reducers serve as one-stop shops for adversaries trying to link people to ruinous facts, they owe their data subjects a heightened duty of care. When a large entropy reducer loses control of its massive database, it causes much more harm than an entity holding much less data.

More specifically, Ohm identifies as "large entropy reducers" companies such as the credit reporting agencies (i.e., Equifax), data brokers (i.e., LexisNexis), and Internet search engines (i.e., Google). Do you think that a specific set of regulations should be devoted to companies such as the ones that Ohm identifies?

6. *Schwartz and Solove Propose PII 2.0.* In contrast to Ohm, Paul Schwartz and Daniel Solove contend that information privacy law needs a concept of PII.[19] Without such a concept, information privacy law will be a boundless area—it will grow to regulate all information use. At the same time, Schwartz and Solove also propose that PII must be reconceptualized if privacy law is to remain effective in the future.

In their concept of PII 2.0, they propose three different regulatory categories, each of which would be treated differently. Schwartz and Solove write:

Rather than a hard "on-off" switch, this approach allows legal safeguards for both identified and identifiable information, ones that permit tailored FIPs built around the different levels of risk to individuals. In our model of PII 2.0, information refers to (1) an identified, (2) identifiable, or (3) non-identifiable person. The continuum runs from actually being identified to no risk of identification, and our three categories divide up this spectrum and provide three different regimes of regulation. Because these categories do not have hard boundaries and are fluid, we define them in terms of standards.

Information refers to an *identified* person when it singles out a specific individual from others. Put differently, a person has been identified when her identity is ascertained. There is general international agreement about the content of this category, albeit not of the implications of being placed in it. For example, in the U.S., the General Accounting Office, Office of Management and Budget, and National Institute of Standards and Technology associate this concept with information that distinguishes or traces a specific individual's identity.[20] In Europe, the Article 29 Group states that a person is

---

[19] Paul Schwartz & Daniel Solove, *The PII Problem: Privacy and a New Concept of Personally Identifiable Information*, 86 N.Y.U. L. Rev. 1815 (2011).

[20] National Institute of Standards and Technology, *Guide to Protecting the Confidentiality of Personally Identifiable Information* (PII) 2–1 (2010); General Accounting Office, *Privacy: Alternatives Exist for Enhancing Protection of Personally Identifiable Information* (May 2008); Office of Management & Budget, *Memorandum 07-16, Safeguarding Against and Responding to the Breach of Personally Identifiable Information* (2007).

identified "when, within a group of persons, he or she is 'distinguished' from all other members of the group."[21]

In the middle of the risk continuum, information refers to an *identifiable* individual when a specific identification, while possible, is not a significantly probable event. In other words, an individual is identifiable when there is some non-remote possibility of future identification. The risk level is moderate to low. This information should be treated differently than an important sub-category of nominally identifiable information, where a linkage to a specific person has not yet been made, but where such a connection is more likely. . . . [S]uch nominally identifiable data should be treated the same as identified data.

At the other end of the risk continuum, *non-identifiable* information carries only a remote risk of identification. Such data cannot be said to be relatable to a person taking account of the means reasonably likely to be used for identification. In certain kinds of data sets, for example, the original sample is so large that other information will not enable the identification of individuals.

Schwartz and Solove argue that re-identification is a risk rather than a certainty, and the law should be based upon the degree of risk. That risk, however, is changing, because the ability to transform non-PII into identified information depends in part on the amount of personal data about people that is available — the more data, the easier it is to find a match. The risk also depends upon technology, which is changing. How should privacy regulation deal with this evolving landscape? Does PII 2.0 adequately address this problem?

7. *Risks in De-Identified Data?* For Jane Yakowitz, the key question is "how much marginal risk does a public research database create in comparison to the background risks we already endure?"[22] Yakowitz assesses this marginal risk from data-sharing involving de-identified data as "trivially small." She reaches this conclusion by arguing that actual "adversaries" who will seek to de-identify are scarce, in part because of "lower hanging fruit," such as consumer databases that can be purchased, compared to anonymized databases. Yakowitz also points out that re-identifying subjects in anonymized databases is far from easy, but requires statistical expertise, and that "large repeat players" who share anonymized databases do not make "rookie mistakes."

A white paper by Ann Cavoukian, the Information and Privacy Commissioner of Ontario, Canada, and Khaled El Emam has argued along similar lines.[23] In their view, despite "a residual risk of re-identification, in the vast majority of cases, de-identification will protect the privacy of individuals, as long as additional safeguards are in place." In their four-step process, the re-identification risk exposure of a data disclosure depends upon: "the re-identification probability; the mitigating controls that are in place; the motives

---

[21] Article 29 Data Protection Working Party, *Opinion 4/2007 on the Concept of Personal Data* 12 (June, 20, 2007).

[22] Jane Yakowitz, *Tragedy of the Data Commons*, 25 Harv. J.L. & Tech.1 (2011).

[23] Ann Cavoukian & Khaled El Emam, *Dispelling the Myths Surrounding De-Identification: Anonymization Remains a Strong Tool for Protecting Privacy* (Information and Privacy Commissioner of Ontario, June 2011).

and capacity of the data recipient to re-identify the data; and the extent to which an inappropriate disclosure would be an invasion of privacy."

Data security breach laws also rely on definitions of PII. We examine this area of law in the next chapter.

4. INJURY AND STANDING

An overarching issue in privacy cases is whether the privacy violation caused any harm. Suppose a company violates a promise made in its privacy policy not to share data with third parties. The company shares personal data about consumers with a marketing company that uses the data to create more tailored ad profiles and deliver targeted advertisements to consumers. Did the consumers suffer any harm?

Plaintiffs must typically allege a cognizable injury in order to have a viable cause of action. In federal courts, in order to have standing, the plaintiff

> must show that (1) it has suffered an 'injury in fact' that is (a) concrete and particularized and (b) actual or imminent, not conjectural or hypothetical; (2) the injury is fairly traceable to the challenged action of the defendant; and (3) it is likely, as opposed to merely speculative, that the injury will be redressed by a favorable decision. *Friends of the Earth, Inc. v. Laidlaw Envtl. Sys. (TOC), Inc.,* 528 U.S. 167 (2000).

If a plaintiff cannot establish standing, then a plaintiff's lawsuit cannot proceed forward in federal court.

Sometimes, statutes define the elements of a cognizable injury, but in the absence of such a statutorily defined harm, courts will look to general legal principles to determine if an injury occurred. In both data security breach cases and privacy cases, courts have struggled to recognize harm. Daniel Solove argues that courts often look for harms that are "visceral and vested":

> Harms must be *visceral* — they must involve some dimension of palpable physical injury or financial loss. And harms must be *vested* — they must have already occurred.
>
> For harms that involve emotional distress, courts are skeptical because people can too easily say they suffered emotional distress. It can be hard to prove or disprove statements that one suffered emotional distress, and these difficulties make courts very uneasy.
>
> For the future risk of harm, courts generally want to see harm that has actually manifested rather than harm that is incubating. Suppose you're exposed to a virus that silently waits in your bloodstream for 10 years and then suddenly might kill you. Most courts would send you away and tell you to come back after you've dropped dead, because then we would know for sure you're injured. But then, sadly, the statute of limitations will have run out, so it's too late to sue. Tough luck, the courts will say.[24]

---

[24] Daniel J. Solove, *Privacy and Data Security Violations: What's the Harm*, LinkedIn (June 25, 2014), https://www.linkedin.com/today/post/article/20140625045136-2259773-privacy-and-data-security-violations-what-s-the-harm.

IN RE GOOGLE, INC. PRIVACY POLICY LITIGATION

2013 WL 6248499 (N.D. Cal. 2013)

GREWAL, MAGISTRATE J. . . . By now, most people know who Google is and what Google does. Google serves billions of online users in this country and around the world. What started as simply a search engine has expanded to many other products such as YouTube and Gmail. Google offers these products and most others without charge. With little or no revenue from its users, Google still manages to turn a healthy profit by selling advertisements within its products that rely in substantial part on users' personal identification information ("PII"). As some before have observed, in this model, the users are the real product.

Before March 1, 2012, Google maintained separate privacy policies for each of its products, each of which confirmed that Google used a user's PII to provide that particular product. These policies also confirmed that Google would not use the PII for any other purpose without the user's explicit consent. As Google put it, "[w]hen you sign up for a particular service that requires registration, we ask you to provide personal information. If we use this information in a manner different than the purpose for which it was collected, then we will ask for your consent prior to such use." . . .

On March 1, 2012, Google announced a new policy. The majority of its separate privacy policies were eliminated in favor of a single, universal privacy policy that spells out that Google may combine a user's PII across multiple Google products. Google explained the basis for the change in policy as follows:

> Our new Privacy Policy makes clear that, if you're signed in, we may combine information that you've provided from one service with information from other services. In short, we'll treat you as a single user across all our products, which will mean simpler, more intuitive Google experience.

In other words, through the new policy, Google is explicit that it may combine PII collected from a user's Gmail or YouTube account, including the content of that account, with PII collected from that user's Google search queries, along with the user's activities on other Google products, such as Picasa, Maps, Docs, and Reader. This PII includes:

- first and last name;
- home or other physical address (including street name and city);
- current, physical location, a user's email address, and other online contact information (such as the identifier or screen name);
- IP address;
- telephone number (both home and mobile numbers);
- list of contacts;
- search history from Google's search engine;
- web surfing history from cookies placed on the computer; and
- posts on Google+.

Plaintiffs contend that Google's new policy violates its prior policies because the new policy no longer allows users to keep information gathered from one

Google product separate from information gathered from other Google products. Plaintiffs further contend that Google's new policy violates users' privacy rights by allowing Google to take information from a user's Gmail account, for which users may have one expectation of privacy, for use in a different context, such as to personalize Google search engine results, or to personalize advertisements shown while a user is surfing the internet, products for which a user may have an entirely different expectation of privacy. In addition to commingling Plaintiffs' PII across the various Google products, Plaintiff contend Google has shared Plaintiffs' PII with third-party entities who have partnered with Google in order to develop applications for the Google Play app store to help it place targeted advertisements. . . .

To satisfy Article III, a plaintiff "must show that (1) it has suffered an 'injury in fact' that is (a) concrete and particularized and (b) actual or imminent, not conjectural or hypothetical; (2) the injury is fairly traceable to the challenged action of the defendant; and (3) it is likely, as opposed to merely speculative, that the injury will be redressed by a favorable decision." A suit brought by a plaintiff without Article III standing is not a "case or controversy," and an Article III court therefore lacks subject matter jurisdiction over the suit. In that event, the suit should be dismissed under Fed. R. Civ. Pro. 12(b)(1). The injury required by Article III may exist by virtue of "statutes creating legal rights, the invasion of which creates standing." In such cases, the "standing question . . . is whether the constitutional or standing provision on which the claim rests properly can be understood as granting persons in the plaintiff's position a right to judicial relief." At all times the threshold question of standing "is distinct from the merits of [a] claim" and does not require "analysis of the merits." The Supreme Court also has instructed that the "standing inquiry requires careful judicial examination of a complaint's allegations to ascertain whether the particular plaintiff is entitled to an adjudication of the particular claims asserted."

A complaint must state a "short plain statement of the claim showing that the pleader is entitled to relief." While "detailed factual allegations" are not required, a complaint must include more than an unadorned, the defendant-unlawfully-harmed-me accusation." In other words, a complaint must have sufficient factual allegations to "state a claim to relief that is plausible on its face." A claim is facially plausible "when the pleaded factual content allows the court to draw the reasonable inference that the defendant is liable for the misconduct alleged." Accordingly, under Fed. R. Civ. P. 12(b)(6), which tests the legal sufficiency of the claims alleged in the complaint, "[d]ismissal can be based on the lack of cognizable legal theory or the absence of sufficient facts alleged under a cognizable legal theory."

When evaluating a Rule 12(b)(6) motion, the court must accept all material allegations in the complaint as true and construe them in the light most favorable to the non-moving party. . . .

"Dismissal with prejudice and without leave to amend is not appropriate unless it is clear that the complaint could not be saved by amendment. A dismissal with prejudice, except one for lack of jurisdiction, improper venue, or failure to join a party operates as an adjudication on the merits. . . .

Before considering the standing question, however, the court cannot help but make a few observations. First, despite generating little or no discussion in most other cases, the issue of injury-in-fact has become standard fare in cases involving data privacy. In fact, the court is hard-pressed to find even one recent data privacy case, at least in this district, in which injury-in-fact has not been challenged. Second, in this district's recent case law on data privacy claims, injury-infact has proven to be a significant barrier to entry. And so even though injury-in-fact may not generally be Mount Everest, as then-Judge Alito observed, in data privacy cases in the Northern District of California, the doctrine might still reasonably be described as Kilimanjaro. *Danvers Motor Co., Inc. v. Ford Motor Co.*, 432 F.3d 286, 294 (3d Cir. 2005).

1. *Personal Identification Information.* Plaintiffs claim that when Google combined information that Plaintiffs provided to discrete Google products, without Plaintiffs' consent, Google injured them in two different ways. First, Google did not compensate them for the substantial economic value of the combined information. Second, Google's unauthorized comingling of their information, especially their likeness, was a breach of contract. Neither alleged harm, however, is sufficient to establish an injury-in-fact.

. . . [I]njury-in-fact in this context requires more than an allegation that a defendant profited from a plaintiff's personal identification information. Rather, a plaintiff must allege how the defendant's use of the information deprived the plaintiff of the information's economic value. Put another way, a plaintiff must do more than point to the dollars in a defendant's pocket; he must sufficient allege that in the process he lost dollars of his own. Plaintiffs' allegations certainly plead that Google made money using information about them for which they were provided no compensation beyond free access to Google's services. But an allegation that Google profited is not enough equivalent to an allegation that such profiteering deprived Plaintiffs' of economic value from that same information.

As before, the court finds the reasoning in *LaCourt v. Specific Media,* [2011 WL 1661532, at *5 (C.D. Cal. 2011),] instructive. There the plaintiffs alleged that the defendant installed cookies to track users' internet browsing to build behavior profiles to better target advertisements. The court found the tracked users lacked standing because, among other reasons, they did not "explain how they were 'deprived' of the economic value of their personal information simply because their unspecified personal information was purportedly collected by a third party." Other courts have agreed.

Addressing a set of facts similar to the present case, in *In re Google Android User Privacy Litig.,* [No. 11–MD–02264 JSW, 2013 WL 1283236, at *4 (N.D. Cal. Mar. 26, 2013)] the court found no Article III standing where plaintiffs alleged that Google's unauthorized use of PII reduced its value to them because the plaintiffs failed to tie Google's use to their alleged loss, such as being foreclosed from capitalizing on its value. Here, Plaintiffs similarly have not alleged how Google's use of PII in any way deprives them of the ability to profit from the same information. . . .

Finally, although Plaintiffs assert that the breach of contract arising from Google's unauthorized commingling activities offers a separate basis for injury-in-fact, they still fail to articulate a sufficient contract injury. Nominal damages are not available in California for breach of contract, and the amended complaint does not allege any other injury based on the breach. In their opposition,

Plaintiffs assert that "one of the most egregious ways in which Google breaches its contracts . . . is by misusing Plaintiffs' information to misappropriate their likeness. But even if this point in opposition were presented in the complaint itself, which it is not, Plaintiffs still cite no case law holding that a contract breach by itself constitutes an injury in fact. This is insufficient.

2. *Direct Economic Injuries.* The court next considers whether Plaintiffs have alleged direct economic injuries sufficient to establish injury-in-fact. As the Supreme Court has noted, "palpable economic injuries have long been recognized as sufficient to lay the basis for standing." Plaintiffs each allege that they were injured when their Android devices sent their respective names, email addresses, and locations to the developer of each app they purchased or downloaded because they had to pay for the battery and bandwidth consumed by the unauthorized transmissions. Mr. Nisenbaum, representing the Android Device Switch Subclass, claims further injury in that he overpaid for his Android phone in 2010 because he would not have bought the phone had Google disclosed its intention to use his information as alleged in the complaint. Mr. Nisenbaum also claims that he replaced his Android phone with an iPhone in 2012 as a result of Google's policy change, causing him further economic injury.

The Court will consider each of these direct economic injury theories in turn to determine if they articulate "something more" than pure economic harm to support subject-matter jurisdiction under Rule 12(b)(1).

With respect to Plaintiffs' injury claims based on battery and bandwidth consumption, courts have found that the unauthorized use of system resources can suffice to establish a cognizable injury. For example, in *Goodman* [*vs. HTC*, No. C11–1793MJP, 2012 WL 2412070, at *5 (W.D. Wash. Jun. 26, 2012)], the court found standing based upon battery discharge where the application at issue sent fine location data every three hours or whenever the device's screen was refreshed. Similarly, in *In re iPhone Application Litigation* [844 F. Supp. 2d 1040, 1054–56 (N.D. Cal. 2012)], the court found standing where the device systematically collected and transmitted location information. In *In re Google Android User Privacy Litigation* [2013 WL 1283236, at *2, 4 (N.D. Cal. Mar. 26, 2013)], the plaintiffs did not clearly allege how frequently Google collected geolocation data from a phone, but did allege that collecting relocation data was particularly battery intensive, that "their batteries discharged more quickly[,] and that their services were interrupted." This latter allegation was deemed sufficient to establish standing. At the same time, in *Hernandez v. Path, Inc.* [2012 WL 5194120, at *8 (N.D. Cal. Oct. 19, 2012)], the court found that any harm from the use of phone resources in an app's uploading a user's address book a single time upon first running the app was *de minimis* and thus insufficient to establish injury.

Plaintiffs' allegations here are closer to *Goodman, iPhone I* and *Android* than *Hernandez.* Like *Hernandez,* Plaintiffs' alleged unauthorized battery consumption only happened infrequently, when a plaintiff first downloaded an app. But in *Hernandez* the allegedly unauthorized upload only happened once, when a plaintiff downloaded the Path app. Here, it happens each time a user downloads any app. The plaintiff who downloaded the most apps, according to the amended complaint, did so at least 27 times. In addition, like the plaintiffs in *Goodman* and *Android,* Plaintiffs here specifically allege a greater discharge of battery power as a result of unauthorized conduct and as in *iPhone I* the discharge is systemic rather than episodic. This is sufficient to establish more than a *de minimis* injury.

With respect to Mr. Nisenbaum's further allegations of injury, they, too, support standing for purposes of Article III.

First, the allegation that Mr. Nisenbaum bought a new phone after the policy change and that his motivation for choosing an iPhone over the Android device was substantially for privacy reasons, establishes that he was injured by making the purchase. To be sure, users frequently replace old phones for all kinds of reasons beyond privacy. For example, from the complaint, it appears Mr. Nisenbaum had his Android device for approximately two years, the length of most phone contracts that often include a discount for bundled phones, before purchasing a new phone. But Mr. Nisenbaum specifically alleges that but for the policy switch he would not have otherwise have bought a new phone. The alleged injury is fairly traceable to Google based on Mr. Nisenbaum's allegation that he relied on Google's previous policies in purchasing the Android phone in the first place.

Second, Mr. Nisembaum's allegations regarding overpayment establish injury. In *Pirozzi v. Apple* [913 F. Supp. 2d 840, 846–47 (N.D. Cal. 2012)], the court explained that Article III standing under an overpayment theory may be supported by "allegations [by plaintiffs] that, when they purchased their [ ] devices, they relied upon representations regarding privacy protection, which caused them to pay more than they would have for their devices." Similarly, in *Goodman,* the court found standing for overpayment of a smartphone where plaintiffs alleged they would have "paid less for the phones had [d]efendant's not misrepresented the relevant features." The court held that a "general averment of quality, alleged to be false, was sufficient to constitute an alleged injury in the form of overpayment." The allegations here are equally sufficient.

Google highlights that Mr. Nisenbaum has not alleged that he bought his phone from Google or that Google manufactured the phone. But the complaint is clear that Mr. Nisenbaum's phone ran on Android, Google's open-source operating system, and that in order to access the Google Play marketplace included in Android, Mr. Nisenbaum had to create a Google account. Under such circumstances, the alleged harm of overpayment to a third party is fairly traceable to Google. . . .

NOTES & QUESTIONS

1. *Postscript.* The *Google* court went on to analyze the various claims, and it found that none of the claims was viable, so the court granted Google's motion to dismiss. Note that in federal court, plaintiffs must establish sufficient injury for standing, and then must still establish sufficient facts to justify a prima facie case on various causes of action.

2. *Financial Harm.* Is the *Google* court looking for the appropriate type of harm? Recall that Warren and Brandeis defined privacy as primarily an emotional injury, not a financial one. Should courts be focusing on financial harm? Was there non-financial harm when Google changed its privacy

policies? Should courts recognize such harm?

In *In Re Google, Inc. Cookie Placement Consumer Privacy Litigation*, 988 F. Supp. 2d 434 (D. Del. 2013), plaintiffs alleged that Google " 'tricked' their Apple Safari and/or Internet Explorer browsers into accepting cookies, which then allowed defendants to display targeted advertising." The court held that the plaintiffs couldn't prove a harm because they couldn't demonstrate that Google interfered with their ability to "monetize" their personal data:

> Examining the facts alleged in the light most favorable to plaintiffs, the court concludes that, while plaintiffs have offered some evidence that the online personal information at issue has some modicum of identifiable value to an individual plaintiff, plaintiffs have not sufficiently alleged that the ability to monetize their PII has been diminished or lost by virtue of Google's previous collection of it.

3. *The EU Reaction.* Google's consolidation of its privacy policies also led to a reaction in the European Union. On December 19, 2013, the Spanish Data Protection Authority fined it 900,000 Euros, or approximately $1.2 million, for violating Spanish data protection provisions. The *Agencia Española de Protección de Datos* (AEPD) found that the combination of data by the different Google services widely exceeded the reasonable expectations of the majority of users. It also noted that Google hindered and, in some cases, prevented rights of access, rectification, and cancellation. Finally, the AEPD declared that Google did not obtain valid consent from the concerned individuals.

In France, the French Data Protection authority fined Google 150,000 Euros, or approximately $200,000, which was the maximum fine that French law permitted to be placed on first time violators. The *Commission nationale de l'information et des libertés* (CNIL) also required Google to publish a copy of its order on its website in France. The CNIL found that Google "did not sufficiently inform its users of the conditions in which their personal data are processed, nor of the purposes of this processing." Google also failed to comply with its obligation to obtain user consent and to define retention periods for the data that it processes. As a final matter, Google "permits itself to combine all the data it collects about its users across all its services without any legal basis."[25]

What lessons do you draw from the different reactions in the EU and United States to this same action by Google?

4. *Possible Future Harm and Mitigation Expenses.* In privacy cases, plaintiffs have alleged that defendants' activities create risks of possible future harm. Courts have generally not been receptive to this argument. In *Clapper v. Amnesty International*, 133 S. Ct. 1138 (2013), which we excerpted in Chapter 5, the U.S. Supreme Court held that plaintiffs failed to allege a legally cognizable injury when they challenged a provision of the law that permits the government to engage in surveillance of their communications.

---

[25] CNIL, *Deliberation No. 2013-420 of the Sanctions Committee of CNIL imposing a financial penalty against Google Inc.* (Jan. 3, 2014).

Although this case does not involve consumer privacy issues, its reasoning has applicability for consumer privacy cases.

The plaintiffs claimed that there was an "objectively reasonable likelihood" that their communications would be monitored, and as a result, they had to take "costly and burdensome measures to protect the confidentiality of their international communications." The Supreme Court concluded that the plaintiffs were speculating and that "allegations of possible future injury are not sufficient" to establish an injury. According to the Court, "fears of hypothetical future harm" cannot justify the countermeasures the plaintiffs took. "Enterprising" litigants could establish an injury "simply by making an expenditure based on a nonparanoid fear."

In data breach cases, most courts have rejected claims that the breach increased the risk of future identity theft. *See, e.g., Amburgy v. Express Scripts, Inc.,* 671 F.Supp.2d 1046 (E.D. Mo. 2009); *Key v. DSW, Inc.,* 454 F. Supp. 2d 684 (S.D. Ohio 2006). Likewise, courts reject cases when plaintiffs spend money for mitigation expenses — measures to protect themselves against future harm. One case, however, accepted this theory. In *Anderson v. Hannaford Bros. Co.,* 659 F.3d 151 (1st Cir. 2011), the court held:

> Under Maine negligence law, damages must be both reasonably foreseeable, and, even if reasonably foreseeable, of the type which Maine has not barred for policy reasons. Generally, under Maine law, "the fundamental test [for both tort and contract recovery] is one of reasonable foreseeability: if the loss or injury for which damages are claimed was not reasonably foreseeable under the circumstances, there is no liability." But liability in negligence also "ordinarily requires proof of personal injury or property damage." . . . In cases of nonphysical harm, Maine courts limit recovery by considering not only reasonable foreseeability, but also relevant policy considerations such as "societal expectations regarding behavior and individual responsibility in allocating risks and costs." . . .
>
> It is clear that, as a matter of policy, Maine law "encourages plaintiffs to take reasonable steps to minimize losses caused by a defendant's negligence." To recover mitigation damages, plaintiffs need only show that the efforts to mitigate were reasonable, and that those efforts constitute a legal injury, such as actual money lost, rather than time or effort expended.
>
> Maine has interpreted this "reasonableness" requirement for mitigation, judging whether the decision to mitigate was reasonable "at the time it was made." . . .
>
> The Seventh Circuit, for example, has held that under Restatement § 919 incidental costs expended in good faith to mitigate harm are recoverable— even if the costs turn out to exceed the savings. . . .
>
> The Fourth Circuit has noted, applying Restatement § 919, that plaintiffs should not face "a Hobson's choice" between allowing further damage to occur or mitigating the damage at their own expense. Toll Bros., Inc. v. Dryvit Sys., Inc., 432 F.3d 564, 570 (4th Cir.2005) (applying Connecticut law). In Toll, a real estate developer removed and replaced defective stucco from homes that it built, and sued the stucco manufacturer in negligence to recover its costs. The court concluded that, as a matter of policy, a plaintiff may recover the cost of its reasonable attempts to mitigate, even if the injury is "wholly financial" in nature.

However, in the *Hannaford Brothers* case the information was obtained by a ring of identity thieves and some people were already victimized. The court noted that the plaintiffs "were not merely exposed to a hypothetical risk, but to a real risk of misuse." Another case that found standing in a data breach case is *Resnick v. Avmed Inc.* (11th Cir. 2012), which is excerpted in Chapter 10.

B. TORT LAW

DWYER V. AMERICAN EXPRESS CO.

652 N.E.2d 1351 (Ill. App. 1995)

BUCKLEY, J. Plaintiffs, American Express cardholders, appeal the circuit court's dismissal of their claims for invasion of privacy and consumer fraud against defendants, American Express Company, American Express Credit Corporation, and American Express Travel Related Services Company, for their practice of renting information regarding cardholder spending habits.

On May 13, 1992, the New York Attorney General released a press statement describing an agreement it had entered into with defendants. The following day, newspapers reported defendants' actions which gave rise to this agreement. According to the news articles, defendants categorize and rank their cardholders into six tiers based on spending habits and then rent this information to participating merchants as part of a targeted joint-marketing and sales program. For example, a cardholder may be characterized as "Rodeo Drive Chic" or "Value Oriented." In order to characterize its cardholders, defendants analyze where they shop and how much they spend, and also consider behavioral characteristics and spending histories. Defendants then offer to create a list of cardholders who would most likely shop in a particular store and rent that list to the merchant.

Defendants also offer to create lists which target cardholders who purchase specific types of items, such as fine jewelry. The merchants using the defendants' service can also target shoppers in categories such as mail-order apparel buyers, home-improvement shoppers, electronics shoppers, luxury lodgers, card members with children, skiers, frequent business travelers, resort users, Asian/European travelers, luxury European car owners, or recent movers. Finally, defendants offer joint-marketing ventures to merchants who generate substantial sales through the American Express card. Defendants mail special promotions devised by the merchants to its cardholders and share the profits generated by these advertisements. . . .

Plaintiffs have alleged that defendants' practices constitute an invasion of their privacy [in particular, a violation of the intrusion upon seclusion tort]. . . .

. . . [There are] four elements [to intrusion upon seclusion] which must be alleged in order to state a cause of action: (1) an unauthorized intrusion or prying into the plaintiff's seclusion; (2) an intrusion which is offensive or objectionable to a reasonable man; (3) the matter upon which the intrusion occurs is private; and (4) the intrusion causes anguish and suffering. . . .

Plaintiffs' allegations fail to satisfy the first element, an unauthorized intrusion or prying into the plaintiffs' seclusion. The alleged wrongful actions involve the defendants' practice of renting lists that they have compiled from information contained in their own records. By using the American Express card, a cardholder is voluntarily, and necessarily, giving information to defendants that, if analyzed, will reveal a cardholder's spending habits and shopping preferences. . . .

Plaintiffs claim that because defendants rented lists based on this compiled information, this case involves the disclosure of private financial information and most closely resembles cases involving intrusion into private financial dealings, such as bank account transactions. Plaintiffs cite several cases in which courts have recognized the right to privacy surrounding financial transactions.

However, we find that this case more closely resembles the sale of magazine subscription lists, which was at issue in *Shibley v. Time, Inc.* In *Shibley*, the plaintiffs claimed that the defendant's practice of selling and renting magazine subscription lists without the subscribers' prior consent "constitut[ed] an invasion of privacy because it amount[ed] to a sale of individual 'personality profiles,' which subjects the subscribers to solicitations from direct mail advertisers." The plaintiffs also claimed that the lists amounted to a tortious appropriation of their names and "personality profiles." . . .

The *Shibley* court found that an Ohio statute, which permitted the sale of names and addresses of registrants of motor vehicles, indicated that the defendant's activity was not an invasion of privacy. . . .

Defendants rent names and addresses after they create a list of cardholders who have certain shopping tendencies; they are not disclosing financial information about particular cardholders. These lists are being used solely for the purpose of determining what type of advertising should be sent to whom. We also note that the Illinois Vehicle Code authorizes the Secretary of State to sell lists of names and addresses of licensed drivers and registered motor-vehicle owners. Thus, we hold that the alleged actions here do not constitute an unreasonable intrusion into the seclusion of another. We so hold without expressing a view as to the appellate court conflict regarding the recognition of this cause of action.

Considering plaintiffs' appropriation claim, the elements of the tort are: an appropriation, without consent, of one's name or likeness for another's use or benefit. This branch of the privacy doctrine is designed to protect a person from having his name or image used for commercial purposes without consent. According to the Restatement, the purpose of this tort is to protect the "interest of the individual in the exclusive use of his own identity, in so far as it is represented by his name or likeness." Illustrations of this tort provided by the Restatement include the publication of a person's photograph without consent in an advertisement; operating a corporation named after a prominent public figure without the person's consent; impersonating a man to obtain information regarding the affairs of the man's wife; and filing a lawsuit in the name of another without the other's consent.

Plaintiffs claim that defendants appropriate information about cardholders' personalities, including their names and perceived lifestyles, without their consent. Defendants argue that their practice does not adversely affect the interest of a cardholder in the "exclusive use of his own identity," using the language of the Restatement. Defendants also argue that the cardholders' names lack value and that the lists that defendants create are valuable because "they identify a useful aggregate of potential customers to whom offers may be sent.". . .

To counter defendants' argument, plaintiffs point out that the tort of appropriation is not limited to strictly commercial situations.

Nonetheless, we again follow the reasoning in *Shibley* and find that plaintiffs have not stated a claim for tortious appropriation because they have failed to allege the first element. Undeniably, each cardholder's name is valuable to defendants. The more names included on a list, the more that list will be worth. However, a single, random cardholder's name has little or no intrinsic value to defendants (or a merchant). Rather, an individual name has value only when it is associated with one of defendants' lists. Defendants create value by categorizing and aggregating these names. Furthermore, defendants' practices do not deprive any of the cardholders of any value their individual names may possess. . . .

NOTES & QUESTIONS

1. **Shibley v. Time.** In *Shibley v. Time, Inc.,* 341 N.E.2d 337 (Ohio Ct. App. 1975), the plaintiff sued the publishers of a number of magazines for selling subscription lists to direct mail advertising businesses. The plaintiff sued under the public disclosure tort and the appropriation tort. Despite the fact that the purchasers of the lists can learn about the plaintiff's lifestyle from the data, the court dismissed the plaintiff's public disclosure action. The court found that the sale of the lists did not "cause mental suffering, shame or humiliation to a person of ordinary sensibilities." The court also rejected the plaintiff's argument that by selling the lists, the defendants were appropriating his name and likeness because the tort of appropriation is available only in those "situations where the plaintiff's name or likeness is displayed to the public to indicate that the plaintiff indorses the defendant's product or business."

   According to *Shibley* and *Dwyer*, why does the public disclosure tort fail to provide a remedy for the disclosure of personal information to other companies? Why does the tort of intrusion upon seclusion fail? Why does the tort of appropriation fail? More generally, can tort law adequately remedy the privacy problems created by profiling and databases?[26]

2. *A Fair Information Practices Tort?* Sarah Ludington recommends that a new tort should be developed in the common law, one that "would impose on data traders a duty to use Fair Information Practices (based on the principles of

---

[26] For an interesting argument about how the tort of breach of confidentiality might provide a weak but potential solution to the problem, see Jessica Litman, *Information Privacy/Information Property*, 52 Stan. L. Rev. 1283 (2000). For a discussion of the use of the tort of appropriation, see Andrew J. McClurg, *A Thousand Words Are Worth a Picture: A Privacy Tort Response to Consumer Data Profiling*, 98 Nw. U. L. Rev. 63 (2003).

notice, choice, access, and security)." Why the common law rather than legislation? Ludington argues:

> [B]ecause it is now clear that industry lobbying has succeeded while self-regulation has failed, and that legislatures have either failed to act or provided solutions that inadequately address the injuries, individuals must — indeed, should — look to the judiciary to help resolve the misuse of personal information.[27]

Would the use of the common law to regulate the collection and use of personal data be effective or appropriate? What would be the strengths and weaknesses of such a regulatory approach?

3. ***Defining the Harm.*** What is the harm of commercial entities collecting and using personal information? One might contend that the kind of information that companies collect about individuals is not very sensitive or intimate. How much is a person harmed by sharing data that she prefers Coke to Pepsi or Puffs to Kleenex? Is there a significant privacy problem in revealing that a person has purchased tennis products, designer sunglasses, orange juice, or other things? One might view the harm as so minimal as to be trivial.

Does information about a person's consumption patterns reveal something about that person's identity? Stan Karas argues that "consumption patterns may identify one as a liberal, moderate Republican, radical feminist or born-again Christian. . . . For some individuals, consumption is no longer a way of expressing identity but is synonymous with identity. . . . [T]he identity of many subcultures is directly related to distinctive patterns of consumption. One need only think of the personal styles of punk rockers, hip-hoppers, or Harley-fetishizing bikers."[28]

According to Jerry Kang, data collection and compiling is a form of surveillance that inhibits individual freedom and choice: "[I]information collection in cyberspace is more like surveillance than like casual observation." He notes that "surveillance leads to self-censorship. This is true even when the observable information would not be otherwise misused or disclosed."[29]

Daniel Solove contends that the problem of computer databases does not stem from surveillance. He argues that numerous theorists describe the problem in terms of the metaphor of Big Brother, the ruthless totalitarian government in George Orwell's *1984*, which constantly monitors its citizens. Solove contends that the Big Brother metaphor fails to adequately conceptualize the problem:

> A large portion of our personal information involves facts that we are not embarrassed about: our financial information, race, marital status, hobbies, occupation, and the like. Most people surf the web without wandering into its dark corners. The vast majority of the information collected about us concerns

---

[27] Sarah Ludington, *Reining in the Data Traders: A Tort for the Misuse of Personal Information*, 66 Md. L. Rev. 140, 172-73 (2007).

[28] Stan Karas, *Privacy, Identity, Databases,* 52 Am. U. L. Rev. 393, 438-39 (2002).

[29] Jerry Kang, *Information Privacy in Cyberspace Transactions*, 50 Stan. L. Rev. 1193 (1998).

relatively innocuous details. The surveillance model does not explain why the recording of this non-taboo information poses a problem.[30]

In contrast, Solove proposes that data collection and processing is most aptly captured by Franz Kafka's *The Trial*, where the protagonist (Joseph K.) is arrested by officials from a clandestine court system but is not informed of the reason for his arrest. From what little he manages to learn about the court system, which operates largely in secret, Joseph K. discovers that a vast bureaucratic court has examined his life and assembled a dossier on him. His records, however, are "inaccessible," and K.'s life gradually becomes taken over by his frustrating quest for answers:

> *The Trial* captures the sense of helplessness, frustration, and vulnerability one experiences when a large bureaucratic organization has control over a vast dossier of details about one's life. At any time, something could happen to Joseph K.; decisions are made based on his data, and Joseph K. has no say, no knowledge, and no ability to fight back. He is completely at the mercy of the bureaucratic process. . . .
>
> The problem with databases emerges from subjecting personal information to the bureaucratic process with little intelligent control or limitation, resulting in a lack of meaningful participation in decisions about our information. . . .
>
> Under this view, the problem with databases and the practices currently associated with them is that they disempower people. They make people vulnerable by stripping them of control over their personal information. There is no diabolical motive or secret plan for domination; rather, there is a web of thoughtless decisions made by low-level bureaucrats, standardized policies, rigid routines, and a way of relating to individuals and their information that often becomes indifferent to their welfare.[31]

Joel Reidenberg points out that the lack of protection of information privacy will "destroy anonymity" and take away people's "freedom to choose the terms of personal information disclosure."[32] According to Paul Schwartz, the lack of privacy protection can threaten to expose not just information about what people purchase, but also information about their communication and consumption of ideas:

> In the absence of strong rules for information privacy, Americans will hesitate to engage in cyberspace activities—including those that are most likely to promote democratic self-rule. . . . Current polls already indicate an aversion on the part of some people to engage even in basic commercial activities on the Internet. Yet, deliberative democracy requires more than shoppers; it demands speakers and listeners. But who will speak or listen when this behavior leaves finely-grained data trails in a fashion that is difficult to understand or anticipate?[33]

---

[30] Daniel J. Solove, *Privacy and Power: Computer Databases and Metaphors for Information Privacy*, 53 Stan. L. Rev. 1393 (2001).

[31] *Id.*

[32] Joel R. Reidenberg, *Setting Standards for Fair Information Practice in the U.S. Private Sector*, 80 Iowa L. Rev. 497 (1995).

[33] Paul M. Schwartz, *Privacy and Democracy in Cyberspace*, 52 Vand. L. Rev. 1609, 1651 (1999).

4. ***Using Consumers in Ads: Facebook's Sponsored Stories.*** In *Fraley v. Facebook*, 830 F. Supp. 2d 785 (N.D. Cal. 2011), plaintiffs sued Facebook for its "Sponsored Stories" advertising program. A Sponsored Story is a paid ad appearing on a person's Facebook page. It uses the name and photo of a person's friend who "likes" the advertiser:

> For example, Plaintiff Angel Fraley, who registered as a member with the name Angel Frolicker, alleges that she visited Rosetta Stone's Facebook profile page and clicked the "Like" button in order to access a free software demonstration. Subsequently, her Facebook user name and profile picture, which bears her likeness, appeared on her Friends' Facebook pages in a "Sponsored Story" advertisement consisting of the Rosetta Stone logo and the sentence, "Angel Frolicker likes Rosetta Stone."

Among the causes of action plaintiffs brought was appropriation of name or likeness under Cal. Civ. Code § 3344. Facebook moved to dismiss. Facebook argued that the plaintiffs consented to being used in the ads because it had stated in its Terms of Use:

> You can use your privacy settings to limit how your name and profile picture may be associated with commercial, sponsored, or related content (such as a brand you like) served or enhanced by us. You give us permission to use your name and [Facebook] profile picture in connection with that content, subject to the limits you place.

The plaintiffs argued that Sponsored Stories did not exist when they signed up with Facebook and were never informed before they were suddenly used in the ads. The court held that there were factual issues in dispute on the consent issue that prevented dismissal.

Facebook also argued that there was no injury. The court however, concluded that plaintiffs had alleged sufficient facts to establish injury to withstand a motion to dismiss:

> Here, Plaintiffs allege not that they suffered mental anguish as a result of Defendant's actions, but rather that they suffered economic injury because they were not compensated for Facebook's commercial use of their names and likenesses in targeted advertisements to their Facebook Friends. Defendant does not deny that Plaintiffs may assert economic injury, but insists that, because they are not celebrities, they must demonstrate some preexisting commercial value to their names and likenesses, such as allegations that they "previously received remuneration for the use of their name or likeness, or that they have ever sought to obtain such remuneration."
>
> First, the Court finds nothing in the text of the statute or in case law that supports Defendant's interpretation of § 3344 as requiring a plaintiff pleading economic injury to provide proof of *preexisting* commercial value and efforts to capitalize on such value in order to survive a motion to dismiss. The plain text of § 3344 provides simply that "[a]ny person who knowingly uses another's name, voice, signature, photograph, or likeness, in any manner . . . for purposes of advertising or selling . . . without such person's consent . . . shall be liable for any damages sustained by the person or persons injured as a result thereof." The statutory text makes no mention of preexisting value, and in fact can be read to presume that a person whose name, photograph, or

likeness is used by another for commercial purposes without their consent is "injured as a result thereof."

Nor does the Court find any reason to impose a higher pleading standard on non-celebrities than on celebrities. California courts have clearly held that "the statutory right of publicity exists for celebrity and non-celebrity plaintiffs alike."

Moreover, . . . the Court finds that Plaintiffs' allegations satisfy the requirements for pleading a claim of economic injury under § 3344. Plaintiffs quote Facebook CEO Mark Zuckerberg stating that "[n]othing influences people more than a recommendation from a trusted friend. A trusted referral influences people more than the best broadcast message. A trusted referral is the Holy Grail of advertising." . . .

In August 2013, the court in this case approved a $20 million settlement with Facebook. As this casebook goes to press, there is an appeal to the settlement that argues that it violates state law in allowing Facebook to use images of minors without parental consent.[34]

REMSBURG V. DOCUSEARCH, INC.

816 A.2d 1001 (N.H. 2003)

DALIANIS, J. . . . [Liam Youens contacted Docusearch and purchased the birth date of Amy Lynn Boyer for a fee. He again contacted Docusearch and placed an order for Boyer's SSN. Docusearch obtained Boyer's SSN from a credit reporting agency and provided it to Youens. Youens then asked for Boyer's employment address. Docusearch hired a subcontractor, Michele Gambino, who obtained it by making a "pretext" phone call to Boyer. Gambino lied about her identity and the purpose of the call, and she obtained the address from Boyer. The address was then given to Youens. Shortly thereafter, Youens went to Boyer's workplace and shot and killed her and then killed himself.]

All persons have a duty to exercise reasonable care not to subject others to an unreasonable risk of harm. Whether a defendant's conduct creates a risk of harm to others sufficiently foreseeable to charge the defendant with a duty to avoid such conduct is a question of law, because "the existence of a duty does not arise solely from the relationship between the parties, but also from the need for protection against reasonably foreseeable harm." Thus, in some cases, a party's actions give rise to a duty. Parties owe a duty to those third parties foreseeably endangered by their conduct with respect to those risks whose likelihood and magnitude make the conduct unreasonably dangerous.

In situations in which the harm is caused by criminal misconduct, however, determining whether a duty exists is complicated by the competing rule "that a private citizen has no general duty to protect others from the criminal attacks of third parties." This rule is grounded in the fundamental unfairness of holding private citizens responsible for the unanticipated criminal acts of third parties, because "[u]nder all ordinary and normal circumstances, in the absence of any

---

[34] For more on the case and a proposed "holistic economic and non-economic approach to the right of publicity" in online social networks, see Jesse Koehler, Fraley v. Facebook: *The Right of Publicity in Online Social Networks*, 28 Berkeley Tech. L.J. 963 (2013).

reason to expect the contrary, the actor may reasonably proceed upon the assumption that others will obey the law."

In certain limited circumstances, however, we have recognized that there are exceptions to the general rule where a duty to exercise reasonable care will arise. We have held that such a duty may arise because: (1) a special relationship exists; (2) special circumstances exist; or (3) the duty has been voluntarily assumed. The special circumstances exception includes situations where there is "an especial temptation and opportunity for criminal misconduct brought about by the defendant." This exception follows from the rule that a party who realizes or should realize that his conduct has created a condition which involves an unreasonable risk of harm to another has a duty to exercise reasonable care to prevent the risk from occurring. The exact occurrence or precise injuries need not have been foreseeable. Rather, where the defendant's conduct has created an unreasonable risk of criminal misconduct, a duty is owed to those foreseeably endangered.

Thus, if a private investigator or information broker's (hereinafter "investigator" collectively) disclosure of information to a client creates a foreseeable risk of criminal misconduct against the third person whose information was disclosed, the investigator owes a duty to exercise reasonable care not to subject the third person to an unreasonable risk of harm. In determining whether the risk of criminal misconduct is foreseeable to an investigator, we examine two risks of information disclosure implicated by this case: stalking and identity theft.

It is undisputed that stalkers, in seeking to locate and track a victim, sometimes use an investigator to obtain personal information about the victims.

Public concern about stalking has compelled all fifty States to pass some form of legislation criminalizing stalking. Approximately one million women and 371,000 men are stalked annually in the United States. Stalking is a crime that causes serious psychological harm to the victims, and often results in the victim experiencing post-traumatic stress disorder, anxiety, sleeplessness, and sometimes, suicidal ideations.

Identity theft, *i.e.*, the use of one person's identity by another, is an increasingly common risk associated with the disclosure of personal information, such as a SSN. A person's SSN has attained the status of a quasi-universal personal identification number. At the same time, however, a person's privacy interest in his or her SSN is recognized by state and federal statutes. . . .

Like the consequences of stalking, the consequences of identity theft can be severe. . . . Victims of identity theft risk the destruction of their good credit histories. This often destroys a victim's ability to obtain credit from any source and may, in some cases, render the victim unemployable or even cause the victim to be incarcerated.

The threats posed by stalking and identity theft lead us to conclude that the risk of criminal misconduct is sufficiently foreseeable so that an investigator has a duty to exercise reasonable care in disclosing a third person's personal information to a client. And we so hold. This is especially true when, as in this case, the investigator does not know the client or the client's purpose in seeking the information. . . .

[The plaintiff also brought an action for intrusion upon seclusion.] A tort action based upon an intrusion upon seclusion must relate to something secret, secluded or private pertaining to the plaintiff. Moreover, liability exists only if the defendant's conduct was such that the defendant should have realized that it would be offensive to persons of ordinary sensibilities.

In addressing whether a person's SSN is something secret, secluded or private, we must determine whether a person has a reasonable expectation of privacy in the number. . . . As noted above, a person's interest in maintaining the privacy of his or her SSN has been recognized by numerous federal and state statutes. As a result, the entities to which this information is disclosed and their employees are bound by legal, and, perhaps, contractual constraints to hold SSNs in confidence to ensure that they remain private. Thus, while a SSN must be disclosed in certain circumstances, a person may reasonably expect that the number will remain private.

Whether the intrusion would be offensive to persons of ordinary sensibilities is ordinarily a question for the fact-finder and only becomes a question of law if reasonable persons can draw only one conclusion from the evidence. The evidence underlying the certified question is insufficient to draw any such conclusion here, and we therefore must leave this question to the fact-finder. In making this determination, the fact-finder should consider "the degree of intrusion, the context, conduct and circumstances surrounding the intrusion as well as the intruder's motives and objectives, the setting into which he intrudes, and the expectations of those whose privacy is invaded." Accordingly, a person whose SSN is obtained by an investigator from a credit reporting agency without the person's knowledge or permission may have a cause of action for intrusion upon seclusion for damages caused by the sale of the SSN, but must prove that the intrusion was such that it would have been offensive to a person of ordinary sensibilities.

We next address whether a person has a cause of action for intrusion upon seclusion where an investigator obtains the person's work address by using a pretextual phone call. We must first establish whether a work address is something secret, secluded or private about the plaintiff.

In most cases, a person works in a public place. "On the public street, or in any other public place, [a person] has no legal right to be alone." . . . Thus, where a person's work address is readily observable by members of the public, the address cannot be private and no intrusion upon seclusion action can be maintained.

[Additionally, the plaintiff brought a cause of action for appropriation.] "One who appropriates to his own use or benefit the name or likeness of another is subject to liability to the other for invasion of his privacy." *Restatement (Second) of Torts* § 652E.

. . . Appropriation is not actionable if the person's name or likeness is published for "purposes other than taking advantage of [the person's] reputation, prestige or other value" associated with the person. Thus, appropriation occurs most often when the person's name or likeness is used to advertise the defendant's product or when the defendant impersonates the person for gain.

An investigator who sells personal information sells the information for the value of the information itself, not to take advantage of the person's reputation or prestige. The investigator does not capitalize upon the goodwill value associated with the information but rather upon the client's willingness to pay for the information. In other words, the benefit derived from the sale in no way relates to the social or commercial standing of the person whose information is sold. Thus, a person whose personal information is sold does not have a cause of action for appropriation against the investigator who sold the information. . . .

NOTES & QUESTIONS

1. *The Scope of the Duty.* The court concludes that Docusearch has a duty to people "foreseeably endangered" by its disclosure of personal information. Is this too broad a duty to impose on those who collect and disseminate personal data? What could Docusearch have done to avoid being negligent in this case? Suppose Jill tells Jack the address of Roe. Jack goes to Roe's house and kills her. Based on *Remsburg*, can Jill be liable?
2. *Tort Liability and the First Amendment.* Does liability for Docusearch implicate the First Amendment?

C. CONTRACT LAW

1. PRIVACY POLICIES

Privacy policies are statements made by companies about their practices regarding personal information. Privacy policies are also referred to as "privacy notices." Increasingly, companies on the Internet are posting privacy policies, and statutes such as the Gramm-Leach-Bliley Act require certain types of companies (financial institutions, insurance companies, and brokerage companies) to maintain privacy policies.

One of the common provisions of many privacy policies is an "opt-out" provision. An opt-out provision establishes a default rule that the company can use or disclose personal information in the ways it desires so long as the consumer does not indicate otherwise. The consumer must take affirmative steps, such as checking a box, calling the company, or writing a letter, to express her desire to opt out of a particular information use or disclosure. In contrast, an "opt-in" provision establishes a default rule that the company cannot use or disclose personal information without first obtaining the express consent of the individual.

JEFF SOVERN, *OPTING IN, OPTING OUT, OR NO OPTIONS AT ALL: THE FIGHT FOR CONTROL OF PERSONAL INFORMATION*

74 Wash. L. Rev. 1033 (1999)

. . . [F]ew consumers understand how much of their personal information is for sale, although they may have a general idea that there is a trade in personal data and that the specifics about that trade are kept from them. . . .

. . . [C]onsumers cannot protect their personal information when they are unaware of how it is being used by others. . . .

The second reason consumers have not acted to protect their privacy, notwithstanding surveys that suggest considerable consumer concern with confidentiality, has to do with how difficult it is to opt out. . . .

. . . Even if consumers can obtain the information needed to opt out, the cost in time and money of communicating and negotiating with all the relevant information gatherers may be substantial. . . .

Companies may not be eager to offer opt-outs because they may rationally conclude that they will incur costs when consumers opt out, while receiving few offsetting benefits. When consumers exercise the option of having their names deleted, mailing lists shrink and presumably become less valuable. . . .

Because of these added costs, companies might decide that while they must offer an opt-out plan, they do not want consumers to take advantage of it. . . . [C]ompanies that offer opt-outs have an incentive to increase the transaction costs incurred by consumers who opt out. . . .

Companies can increase consumers' transaction costs in opting out in a number of ways. A brochure titled "Privacy Notice," which my local cable company included with its bill, provides an example. This Privacy Notice discussed, among other things, how cable subscribers could write to the company to ask that the company not sell their names and other information to third parties. There are at least four reasons why this particular notice may not be effective in eliciting a response from consumers troubled by the sale of their names to others.

First, the Privacy Notice may be obscured by other information included in the mailing. . . .

The second reason why consumers may not respond to the Privacy Notice is its length. The brochure is four pages long and contains 17 paragraphs, 36 sentences, and 1062 words. . . .

Some companies have gone in the other direction, providing so little information in such vague terms that consumers are unable to discern what they are being told. . . .

A third reason why the Privacy Notice may not be effective stems from its prose. Notwithstanding the Plain Language Law in my home state, computer analysis of the text found it extremely difficult, requiring more than a college education for comprehension. By comparison, a similar analysis of this Article found that it required a lower reading level than that of the Privacy Notice.

Fourth, the Privacy Notice may be ineffective because it does not provide an easy or convenient mechanism for opting out. For example, the Privacy Notice invites consumers who object to the sale of their personal information to write to the cable company in a separate letter. By contrast, cable subscribers desiring to add a new premium channel can do so over the telephone, speaking either to a person or tapping buttons on their telephone, depending on their preference. The more difficult the opt-out process, the less likely consumers are to avail themselves of it. . . .

A third explanation for the failure of consumers to opt out as often as their survey answers might suggest is the consumers themselves. Extensive literature on consumer complaint behavior makes clear that many consumers who are distressed by merchant conduct cannot bring themselves to tell the merchant about it. This inability to communicate might translate into failure by consumers to add their names to opt-out lists. . . .

[Sovern suggests that an opt-in system would be more preferable than an opt-out system.]

One benefit of an opt-in system is that it minimizes transaction costs. While some transaction costs are inevitable in any system in which consumers can opt out or opt in, strategic-behavior transaction costs, at least, can be avoided by using a system which discourages parties from generating such costs. The current system encourages businesses to inflate strategic-behavior costs to increase their own gains, albeit at the expense of consumers and the total surplus from exchange. An opt-in system would encourage businesses to reduce strategic-behavior costs without giving consumers an incentive to increase these costs. Instead of an opt-out situation in which merchants are obligated to provide a message they do not wish consumers to receive, an opt-in regime would harness merchants' efforts in providing a message they want the consumer to receive. . . .

An opt-in system thus increases the likelihood that consumers will choose according to their preferences rather than choosing according to the default. . . .

An opt-in system also increases the prospect that direct mailing would be tailored to what consumers wish to receive, thus benefiting consumers who want to receive some, but not all, solicitations. . . .

The sale of information is troublesome in part because it creates externalities, or costs borne by others. Externalities are created when a person engages in an activity that imposes costs on others but is not required to take those costs into account when deciding whether to pursue the activity. The feelings experienced by consumers whose information is sold and used against their wishes constitute just such externalities. An opt-in system — or an opt-out system in which consumers who object to the trade in their personal information have a genuine opportunity to opt out — can shift costs and thereby "internalize" this externality. To put it another way, consumers could bar the sale of their information unless businesses paid them an amount they deemed adequate, thereby requiring businesses selling personal information to incur a cost otherwise borne by consumers. . . .

A regulated opt-out system is less likely than an opt-in system to solve the problem. Opt-out systems do not give businesses the incentive to minimize consumer transaction costs. Consequently, firms might respond to such regulation by generating formal, legalistic notices that consumers would likely ignore. An opt-out system might thus create only the illusion of a cure.

Accordingly, an opt-in system is preferable, chiefly because it eliminates the incentive firms have to engage in strategic behavior and thus inflate consumer transaction costs. An opt-in system would permit consumers who wish to protect their privacy to do so without incurring transaction costs. Consumers who permit the use of their personal information should also be able to realize their wish easily. Indeed, because firms profit from the use of consumer information, firms would have an incentive to make it as easy as possible for consumers to consent to the use of their personal information. . . . An opt-in system, therefore, seems to offer the best hope of accommodating consumer preferences while minimizing transaction costs. . . .

MICHAEL E. STATEN & FRED H. CATE, *THE IMPACT OF OPT-IN PRIVACY RULES ON RETAIL MARKETS: A CASE STUDY OF MBNA*

52 Duke L.J. 745, 750-51, 766, 770-74, 776 (2003)

To illustrate the costs of moving to an opt-in system, we examine MBNA Corporation, a financial institution that offers consumers a variety of loan and insurance products (primarily credit cards), takes deposits, but operates entirely without a branch network. Incorporated in 1981 and publicly traded since 1991, the company has compiled a stunning growth record in just two decades. As of the end of 2000, the company provided credit cards and other loan products to 51 million consumers, had $89 billion of loans outstanding, and serviced 15 percent of all Visa/MasterCard credit card balances outstanding in the United States.

MBNA's ability to access and use information about potential and existing customers is largely responsible for it becoming the second largest credit card issuer in the United States in less than twenty years. To appreciate the critical role that the sharing of information has played in MBNA's remarkable history, one need only reflect on the challenge of acquiring 51 million customers with no brick-and-mortar stores or branches. Like firms in a variety of businesses, but especially financial services, MBNA harnessed information technology as the engine for establishing and building customer relationships without ever physically meeting its customers. By using direct mail, telephone and, most recently, Internet contacts, the company has reached out to new prospects throughout the population, regardless of where they live, with offers tailored to their individual interests. . . .

At the core of its marketing and targeting strategies is the proposition that consumers who share a common institutional bond or experience will have an affinity for using a card that lets them demonstrate their affiliation each time they use it to pay for a purchase. The affinity for the institution raises the probability that a prospect will be converted to a customer. Equally important, the institution or organization usually maintains a list of members on which MBNA can focus its marketing efforts. Following this "affinity group" marketing strategy, MBNA designs a card product tailored to members of a particular group, negotiates a financial arrangement with the organization for the exclusive rights to market an affinity card to its members, and uses the member list as a source of potential names to contact via direct mail or telemarketing. . . .

Design of new affinity cards is an ongoing process. In 2000 alone, MBNA acquired the endorsements of 459 new groups, including the United States Tennis Association, the Atlanta Braves, National Audubon Society, barnesand-noble.com, and the Thurgood Marshall Scholarship Fund.

Although targeting prospects through affinity groups has proven to be a clever strategy, not every group member is offered a card product. The key to the company's profitability and earnings growth, especially given the rapid growth in the size of the customer base, has been in screening the prospects from each affinity group to identify those likely to be quality customers. Given that MBNA's fundamental business is lending money via an unsecured credit card with a revolving line of credit attached, the company wants to put the card in the hands of customers who will use it, but who will not default on their balances.

Consequently, MBNA uses information to screen prospects both before it makes card offers (the targeting process) and after it receives applications (the underwriting process). . . .

How large a drag does an "explicit-consent" system impose on economic efficiency? According to the U.S. Postal Service, 52 percent of unsolicited mail in this country is never read. If that figure translates to opt-in requests, then more than half of all consumers in an opt-in system would lose the benefits or services that could result from the use of personal information because the mandatory request for consent would never receive their attention. Moreover, even if an unsolicited offer is read, experience with company-specific and industry-wide opt-out lists demonstrates that less than 10 percent of the U.S. population ever opts out of a mailing list — often the figure is less than 3 percent. Indeed, the difficulty (and cost) of obtaining a response of any sort from consumers is the primary drawback of an opt-in approach. . . .

MBNA's core product is the affinity card tailored for and marketed to each of more than 4,700 affinity groups. . . . [T]he foundation of MBNA's affinity strategy is access to the member lists of each of its affinity organizations. This marketing partnership with thousands of member organizations nationwide makes MBNA unique among major credit card issuers and accounts for much of the company's superior financial performance and reputation for outstanding customer service. However, in the absence of an explicit joint-marketing exception in an opt-in law, a third-party opt-in regime could effectively end MBNA's unique direct marketing approach by sharply limiting an organization's ability to share its member list. . . .

Like all major credit card issuers, MBNA uses personal information to increase the chance that its credit card offer will reach an interested and qualified customer. This process greatly reduces the number of solicitations that must be sent to achieve a given target volume of new accounts, thereby reducing the cost of account acquisition. It also reduces the volume of junk mail in the form of card offers sent to consumers who are not qualified. Third-party or affiliate opt-in systems would eliminate MBNA's access to a significant portion of the information that it currently uses to identify which individuals on the member lists it receives would be good prospects for a given credit card or other product. A blanket opt-in system applicable to marketing activities would impose similar limits.

The MBNA direct mail marketing operations obtain and consider about 800 million consumer "leads" during the course of a year. The vast majority of these leads are names that appear on affinity group member lists (e.g., university alumni groups and professional associations), or names of consumers who are customers of institutions that have endorsed MBNA's credit card product. Because this is an annual figure, many names appear more than once because the individuals are on more than one list acquired during the course of a year, or may be considered in conjunction with a specific group's marketing campaign several times during the year. The most creditworthy names among them may receive multiple solicitations during the year.

MBNA does not wish to mail to all names on the list. Not all are equally likely to respond to a solicitation, nor will all meet the credit underwriting standards for a particular card product. In 2000, the MBNA direct marketing budget supported approximately 400 million mailings of card offers. The challenge to the company in managing the acquisition of new accounts is to cull the "lead list" of 800 million prospect names to identify and target the 400 million direct mail solicitations to consumers who are most likely to become new cardholders. Generally speaking, MBNA has developed a set of targeting criteria such that names reaching the final mailing list of 400 million: (1) are most likely to respond to the offer and the use of the credit card, and (2) are most likely to meet MBNA's creditworthiness standards for the card.

MBNA prepares hundreds of distinct solicitations throughout the year for its various affinity groups. As part of the targeting process for each new solicitation, the prospect list is scrubbed via comparison to a series of "suppression files" that the company maintains and routinely updates. These files pull information about either individuals or addresses from a variety of internal and external data sources. A few examples of the specific criteria illustrate the process.

[The authors describe how MBNA has proprietary response models to help it determine which customers are most likely to respond to its offer. It uses credit history information to find individuals who are likely to repay, but, at the same time, do not have "extraordinary creditworthiness" and are, hence, likely to be frequently solicited by card issuers and unlikely to respond to an MBNA offer.]

The bottom line from the culling process is that approximately 40 percent of the eight hundred million names are suppressed. The initial lead list is typically reduced by an additional 10 percent through a combination of eliminating duplicate records, suppressing undeliverable addresses, and dropping customer names that appear on various "do not mail" lists that record customer preferences not to be solicited. . . . The approximately four hundred million names remaining on the lead list receive targeted direct mail offers with the endorsement of the affinity group to which they belong. . . .

MBNA's proprietary response models indicate that its use of information in these three categories to cull likely prospects accounts for approximately a 19 percent reduction in names from the annual prospect list. In other words, by targeting offers under current rules, about 150 million names on the prospect list during the course of a typical annual solicitation cycle do not receive solicitations, because the direct mail piece would otherwise reach a consumer who was either not interested or not qualified for the card product. . . .

[Under an opt-in approach,] approximately 550 million names would remain, instead of 400 million under the current rules. Lacking the information necessary to further distinguish good prospects from poor prospects, the company's targeting efficiency would be impaired.

MBNA would have two choices. It could increase its direct mail volume to send solicitations to all 550 million names remaining on the prospect list after the culling process, or it could arbitrarily remove 150 million names from the list after the culling process so that its direct mail volume remained unchanged at 400 million. Under either scenario, approximately 27 percent of the solicitations (150 million of 550 million) would go to consumers who were less interested in, and/or less qualified for, the offer, and who would have been dropped from the target list had MBNA been allowed to access and use the information on which its presently relies under current privacy rules. . . .

Although MBNA's actual response rate and cost per account booked is proprietary, we can illustrate the impact of the decline by utilizing the credit card industry average response rate to direct mail solicitations for 2000, which was 0.6 percent. For every 100 million solicitations mailed to individuals under the opt-in scenario, only 492 thousand new accounts would be booked, as compared to 600 thousand if the offers were targeted under existing rules, an 18 percent reduction in new accounts for the same expenditure on direct mail solicitations. Of course, the higher cost per account booked is borne not only by MBNA, but by MBNA's customers as well, in the form of higher prices, reduced benefits, diminished service, and higher acceptance standards for new credit products.

But, the negative impact does not stop there. Regardless of whether MBNA's response to opt-in is to mail more solicitations or mail the same number to a less-targeted prospect list, under either scenario, the recipient group of four hundred million individuals will — on average — be more risky and less profitable than MBNA's target group reached under the current rules. As a result, MBNA's delinquency and charge-off rates will rise, relative to its current experience, thereby imposing additional costs that will be passed along to all of MBNA's customers. Card usage will also be affected by booking cardholders who are less likely to use the card.

NOTES & QUESTIONS

1. *Opt Out vs. Opt In.* Do you agree with Sovern that an opt-in policy is more efficient than an opt-out policy? Do you think that an opt-in policy is feasible? Are the views of Staten and Cate convincing on this score? Do you think opt out or opt in should be required by law?

2. *Internalizing Costs.* Staten and Cate claim that MBNA's business model will be threatened by opt in. This business model relies in part, however, on sending out 400 million of mostly unwanted solicitations for credit in order to receive a 0.6 percent response rate. In other words, this model views as an externality the added cost of sorting through mail for 99.4 percent of those individuals solicited. Should MBNA be obliged to internalize these costs?

3. *Does Privacy-Self Management Work?* Privacy policies form the backbone of what Daniel Solove calls "privacy self-management" where the law seeks to foster people's ability to make choices about their personal data. The privacy policy describes the ways that a business will collect, use, and share personal data, and people can either consent to these practices or not engage in transactions with businesses whose practices they do not find acceptable. Solove finds severe problems with this approach:

> Although privacy self-management is certainly a laudable and necessary component of any regulatory regime, I contend that it is being tasked with doing work beyond its capabilities. Privacy self-management does not provide people with meaningful control over their data. First, empirical and social science research demonstrates that there are severe cognitive problems that undermine privacy self-management. These cognitive problems impair individuals' ability to make informed, rational choices about the costs and

benefits of consenting to the collection, use, and disclosure of their personal data.

Second, and more troubling, even well-informed and rational individuals cannot appropriately self-manage their privacy due to several structural problems. There are too many entities collecting and using personal data to make it feasible for people to manage their privacy separately with each entity. Moreover, many privacy harms are the result of an aggregation of pieces of data over a period of time by different entities. It is virtually impossible for people to weigh the costs and benefits of revealing information or permitting its use or transfer without an understanding of the potential downstream uses, further limiting the effectiveness of the privacy self-management framework.[35]

4. **Visceral Notice.** Ryan Calo argues that policymakers should explore "innovative new ways to deliver privacy notice." He contends that notice can be made more "visceral" so that people are more aware of it and understand it better. For example, a "regulation might require that a cell phone camera make a shutter sound so people know their photo is being taken."[36] Can you think of ways that privacy notices might be made more visceral? Would visceral notice address the problems that Solove has identified?

As a related approach, there has been a discussion about "just-in-time" notice. A Staff Report from the FTC has noticed that "a disclosure (*e.g.*, "why did I get this ad?") located in close proximity to an advertisement and links to the pertinent section of a privacy policy explaining how data is collected for purposes of delivering targeted advertising, could be an effective way to communicate with consumers."[37] Is "just-in-time" notice a promising approach?

2. CONTRACT AND PROMISSORY ESTOPPEL

A privacy policy can be thought of as a type of contract, though the terms are typically dictated by the company and are non-negotiable. Consider the following advice of Scott Killingsworth to the drafters of website privacy policies:

Considering enforcement leads to the question: what is the legal effect of a privacy policy? As between the website and the user, a privacy policy bears all of the earmarks of a contract, but perhaps one enforceable only at the option of the user. It is no stretch to regard the policy as an offer to treat information in specified ways, inviting the user's acceptance, evidenced by using the site or submitting the information. The website's promise and the user's use of the site and submission of personal data are each sufficient consideration to support a contractual obligation. Under this analysis, users would have the right to sue and

---

[35] Daniel J. Solove, *Privacy Self-Management and the Consent Dilemma,* 126 Harv. L. Rev. 1880 (2013).

[36] *See* M. Ryan Calo, *Against Notice Skepticism in Privacy (and Elsewhere),* 87 Notre Dame L. Rev. 1027 (2012).

[37] FTC Staff Report, *Self-Regulatory Principles for Online Behavioral Advertising* 35-36 (Feb. 12, 2009).

seek all available remedies for breach of the privacy policy, without the need for private rights of action under such regulatory statutes as the FTC Act.[38]

Privacy policies can also be viewed simply as notices that warn consumers about the use of their personal information. Assuming that these notices are subject to change as business practices evolve, how effective are privacy policies as a means to protect privacy?

IN RE NORTHWEST AIRLINES PRIVACY LITIGATION

2004 WL 1278459 (D. Minn. 2004) (not reported in F. Supp. 2d)

MAGNUSON, J. . . . . Plaintiffs are customers of Defendant Northwest Airlines, Inc. ("Northwest"). After September 11, 2001, the National Aeronautical and Space Administration ("NASA") requested that Northwest provide NASA with certain passenger information in order to assist NASA in studying ways to increase airline security. Northwest supplied NASA with passenger name records ("PNRs"), which are electronic records of passenger information. PNRs contain information such as a passenger's name, flight number, credit card data, hotel reservation, car rental, and any traveling companions.

Plaintiffs contend that Northwest's actions constitute violations of the Electronic Communications Privacy Act ("ECPA"), 18 U.S.C. § 2701 *et seq.*, the Fair Credit Reporting Act ("FCRA"), 15 U.S.C. § 1681, and Minnesota's Deceptive Trade Practices Act ("DTPA"), Minn. Stat. § 325D.44, and also constitute invasion of privacy, trespass to property, negligent misrepresentation, breach of contract, and breach of express warranties. The basis for most of Plaintiffs' claims is that Northwest's website contained a privacy policy that stated that Northwest would not share customers' information except as necessary to make customers' travel arrangements. Plaintiffs contend that Northwest's provision of PNRs to NASA violated Northwest's privacy policy, giving rise to the legal claims noted above.

Northwest has now moved to dismiss the Amended Consolidated Class Action Complaint (hereinafter "Amended Complaint"). . . .

The ECPA prohibits a person or entity from

(1) intentionally access[ing] without authorization a facility through which an electronic communication service is provided; or

(2) intentionally exceeds an authorization to access that facility; and thereby obtains, alters, or prevents authorized access to a wire or electronic communication while it is in electronic storage in such system shall be punished. 18 U.S.C. § 2701(a).

Plaintiffs argue that Northwest's access to its own electronic communications service is limited by its privacy policy, and that Northwest's provision of PNRs to NASA violated that policy and thus constituted unauthorized access to the "facility through which an electronic communication service is provided" within the meaning of this section. Plaintiffs also allege that Northwest violated § 2702

---

[38] Scott Killingsworth, *Minding Your Own Business: Privacy Policies in Principle and in Practice*, 7 J. Intell. Prop. L. 57, 91-92 (1999).

of the ECPA, which states that "a person or entity providing an electronic communications service to the public shall not knowingly divulge to any person or entity the contents of a communication while in electronic storage by that service." 18 U.S.C. § 2702(a)(1). Northwest argues first that it cannot violate § 2702 because it is not a "person or entity providing an electronic communications service to the public." . . .

Defining electronic communications service to include online merchants or service providers like Northwest stretches the ECPA too far. Northwest is not an internet service provider. . . .

Similarly, Northwest's conduct as outlined in the Amended Complaint does not constitute a violation of § 2701. Plaintiffs' claim is that Northwest improperly disclosed the information in PNRs to NASA. Section 2701 does not prohibit improper disclosure of information. Rather, this section prohibits improper access to an electronic communications service provider or the information contained on that service provider. . . .

Finally, Northwest argues that Plaintiffs' remaining claims fail to state a claim on which relief can be granted. These claims are: trespass to property, intrusion upon seclusion, breach of contract, and breach of express warranties.

To state a claim for trespass to property, Plaintiffs must demonstrate that they owned or possessed property, that Northwest wrongfully took that property, and that Plaintiffs were damaged by the wrongful taking. Plaintiffs contend that the information contained in the PNRs was Plaintiffs' property and that, by providing that information to NASA, Northwest wrongfully took that property.

As a matter of law, the PNRs were not Plaintiffs' property. Plaintiffs voluntarily provided some information that was included in the PNRs. It may be that the information Plaintiffs provided to Northwest was Plaintiffs' property. However, when that information was compiled and combined with other information to form a PNR, the PNR itself became Northwest's property. Northwest cannot wrongfully take its own property. Thus, Plaintiffs' claim for trespass fails. . . .

Intrusion upon seclusion exists when someone "intentionally intrudes, physically or otherwise, upon the solitude or seclusion of another or his private affairs or concerns . . . if the intrusion would be highly offensive to a reasonable person." . . . In this instance, Plaintiffs voluntarily provided their personal information to Northwest. Moreover, although Northwest had a privacy policy for information included on the website, Plaintiffs do not contend that they actually read the privacy policy prior to providing Northwest with their personal information. Thus, Plaintiffs' expectation of privacy was low. Further, the disclosure here was not to the public at large, but rather was to a government agency in the wake of a terrorist attack that called into question the security of the nation's transportation system. Northwest's motives in disclosing the information cannot be questioned. Taking into account all of the factors listed above, the Court finds as a matter of law that the disclosure of Plaintiffs' personal information would not be highly offensive to a reasonable person and that Plaintiffs have failed to state a claim for intrusion upon seclusion. . . .

Northwest contends that the privacy policy on Northwest's website does not, as a matter of law, constitute a unilateral contract, the breach of which entitles Plaintiffs to damages. Northwest also argues that, even if the privacy policy constituted a contract or express warranty, Plaintiffs' contract and warranty claims fail because Plaintiffs have failed to plead any contract damages. . . .

Plaintiffs' rely on the following statement from Northwest's website as the basis for their contract and warranty claims:

> When you reserve or purchase travel services through Northwest Airlines nwa.com Reservations, we provide only the relevant information required by the car rental agency, hotel, or other involved third party to ensure the successful fulfillment of your travel arrangements. . . .

The usual rule in contract cases is that "general statements of policy are not contractual." . . .

The privacy statement on Northwest's website did not constitute a unilateral contract. The language used vests discretion in Northwest to determine when the information is "relevant" and which "third parties" might need that information. Moreover, absent an allegation that Plaintiffs actually read the privacy policy, not merely the general allegation that Plaintiffs "relied on" the policy, Plaintiffs have failed to allege an essential element of a contract claim: that the alleged "offer" was accepted by Plaintiffs. Plaintiffs' contract and warranty claims fail as a matter of law.

Even if the privacy policy was sufficiently definite and Plaintiffs had alleged that they read the policy before giving their information to Northwest, it is likely that Plaintiffs' contract and warranty claims would fail as a matter of law. Defendants point out that Plaintiffs have failed to allege any contractual damages arising out of the alleged breach. . . .

[The case is dismissed.]

NOTES & QUESTIONS

1. ***Breach of Contract.*** In *Dyer v. Northwest Airlines Corp.*, 334 F. Supp. 2d 1196 (D.N.D. 2004), another action involving Northwest Airlines' disclosure of passenger records to the government, the court reached a similar conclusion on the plaintiffs' breach of contract claim:

   > To sustain a breach of contract claim, the Plaintiffs must demonstrate (1) the existence of a contract; (2) breach of the contract; and (3) damages which flow from the breach. . . .
   >   . . . [T]he Court finds the Plaintiffs' breach of contract claim fails as a matter of law. First, broad statements of company policy do not generally give rise to contract claims. . . . Second, nowhere in the complaint are the Plaintiffs alleged to have ever logged onto Northwest Airlines' website and accessed, read, understood, actually relied upon, or otherwise considered Northwest Airlines' privacy policy. Finally, even if the privacy policy was sufficiently definite and the Plaintiffs had alleged they did read the policy prior to providing personal information to Northwest Airlines, the Plaintiffs have failed to allege any contractual damages arising out of the alleged breach.

2. ***Damages.*** In *In re Jet Blue Airways Corp. Privacy Litigation*, 379 F. Supp. 2d 299 (E.D.N.Y. 2005), a group of plaintiffs sued Jet Blue Airlines for breach of

contract for sharing passenger records with the government. The court granted Jet Blue's motion to dismiss:

> An action for breach of contract under New York law requires proof of four elements: (1) the existence of a contract, (2) performance of the contract by one party, (3) breach by the other party, and (4) damages. . . .
>
> JetBlue . . . argues that plaintiffs have failed to meet their pleading requirement with respect to damages, citing an absence of any facts in the Amended Complaint to support this element of the claim. Plaintiffs' sole allegation on the element of contract damages consists of the statement that JetBlue's breach of the company privacy policy injured plaintiffs and members of the class and that JetBlue is therefore liable for "actual damages in an amount to be determined at trial." . . . At oral argument, when pressed to identify the "injuries" or damages referred to in the Amended Complaint, counsel for plaintiffs stated that the "contract damage could be the loss of privacy," acknowledging that loss of privacy "may" be a contract damage. It is apparent based on the briefing and oral argument held in this case that the sparseness of the damages allegations is a direct result of plaintiffs' inability to plead or prove any actual contract damages. As plaintiffs' counsel concedes, the only damage that can be read into the present complaint is a loss of privacy. At least one recent case has specifically held that this is not a damage available in a breach of contract action. *See Trikas v. Universal Card Services Corp.,* 351 F. Supp. 2d 37 (E.D.N.Y. 2005). This holding naturally follows from the well-settled principle that "recovery in contract, unlike recovery in tort, allows only for economic losses flowing directly from the breach."
>
> Plaintiffs allege that in a second amended complaint, they could assert as a contract damage the loss of the economic value of their information, but while that claim sounds in economic loss, the argument ignores the nature of the contract asserted. . . . [T]he "purpose of contract damages is to put a plaintiff in the same economic position he or she would have occupied had the contract been fully performed." Plaintiffs may well have expected that in return for providing their personal information to JetBlue and paying the purchase price, they would obtain a ticket for air travel and the promise that their personal information would be safeguarded consistent with the terms of the privacy policy. They had no reason to expect that they would be compensated for the "value" of their personal information. In addition, there is absolutely no support for the proposition that the personal information of an individual JetBlue passenger had any value for which that passenger could have expected to be compensated. . . . There is likewise no support for the proposition that an individual passenger's personal information has or had any compensable value in the economy at large.

If you were the plaintiffs' attorney, how would you go about establishing the plaintiffs' injury? Is there any cognizable harm when an airline violates its privacy policy by providing passenger information to the government?

3. *Promissory Estoppel.* Under the Restatement (Second) of Contracts § 90:

> A promise which the promisor should reasonably expect to induce action or forbearance on the part of the promisee or a third person and which does induce such action or forbearance is binding if injustice can be avoided only

by enforcement of the promise. The remedy granted for breach may be limited as justice requires.

If website privacy policies are not deemed to be contracts, can they be enforced under the promissory estoppel doctrine?

4. *Breach of Confidentiality Tort.* Would the plaintiffs have a cause of action based on the breach of confidentiality tort?

5. *Enforcing Privacy Policies as Contracts Against Consumers.* Suppose privacy policies were enforceable as contracts. Would this be beneficial to consumers? It might not be, Allyson Haynes argues:

> [T]here is a distinct possibility that as website operators grow savvier with respect to the law, they will respond to the lack of substantive privacy protection (and lack of consumer awareness) by including in privacy policies terms that are not favorable to consumers.

On the flip side of consumers seeking to enforce privacy policies as contracts, companies might also desire to hold customers to be contractually bound to the companies' privacy policies. Would a privacy policy be enforceable as a contract against the customer? Haynes contends:

> [P]articularly in cases where consumers are deemed to have assented to privacy policies by virtue of their presence on the site or by giving information without affirmatively clicking acceptance, the consumer has a good argument that he or she did not assent to the privacy policy, preventing the formation of a binding contract, and preventing the website from enforcing any of its terms against the consumer.[39]

6. *Standing in Misrepresentation Claims.* In *In re iPhone Application Litigation*, 2013 WL 6212591 (N.D. Cal. Nov. 25, 2013), plaintiffs sued Apple in a class action alleging, among other things, that Apple made misrepresentations about iPhone privacy:

> Plaintiffs claim that they relied upon Apple's representations about privacy and data collection in purchasing their iPhones. In light of Apple's statements about protecting users' privacy, Plaintiffs did not consent to the App developers transmitting Plaintiffs' information to third parties. Plaintiffs assert that as a result of Apple's misrepresentations regarding its privacy and data collection practices, Plaintiffs both overpaid for their iPhones and suffered diminishment to their iPhones' battery, bandwidth, and storage "resources."

Some of the statements Apple made in its privacy policy included:

> Your privacy is important to Apple. So we've developed a Privacy Policy that covers how we collect, use, disclose, transfer, and store your information. . . .

> To make sure your personal information is secure, we communicate our privacy and security guidelines to Apple employees and strictly enforce privacy safeguards within the company. . . .

---

[39] Allyson W. Haynes, *Online Privacy Policies: Contracting Away Control Over Personal Information?*, 111 Penn. St. L. Rev. 587, 612, 618 (2007).

Apple takes precautions—including administrative, technical, and physical measures—to safeguard your personal information against loss, theft, and misuse as well as against unauthorized access, disclosure, alteration, and destruction. . . .

The court held:

While the iDevice Plaintiffs identify numerous purported misrepresentations and argue that they relied on them in purchasing their iPhones the evidentiary record is devoid of "specific facts" to support Plaintiffs' assertions. Critically, *none* of the Plaintiffs presents evidence that he or she even saw, let alone read and relied upon, the alleged misrepresentations contained in the Apple Privacy Policies . . . or App Store Terms and Conditions, either prior to purchasing his or her iPhone, or at any time thereafter.

In their depositions, Plaintiffs either could not recall having read any of these policies (or any other Apple representation) in connection with obtaining their iPhones, or expressly disavowed having read any Apple policy, or anything else about the iPhone, prior to purchasing one.

The court further reasoned:

First, Plaintiffs suggest that standing is established as long as a plaintiff "receives" a misrepresentation. The implication of this argument seems to be that a plaintiff can show standing as long as the defendant has disseminated the alleged misrepresentation to her in some fashion, regardless of whether the plaintiff ever actually sees, reads, or hears the defendant's statement. The Court questions how one can act in reliance on a statement one does not see, read, or hear. . . .

Second, Plaintiffs argue that the Court should infer reliance from the fact that Plaintiffs had iTunes accounts and therefore had to, at some point, agree to Apple's Terms and Conditions and Privacy Policy. . . . [B]y virtue of having active iTunes accounts, Plaintiffs would have been asked to agree to Apple's updated Privacy Policy at some point during the class period. . . . Plaintiffs ask the Court to infer that Plaintiffs must have read and relied on misrepresentations contained in Apple's Privacy Policy at some point during the class period.

There are two problems with this theory. Most critically, it has no evidentiary support. No Plaintiff, in either a deposition or declaration, identified an Apple Privacy Policy as the source of his or her "understanding" regarding Apple's policies concerning privacy and data collection. . . .

What is more, the mere fact that Plaintiffs had to scroll through a screen and click on a box stating that they agreed with the Apple Privacy Policy in July 2010 does not establish, standing alone, that Plaintiffs actually read the alleged misrepresentations contained in that Privacy Policy, let alone that these misrepresentations subsequently formed the basis for Plaintiffs' "understanding" regarding Apple's privacy practices. Accordingly, the existence of Plaintiffs' iTunes accounts does not, *by itself,* demonstrate that Plaintiffs actually read and relied on any misrepresentations contained in the updated Privacy Policy from July 2010.

7. ***Promises of Anonymity.*** In *Saffold v. Plain Dealer Publishing Co.,* a state court judge (Shirley Strickland Saffold) sued the *Cleveland Plain Dealer* for stating that comments posted on the newspaper's website under the screen

name "lawmiss" originated from a computer used by the judge and her daughter. Some of these comments related to cases before Judge Saffold. Judge Saffold claimed that the newspaper's disclosure of the identity of "lawmiss" violated its website's privacy policy, which stated that "personally identifiable information is protected." Moreover, the user agreement that was part of the registration process to create an account on the website incorporated the privacy policy. The case was settled before any judicial decision was issued. Suppose, however, the litigation had proceeded. Would Judge Saffold have a claim for breach of contract or promissory estoppel?

8. *Website Communities and Promissory Estoppel.* Consider Woodrow Hartzog:

> Suppose a person improperly provides others with access to a friend's Facebook profile. Suppose a member of a dating website copies another's dating profile and discloses the information to the general public. Or suppose a member of an online support community for recovering alcoholics reveals the names and other personal information of other members. Should members of an online community be able to expect and legally enforce the confidentiality of their data? . . .
>
> I contend that the law can ensure confidentiality for members of online communities through promissory estoppel. . . .
>
> One of the immediate difficulties with using promissory estoppel is that members of online communities have not made agreements between each other. They have merely agreed to the terms of use of the website and community. Suppose Member A of an online community discloses the private information of Member B. Would Member B be able to sue Member A for promissory estoppel even though Member A never made a direct promise to Member B?
>
> In order to allow all users within the community the ability to rely on promises of confidentiality, I propose application of either the third-party beneficiary doctrine or the concept of dual agency effectuated through a website's terms of use. Although the implementation of promissory estoppel in this context would be challenging, I conclude that the promissory estoppel theory for confidential disclosure could have positive practical effects and advance both privacy and free speech objectives.[40]

What are the pros and cons of Hartzog's proposal? Should members of online communities have any obligations to each other?

9. *Are Website Privacy Settings Part of a Contract?* Woodrow Hartzog contends that website privacy settings and other design features should be considered as part of the contract between the website and the user:

> When courts seek to determine a website user's privacy expectations and the website's promises to that user, they almost invariably look to the terms of use agreement or to the privacy policy. They rarely look to the privacy settings or other elements of a website where users specify their privacy preferences. These settings and elements are typically not considered to be part of any contract or promise to the user. Yet studies have shown that few users actually

---

[40] Woodrow Hartzog, *Promises and Privacy: Promissory Estoppel and Confidential Disclosure in Online Communities*, 82 Temp. L. Rev. 891, 893-96 (2009).

read or rely upon terms of service or privacy policies. In contrast, users regularly take advantage of and rely upon privacy settings. . . . [T]o the extent website design is incorporated into or consistent with a website's terms of use, or to the extent website design induces reliance, courts should consider these design features as enforceable promises.[41]

Facebook and other social media websites, for example, have privacy settings that allow users to establish how broadly their information will be shared. If Facebook were to expose a person's information more broadly than he set it in his privacy settings, could that be the basis of a contract or promissory estoppel lawsuit? What other design elements might be considered to be part of a website's contract or promise with a user?

10. **Contract and Morality.** In Canada, Gabrielle Nagy sued her cellphone company, Rogers Communications, for breach of contract when it incorporated her cell phone bill into the family phone bill. The result was that her husband discovered that she was frequently calling another man. Nagy eventually confessed to her husband that she was having an affair, and they divorced. Consider David Hoffman:

> I think the breach of contract lawsuit, if filed in an American court applying fairly ordinary domestic contract principles, would be a loser. . . .
>
> The common law generally dislikes punishing breach with liability or damages when the inevitable consequence of performance is to motivate socially wrongful conduct, and nonperformance to retard it. . . .
>
> What about cases where A and B contract not to disclose some fact X, and the nondisclosure will create harm for innocent third parties. These contracts are often enforced (every confidentiality clause probably shelters some fact with the potential for third party harm). But the degree to which the nonbreaching party can recover ought to turn on what's being kept secret: if the secret is particularly socially harmful (oozing toxic sludge!) we might believe that the hiding, non-breaching, party doesn't get to recover for breach. Thus, you sometimes see cases where fraud-revealing employees are protected from consequences of nondisclosure agreements by (effectively) common law whistleblower doctrines.
>
> Where the third-party harm *relates to marriage*, the law appears to be more categorical. Public policy concerns about contracting and third party harm are strongest in agreements touching on issues of family life and infidelity.[42]

Is Hoffman correct that such a breach of contract case would lose under American law? Should courts choose which contracts to enforce based on morality? If a company breaches a contract and reveals that a person is doing something immoral, should that breach go unremedied?

11. **Interpreting Promises.** In *In re iPhone Application Litigation*, 844 F. Supp. 2d 1040 (N.D. Cal. June 12, 2012), plaintiffs sued Apple for the practices of third-party apps. Apple argued that its Privacy Policy and Terms of Use disclaimed liability from third-party conduct. However, the court concluded:

---

[41] Woodrow Hartzog, *Website Design as Contract,* 60 Am. U. L. Rev. 1635 (2011).

[42] David Hoffman, *Contracts and Privacy,* Concurring Opinions (June 21, 2010), http://www.concurringopinions.com/archives/2010/06/contracts-and-privacy.html.

Additionally, to the extent that Apple argues that it has no duty to review or evaluate apps and that it has disclaimed any liability arising from the actions of third parties, this argument both ignores contradictory statements made by Apple itself, and the allegations asserted by Plaintiffs regarding Apple's own conduct with respect to the alleged privacy violations. For one, it is not clear that Apple disclaimed all responsibility for privacy violations because, while Apple claimed not to have any liability or responsibility for any third party materials, websites or services, Apple also made affirmative representations that it takes precautions to protect consumer privacy. Additionally, Plaintiffs' allegations go beyond asserting that Apple had a duty to review or police third party apps. Instead, Plaintiffs allege Apple was responsible for providing user's information to third parties. Plaintiffs allege that Apple is independently liable for any statutory violations that have occurred. At the motion to dismiss stage, then, the Court is not prepared to rule that the Agreement establishes an absolute bar to Plaintiffs' claims.

The court recognized that increased security risks and lessened device resources (storage, battery life, and bandwidth) from third-party apps could constitute concrete injuries.

Should a more general statement that a company protects privacy override more specific statements such as disclaiming responsibility for third-party apps? Or should the more specific statements govern over the more general ones? Suppose a company's founder in an interview states: "We care deeply about our the privacy of our customers and protect it zealously." Could this trump a statement in the privacy policy that allows personal data to be shared with third parties unless people opt out?

12. *The Cost of "Free."* Many online services, such as Google and Facebook, are free. Chris Hoofnagle and Jan Whittington argue that these services are not really free:

> [C]onceiving of transactions as free can harm both consumers and competition. These exchanges often carry a hidden charge: the forfeit of one's personal information. The service provider may expect to earn revenues from the personal information collected about consumers who devote their attention to advertising and other services, such as games, from third parties. The more time the consumer spends using the service and revealing information, the more the service can adjust the product to reveal more information about the consumer and tailor its advertising of products to that consumer's personal information.[43]

Hoofnagle and Wittington contend that many "information-intensive companies misuse the term 'free' to promote products and services that incur myriad hidden, nonpecuniary costs." What are the implications of recognizing that consumers are paying a price for sharing their personal data? To what extent does this fact affect contract law analysis when it comes to privacy policies?

---

[43] Chris Jay Hoofnagle and Jan Whittington, *Free: Accounting for the Costs of the Internet's Most Popular Price*, 61 UCLA L. Rev. 606 (2014).

D. PROPERTY LAW

A number of commentators propose that privacy can be protected by restructuring the property rights that people have in personal information. For example, according to Richard Murphy, personal information "like all information, is property." He goes on to conclude:

> . . . [I]n many instances, privacy rules are in fact implied contractual terms. To the extent that information is generated through a voluntary transaction, imposing nondisclosure obligations on the recipient of the information may be the best approach for certain categories of information. The value that information has ex post is of secondary importance; the primary question is what is the efficient contractual rule. Common-law courts are increasingly willing to impose an implied contractual rule of nondisclosure for many categories of transactions, including those with attorneys, medical providers, bankers, and accountants. Many statutes can also be seen in this light — that is, as default rules of privacy. And an argument can be made for the efficiency of a privacy default rule in the generic transaction between a merchant and a consumer.[44]

Lawrence Lessig also contends that privacy should be protected with property rights. He notes that "[p]rivacy now is protected through liability rules — if you invade someone's privacy, they can sue you and you must then pay." A "liability regime allows a taking, and payment later." In contrast, a property regime gives "control, and power, to the person holding the property right." Lessig argues: "When you have a property right, before someone takes your property they must negotiate with you about how much it is worth."[45]

Jerry Kang proposes a type of fusion between property and contract regulation when he proposes that there be a default rule that individuals retain control over information they surrender during Internet transactions. He contends that this default rule is more efficient than a default rule where companies can use the data as they see fit. The default rule that Kang proposes could be bargained around: "With this default, if the firm valued personal data more than the individual, then the firm would have to buy permission to process the data in functionally unnecessary ways."[46] In essence, Kang is creating a property right in personal data, and people could sell the right to use it to companies.

Other commentators critique the translation of privacy into a form of property right that can be bartered and sold. For example, Katrin Schatz Byford argues that viewing "privacy as an item of trade . . . values privacy only to the extent it is considered to be of personal worth by the individual who claims it." She further contends: "Such a perspective plainly conflicts with the notion that privacy is a collective value and that privacy intrusions at the individual level necessarily have broader social implications because they affect access to social power and stifle public participation."[47]

---

[44] Richard S. Murphy, *Property Rights in Personal Information: An Economic Defense of Privacy*, 84 Geo. L.J. 2381, 2416-17 (1996).

[45] Lawrence Lessig, *Code and Other Laws of Cyberspace* (1999).

[46] Jerry Kang, *Information Privacy in Cyberspace Transactions*, 50 Stan. L. Rev. 1193 (1998).

[47] Katrin Schatz Byford, *Privacy in Cyberspace: Constructing a Model of Privacy for the Electronic Communications Environment*, 24 Rutgers Computer & Tech. L.J. 1 (1998). For an

Consider Pamela Samuelson's argument as to why property rights are inadequate to protect privacy:

> . . . Achieving information privacy goals through a property rights system may be difficult for reasons other than market complexities. Chief among them is the difficulty with alienability of personal information. It is a common, if not ubiquitous, characteristic of property rights systems that when the owner of a property right sells her interest to another person, that buyer can freely transfer to third parties whatever interest the buyer acquired from her initial seller. Free alienability works very well in the market for automobiles and land, but it is far from clear that it will work well for information privacy. . . . Collectors of data may prefer a default rule allowing them to freely transfer personal data to whomever they wish on whatever terms they can negotiate with their future buyers. However, individuals concerned with information privacy will generally want a default rule prohibiting retransfer of the data unless separate permission is negotiated. They will also want any future recipient to bind itself to the same constraints that the initial purchaser of the data may have agreed to as a condition of sale. Information privacy goals may not be achievable unless the default rule of the new property rights regime limits transferability. . . .
>
> . . . From a civil liberties perspective, propertizing personal information as a way of achieving information privacy goals may seem an anathema. Not only might it be viewed as an unnecessary and possibly dangerous way to achieve information privacy goals, it might be considered morally obnoxious. If information privacy is a civil liberty, it may make no more sense to propertize personal data than to commodify voting rights. . . .[48]

Daniel Solove also counsels against protecting privacy as a form of property right because the "market approach has difficulty assigning the proper value to personal information":

> . . . [T]he aggregation problem severely complicates the valuation process. An individual may give out bits of information in different contexts, each transfer appearing innocuous. However, the information can be aggregated and could prove to be invasive of the private life when combined with other information. It is the totality of information about a person and how it is used that poses the greatest threat to privacy. As Julie Cohen notes, "[a] comprehensive collection of data about an individual is vastly more than the sum of its parts." From the standpoint of each particular information transaction, individuals will not have enough facts to make a truly informed decision. The potential future uses of that information are too vast and unknown to enable individuals to make the appropriate valuation. . . .
>
> [Property rights] cannot work effectively in a situation where the power relationship and information distribution between individuals and public and private bureaucracies is so greatly unbalanced. In other words, the problem with market solutions is not merely that it is difficult to commodify information (which it is), but also that a regime of default rules alone (consisting of property

---

argument about the problems of commodifying certain goods and of viewing all human conduct in light of the market metaphor, see Margaret Jane Radin, *Contested Commodities* (1996).

[48] Pamela Samuelson, *Privacy as Intellectual Property?*, 52 Stan. L. Rev. 1125, 1137-47 (2000).

rights in information and contractual defaults) will not enable fair and equitable market transactions in personal information. . . .[49]

In contrast to these skeptics, Paul Schwartz develops a model of propertized personal data that would help fashion a market for data trade that would respect individual privacy and help maintain a democratic order. Schwartz calls for "limitations on an individual's right to alienate personal information; default rules that force disclosure of the terms of trade; a right of exit for participants in the market; the establishment of damages to deter market abuses; and institutions to police the personal information market and punish privacy violations." In his judgment, a key element of this model is its approach of "hybrid inalienability" in which a law allows individuals to share their personal information, but also places limitations on future use of the information. Schwartz explains:

This hybrid consists of a use-transferability restriction plus an opt-in default. In practice, it would permit the transfer for an initial category of use of personal data, but only if the customer is granted an opportunity to block further transfer or use by unaffiliated entities. Any further use or transfer would require the customer to opt in — that is, it would be prohibited unless the customer affirmatively agrees to it.

As an initial example concerning compensated telemarketing, a successful pitch for Star Trek memorabilia would justify the use of personal data by the telemarketing company and the transfer of it both to process the order and for other related purposes. Any outside use or unrelated transfers of this information would, however, require obtaining further permission from the individual. Note that this restriction limits the alienability of individuals' personal information by preventing them from granting one-stop permission for all use or transfer of their information. A data processor's desire to carry out further transfers thus obligates the processor to supply additional information and provides another chance for the individual to bargain with the data collector. . . .

To ensure that the opt-in default leads to meaningful disclosure of additional information, however, two additional elements are needed. First, the government must have a significant role in regulating the way that notice of privacy practices is provided. As noted above, a critical issue will be the "frame" in which information about data processing is presented. . . .

Second, meaningful disclosure requires addressing what Henry Hansmann and Reinier Kraakman term "verification problems." Their scholarship points to the critical condition that third parties must be able to verify that a given piece of personal information has in fact been propertized and then identify the specific rules that apply to it. As they explain, "[a] verification rule sets out the conditions under which a given right in a given asset will run with the asset." In the context of propertized personal information, the requirement for verification creates a role for nonpersonal metadata, a tag or kind of barcode, to provide necessary background information and notice.[50]

---

[49] Daniel J. Solove, *Privacy and Power: Computer Databases and Metaphors for Information Privacy*, 53 Stan. L. Rev. 1393 (2001).

[50] Paul M. Schwartz, *Property, Privacy and Personal Data*, 117 Harv. L. Rev. 2055, 2056, 2098-99 (2004). *See also* Vera Bergelson, *It's Personal But Is It Mine? Toward Property Rights in Personal Information*, 37 U.C. Davis L. Rev. 379 (2003) (although a collector may have rights in individuals' personal information, a property approach would correctly subordinate these rights to the rights of the individuals).

Finally, consider what Warren and Brandeis said about privacy as a property claim:

> The aim of [copyright] statutes is to secure to the author, composer, or artist the entire profits arising from publication. . . .
>
> But where the value of the production is found not in the right to take the profits arising from publication, but in the peace of mind or the relief afforded by the ability to prevent any publication at all, it is difficult to regard the right as one of property, in the common acceptation of that term.[51]

E. FTC SECTION 5 ENFORCEMENT

Beyond private law actions such as contract and promissory estoppel, the promises that companies make regarding their privacy practices can be enforced by the government through public law. Private law actions are initiated on behalf of harmed individuals, who can obtain monetary or other redress for their injuries. In contrast, public law actions are initiated by government agencies or officials, and they typically involve fines and penalties.

In 1995, Congress and privacy experts first asked the Federal Trade Commission (FTC) to become involved with consumer privacy issues. Since 1998, the FTC has maintained the position that the use or dissemination of personal information in a manner contrary to a posted privacy policy is a deceptive practice under the FTC Act, 15 U.S.C. § 45.

The Act prohibits "unfair or deceptive acts or practices in or affecting commerce." § 45(n).

Deception. A deceptive act or practice is a material "representation, omission or practice that is likely to mislead the consumer acting reasonably in the circumstances, to the consumer's detriment."[52]

Unfairness. The FTC Act classifies a trade practice as unfair if it "causes or is likely to cause substantial injury to consumers which is not reasonably avoidable by consumers themselves and is not outweighed by countervailing benefits to consumers or competition." 15 U.S.C. § 45(n). Actions of a company can be both deceptive and unfair.

The Scope of Section 5. Section 5 provides very broad jurisdiction to the FTC. However, the FTC does not have jurisdiction over all companies. Exempt from the FTC's jurisdiction are many types of financial institutions, airlines, telecommunications carriers, and other types of entities. § 45(a)(2). Additionally, non-profit institutions such as schools are often not covered.

---

[51] Samuel Warren & Louis Brandeis, *The Right to Privacy*, 4 Harv. L. Rev. 193 (1890).

[52] Letter from James C. Miller III, Chairman, FTC, to Hon. John D. Dingell, Chairman, House Comm. on Energy & Commerce (Oct. 14, 1983).

The FTC's Structure. The FTC is headed by five commissioners, who are appointed by the President and confirmed by the Senate. They each serve a seven-year term. The commissioners must be a bipartisan group — no more than three can be members of the same political party. One of the commissioners is designated by the President as chairman.

Enforcement. The FTC can obtain injunctive remedies. § 53. The Act does not provide for private causes of action; only the FTC can enforce the Act. The FTC does not have the ability to issue fines for violations of Section 5, but the FTC can issue fines when companies violate a consent decree previously entered into for a violation of Section 5.

Rulemaking. The FTC lacks practical rulemaking authority under Section 5. The FTC has only Magnuson-Moss rulemaking authority, which is highly burdensome as a procedural matter. According to Beth DeSimone and Amy Mudge:

> Right now, the FTC is constrained in its rulemaking by the so-called "Magnuson-Moss" rules. These rules require the FTC Staff to engage in an industry-wide investigation, prepare draft staff reports, propose a rule, and engage in a series of public hearings, including cross-examination opportunities prior to issuing a final rule in any area. These processes are so burdensome that the FTC has not engaged in a Magnuson-Moss rule-making in 32 years.[53]

The Growing Role of the FTC. Since it began enforcing the FTC Act for breaches of privacy policies in 1998, the FTC has brought a number of actions, most of which have settled. The FTC has brought about 170 privacy and data security actions under Section 5, averaging about 10 per year, though the number per year has increased throughout the years.

According to Daniel Solove and Woodrow Hartzog:

> Despite over fifteen years of FTC enforcement, there are hardly any judicial decisions to show for it. The cases have nearly all resulted in settlement agreements. Nevertheless, companies look to these agreements to guide their decisions regarding privacy practices. Those involved with helping businesses comply with privacy law—from chief privacy officers to inside counsel to outside counsel—parse and analyze the FTC's settlement agreements, reports, and activities as if they were pronouncements by the Chairman of the Federal Reserve. Thus, in practice, FTC privacy jurisprudence has become the broadest and most influential regulating force on information privacy in the United States—more so than nearly any privacy statute or common law tort.[54]

Companies that violate settlement orders are liable for a civil penalty of up to $16,000 for each violation. Injunctive or other equitable relief is also available.

---

[53] Beth DeSimone & Amy Mudge, *Is Congress Putting the FTC on Steroids?*, Seller Beware Blog, Arnold & Porter (Apr. 26, 2010), http://www.consumeradvertisinglawblog.com/2010/04/is-congress-putting-the-ftc-on-steroids.html.

[54] Daniel J. Solove & Woodrow Hartzog, *The FTC and the New Common Law of Privacy*, 114 Colum. L. Rev. 583, 585-86 (2014).

FTC Privacy Enforcement Beyond Section 5. Beyond Section 5, the FTC also enforces the Gramm-Leach-Bliley Act (GLBA) and the Children's Online Privacy Protection Act (COPPA). Additionally, it enforces the US-EU Safe Harbor Arrangement. The FTC used to be the primary enforcer of the Fair Credit Reporting Act (FCRA), but that responsibility has largely been passed to the Consumer Financial Protection Bureau (CFPB). The FTC still retains some limited enforcement power over FCRA that is shared with CFPB. Although the FTC cannot issue fines under Section 5, it has the power to issue fines under the GLBA, COPPA, and FCRA.

IN THE MATTER OF SNAPCHAT, INC.

2014 WL 1993567 (FTC May 8, 2014)

COMPLAINT

The Federal Trade Commission, having reason to believe that Snapchat, Inc. ("respondent") has violated the provisions of the Federal Trade Commission Act, and it appearing to the Commission that this proceeding is in the public interest, alleges: . . . .

3. Snapchat provides a mobile application that allows consumers to send and receive photo and video messages known as "snaps." Before sending a snap, the application requires the sender to designate a period of time that the recipient will be allowed to view the snap. Snapchat markets the application as an "ephemeral" messaging application, having claimed that once the timer expires, the snap "disappears forever." . . .

6. Snapchat marketed its application as a service for sending "disappearing" photo and video messages, declaring that the message sender "control[s] how long your friends can view your message." Before sending a snap, the application requires the sender to designate a period of time — with the default set to a maximum of 10 seconds — that the recipient will be allowed to view the snap. . . .

8. From October 2012 to October 2013, Snapchat disseminated, or caused to be disseminated, to consumers the following statement on the "FAQ" page on its website:

Is there any way to view an image after the time has expired?

No, snaps disappear after the timer runs out. . . .

9. Despite these claims, several methods exist by which a recipient can use tools outside of the application to save both photo and video messages, allowing the recipient to access and view the photos or videos indefinitely.

10. For example, when a recipient receives a video message, the application stores the video file in a location outside of the application's "sandbox" (*i.e.*, the application's private storage area on the device that other applications cannot access). Because the file is stored in this unrestricted area, until October 2013, a recipient could connect his or her mobile device to a computer and use simple

file browsing tools to locate and save the video file. This method for saving video files sent through the application was widely publicized as early as December 2012. Snapchat did not mitigate this flaw until October 2013, when it began encrypting video files sent through the application.

11. Furthermore, third-party developers have built applications that can connect to Snapchat's application programming interface ("API"), thereby allowing recipients to log into the Snapchat service without using the official Snapchat application. Because the timer and related "deletion" functionality is dependent on the recipient's use of the official Snapchat application, recipients can instead simply use a third-party application to download and save both photo and video messages. As early as June 2012, a security researcher warned Snapchat that it would be "pretty easy to write a tool to download and save the images a user receives" due to the way the API functions. Indeed, beginning in spring 2013, third-party developers released several applications on the iTunes App Store and Google Play that recipients can use to save and view photo or video messages indefinitely. On Google Play alone, ten of these applications have been downloaded as many as 1.7 million times. . . .

13. In addition to the methods described in paragraphs 10-12, a recipient can use the mobile device's screenshot capability to capture an image of a snap while it appears on the device screen.

14. Snapchat claimed that if a recipient took a screenshot of a snap, the sender would be notified. On its product description pages, as described in paragraph 7, Snapchat stated: "We'll let you know if [recipients] take a screenshot!" In addition, from October 2012 to February 2013, Snapchat disseminated, or caused to be disseminated, to consumers the following statement on the "FAQ" page on its website:

> What if I take a screenshot?
>
> Screenshots can be captured if you're quick. The sender will be notified immediately.

15. However, recipients can easily circumvent Snapchat's screenshot detection mechanism. For example, on versions of iOS prior to iOS 7, the recipient need only double press the device's Home button in rapid succession to evade the detection mechanism and take a screenshot of any snap without the sender being notified. This method was widely publicized.

16. As described in Paragraphs 6, 7, and 8, Snapchat has represented, expressly or by implication, that when sending a message through its application, the message will disappear forever after the user-set time period expires.

17. In truth and in fact, as described in Paragraph 9-12, when sending a message through its application, the message may not disappear forever after the user-set time period expires. Therefore, the representation set forth in Paragraph 16 is false or misleading.

18. As described in Paragraphs 7 and 14, Snapchat has represented, expressly or by implication, that the sender will be notified if the recipient takes a screenshot of a snap.

19. In truth and in fact, as described in Paragraph 15, the sender may not be notified if the recipient takes a screenshot of a snap. Therefore, the representation set forth in Paragraph 18 is false or misleading. . . .

20. From June 2011 to February 2013, Snapchat disseminated or caused to be disseminated to consumers the following statements in its privacy policy:

> We do not ask for, track, or access any location-specific information from your device at any time while you are using the Snapchat application.

21. In October 2012, Snapchat integrated an analytics tracking service in the Android version of its application that acted as its service provider. While the Android operating system provided notice to consumers that the application may access location information, Snapchat did not disclose that it would, in fact, access location information, and continued to represent that Snapchat did "not ask for, track, or access any location-specific information . . . ."

22. Contrary to the representation in Snapchat's privacy policy, from October 2012 to February 2013, the Snapchat application on Android transmitted Wi-Fi-based and cell-based location information from users' mobile devices to its analytics tracking service provider.

23. As described in Paragraph 21, Snapchat has represented, expressly or by implication, that it does not collect users' location information.

24. In truth and in fact, as described in Paragraph 22, Snapchat did collect users' location information. Therefore, the representation set forth in Paragraph 23 is false or misleading. . . .

AGREEMENT CONTAINING CONSENT ORDER

The Federal Trade Commission ("Commission") has conducted an investigation of certain acts and practices of Snapchat, Inc. ("Snapchat" or "proposed respondent"). Proposed respondent, having been represented by counsel, is willing to enter into an agreement containing a consent order resolving the allegations contained in the attached draft complaint. Therefore,

IT IS HEREBY AGREED by and between Snapchat, Inc., by its duly authorized officers, and counsel for the Federal Trade Commission that: . . .

2. Proposed respondent neither admits nor denies any of the allegations in the draft complaint, except as specifically stated in this order. Only for purposes of this action, proposed respondent admits the facts necessary to establish jurisdiction. . . .

IT IS ORDERED that respondent and its officers, agents, representatives, and employees, directly or indirectly, shall not misrepresent in any manner, expressly or by implication, in or affecting commerce, the extent to which respondent or its products or services maintain and protect the privacy, security, or confidentiality of any covered information, including but not limited to: (1) the extent to which a message is deleted after being viewed by the recipient; (2) the extent to which respondent or its products or services are capable of detecting or notifying the sender when a recipient has captured a screenshot of, or otherwise saved, a message; (3) the categories of covered information collected; or (4) the steps taken to protect against misuse or unauthorized disclosure of covered information.

IT IS FURTHER ORDERED that respondent, in or affecting commerce, shall, no later than the date of service of this order, establish and implement, and thereafter maintain, a comprehensive privacy program that is reasonably designed to: (1) address privacy risks related to the development and management of new and existing products and services for consumers, and (2) protect the privacy and confidentiality of covered information, whether collected by respondent or input into, stored on, captured with, or accessed through a computer using respondent's products or services. Such program, the content and implementation of which must be fully documented in writing, shall contain privacy controls and procedures appropriate to respondent's size and complexity, the nature and scope of respondent's activities, and the sensitivity of the covered information, including:

A. the designation of an employee or employees to coordinate and be accountable for the privacy program;

B. the identification of reasonably foreseeable, material risks, both internal and external, that could result in the respondent's unauthorized collection, use, or disclosure of covered information, and assessment of the sufficiency of any safeguards in place to control these risks. At a minimum, this privacy risk assessment should include consideration of risks in each area of relevant operation, including, but not limited to: (1) employee training and management, including training on the requirements of this order; and (2) product design, development and research;

C. the design and implementation of reasonable privacy controls and procedures to address the risks identified through the privacy risk assessment, and regular testing or monitoring of the effectiveness of the privacy controls and procedures;

D. the development and use of reasonable steps to select and retain service providers capable of maintaining security practices consistent with this order, and requiring service providers by contract to implement and maintain appropriate safeguards;

E. the evaluation and adjustment of respondent's privacy program in light of the results of the testing and monitoring required by subpart C, any material changes to respondent's operations or business arrangements, or any other circumstances that respondent knows, or has reason to know, may have a material impact on the effectiveness of its privacy program.

IT IS FURTHER ORDERED that, in connection with its compliance with Part II of this order, respondent shall obtain initial and biennial assessments and reports ("Assessments") from a qualified, objective, independent third-party professional, who uses procedures and standards generally accepted in the profession. A person qualified to prepare such Assessments shall have a minimum of three (3) years of experience in the field of privacy and data protection. . . .

This order will terminate twenty (20) years from the date of its issuance. . . .

NOTES & QUESTIONS

1. *FTC Consent Decrees.* When FTC cases are settled, the complaint and consent decree are typically issued together. The complaint is not released during the investigation or settlement negotiations.

   FTC consent decrees often contain at least some of the following elements: (1) prohibition on the activities in violation of the FTC Act; (2) steps to remediate the problematic activities, such as software patches or notice to consumers; (3) deletion of wrongfully-obtained consumer data; (4) modifications to privacy policies; (5) establishment of a comprehensive privacy program, including risk assessment, appointment of a person to coordinate the program, and employee training, among other things; (6) biennial assessment reports by independent auditors; (7) recordkeeping to facilitate FTC enforcement of the order; (8) obligation to alert the FTC of any material changes in the company that might affect compliance obligations (such as mergers or bankruptcy filings).

2. *Types of Section 5 Privacy and Security Violations.* What are the types of cases the FTC brings? Under the "deception" prong of its authority, the FTC brings cases for broken promises of privacy, general deception, insufficient notice, and unreasonable data security practices. Under the "unfairness" prong, the FTC brings cases for retroactive changes to privacy policies, deceitful data collection, improper use of data, unfair design or unfair default settings, and unfair data security practices.[55]

3. *Broken Promises and Deception.* Snapchat represents a classic privacy deception case, where a company is found to be in violation of promises it makes in its privacy policy. Recall the definition of a deceptive practice: it is a material "representation, omission or practice that is likely to mislead the consumer acting reasonably in the circumstances, to the consumers' detriment." Can the FTC bring a deception action for statements that are not made in a company's privacy policy? Suppose the founder of a company states in an interview that her company will never provide consumer data to a third party. This statement contradicts the company's own privacy policy, which correctly indicates that the company does provide consumer to data to certain third parties. Could the founder's statement be the basis of an FTC action for deception?

4. *FTC Enforcement: A Slap on the Wrist?* The FTC does not have the power to issue fines under Section 5. The FTC can issue fines if enforcing other statutory regimes that permit such monetary sanctions, such as the GLBA.

   Does the FTC have sufficient enforcement teeth to deter companies from engaging in privacy violations. To what extent does the FTC's settlement with Snapchat require more than complying appropriately with the law in the future?

   Farhad Manjoo, in commenting on Snapchat notes that FTC consent agreements "have become something of a rite of passage for tech companies." He goes on to argue:

---

[55] Solove & Hartzog, *FTC and the New Common Law of Privacy, supra.*

But there is little evidence that these agreements have led to a wholesale shift in how tech companies handle private data. While the F.T.C. deals might push the companies to be more careful about privacy changes, being careful is not the same as being private. It's possible — and seems likely — that agreements with the government serve mainly to add a veneer of legitimacy over whatever moves the companies planned to make anyway.[56]

Manjoo also comments on a case when the FTC found that Google has violated a 2011 consent decree Google had made with the FTC. The FTC issued the largest-ever fine against a company. Manjoo writes:

> How much was that record-setting fine? $22.5 million. Note that in 2012, Google made a profit of $10.7 billion, most of it through advertising that was based in some way on data it collected from users. If you do the math, the agency's fine represented about 0 percent of Google's income that year.[57]

One aspect of the settlement to note is that the consent order lasts for 20 years. This is quite a long period of time. In comparison, an HHS consent order typically lasts for 1 to 3 years. Is 20 years too long? Or appropriate?

5. ***If People Do Not Read Privacy Policies, Why Enforce Them?*** Daniel Solove points out that people rarely read privacy policies:

> Most people do not read privacy notices on a regular basis. As for other types of notices, such as end-user license agreements and contract boilerplate terms, studies show only a miniscule percentage of people read them. Moreover, few people opt out of the collection, use, or disclosure of their data when presented with the choice to do so. Most people do not even bother to change the default privacy settings on websites.[58]

Why should the FTC enforce privacy policies if people do not read them? Solove points out that privacy policies are often difficult for consumers to understand and there is a tradeoff between making policies understandable and providing sufficient detail to explain the complex ways personal data is used and protected:

> The evidence suggests that people are not well informed about privacy. Efforts to improve education are certainly laudable, as are attempts to make privacy notices more understandable. But such efforts fail to address a deeper problem — privacy is quite complicated. This fact leads to a tradeoff between providing a meaningful notice and providing a short and simple one.

Privacy policies not only serve to inform consumers; they also serve to inform privacy advocates and regulators, and they are a way to hold

---

[56] Farhad Manjoo, *Another Tech Company Finds the F.T.C. Looking Over Its Shoulder*, N.Y. Times Bits Blog, May 8, 2014, http://bits.blogs.nytimes.com/2014/05/08/will-a-government-settlement-improve-snapchats-privacy-dont-count-on-it/.

[57] *Id.* Editors' Note: the 0 percent estimation may seem surprising. But in 2012, Google reported $10.74 billion in total profits. That year, online advertising accounted for about 95 percent of Google's profits. Ninety-five percent of $10.74 billion is approximately $10.203 billion. A $22.5 million dollar fine represents 0.002205 percent of Google profits. Hence, a 0 percent estimation follows normal rounding conventions.

[58] Daniel J. Solove, *Privacy Self-Management and the Consent Dilemma*, 126 Harv. L. Rev. 1880 (2013).

companies to their word. But if experts are the audience for privacy policies, then doesn't this conflict with the needs of the consumer audience, from whom simpler is better?

6. **Why Did the FTC Become the Leading U.S. Privacy Agency?** In 2000, Steven Hetcher assessed the FTC's behavior in enforcing privacy in these terms:

> By the Agency's lights, its promotion of the fair practice principles should satisfy privacy advocates, as the fair information practice principles are derived from pre-existing norms of the advocacy community. Public interest advocates contend to the contrary, however, that privacy policies ill serve their aspirational privacy norms. They argue that privacy policies are typically not read by website users. They are written in legalese such that even if people read them, they will not understand them. Hence, they do not provide notice and thus cannot lead to consent. In addition, there is evidence that many sites do not adhere to their own policies. The policies are subject to change when companies merge, such that one company's policy is likely to go unheeded. Finally, very few privacy policies guarantee security or enforcement. Thus, the provision of a privacy policy by a website does not automatically promote the fair practice principles.
>
> Despite these problems, the FTC has strongly endorsed privacy policies. This raises a puzzle as to why the Agency should do so, given the severe criticism privacy policies have received. Why, for instance, is the FTC not coming out in support of the creation of a new agency to oversee privacy protection? . . .
>
> There is a public choice answer as to why the Agency has promoted privacy policies, despite their problems (and despite the fact that they do not appear to promote the interests of any industry groups whose favor the FTC might be seeking). It is through privacy policies that the FTC is gaining jurisdiction over the commercial Internet. Jurisdiction is power. In other words, the FTC acts as if it has a plan to migrate its activities to the Internet, and privacy policies have been at the core of this plan. . . .[59]

After the writings by Hetcher, however, the FTC developed an additional role — the agency began to enforce standards of data security. Does this role fit in with Hetcher's analysis ("through privacy policies . . . the FTC is gaining jurisdiction over the commercial Internet")?

7. **The Scope of the FTC's Power.** How much power does Section 5 provide to the FTC to regulate the way companies collect, use, and share personal data? In *FTC v. Wyndham Worldwide Corp/,* ___ F. Supp. 2d ___ 2014 WL 1349019 (D.N.J. 2014), Wyndham Hotels challenged the scope of the FTC's power.

The *Wyndham* case arose from a series of data breaches suffered by Wyndham. In its complaint against Wyndham, the FTC alleged a variety of poor data security practices by Wyndham that led to the breaches. Although

---

[59] Steven Hetcher, *The FTC as Internet Privacy Norm Entrepreneur*, 53 Vand. L. Rev. 2041 (2000). *See also* Steven Hetcher, *Norms in a Wired World* (2004); Steven Hetcher, *Changing the Social Meaning of Privacy in Cyberspace*, 15 Harv. J.L. & Tech. 149 (2001); Steven A. Hetcher, *Norm Proselytizers Create a Privacy Entitlement in Cyberspace*, 16 Berkeley Tech. L.J. 877 (2001).

the case involves data security and is excerpted and discussed in more depth in Chapter 10, the arguments in the case could apply to the FTC's privacy enforcement. One of the arguments made by Wyndham was that because Congress enacted targeted data security legislation elsewhere yet failed to create a statute explicitly authorizing the FTC to regulate data security, the FTC lacked the power to regulate. The court rejected this argument, concluding that the FTC's Section 5 power is very broad and that the context-specific data security statutes simply enhance data security protection in certain contexts. The court concluded that Wyndham "fails to explain how the FTC's unfairness authority over data security would lead to a result that is incompatible with more recent legislation and thus would 'plainly *contradict* congressional policy.'"

As Hartzog and Solove argue: "Congress gave the FTC very broad and general regulatory authority by design to allow for a more nimble and evolutionary approach to the regulation of consumer protection." They contend that normatively the FTC's broad power is justified and that "the FTC not only should have broad data protection enforcement powers, but that it also should be exercising these powers more robustly. The FTC should enforce more expansively, embrace consensus norms more quickly, and take more of a leadership role in the development of privacy norms and standards."[60] Should the FTC take an even greater role and more aggressively try to develop privacy norms?

8. *Are FTC Consent Decrees Similar to Common Law?* Daniel Solove and Woodrow Hartzog argue that the body of FTC consent decrees has some key similarities to common law. "Practitioners look to FTC settlements as though they have precedential weight. The result is that lawyers consult and analyze these settlements in much the same way as they do judicial decisions."

9. *Fair Notice.* Some commentators critique the FTC for failing to articulate its standards clearly enough. In the context of the FTC's data security cases, Gerard Stegmaier and Wendell Bartnick argue:

> The FTC's current practice. . . relies heavily upon the publication of negotiated resolutions that consist of draft complaints coupled with consent agreements, as well as the release of reports and other interpretive guidance that blend best practices with law. The result is that legal requirements are generally shrouded in mystery and uncertain risk of enforcement discretion. Finally, . . . a standard based on "reasonableness" grounded solely in settlements raises its own questions of whether constitutionally adequate fair notice was provided. Such a standard seems unfair and problematic to those tasked with assisting entities in avoiding unfair and deceptive trade practices.[61]

In another case, LabMD challenged the FTC with an argument quite similar to Stegmaier and Bartnick's. Writing for the FTC in denying LabMD's motion to dismiss, Commissioner Wright stated:

---

[60] Woodrow Hartzog & Daniel J. Solove, *The Scope and Potential of FTC Data Protection*, 83 Geo. Wash. L. Rev. (forthcoming 2015), http://ssrn.com/abstract=2461096.

[61] Gerard M. Stegmaier & Wendell Bartnick, *Psychics, Russian Roulette, and Data Security: The FTC's Hidden Data-Security Requirements*, 20 Geo. Mason L. Rev. 673 (2013).

LabMD's due process claim is particularly untenable when viewed against the backdrop of the common law of negligence. Every day, courts and juries subject companies to tort liability for violating uncodified standards of care, and the contexts in which they make those fact-specific judgments are as varied and fast-changing as the world of commerce and technology itself.

Hartzog and Solove contend:

In a common law system — or any system where matters are decided case-by-case and there is an attempt at maintaining consistency across decisions, any reasonableness standard will evolve into something more akin to a rule with specifics over time. Indeed, any broad standard will follow this evolutionary trajectory. . . .

While some initial uncertainty might be the present at the outset, the clarity provided by each additional legal action virtually guarantees ever increasing determinism for those already charged with a reasonable adherence to commonly shared industry standards.

The FTC is not exceeding its authority because this developmental pattern is practically inevitable and quite predictable given the clarity offered by incorporation of generally accepted industry practices and the wiggle room provided by requiring reasonable but not strict adherence to those practices.[62]

FTC V. TOYSMART.COM

Civ. Action No. 00-11341-RGS (FTC July 21, 2000),

COMPLAINT

. . . . 4. Defendants Toysmart.com, Inc. and Toysmart.com, LLC (collectively "Toysmart" or "defendant") are Delaware corporations. . . .

6. Since at least January 1999, Toysmart has advertised, promoted, and sold toys on the Internet, located at www.toysmart.com. Toysmart markets its products and services throughout the United States and the world via the Internet.

7. In connection with its Web site, Toysmart collects personal customer information including, but not limited to, consumers' names, addresses, billing information, shopping preferences, and family profile information ("Customer Lists").

8. In September 1999, Toysmart became a licensee of TRUSTe, an organization that certifies the privacy policies of online businesses and allows such businesses to display a TRUSTe trustmark or seal.

9. From September 1999 to the present, the privacy policy posted on the Toysmart.com Web site has stated, *inter alia*, (1) "Personal information voluntarily submitted by visitors to our site, such as name, address, billing information and shopping preferences, is never shared with a third party. All information obtained by toysmart.com is used only to personalize your experience online;" and (2) "When you register with toysmart.com, you can rest

---

[62] Solove & Hartzog, *Scope and Potential of FTC, supra.*

assured that your information will never be shared with a third party." A true and correct copy of the Toysmart privacy policy is attached hereto as Exhibit 1.

10. On May 22, 2000, Toysmart announced that, as of midnight on May 19, 2000, it had officially ceased operations. Toysmart also announced that it had retained the services of a Boston-based management consultant, The Recovery Group, to locate parties interested in acquiring Toysmart.com's business and assets.

11. On May 22, 2000, Toysmart began soliciting bids for the purchase of its assets. Bids have been sought for the purchase of all of the company's assets or for individual assets. Among the individual assets offered for sale by Toysmart.com are its Customer Lists (on either an exclusive or non-exclusive basis). Other assets available include inventory; warehouse fixtures and equipment; intangible assets including domain name, product databases, and Web site source code; and a B2B business plan. Bids were due to Toysmart by 6:00 p.m. EST on June 19, 2000.

12. On June 9, 2000, Toysmart's creditors filed a petition for involuntary bankruptcy. *See* In Re: Toysmart.com, LLC, No. 00-13995-CJK (Bankr. D. Mass).

13. On June 19, 2000, bidding for Toysmart's assets concluded. Toysmart informed the Federal Trade Commission that its Customer Lists will not be transferred to a third party absent bankruptcy court approval. . . .

17. From at least September 1999 to the present, defendant Toysmart, directly or through its employees and agents, in connection with its collection of personal consumer information, expressly and/or by implication, represented that it would "never" disclose, sell, or offer for sale customers' or registered members' personal information to third parties.

18. In truth and in fact, Toysmart has disclosed, sold, or offered for sale its customer lists and profiles. Therefore, the representation set forth in Paragraph 17 was, and is, a deceptive practice. . . .

STIPULATION AND ORDER ESTABLISHING CONDITIONS
ON SALE OF CUSTOMER INFORMATION

This Stipulation is entered into this twentieth day of July, 2000, by and between, Toysmart.com, LLC, debtor and debtor-in-possession ("Debtor" or "Toysmart"), and the Federal Trade Commission ("FTC"). . . .

For the purposes of this Agreement, the following definitions shall apply:

"Qualified Buyer" shall mean an entity that (1) concentrates its business in the family commerce market, involving the areas of education, toys, learning, home and/or instruction, including commerce, content, product and services, and (2) expressly agrees to be Toysmart's successor-in-interest as to the Customer Information, and expressly agrees to the obligations set forth in Paragraphs 2, 3 and 4, below. . . .

The Debtor shall only assign or sell its Customer Information as part of the sale of its Goodwill and only to a Qualified Buyer approved by the Bankruptcy Court. In the process of approving any sale of the Customer Information, the Bankruptcy Court shall require that the Qualified Buyer agree to and comply with the terms of this Stipulation.

The Qualified Buyer shall treat Customer Information in accordance with the terms of the Privacy Statement and shall be responsible for any violation by it following the date of purchase. Among other things, the Qualified Buyer shall use Customer Information only to fulfill customer orders and to personalize customers' experience on the Web site, and shall not disclose, sell or transfer Customer Information to any Third Party.

If the Qualified Buyer materially changes the Privacy Statement, prior notice will be posted on the Web site. Any such material change in policy shall apply only to information collected following the change in policy. The Customer Information shall be governed by the Privacy Statement, unless the consumer provides affirmative consent ("opt-in") to the previously collected information being governed by the new policy.

In the event that an order is not entered on or before July 31, 2001, approving the sale of the Customer Information to a Qualified Buyer or approving a plan of reorganization, the Debtor shall, on or before August 31, 2001, delete or destroy all Customer Information in its possession, custody or control, and provide written confirmation to the FTC, sworn to under penalty of perjury, that all such Customer Information has been deleted or destroyed. Pending approval of any sale of the Customer Information to a Qualified Buyer or of a plan of reorganization, the Debtor shall handle Customer Information in accordance with the Privacy Statement.

This Stipulation and Order, after approval by the Bankruptcy Court, shall be attached to and incorporated in full into the terms of any plan of liquidation or reorganization that is ultimately approved in this bankruptcy case.

STATEMENT OF COMMISSIONER MOZELLE W. THOMPSON

. . . I have voted to approve the settlement in this matter resolving the Commission's charges that Toysmart violated Section 5 of the Federal Trade Commission Act because I believe the terms of the settlement are consistent with Toysmart's privacy policy. More specifically, the settlement permits Toysmart to sell its information only to a "qualified buyer," defined as an entity engaged in the family commerce market who *expressly agrees to be Toysmart's successor-in-interest as to that information*. Accordingly, Toysmart may transfer its data only to someone who specifically "stands" in the shoes of Toysmart.

Despite the consistency between the settlement and Toysmart's privacy policy, my decision to approve the settlement is not without reservation. Like my colleagues Commissioner Anthony and Commissioner Swindle, I think that consumers would benefit from notice and choice before a company transfers their information to a corporate successor. Indeed, many of the consumers who disclosed their families' personal information to Toysmart might not have been willing to turn over the same information to the particular corporate entity that ultimately succeeds Toysmart. This is true even where Toysmart's corporate successor must pursue the same line of business as its predecessor.

I urge any successor to provide Toysmart customers with notice and an opportunity to "opt out" as a matter of good will and good business practice. . . .

STATEMENT OF COMMISSIONER SHEILA F. ANTHONY

The settlements attempt to satisfy both the privacy interests of consumers and the business needs of a failing firm by establishing the conditions on the sale of Toysmart's customer list. Specifically, the order proposed to be filed with the bankruptcy court limits to whom Toysmart may sell its customer list. Toysmart may only sell the customer list in connection with its goodwill, not as a stand-alone asset, and only to a qualified buyer. . . .

To accept the bankruptcy settlement would place business concerns ahead of consumer privacy. Although the proposed settlement's definition of a qualified buyer attempts to ensure that only an entity "similar" to Toysmart is eligible to purchase the list, I do not believe that this limitation is an adequate proxy for consumer privacy interests. In my view, consumer privacy would be better protected by requiring that consumers themselves be given notice and choice before their detailed personal information is shared with or used by another corporate entity — especially where, as here, consumers provided that information pursuant to a promise not to transfer it.

DISSENTING STATEMENT OF COMMISSIONER ORSON SWINDLE

Defendant Toysmart.com, Inc. ("Toysmart") represented that it would never disclose, sell, or offer to sell the personal information of its customers to a third party. When faced with severe financial difficulties, however, Toysmart solicited bids for its customer lists, which include or reflect the personal information of its customers. . . .

I agree that a sale to a third party under the terms of the Bankruptcy Order would be a substantial improvement over the sale that likely would have occurred without Commission action. Nevertheless, I do not think that the Commission should allow the sale. If we really believe that consumers attach great value to the privacy of their personal information and that consumers should be able to limit access to such information through private agreements with businesses, we should compel businesses to honor the promises they make to consumers to gain access to this information. Toysmart promised its customers that their personal information would *never* be sold to a third party, but the Bankruptcy Order in fact would allow a sale to a third party. In my view, such a sale should not be permitted because "never" really means never.

I dissent.

NOTES & QUESTIONS

1. *Postscript.* After the FTC approved the settlement in *Toysmart* by a 3-2 vote by the commissioners, the settlement attracted the support of Toysmart's creditors, since it would allow the sale of the database to certain purchasers, and hence could be used to pay back the creditors. However, in August 2000, Judge Carol Kenner of the U.S. Bankruptcy Court rejected the settlement because there were currently no offers on the table to buy the database, and it would hurt the creditors to restrict the sale to certain types of purchasers

without first having a potential buyer. In February 2001, Judge Kenner agreed to let Toysmart sell its customer database to Disney, the primary shareholder, for $50,000. Disney agreed, as part of the deal, to destroy the list.

The Toysmart bankruptcy also led Amazon.com, the Internet's largest retailer, to change its privacy policy. Prior to the Toysmart case, Amazon's privacy policy provided:

> Amazon.com does not sell, trade, or rent your personal information to others. We may choose to do so in the future with trustworthy third parties, but you can tell us not to by sending a blank e-mail message to never@amazon.com.

In its new policy, Amazon.com stated:

> Information about our customers is an important part of our business, and we are not in the business of selling it to others. We share customer information only with the subsidiaries Amazon.com, Inc., controls and as described below. . . .
>
> As we continue to develop our business, we might sell or buy stores or assets. In such transactions, customer information generally is one of the transferred business assets. Also, in the unlikely event that Amazon.com, Inc., or substantially all of its assets are acquired, customer information will of course be one of the transferred assets. . . .

Amazon.com's new policy was criticized by some privacy organizations. One of the criticisms was that the policy did not provide an opt-out right. Suppose Amazon.com went bankrupt and decided to sell all of its customer data. Can it sell data supplied by consumers under the old policy? Can the new policy apply retroactively?

2. ***Bankruptcy: Property Rights vs. Contract Rights.*** Edward Janger proposes that a property rights regime (as opposed to the contractual rights of a privacy policy) will best protect the privacy of personal data when companies possessing such data go bankrupt:

> Property rules are viewed as reflecting undivided entitlements. They allocate, as Carol Rose puts it, the "whole meatball" to the "owner." Liability rules, by contrast are viewed as dividing an entitlement between two parties. One party holds the right, but the other party is given the option to take the right and compensate the right holder for the deprivation (to breach and pay damages). . . .
>
> Propertization has some crucial benefits, but it also has some serious costs. Both the bankruptcy and non-bankruptcy treatment of privacy policies turn on whether a privacy policy creates a right enforceable only through civil damages, or a right with the status of property. If bankruptcy courts treat privacy policies solely as contract obligations [the liability rule], the debtor will be free to breach (or reject) the contract in bankruptcy. Any damage claim will be treated as a prepetition claim, paid, if at all, at a significant discount. Consumer expectations (contractual or otherwise) of privacy are likely to be defeated. By contrast, if personal information is deemed property subject to an encumbrance, then the property interest must be respected, or to use the bankruptcy term, "adequately protected."

In other words, Janger contends that giving individuals property rights in their personal data will provide more protection than giving individuals contract rights in the event a company goes bankrupt.[63]

3. *Customer Databases as Collateral.* Xuan-Thao Nguyen points out that companies are using their customer databases as collateral for loans, since these databases are one of their most significant assets:

> Whether intentional or unintentional, many Internet companies ignore their own privacy policy statements when the companies pledge their customer database as collateral in secured financing schemes. This practice renders online privacy statements misleading because the statements are silent on collateralization of the company's assets. . . .
>
> The secured party can use the consumer database in its business or sell the consumer database to others. The collateralization of the consumer database and its end result may contradict the debtor's consumer privacy statement declaring that the debtor does not sell or lease the consumer information to others. Though there is no direct sale of the consumer database to the secured party, the effect of the collateralization of the consumer database is the same: the consumer database is in the hands of third parties with unfettered control and rights. Essentially, the collateralization of consumer databases violates the privacy policies publicized on debtors' Web sites.[64]

4. *Retroactive Changes to Privacy Policies.* In *In the Matter of Gateway, Inc.,* 2004 WL 261847 (FTC Sept. 10, 2004), Gateway Learning Corp. collected personal information from its consumers pursuant to a privacy policy stating that it would not sell, rent, or loan personal information to third parties unless people consented. It also promised that if it changed its privacy policy, it would give consumers the opportunity to "opt out" of having their data shared.

Subsequently, Gateway altered its privacy policy to allow the renting of personal information to third parties without informing customers and obtaining their explicit consent. The FTC filed a complaint alleging that this practice was an unfair and deceptive act. According to the FTC, Gateway's retroactive application of a materially changed privacy policy to information that it had previously collected constituted an unfair practice. The FTC also charged that Gateway's failure to inform consumers of its changes to its privacy policies, despite its promises to do so, constituted a deceptive practice. Gateway settled with the FTC, agreeing that it would "not misrepresent . . . [t]he manner in which [it] will collect, use, or disclose personal information." It also agreed to pay $4,608, which was the amount it earned from renting the information.

Suppose a company puts the following line in its privacy policy: "Please be aware that we may change this policy at any time." Would this allow for the retroactive application of a revised policy? Or is there an argument that even with a statement such as this one, the revised policy could not be applied retroactively?

---

[63] Edward J. Janger, *Muddy Property: Generating and Protecting Information Privacy Norms in Bankruptcy*, 44 Wm. & Mary L. Rev. 1801 (2002).

[64] Xuan-Thao N. Nguyen, *Collateralizing Privacy,* 78 Tul. L. Rev. 553, 571, 590 (2004).

5. *Apps with Privacy Policies.* Increasingly, users of various websites, software, and mobile devices are using applications (called "apps") developed by third parties. These apps add special features and functions and are quite popular. Many app developers are small companies or individuals without the normal cadre of lawyers, privacy officers, and other experts. At the same time, many apps gather a lot of personal information. In 2011, the Future of Privacy Forum (FPF), a privacy think tank, examined the top paid apps for mobile devices (such as the iPhone, Android, and Blackberry). FPF found that 22 out of 30 did not have a privacy policy. Without a privacy policy, would the FTC have theories upon which it could enforce privacy protections against the app? Could the FTC require apps to have privacy policies?

IN THE MATTER OF FACEBOOK, INC.

2012 WL 3518628 (FTC July 27, 2012)

COMPLAINT

The Federal Trade Commission, having reason to believe that Facebook, Inc., a corporation ("Respondent") has violated the Federal Trade Commission Act ("FTC Act"), and it appearing to the Commission that this proceeding is in the public interest, alleges: . . . .

3. Since at least 2004, Facebook has operated www.facebook.com, a social networking website. Users of the site create online profiles, which contain content about them such as their name, interest groups they join, the names of other users who are their "friends" on the site, photos albums and videos they upload, and messages and comments they post or receive from their friends. Users also may add content to other users' profiles by sharing photos, sending messages, or posting comments. As of March 2012, Facebook had approximately 900 million users.

4. Since approximately May 2007, Facebook has operated the Facebook Platform ("Platform"), a set of tools and programming interfaces that enables third parties to develop, run, and operate software applications, such as games, that users can interact with online ("Platform Applications"). . . .

6. Facebook has collected extensive "profile information" about its users, including, but not limited to [name, gender, email address, birthday, profile picture, photos, friends, and other personal data]. . . .

9. Facebook has designed its Platform such that Platform Applications can access user profile information in two main instances. First, Platform Applications that a user authorizes can access the user's profile information. Second, if a user's "Friend" authorizes a Platform Application, that application can access certain of the user's profile information, even if the user has not authorized that Application. For example, if a user authorizes a Platform Application that provides reminders about Friends' birthdays, that application could access, among other things, the birthdays of the user's Friends, even if these Friends never authorized the application.

10. Since at least November 2009, Facebook has, in many instances, provided its users with a "Central Privacy Page," the same or similar to the one depicted below. Among other things, this page has contained a "Profile" link, with accompanying text that has stated "[c]ontrol who can see your profile and personal information."

11. When users have clicked on the "Profile" link, Facebook has directed them to a "Profile Privacy Page," the same or similar to the one depicted below, which has stated that users could "[c]ontrol who can see your profile and related information." For each "Profile Privacy Setting," depicted below, users could click on a drop-down menu and restrict access to specified users, *e.g.*, "Only Friends," or "Friends of Friends."

12. Although the precise language has changed over time, Facebook's Central Privacy Page and Profile Privacy Page have, in many instances, stated that the Profile Privacy Settings allow users to "control who can see" their profile information, by specifying who can access it, *e.g.*, "Only Friends" or "Friends of Friends."

13. Similarly, although the precise interface has changed over time, Facebook's Profile Privacy Settings have continued to specify that users can restrict access to their profile information to the audience the user selects, *e.g.*, "Only Friends," "Friends of Friends." . . .

14. None of the pages described in Paragraphs 10-13 have disclosed that a user's choice to restrict profile information to "Only Friends" or "Friends of Friends" would be ineffective as to certain third parties. Despite this fact, in many instances, Facebook has made profile information that a user chose to restrict to "Only Friends" or "Friends of Friends" accessible to any Platform Applications that the user's Friends have used (hereinafter "Friends' Apps"). Information shared with such Friends' Apps has included, among other things, a user's birthday, hometown, activities, interests, status updates, marital status, education (*e.g.*, schools attended), place of employment, photos, and videos.

15. Facebook's Central Privacy Page and Profile Privacy Page have included links to "Applications," "Apps," or "Applications and Websites" that, when clicked, have taken users to a page containing "Friends' App Settings," which would allow users to restrict the information that their Friends' Apps could access.

16. However, in many instances, the links to "Applications," "Apps," or "Applications and Websites" have failed to disclose that a user's choices made through Profile Privacy Settings have been ineffective against Friends' Apps. . . .

17. As described in Paragraphs 10-13, Facebook has represented, expressly or by implication, that, through their Profile Privacy Settings, users can restrict access to their profile information to specific groups, such as "Only Friends" or "Friends of Friends." . . .

19. On approximately November 19, 2009, Facebook changed its privacy policy to designate certain user information as "publicly available" ("PAI"). On approximately December 8, 2009, Facebook began implementing the changes referenced in its new policy ("the December Privacy Changes") to make public in new ways certain information that users previously had provided.

20. Before December 8, 2009, users could, and did, use their Friends' App Settings to restrict Platform Applications' access to their PAI. For example, as of

November 2009, approximately 586,241 users had used these settings to "block" Platform Applications that their Friends used from accessing any of their profile information, including their Name, Profile Picture, Gender, Friend List, Pages, and Networks. Following the December Privacy Changes, Facebook users no longer could restrict access to their PAI through these Friends' App Settings, and all prior user choices to do so were overridden.

21. Before December 8, 2009, users could, and did, use their Profile Privacy Settings to limit access to their Friend List. Following the December Privacy Changes, Facebook users could no longer restrict access to their Friend List through their Profile Privacy Settings, and all prior user choices to do so were overridden, making a user's Friend List accessible to other users. Although Facebook reinstated these settings shortly thereafter, they were not restored to the Profile Privacy Settings and instead were effectively hidden.

22. Before December 8, 2009, users could, and did, use their Search Privacy Settings (available through the "Search" link on the Privacy Settings Page depicted in Paragraph 11) to restrict access to their Profile Picture and Pages from other Facebook users who found them by searching for them on Facebook. For example, as of June 2009, approximately 2.5 million users who had set their Search Privacy Settings to "Everyone," still hid their Profile Picture. Following the December Privacy Changes, Facebook users could no longer restrict the visibility of their Profile Picture and Pages through these settings, and all prior user choices to do so were overridden.

23. To implement the December Privacy Changes, Facebook required each user to click through a multi-page notice, known as the Privacy Wizard, which was composed of:

a. an introductory page, which announced:

> We're making some changes to give you more control of your information and help you stay connected. We've simplified the Privacy page and added the ability to set privacy on everything you share, from status updates to photos.

> At the same time, we're helping everyone find and connect with each other by keeping some information — like your name and current city — publicly available. The next step will guide you through choosing your privacy settings.

b. privacy update pages, which required each users to choose, via a series of radio buttons, between new privacy settings that Facebook "recommended" and the user's "Old Settings," for ten types of profile information (*e.g.*, Photos and Videos of Me, Birthday, Family and Relationships, etc.), and which stated:

> Facebook's new, simplified privacy settings give you more control over the information you share. We've recommended settings below, but you can choose to apply your old settings to any of the fields.

and

c. a confirmation page, which summarized the user's updated Privacy Settings.

24. The Privacy Wizard did not disclose adequately that users no longer could restrict access to their newly-designated PAI via their Profile Privacy Settings, Friends' App Settings, or Search Privacy Settings, or that their existing

choices to restrict access to such information via these settings would be overridden. For example, the Wizard did not disclose that a user's existing choice to share his or her Friend List with "Only Friends" would be overridden, and that this information would be made accessible to the public. . . .

26. Facebook's designation of PAI caused harm to users, including, but not limited to, threats to their health and safety, and unauthorized revelation of their affiliations. Among other things:

a. certain users were subject to the risk of unwelcome contacts from persons who may have been able to infer their locale, based on the locales of their Friends (*e.g.*, their Friends' Current City information) and of the organizations reflected in their Pages;

b. each user's Pages became visible to anyone who viewed the user's profile, thereby exposing potentially controversial political views or other sensitive information to third parties — such as prospective employers, government organizations, or business competitors — who sought to obtain personal information about the user;

c. each user's Friend List became visible to anyone who viewed the user's profile, thereby exposing potentially sensitive affiliations, that could, in turn, reveal a user's political views, sexual orientation, or business relationships, to third parties — such as prospective employers, government organizations, or business competitors — who sought to obtain personal information about the user; and

d. each user's Profile Photo became visible to anyone who viewed the user's profile, thereby revealing potentially embarrassing or political images to third parties whose access users previously had restricted.

27. As described in Paragraph 23, Facebook has represented, expressly, or by implication, that its December Privacy Changes provided users with "more control" over their information, including by allowing them to preserve their "Old Settings," to protect the privacy of their profile information.

28. As described in Paragraph 24-26, Facebook failed to disclose, or failed to disclose adequately, that, following the December Privacy Changes, users could no longer restrict access to their Name, Profile Picture, Gender, Friend List, Pages, or Networks by using privacy settings previously available to them. Facebook also failed to disclose, or failed to disclose adequately, that the December Privacy Changes overrode existing user privacy settings that restricted access to a user's Name, Profile Picture, Gender, Friend List, Pages, or Networks. These facts would be material to consumers. Therefore, Facebook's failure to adequately disclose these facts, in light of the representation made, constitutes a deceptive act or practice.

29. As described in Paragraphs 19-26, by designating certain user profile information publicly available that previously had been subject to privacy settings, Facebook materially changed its promises that users could keep such information private. Facebook retroactively applied these changes to personal information that it had previously collected from users, without their informed consent, in a manner that has caused or has been likely to cause substantial injury to consumers, was not outweighed by countervailing benefits to consumers or to competition, and was not reasonably avoidable by consumers. This practice constitutes an unfair act or practice. . . .

34. Facebook has displayed advertisements ("ads") from third-parties ("Platform Advertisers") on its web site.

35. Facebook has allowed Platform Advertisers to target their ads ("Platform Ads") by requesting that Facebook display them to users whose profile information reflects certain "targeted traits," including, but not limited to [location, age, sex, birthday, relationship status, likes, and interests, among other things]. . . .

36. Facebook has disseminated or caused to be disseminated numerous statements that it does not share information about its users with advertisers, including:

> a. Facebook may use information in your profile without identifying you as an individual to third parties. We do this for purposes such as ... personalizing advertisements and promotions so that we can provide you Facebook. We believe this benefits you. You can know more about the world around you and, where there are advertisements, they're more likely to be interesting to you. For example, if you put a favorite movie in your profile, we might serve you an advertisement highlighting a screening of a similar one in your town. But we don't tell the movie company who you are. (Facebook Privacy Policy, November 26, 2008). . . .

> d. Still others asked to be opted-out of having their information shared with advertisers. This reflects a common misconception about advertising on Facebook. We don't share your information with advertisers unless you tell us to ([*e.g.,*] to get a sample, hear more, or enter a contest). Any assertion to the contrary is false. Period ... we never provide the advertiser any names or other information about the people who are shown, or even who click on, the ads. (Facebook Blog, http://blog.facebook.com/blog.php, "Responding to Your Feedback," Barry Schnitt, April 5, 2010). . . .

37. Contrary to the statements set forth in Paragraph 36(a)-(d), in many instances, Facebook has shared information about users with Platform Advertisers by identifying to them the users who clicked on their ads and to whom those ads were targeted. Specifically, from at least September 2008 until May 26, 2010, Facebook designed and operated its web site such that, in many instances, the User ID for a user who clicked on a Platform Ad was shared with the Platform Advertiser.

38. As a result of the conduct described in Paragraph 37, Platform Advertisers potentially could take steps to get detailed information about individual users. . . .

41. As set forth in Paragraph 36, Facebook has represented, expressly or by implication, that Facebook does not provide advertisers with information about its users.

42. In truth and in fact, as described in Paragraphs 37-40, Facebook has provided advertisers with information about its users. Therefore, the representation set forth in Paragraph 41 constitutes a false or misleading representation. . . .

50. As described above, Facebook has collected and stored vast quantities of photos and videos that its users upload, including, but not limited to: at least one

such photo from approximately ninety-nine percent of its users, and more than 100 million photos and 415,000 videos from its users, collectively, every day.

51. Facebook has stored users' photos and videos such that each one is assigned a Content URL — a uniform resource locator that specifies its location on Facebook's servers. Facebook users and Platform Applications can obtain the Content URL for any photo or video that they view on Facebook's web site by, for example, right-clicking on it. If a user or Application further disseminates this URL, Facebook will "serve" the user's photo or video to anyone who clicks on the URL.

52. Facebook has disseminated or caused to be disseminated statements communicating that a user can restrict access to his or her profile information — including, but not limited to, photos and videos that a user uploads — by deleting or deactivating his or her user account. Such statements include:

> a. Deactivating or deleting your account. If you want to stop using your account you may deactivate it or delete it. When you deactivate an account, no user will be able to see it, but it will not be deleted. . . . When you delete an account, it is permanently deleted from Facebook. . . .
>
> Backup copies. Removed and deleted information may persist in backup copies for up to 90 days, but will not be available to others; (Facebook Privacy Policy, November 19, 2009). . . .

53. Contrary to the statements set forth in Paragraph 52, Facebook has continued to display users' photos and videos to anyone who accesses Facebook's Content URLs for them, even after such users have deleted or deactivated their accounts. . . .

NOTES & QUESTIONS

1. *Postscript.* Facebook settled with the FTC, agreeing to refrain from misrepresenting the privacy of consumer personal data, obtain consent before changing consumer privacy preferences, and establish a comprehensive privacy program, among other things.

2. *Statements Beyond the Privacy Policy.* In *Facebook*, the FTC cites statements made in blog posts by Facebook employees when listing various false or misleading claims made by Facebook. When should statements by a company's employees count as official statements of the company? Suppose a company allows employees to have blogs hosted by the company and each blog does not contain any language that indicates that employees are speaking for themselves only. Should statements the employees write on these blogs be considered promises made by the company?

   How specific do statements need to be? In an interview, Mark Zuckerberg assured Facebook users that "[p]rivacy is very important to us."[65] Could vague or broad statements like this one be used by the FTC against Facebook?

   Consider Solove and Hartzog:

---

[65] John Paczkowski, *Facebook CEO Mark Zuckerberg in the Privacy Hot Seat*, All Things D (June 2, 2010), http://allthingsd.com/20100602/mark-zuckerberg-session/.

These cases have made it clear that the question of what constitutes a deceptive trade practice is holistic. Not only does the FTC consider representations beyond what exists in a privacy policy, but it considers consumer expectations as well. This raises a number of interesting questions. The first is the extent to which other representations can contradict explicit representations in the privacy policy. While contract law tends to give great weight to the boilerplate terms of a contract, the FTC does not appear to recognize any kind of significant presumption to exculpatory representations buried in dense legalese that run contrary to other representations or consumer expectations. . . .

Finally, given the universe of potential privacy-related statements the FTC could have (and has) drawn from to find deception, has there been a shift from explicit, insular representations to larger framing effects that create consumer trust? In other words, it appears that what a company has promised is simply one factor in a larger approach to determining whether a company has been deceptive. The FTC looks at architecture, shared norms, and cultural assumptions likely held by consumers to determine consumer expectations. This framework developed by the FTC logically would also consider any statement made by the company that would materially contribute to the creation of trust on the part of the consumer.[66]

3. *Website Design Elements.* Woodrow Hartzog argues that the privacy expectations of many users of websites is formed not by the privacy policy but by the various privacy settings and design elements of the site.[67] Websites such as Facebook have multiple privacy settings on a page distinct from the privacy policy or terms of use. More people might interact with the privacy settings page than read the privacy policy page.

Suppose certain forms of data sharing are disclosed in the privacy policy but not on the privacy settings page. These forms of data sharing exist no matter what a person's settings are. A user might argue that she did not expect this data sharing because based on the privacy settings page, it appeared as though all her data would only be shared per the settings she set. On the settings page, the company has the following statement, with a link to the privacy policy page: "Please refer to our privacy policy for information about how we collect, use, and share your data." Is this sufficient?

4. *Is Touting a Service as "Free" a Deceptive Trade Practice?* Recall Chris Hoofnagle and Jan Whittington's argument that many online services that are purportedly "free" actually have a cost because they gather personal data about consumers and sell this data to advertisers.[68] The FTC, however, has allowed free offers that require a purchase. As Hoofnagle and Whittington describe the FTC's approach:

[T]he FTC will generally consider the use of free offers to be unfair and deceptive unless two conditions are met. First, the conditions and obligations accompanying the free offer must be set forth at the outset, "so as to leave no

---

[66] Solove & Hartzog, *FTC and the New Common Law of Privacy, supra.*

[67] Woodrow Hartzog, *Website Design as Contract*, 60 Am. U. L. Rev. 1635 (2011).

[68] Chris Jay Hoofnagle and Jan Whittington, *Free: Accounting for the Costs of the Internet's Most Popular Price*, 61 UCLA L. Rev. 606 (2014).

reasonable probability that the terms of the advertisement or offer might be misunderstood." Second, sellers cannot offset the cost of providing a free product by increasing the ordinary price, quality, or size of the product that must be purchased in order to obtain the free offer.

According to Hoofnagle and Whittington, under the guidance of the 1971 FTC Guide and subsequent decisions, "sites such as Facebook.com [can] continue to use the term 'free' even when offers are contingent on the consumer's performance of certain obligations, so long as Facebook clearly discloses those obligations." Hoofnagle and Whittington suggest that the FTC should change its approach and take measures to help consumers realize the true nature of online services. For example, they suggest that the FTC could mandate "notice at the time the transaction occurs that the consumer's personal information is the basis of the bargain and that such information may be used for tracking or other secondary purposes." Another solution might be to require free services to offer a paid alternative where personal data would not be used.

IN THE MATTER OF SEARS HOLDINGS MANAGEMENT CORP.

2009 WL 2979770 (FTC Aug. 31, 2009)

COMPLAINT

The Federal Trade Commission, having reason to believe that Sears Holdings Management Corporation, a corporation, has violated the provisions of the Federal Trade Commission Act, and it appearing to the Commission that this proceeding is in the public interest, alleges:

1. Respondent Sears Holdings Management Corporation ("respondent" or "SHMC") is a Delaware corporation with its principal office or place of business at 3333 Beverly Road, Hoffman Estates, Illinois 60179. SHMC, a subsidiary of Sears Holdings Corporation ("SHC") with shares owned by Sears, Roebuck and Co. and Kmart Management Corporation, handles marketing operations for the Sears Roebuck and Kmart retail stores, and operates the sears.com and kmart.com retail Internet websites. . . .

3. From on or about April 2007 through on or about January 2008, SHMC disseminated or caused to be disseminated via the Internet a software application for consumers to download and install onto their computers (the "Application"). The Application was created, developed, and managed for respondent by a third party in connection with SHMC's "My SHC Community" market research program.

4. The Application, when installed, runs in the background at all times on consumers' computers and transmits tracked information, including nearly all of the Internet behavior that occurs on those computers, to servers maintained on behalf of respondent. Information collected and transmitted includes: web browsing, filling shopping baskets, transacting business during secure sessions, completing online application forms, checking online accounts, and, through

select header information, use of web-based email and instant messaging services.

5. SHMC, during the relevant time period, presented fifteen out of every hundred visitors to the sears.com and kmart.com websites with a "My SHC Community" pop-up box that said:

> Ever wish you could talk directly to a retailer? Tell them about the products, services and offers that would really be right for you?
>
> If you're interested in becoming part of something new, something different, we'd like to invite you to become a member of My SHC Community. My SHC Community, sponsored by Sears Holdings Corporation, is a dynamic and highly interactive on-line community. It's a place where your voice is heard and your opinion matters, and what you want and need counts!

The pop-up box made no mention of the Application. Likewise, the general "Privacy Policy" statement accessed via the hyperlink in the pop-up box did not mention the Application.

6. The pop-up box message further invited consumers to enter their email address to receive a follow-up email from SHMC with more information. Subsequently, invitation messages were emailed to those consumers who supplied their email address. These emails stated, in pertinent part:

> From shopping, current events, social networking, to entertainment and email, it seems that the Internet is playing a bigger and bigger role in our daily lives these days.
>
> If you're interested in becoming part of something new, something different, we'd like to invite you to join a new and exciting online community; My SHC Community, sponsored by Sears Holdings Corporation. *Membership is absolutely free!*
>
> My SHC Community is a dynamic and highly interactive online community. It's a place where your voice is heard and your opinion matters, and what you want and need counts! As a member of My SHC Community, you'll partner directly with the retail industry. You'll participate in exciting, engaging and on-going interactions — always on your terms and always by your choice. My SHC Community gives you the chance to help shape the future by sharing and receiving information about the products, services and offers that would really be right for you.
>
> To become a member of My SHC Community, we simply ask you to complete the registration process which includes providing us with your contact information as well as answering a series of profile questions that will help us get to know you better. You'll also be asked to take a few minutes to download software that is powered by (VoiceFive). This research software will confidentially track your online browsing. This will help us better understand you and your needs, enabling us to create more relevant future offerings for you, other community members, and eventually all shoppers. You can uninstall the software at any time through the Add/Remove program utility on your computer. During the registration process, you'll learn more about this application software and you'll always have the opportunity to ask any and every question you may have.
>
> Once you're a member of My SHC Community, you'll regularly interact with My SHC Community members as well as employees of Sears Holdings

Corporation through special online engagements, surveys, chats and other fun and informative online techniques. We'll ask you to journal your shopping and purchasing behavior. Again, this will be when you want and how you want to record it — always on your terms and always by your choice. We'll also collect information on your internet usage. Community engagements are always fun and always voluntary!

The email invitation message then described what consumers would receive in exchange for becoming a member of the My SHC Community, including a $10 payment for joining the "online community," contingent upon the consumer retaining the Application on his or her computer for at least one month. Consumers who wished to proceed further would need to click a button, at the bottom, center portion of the invitation email, that said "Join Today!"

7. Consumers who clicked on the "Join Today!" button in the email invitation were directed to a landing page that restated many of the aforementioned representations about the potential interactions between members and the "community" and about the putative benefits of membership. The landing page did not mention the Application.

8. Consumers who clicked on the "Join Today" button in the landing page were directed to a registration page. To complete registration, consumers needed to enter information, including their name, address, age, and email address. Below the fields for entering information, the registration page presented a "Privacy Statement and User License Agreement" ("PSULA") in a "scroll box" that displayed ten lines of the multi-page document at a time. A description of the Application's specific functions begins on approximately the 75 line down in the scroll box:

> Computer hardware, software, and other configuration information: Our application may collect certain basic hardware, software, computer configuration and application usage information about the computer on which you install our application, including such data as the speed of the computer processor, its memory capacities and Internet connection speed. In addition, our application may report on devices connected to your computer, such as the type of printer or router you may be using.
>
> Internet usage information: Once you install our application, it monitors all of the Internet behavior that occurs on the computer on which you install the application, including both your normal web browsing and the activity that you undertake during secure sessions, such as filling a shopping basket, completing an application form or checking your online accounts, which may include personal financial or health information. We may use the information that we monitor, such as name and address, for the purpose of better understanding your household demographics; however we make commercially viable efforts to automatically filter confidential personally identifiable information such as UserID, password, credit card numbers, and account numbers. Inadvertently, we may collect such information about our panelists; and when this happens, we make commercially viable efforts to purge our database of such information.
>
> The software application also tracks the pace and style with which you enter information online (for example, whether you click on links, type in webpage names, or use shortcut keys), the usage of cookies, and statistics about your use of online applications (for example, it may observe that during a given period of

use of a computer, the computer downloaded X number of bytes of data using a particular Internet enabled gaming application).

Please note: Our application does not examine the text of your instant messages or e-mail messages. We may, however, review select e-mail header information from web-based e-mails as a way to verify your contact information and online usage information.

The PSULA went on to describe how the information the Application would collect was transmitted to respondent's servers, how it might be used, and how it was maintained. It also described how consumers could stop participating in the online community and remove the Application from their computers. Respondent stated in the PSULA that it reserved the right to continue to use information collected prior to a consumer's "resignation."

9. Below the scroll box on the registration page was a link that consumers could click to access a printable version of the PSULA, and a blank checkbox next to the statement: "I am the authorized user of this computer and I have read, agree to, and have obtained the agreement of all computer users to the terms and conditions of the Privacy Statement and User License Agreement." To continue with the registration process, consumers needed to check the box and click the "Next" button at the bottom of the registration page.

10. Consumers who completed the required information, checked the box, and clicked the "Next" button on the registration page, were directed to an installation page that explained the Application download and installation process. Consumers were required to click a "Next" button to begin the download, and then click an "Install" or "Yes" button in a "security warning" dialog box to install the Application. Nothing on the installation page provided information on the Application.

11. When installed, the Application functioned and transmitted information substantially as described in the PSULA. The Application, when installed, would run in the background at all times on consumers' computers. Although the Application would be listed (as "mySHC Community") in the "All Programs" menu and "Add/Remove" utilities of those computers, and the Application's executable file name ("srhc.exe") would be listed as a running process in Windows Task Manager, the Application would display to users of those computers no visible indication, such as a desktop or system tray icon, that it was running.

12. The Application transmitted, in real time, tracked information to servers maintained on behalf of respondent. The tracked information included not only information about websites consumers visited and links that they clicked, but also the text of secure pages, such as online banking statements, video rental transactions, library borrowing histories, online drug prescription records, and select header fields that could show the sender, recipient, subject, and size of web-based email messages.

13. Through the means described in paragraphs 3-12, respondent has represented, expressly or by implication, that the Application would track consumers' "online browsing." Respondent failed to disclose adequately that the software application, when installed, would: monitor nearly all of the Internet behavior that occurs on consumers' computers, including information exchanged between consumers and websites other than those owned, operated, or affiliated

with respondent, information provided in secure sessions when interacting with third-party websites, shopping carts, and online accounts, and headers of web-based email; track certain non-Internet-related activities taking place on those computers; and transmit nearly all of the monitored information (excluding selected categories of filtered information) to respondent's remote computer servers. These facts would be material to consumers in deciding to install the software. Respondent's failure to disclose these facts, in light of the representations made, was, and is, a deceptive practice.

14. The acts and practices of respondent as alleged in this complaint constitute unfair or deceptive acts or practices in or affecting commerce in violation of Section 5(a) of the Federal Trade Commission Act. . . .

NOTES & QUESTIONS

1. *Adequate Notice.* Sears did disclose how the application worked, though it was buried in a lengthy statement. How prominently must something be mentioned for notice to be adequate? One factor in this case involved the highly invasive functions of the application. Perhaps the prominence of notice should be proportionate to the invasiveness to privacy. But who decides? If many people do not read privacy notices at all, does it matter if a statement appears in line 5 or line 75?

2. *From Broken Promises to Broken Expectations?* Solove and Hartzog contend that the FTC has begun to focus away from the explicit promises a company makes and towards ways in which consumer expectations are being thwarted:

> Although the FTC began enforcing broken *promises* of privacy, its focus seems to have shifted to broken *expectations* of consumer privacy. The shift might seem subtle, but it is dramatic in effect. Instead of the core question being what was promised, which largely focuses on a company's language, the core question has become what was expected, which incorporates the universe of preexisting consumer backgrounds, norms, and dispositions, as well as elements of design, functionality, and other nonlinguistic factors besides privacy-related statements that shape a consumer's expectations.
>
> The FTC could simply look at what a company's polices and design/architecture are and compare that with the company's actions. But it is not doing that. Instead, it seems to be taking consumers as it finds them, full of preexisting expectations, contextual norms, and cognitive limitations, and prohibiting companies from exploiting these assumptions and rational ignorance. . . .
>
> If the FTC takes into account the growing evidence about how consumers form their expectations, then it could increasingly demand that companies engage in practices that will correct mistaken consumer assumptions, or at the very least not exploit such assumptions. Existing forms of notice might not be deemed sufficient because the empirical evidence shows that consumers are not really being notified.[69]

3. *Constructive Sharing of Personally Identifiable Information. In the Matter*

---

[69] Solove & Hartzog, *FTC and the New Common Law of Privacy, supra.*

of MySpace, LLC (FTC 2012) involved the "constructive sharing" of non-personally identifiable information (PII) — sharing non-PII with third parties that can be used by third parties to access PII. The FTC alleged that MySpace shared non-PII in this manner without indicating to users that the non-PII could be used by third parties to obtain PII. Hence, MySpace's statement that it does not share PII with third parties was misleading.

4. ***Violating the Privacy Policies of Others.*** Most FTC enforcement actions against companies are for violating their own privacy policies. What if a company violates the privacy policy of another company? In *In re Vision I Properties* (FTC 2005), Vision I Properties licensed shopping cart software and provided related services to small online retail merchants. The company's software created customizable shopping cart pages for client merchants' websites. The resulting pages resided on websites managed by Vision I Properties, but resembled the other pages on its client merchants' websites. Vision I Properties violated the privacy promises of some of these client merchants as stated in their websites; it rented consumers' personal information collected through its shopping cart software. This personal information was then used by third parties to send direct mail and make telemarketing calls to consumers. For the FTC, it was reasonable for consumers to rely on merchants' privacy policies. Moreover, Vision I Properties did not adequately inform merchants of its information sharing. Vision I settled, agreeing to cease selling the data, to provide better notice and to disgorge $9,101 of profits.

5. ***Duties When Contracting with Data Service Providers.*** In the Matter of GMR Transcription Services, Inc. (FTC 2014) concerned the inadvertent disclosure of medical data by a data service provider hired by GMR, a company that provides medical transcription services. The FTC faulted GMR for its data service provider management practices. According to the FTC complaint, GMR failed to "adequately verify that their service provider, Fedtrans, implemented reasonable and appropriate security measures to protect personal information in audio and transcript files on Fedtrans' network and computers used by Fedtrans' typists."

Moreover, the FTC faulted GMR for failures in contracting with its data service provider. The FTC complaint alleged that GMR failed to "require Fedtrans by contract to adopt and implement appropriate security measures to protect personal information in medical audio and transcript files, such as by requiring that files be securely stored and securely transmitted to typists (e.g., through encryption) and authenticating typists (e.g., through unique user credentials) before granting them access to such files; take adequate measures to monitor and assess whether Fedtrans employed measures to appropriately protect personal information under the circumstances."

The FTC additionally found GMR to be deficient in doing due diligence before hiring its data service provider: "Respondents did not request or review relevant information about Fedtrans' security practices, such as, for example, Fedtrans' written information security program or audits or assessments Fedtrans may have had of its computer network."

Looking broadly at the complaint, there are three key things that the FTC requires companies to do when it comes to contracting with data service providers: (1) exercise due diligence before hiring these third parties; (2) have appropriate protections of data in their contracts with data service providers; and (3) take steps to verify that the data service providers are adequately protecting data.

6. ***State Deceptive Trade Practices Acts.*** In addition to the FTC Act, which is enforced exclusively by the FTC, every state has some form of deceptive trade practices act of its own. Many of these statutes not only enable a state attorney general to bring actions but also provide a private cause of action to consumers. Several of these laws have provisions for statutory minimum damages, punitive damages, and attorneys' fees. *See, e.g.,* Cal. Civ. Code § 1780(a)(4) (punitive damages); Conn. Gen. Stat. § 42-110g(a) (punitive damages); Mich. Comp. Laws § 445.911(2) (minimum damages); N.Y. Gen. Bus. Law § 349(h) (minimum damages). In interpreting these state laws, many state courts have been heavily influenced by FTC Act jurisprudence. However, as Jeff Sovern notes, many states "have been more generous to consumers than has the FTC," and "even if the FTC concludes that practices pass muster under the FTC Act, it is still at least theoretically possible for a state to find the practices deceptive under their own legislation." Thus, Sovern concludes, "information practices that are currently in widespread use may indeed violate state little FTC Acts. Marketers should think carefully about whether they wish to alter their practices."[70]

F. STATUTORY REGULATION

Numerous statutes are directly and potentially applicable to the collection, use, and transfer of personal information by commercial entities. Congress's approach is best described as "sectoral," as each statute is narrowly tailored to particular types of businesses and services. The opposite of sectoral in this context is omnibus, and the United States lacks such a comprehensive statute regulating the private sector's collection and use of personal information. Such omnibus statutes are standard in much of the rest of the world. All member nations of the European Union have enacted omnibus information privacy laws.

In the United States, sectoral laws also do not regulate all commercial entities in their collection and use of personal information. Thus far, federal statutes regulate three basic areas: (a) entertainment records (video and cable television); (b) Internet use and electronic communications; and (c) marketing (telemarketing and spam). As you examine the existing statutes, think about the kinds of commercial entities that the law does not currently regulate. Consider whether these entities should be regulated. Also consider whether one omnibus privacy law can adequately apply to all commercial entities. Would the differences

---

[70] Jeff Sovern, *Protecting Privacy with Deceptive Trade Practices Legislation*, 69 Fordham L. Rev. 1305, 1352-53, 1357 (2001).

between types of commercial entities make a one-size-fits-all privacy law impractical?

The sectoral statutes embody the Fair Information Practices originally developed by HEW and incorporated into the Privacy Act. However, not all statutes embody all of the Fair Information Practices. As you study each statute, examine which of the Fair Information Practices are required by each statute and which are not.

1. ENTERTAINMENT RECORDS

(a) The Video Privacy Protection Act

Incensed when a reporter obtained a list of videos that Supreme Court Justice Nominee Robert Bork and his family had rented from a video store, Congress passed the Video Privacy Protection Act (VPPA) of 1988, Pub. L. No. 100-618. The VPPA is also known as the "Bork Bill."

Scope. The VPPA is written in technology-neutral terms. It defines a "video tape service provider" as "any person engaged in the business, in or affecting interstate or foreign commerce, of rental, sale, or delivery of prerecorded video cassette tapes or similar audio visual materials. . . ." § 2710(a)(4). This statutory language allows the VPPA to extend to DVDs (as opposed to video cassette tapes) and also covers online delivery of movies and other content.

Opt in for Disclosure. The VPPA prohibits videotape service providers from knowingly disclosing personal information, such as titles of videocassettes rented or purchased, without the individual's written consent.

Online providers of video content lobbied Congress, contending that VPPA's opt-in requirement prevented them from integrating into Facebook. They complained that VPPA required consent before each instance where video preferences were shared on social networks. They wanted a single consent to the practice of displaying video "likes" rather than a requirement of consent for each video.

In 2012, Congress passed the Video Privacy Protection Act Amendments Act, which was signed into law in early 2013. These amendments make it easier to obtain consent. Now, consumers can consent via electronic means. Additionally, consent can be obtained in advance for a period of two years. People can later withdraw consent if they choose. A videotape service provider must provide an opportunity "in a clear and conspicuous manner, for the consumer to withdraw on a case-by-case basis or to withdraw from ongoing disclosures, at the consumer's election."

Exceptions Allowing Disclosure Without Consent. The VPPA contains several exceptions, permitting videotape providers to disclose "to any person if the disclosure is incident to the ordinary course of business of the video tape service provider." § 2710(b)(2)(E).

The statute provides that "the subject matter of such materials may be disclosed if the disclosure is for the exclusive use of marketing goods and services directly to the consumer." § 2710(b)(2)(D)(ii). Videotape service providers can disclose the names and addresses of consumers if the consumer has been given the right to opt out, and the disclosure does not identify information about the videos the consumer rents. § 2710(b)(2)(D).

The statute also permits disclosure to the consumer, § 2710(b)(2)(A); disclosure with the informed written consent of the consumer, § 2710(b)(2)(B); disclosure to a law enforcement agency pursuant to a warrant or subpoena, § 2710(b)(2)(C); and disclosure for civil discovery if there is notice and an opportunity to object, § 2710(b)(2).

Destruction of Records. The VPPA requires that records of personal information be destroyed as soon as practicable. § 2710(e).

Preemption. VPPA does not block states from enacting statutes that are more protective of privacy. § 2710(f).

Enforcement. The VPPA creates a private cause of action when a videotape service provider "knowingly discloses . . . personally identifiable information concerning any consumer of such provider." 18 U.S.C. § 2710(b)(1). VPPA permits recovery of actual damages and provides for liquidated damages in the amount of $2,500. The Act also authorizes recovery for punitive damages, attorneys' fees, and enables equitable and injunctive relief. § 2710(c). The VPPA also includes a statutory exclusionary rule that prevents the admission into evidence of any information obtained in violation of the statute. § 2710(d).

VPPA damages are only available for unauthorized disclosures, not failure to meet other requirements of the act such as the destruction of records. In *Sterk v. Redbox Automated Retail LLC,* 672 F.3d 535 (2012), the court rejected a plaintiff's lawsuit for failure to destroy plaintiff's records in a timely manner, concluding that "[u]nlawful disclosure is the only misconduct listed in the statute for which an award of damages is an appropriate remedy."

NOTES & QUESTIONS

1. *Netflix and Frictionless Sharing.* William McGeveran criticizes the Video Privacy Protection Act Amendments Act, which permits Netflix and other online video service providers to obtain a broad ongoing consent from consumers to display the videos they like on Facebook and other social media sites. According to McGeveran, the former requirement of VPPA that users must provide consent for each and every disclosure of videos they watch created a type of "friction" on sharing information. The change to VPPA makes sharing videos more "frictionless."[71] McGeveran warns that frictionless sharing interfaces can be "badly designed" leading to misdisclosures and a lack of clear notice to consumers. People can readily forget that their actions are being broadcast and might end up disclosing things they did not want to disclose. McGeveran suggests that friction can be

---

[71] William McGeveran, *The Law of Friction*, 2013 U. Chi. Legal F. 15, 18.

a good thing and should not be removed entirely from sharing. He suggests one way that friction could be added:

> Netflix could simply put a "PLAY AND SHARE" button next to the "PLAY" button that viewers already must click to stream any video. An interface would not satisfy this law of friction if it required more effort for customers to start viewing a movie than to inform all their Facebook friends what they are watching.

To what extent should the law mandate that friction be included in the design of online sharing technologies?

2. ***Private Right of Action vs. Agency Enforcement.*** VPPA is enforced by a private right of action. Other privacy laws are enforced by agencies, such as HIPAA which is enforced by HHS and COPPA which is enforced by the FTC. Should VPPA have been written to not include a private right of action and be enforced by the FTC instead? Is a private right of action a better or worse method of enforcement than agency enforcement? If the answer depends upon specific contexts and types of data, what factors should be considered in evaluating the desirability of having a private right of action?

3. ***The Narrow Focus of VPPA.*** VPPA was passed in reaction to an attempt to obtain data on what videos Judge Bork watched. The law has been criticized for being too specifically focused on videos and ignoring other forms of media, such as books, magazines, and music. Should VPPA be expanded to cover such things? What about the Internet sites one visits? Or other merchandise one buys, including food, furniture, cars, etc.? Is there a reasonable limiting principle that would limit such an expanded law's scope?

DANIEL V. CANTELL

375 F.3d 377 (6th Cir. 2004)

CUDAHY, J. The plaintiff, Alden Joe Daniel, Jr. (Daniel) was charged with and eventually pleaded guilty to the sexual molestation of three underage girls. Allegedly, part of his *modus operandi* was showing pornographic movies to the underage girls. . . . Therefore, as part of the criminal investigation into his conduct, law enforcement officials sought and were able to obtain his video rental records. . . .

Daniel brings this suit against (1) various police officers, attorneys, and the parents of one of Daniel's victims, as well as (2) the employees and owners of two video stores where Daniel rented pornographic videos. There is no dispute that the defendants making up this second category are proper parties under the Act. The only question which we must answer is whether the defendants not associated with the video stores are proper parties under the Act. We believe that based on the plain language of the Act, this first group of defendants are *not* proper parties. . . .

Section (b) provides that "[a] *video tape service provider* who knowingly discloses, to any person, personally identifiable information concerning any consumer of such provider shall be liable to the aggrieved person for the relief provided in subsection (d)." 18 U.S.C. § 2710(b)(1) (emphasis added). Therefore, under the plain language of the statute, only a "video tape service provider" (VTSP) can be liable. The term VTSP is defined by the statute to mean "any person, engaged in the business, in or affecting interstate or foreign commerce, of rental, sale, or delivery of prerecorded video cassette tapes or similar audio video materials, or any person or other entity to whom a disclosure is made under subparagraph (D) or (E) of subsection (b)(2), but only with respect to the information contained in the disclosure." *Id.* at § 2710(a)(4). Daniel does not allege that the defendants in question are engaged in the business of rental, sale or delivery of prerecorded video cassette tapes. Therefore, the defendants may only be VTSPs if personal information was disclosed to them under subparagraph (D) or (E) of subsection (b)(2).

Subparagraph (D) applies "if the disclosure is solely the names and addresses of consumers." *Id.* at § 2710(b)(2)(D). Moreover, disclosure under subparagraph (D) must be "for the exclusive use of marketing goods and services directly to the consumer." *Id.* at § 2710(b)(2)(D)(ii). For instance, if a video store provided the names and addresses of its patrons to a movie magazine publisher, the publisher would be considered a VTSP, but only with respect to the information contained in the disclosure. No disclosure in this case was made under subparagraph (D). The information provided was not limited to Daniel's name and address. Instead, the disclosure was of Daniel's history of renting pornographic videotapes and included the specific titles of those videos. Additionally, the disclosure was not for marketing purposes but for purposes of a criminal investigation. Therefore, subparagraph (D) is inapplicable in this case.

Daniel properly does not argue that the disclosure falls within subparagraph (E). . . . Subparagraph (E) applies only to disclosures made "incident to the ordinary course of business" of the VTSP. *Id.* at § 2710(b)(2)(E). The term "ordinary course of business" is "narrowly defined" in the statute to mean "only debt collection activities, order fulfillment, request processing, and the transfer of ownership." *Id.* at § 2710(a)(2) . . . In sum, because Daniel has presented no evidence suggesting that a disclosure was made under subparagraph (D) or (E) in this case, the non-video store defendants are not VTSPs under the Act and therefore, are not proper parties to this litigation.

Daniel argues, however, that any person, not just a VTSP, can be liable under the Act based on *Dirkes v. Borough of Runnemede,* 936 F. Supp. 235 (D.N.J. 1996). *Dirkes* did reach this conclusion but only by misreading the Act. The court in *Dirkes* was focused on language in the Act stating that "[a]ny person aggrieved by any act of *a person* in violation of this section may bring a civil action in the United States district court." 18 U.S.C. § 2710(c)(1) (emphasis added). Because the statute states that a suit can be based upon an act of "a person" rather than an act of "a VTSP," *Dirkes* found that any person can be liable under the Act. *Dirkes,* however, ignored the rest of the sentence. A lawsuit under the Act must be based on an "act of a person *in violation of this section.* . . ." 18 U.S.C. § 2710(c)(1) (emphasis added). The statute makes it clear that only a VTSP can be in violation of section 2710(b). *See* § 2710(b)(1) ("A video tape service provider who knowingly discloses . . . personally identifiable information . . . shall be liable. . . ."). Moreover, if any person could be liable under the Act, there would be no need for the Act to define a VTSP in the first place. More tellingly, if any person could be liable under the Act, there is no reason that the definition of a VTSP would be limited to "any person . . . to whom a disclosure is made under subparagraph (D) or (E) of subsection (b)(2)." *Dirkes* would have us ignore this limitation and find that any person can be liable under the Act whether or not a disclosure was made to him under subparagraph (D) or (E). We avoid interpretations of a statute which would render portions of it superfluous.

The court in *Dirkes* found otherwise because the "clear intent of the Act," as demonstrated by its legislative history, "is to prevent the disclosure of private information." Where the plain language of a statute is clear, however, we do not consult the legislative history. . . . In any case, our interpretation of the statute — that only a VTSP can be liable under § 2710(b) — does not conflict with Congress' purpose in adopting the Act. One can "prevent the disclosure of private information" simply by cutting off disclosure at its source, i.e., the VTSP. Just because Congress' goal was to prevent the disclosure of private information, does not mean that Congress intended the implementation of every conceivable method of preventing disclosures. Printing all personal information in hieroglyphics instead of English would also help prevent the disclosure of such information. However, nothing in the legislative history suggests that Congress was encouraging hieroglyphics and, similarly, nothing suggests that Congress intended that anyone other than VTSPs would be liable under the Act. In sum, the Act is clear that only a VTSP can be liable under § 2710(b). Because the non-video store defendants do not fit within the definition of a VTSP, they are not proper parties.

NOTES & QUESTIONS

1. *To Whom Does VPPA Apply?* The key question in *Dirkes* and *Daniel* is whether the VPPA *only* regulates videotape service providers. The *Daniel* court answered this question affirmatively; the *Dirkes* court would apply the VPPA to additional parties, including law enforcement officers. Which interpretation of the statutory language do you find most convincing? Would policy reasons support a broader or narrower application of the statute?

2. *Facebook, Beacon, Blockbuster, and a VPPA Violation?* In April 2008, Cathryn Elain Harris filed a lawsuit against Blockbuster Video (a video tape service provider) and Facebook claiming violations of the VPPA. The complaint objected to Blockbuster reporting its customers' activities to Facebook through the Beacon program.

   Facebook introduced Beacon in November 2007; under it, partner companies shared information with Facebook about Facebook user activity that took place on their websites. Initially, this information became part of one's Facebook profile unless the user opted out. After consumer protest, Facebook changed its policy to require that a Facebook user would have to opt in to Beacon before information was disclosed on her Facebook page. It is not clear, however, whether opting out of Beacon stops partner companies from sharing information with Facebook.

The Harris complaint alleges that Blockbuster's website is still reporting a user's activities back to Facebook, whether or not the consumer opts out of having the information associated with her Facebook profile. Does the Blockbuster-Beacon-Facebook behavior, if as alleged, violate the VPPA? If so, what measure of damages should be used?

IN RE HULU PRIVACY LITIGATION

2012 WL 3282960 (N.D. Cal. 2012)

BEELER, MAGISTRATE J. . . . In this putative class action, viewers of Hulu's on-line video content allege that Hulu wrongfully disclosed their video viewing selections and personal identification information to third parties such as online ad networks, metrics companies (meaning, companies that track data), and social networks, in violation of the Video Privacy Protection Act, 18 U.S.C. § 2710. . . .

Defendant Hulu moves to dismiss the claim under Federal Rule of Civil Procedure 12(b)(1). . . .

Hulu operates a website called Hulu.com that provides video content, both previously released and posted and originally developed. . . .

Plaintiffs and Class Members used their Internet-connected computers and browsers to visit hulu.com and view video content. They were renters, purchasers, and/or subscribers of goods and/or services from Hulu and so were consumers as defined in the Video Privacy Protection Act. . . .

Plaintiffs value their privacy while web-browsing; they do not want to be tracked online; their web browsing (including their viewing choices) involves personal information that is private. . . .

Hulu allowed a metrics company called KISSmetrics to place code containing tracking identifiers on Plaintiffs' computers in the browser cache, Adobe Flash local storage, or DOM local storage. This code allegedly "respawned" or "resurrected" previously-deleted cookies. This code was "inescapable" and allowed Plaintiffs' data to be "retained ... so that they could be tracked over long periods of time and across multiple websites, regardless of whether they were registered and logged in." As a result, when Class Members viewed video content on Hulu.com, Hulu transmitted their video viewing choices and personally identifiable information to third parties without obtaining their written consent before the disclosure. The third parties included online ad networks, metrics companies, and social networks such as Scorecard Research ("Scorecard") (an online market research company), Facebook (the online social network), DoubleClick (an online ad network), Google Analytics (an online web analytics company), and QuantCast (an online ad network and web analytics company).

The information transmitted to Scorecard and Facebook included information that identified Plaintiffs and Class Members personally. As to Facebook, Hulu included their Facebook IDs, connecting the video content information to Facebook's personally identifiable user registration information. As to Scorecard, Hulu provided Plaintiffs' "Hulu profile identifiers" linked to their "individual Hulu profile pages that included name, location, preference information designated by the user as private, and Hulu username (which, in the case of many individuals, is the same screen name used in other online environments.)" . . . .

Plaintiffs allege that Hulu "knowingly and without . . . [their] consent disclosed to third parties . . . [their] video viewing selections and personally identifiable information, knowing that such disclosure included the disclosure of [their] personally identifying information . . . and their requests for and/or obtaining of specific video materials and/or services from Hulu," in violation of the Video Privacy Protection Act ("VPPA"), 18 U.S.C. § 2710(b)(1).

The Act prohibits a "video tape service provider" from (1) knowingly disclosing to any person (2) personally identifiable information concerning any consumer of such provider (3) except for certain disclosures—such as to the consumer or law enforcement—allowed under section 2710(b)(2). 18 U.S.C. § 2710. "'Personally identifiable information' includes information which identifies a person as having requested or obtained specific video materials or services." Such disclosures are not prohibited if they are "incident to the ordinary course of business" of the video tape service provider. The VPPA defines "ordinary course of business" as "debt collection activities, order fulfillment, request processing, and the transfer of ownership."

VPPA defines "video tape service provider" as "any person, engaged in the business, in or affecting interstate or foreign commerce, of rental, sale, or delivery of prerecorded video cassette tapes or similar audio visual materials."18 U.S.C. § 2710(a)(4).

Hulu does not deal in prerecorded video cassette tapes. Thus, whether Hulu is a "video tape service providers" turns on the scope of the phrase "similar audio visual materials."

Citing dictionary definitions, Hulu contends that "materials" are things "composed of physical matter." . . . As drafted, Hulu contends, the VPPA "only regulates businesses that sell or rent physical objects (i.e,'video cassettes or other similar audio visual materials') . . . and not businesses that transmit digital content over the Internet." . . . Had Congress wanted to regulate businesses dealing in digital content, it would have defined "video tape service provider" to include businesses that "traffic in audio-visual information or data."

To this reader, a plain reading of a statute that covers videotapes and "similar audio visual materials" is about the video content, not about how that content was delivered (e.g. via the Internet or a bricks-and-mortar store). Still, the online streaming mechanism of delivery here did not exist when Congress enacted the statute in 1988. A dictionary definition helps some. The undersigned looked at the third edition of Oxford English Dictionary, which defines "material" both as "relating to substance" and as "Text or images in printed or electronic form; also with distinguishing word, as reading material, etc." . . .

Also, the Senate Report confirms that Congress was concerned with protecting the confidentiality of private information about viewing preferences regardless of the business model or media format involved. . . .

The court concludes that Congress used "similar audio video materials" to ensure that VPAA's protections would retain their force even as technologies evolve. . . .

The court denies Hulu's motion to dismiss.

IN RE HULU PRIVACY LITIGATION

2014 WL 1724344 (N.D. Cal. 2014)

BEELER, MAGISTRATE J. . . . In this putative class action, viewers of Hulu's on-line video content allege that Hulu wrongfully disclosed their video viewing selections and personal identification information to third parties such as metrics companies (meaning, companies that track data) and social networks, in violation of the Video Privacy Protection Act ("VPPA"), 18 U.S.C. § 2710. . . .

The Act prohibits a "video tape service provider" from knowingly disclosing "personally identifiable information of a consumer of the provider" to third parties except under identified exceptions that do not apply here. See 18 U.S.C. § 2710. "The term 'personally identifiable information' includes information that identifies a person as having requested or obtained specific video materials or services from a video tape service provider." Id. § 2710(a)(3).

Hulu argues that it did not violate the VPPA because (I) it disclosed only anonymous user IDs and never linked the user IDs to identifying data such as a person's name or address; (II) it did not disclose the information "knowingly" and thus is not liable. . . .

The issue is whether Hulu's disclosures here (unique numeric identifications tied to video watching) are PII under the VPPA. The statute's plain language prohibits disclosure of information that "identifies a person" as having (in the Hulu context) viewed specific video content. 28 U.S.C. § 2710(a)(3). It does not say "identify by name" and thus plainly encompasses other means of identifying a person. Indeed, PII is not given one definition: "the term . . . includes information which identifies a person.". . .

The plain language of the statute suggests, and the Senate Report confirms, that the statute protects personally identifiable information that identifies a specific person and ties that person to particular videos that the person watched.

The issue then is whether the disclosures here are merely an anonymized ID or whether they are closer to linking identified persons to the videos they watched. A summary of the alleged disclosures is as follows:

1. Disclosure to comScore of Watch Page and Hulu User ID. The disclosure to comScore is of a "watch page" URL web address containing the video name and the Hulu user's unique seven-digit Hulu User ID. The ID also appeared in unencrypted form in the URL web address for the user's profile page in the standard format http://www.hulu.com/profiles/u/[User ID]. The profile page also listed the user's name (or at least the first and last name used to register with Hulu). This meant that comScore could access the profile page and see the user's first and last names.

2. Disclosure to comScore of the comScore UID (User ID) Cookie. Hulu sent comScore a "comScore ID" that was unique to each registered user. This allowed comScore to link the identified user and the user's video choices with information that comScore gathered from other websites that the same user visited.

3. Disclosure to Facebook of Watch Page and Transmission of Facebook Cookies to Facebook. These disclosures included unique identifiers that sometimes included the user's IP address and sometimes contained the user's Facebook ID. Because the URL web address had the video name, Facebook could see its users and what they were watching.

Hulu argues that it is not liable for these three disclosures because it never combined or linked the user IDs to identifying data such as a person's name or address. It characterizes Plaintiffs' comScore case as "the theoretical possibility that comScore could have used the anonymous ID . . . to find the user's name." It characterizes the Facebook case as "plaintiffs' evidence does not show that Facebook was gathering the actual name of its users from Hulu pages" and "there is no evidence that Facebook ever linked the anonymized identifier to a person's name, or to the title of a video that person watched." . . .

No case has addressed directly the issues raised by Plaintiffs: the disclosure of their unique identifiers and the videos they are watching. Most cases involve identified customers linked to the videos they watch. . . .

Hulu . . . argues that the disclosure has to be the person's actual name. That position paints too bright a line. One could not skirt liability under the VPPA, for example, by disclosing a unique identifier and a correlated look-up table. The statute does not require a name. It defines PII as a term that "includes information which identifies a person." The legislative history shows Congress used the word "includes" when it defined PII to establish a minimum, but not exclusive, definition. It is information that "identifies a particular person as having engaged in a specific transaction with a video tape service provider" by retaining or obtaining specific video materials or services. It does not require identification by a name necessarily. One can be identified in many ways: by a picture, by pointing, by an employee number, by the station or office or cubicle where one works, by telling someone what "that person" rented. In sum, the statute, the legislative history, and the case law do not require a name, instead require the identification of a specific person tied to a specific transaction, and support the conclusion that a unique anonymized ID alone is not PII but context could render it not anonymous and the equivalent of the identification of a specific person. . . .

Hulu's liability here is based on the hypothetical that comScore could use the Hulu ID to access the Hulu user's profile page to obtain the user's name. Hulu characterizes this argument as "reverse engineering" its data. The idea is that comScore could capture the data from the watch page, extract the relevant information (the video name and Hulu User ID), and plug the data into the standard-format URL for the profile page to capture the user's name from that page. There is no evidence that comScore did this. The issue is only that it could. . . .

. . . [The evidence] does not suggest any linking of a specific, identified person and his video habits. The court grants summary judgment in Hulu's favor on this theory. . . .

For similar reasons, the court grants Hulu summary judgment on [the cookies that could allow comScore to recognize users.] . . .

[Regarding the Facebook disclosures,] Hulu argues that it never sent the "actual" name of any Facebook user. Instead, the name came from the user's web browser and the interaction that Facebook had with its users. . . .

It may be true—as Hulu says—that accessing a remote browser involves sending that browser's cookies. But according to Plaintiffs' expert, it was straightforward to develop a webpage that would not communicate information to Facebook. Put another way, it was not necessary to send the "Facebook user" cookies, and they were sent because Hulu chose to include the Like button on watch pages. . . .

Hulu argues that it needed to send an actual name to be liable and that it sent only cookies. The statute does not require an actual name and requires only something akin to it. If the cookies contained a Facebook ID, they could show the Hulu user's identity on Facebook. . . .

Hulu also argues that there is no evidence that Facebook took any actions with the cookies after receiving them. It also says that there is no evidence that Facebook tied its Facebook user cookies to the URL for the watch page (and the accompanying title). In contrast to comScore, where the user was not tied to the video in one transmission, the transmission to Facebook included the video name and Facebook user cookies. Thus, the link between user and video was more obvious. But Hulu's point is that the information really was not disclosed to Facebook in the sense that the information about Judge Bork's video viewing was disclosed to the Washington Post.

Whether this link was the equivalent of a disclosure under the VPPA depends on the facts. One can think of analogies in a paper world. Throwing Judge Bork's video watch list in the recycle bin is not a disclosure. Throwing it in the bin knowing that the Washington Post searches your bin every evening for intelligence about local luminaries might be. The issue is whether Hulu made a "knowing" disclosure.

The statute requires a "knowing" disclosure "to any person." See 18 U.S.C. § 2710(b)(1). The emphasis is on disclosure, not comprehension by the receiving person. See S. Rep. 100–599, at *12 ("[s]ection 2710(b)(1) establishes a statutory presumption that the disclosure of personally identifiable information is a violation" unless a statutory exception applies). Thus, the Seventh Circuit held that the practice of placing PII on parking tickets in the view of the public was a disclosure that violated the analogous Driver's Privacy Protection Act, regardless of whether anyone viewed the PII. *See Senne v. Village of Palatine Ill.*, 695 F.3d 597 (7th Cir.2012) (en banc). By analogy, if a video store knowingly hands a list of Judge Bork's rented videos to a Washington Post reporter, it arguably violates the VPPA even if the reporter does not look at the list.

Still, disclosure of information on traffic tickets in public view or providing a list of videos is different than transmission of cookies tied to a watch page. The first disclosures transmit obvious PII. The second transmits cookies with identifying information that is the equivalent of a name only to someone who has the ability to read it. Moreover, the VPPA prohibits a knowing disclosure to "any person," and the point of that prohibition is to prevent disclosure of a person's video viewing preferences to someone else.

No case has construed the word "knowingly" as it appears in the VPPA. Other cases involving violations of privacy statutes show that in the context of a disclosure of private information, "knowingly" means consciousness of transmitting the private information. It does not mean merely transmitting the code. . . .

If Hulu did not know that it was transmitting both an identifier and the person's video watching information, then there is no violation of the VPPA. By contrast, if it did know what it was transmitting, then (depending on the facts) there might be a VPPA violation. . . .

. . . [A]rguing that transmitting cookies is just the normal way that webpages and the Like button load is not enough to negate knowledge or show the absence of evidence about knowledge. . . .

The court denies Hulu's summary judgment motion regarding the disclosures to Facebook. . . .

NOTES & QUESTIONS

1. *What Is a "Video Tape Service Provider"?* The court holds that Hulu is a videotape service provider, even though the statutory language refers to videotapes and was written in 1994, long before online streaming video. Should the phrase "rental, sale, or delivery of prerecorded video cassette tapes or similar audio visual materials" be interpreted broadly as the court interprets it?

2. *What Is PII?* The second opinion excerpted above involves what constitutes personally identifiable information (PII) under VPPA. The court recognizes that VPPA does not require actual names in order for a disclosure to be of PII — disclosing an ID could be the "equivalent to the identification of a specific person" depending upon the context. However, the court grants summary judgment to Hulu regarding the comScore disclosure because of a lack of evidence comScore was re-identifying the data by linking the ID to a person's name. Why is sending the cookies to Facebook different? The court writes:

> Hulu also argues that there is no evidence that Facebook took any actions with the cookies after receiving them. It also says that there is no evidence that Facebook tied its Facebook user cookies to the URL for the watch page (and the accompanying title). In contrast to comScore, where the user was not tied to the video in one transmission, the transmission to Facebook included the video name and Facebook user cookies. Thus, the link between user and video was more obvious.

Do you agree with this distinction? In dismissing comScore, the court also focused on the lack of actions comScore took after receiving the ID information. The court noted that "if a video store knowingly hands a list of Judge Bork's rented videos to a Washington Post reporter, it arguably violates the VPPA even if the reporter does not look at the list." Suppose a video store hands a list of rented videos to a *Washington Post* reporter with a unique ID number of the customer on the list. The *Washington Post* reporter can readily look up the unique ID number to figure out who the individual is. Why is the reporter who does not look at the list treated differently from the reporter who does not look up the unique ID number?

(b) The Cable Communications Policy Act

In 1984, Congress passed the Cable Communications Policy Act (CCPA or "Cable Act"), Pub. L. No. 98-549. The Act applies to cable operators and service providers. 47 U.S.C. § 551(a)(1).

Notice and Access. The Cable Act requires cable service providers to notify subscribers (in a written privacy policy) of the nature and uses of personal information collected. § 551(a)(1). Subscribers must have access to their personal data held by cable operators. § 551(d).

Limitations on Data Collection. Cable operators "shall not use the cable system to collect personally identifiable information concerning any subscriber without the prior written or electronic consent of the subscriber concerned." § 551(b)(1).

Limitations on Data Disclosure. Cable operators cannot disclose personally identifiable information about any subscriber without the subscriber's consent:

> [A] cable operator shall not disclose personally identifiable information concerning any subscriber without the prior written or electronic consent of the subscriber concerned and shall take such actions as are necessary to prevent unauthorized access to such information by a person other than the subscriber or cable operator. § 551(c)(1).

However, cable operators can disclose personal data under certain circumstances, such as when necessary for a "legitimate business activity" or pursuant to a court order if the subscriber is notified. Cable operators may disclose subscriber names and addresses if "the cable operator has provided the subscriber the opportunity to prohibit or limit such disclosure." § 551(c)(2).

Data Destruction. Cable operators must destroy personal data if the information is no longer necessary for the purpose for which it was collected. § 551(e).

Government Access to Cable Information. Pursuant to § 551(h):

> A governmental entity may obtain personally identifiable information concerning a cable subscriber pursuant to a court order only if, in the court proceeding relevant to such court order —
>
> > (1) such entity offers clear and convincing evidence that the subject of the information is reasonably suspected of engaging in criminal activity and that the information sought would be material evidence in the case; and
> > (2) the subject of the information is afforded the opportunity to appear and contest such entity's claim.

Note that a court order to obtain cable records requires "clear and convincing evidence," a standard higher than probable cause. There is no exclusionary rule for information obtained in violation of the Cable Act.

Enforcement. The Cable Act provides for a private cause of action and actual damages, with a minimum of $1,000 or $100 for each day of the violation, whichever is higher. The plaintiff can collect any actual damages that are more than the statutory minimum. Further, the Cable Act provides for punitive damages and attorneys' fees. § 551(f).

Cable Internet Service. Section 211 of the USA PATRIOT Act amended the Cable Act, 47 U.S.C. § 551(c)(2)(D), to provide disclosure to a government entity under federal wiretap law when the government seeks information from cable companies except that "such disclosure shall not include records revealing cable subscriber selection of video programming from a cable operator." This provision of the PATRIOT Act will not sunset.

New Cable Services and Products? In March 2011, the *Wall Street Journal* reported on the testing by cable companies of new systems that are designed to show households highly targeted ads.[72] The goal is to "emulate the sophisticated tracking widely used on people's personal computers with new technology that reaches the living room." In one test of Cablevision's technology, for example, the U.S. Army used it to target four different recruitment ads to different categories of viewers. In many of these systems, companies generally seek to remove personal data, including names, before data is sent to third party companies who match ads to households.

In August 2014, the *Washington Post* predicted that the cable industry was about to start serving targeted ads on a large scale. It discussed how a cable-owned service, called NBCU+, was planning to combine cable subscriber information with data from other sources, "such as loyalty card purchases, box office sales, and even car registrations."[73] The plan was said likely to involve purchasing data from data brokers, such as Acxiom and Experian.

Does these practices comport with the Cable Act?

2. INTERNET USE AND ELECTRONIC COMMUNICATIONS

(a) The Children's Online Privacy Protection Act

Passed in 1998, the Children's Online Privacy Protection Act (COPPA), Pub. L. No. 106-170, 15 U.S.C. §§ 6501–6506, regulates the collection and use of children's information by Internet websites. In January 2013, the FTC issued an important amendments to its COPPA Rule, which it included in a complete re-issued Final COPPA Rule. 16 C.F.R. Part 312. These Rules took effect in July 2013.

Scope. COPPA applies to "an operator of a website or online service directed to children, or any operator that has actual knowledge that it is collecting personal information from a child." 15 U.S.C. § 6502(a)(1). COPPA only applies to websites that collect personal information from children under age 13.

---

[72] Jessica E. Vascellaro, *TV's Next Wave: Tuning into You*, Wall St. J., Mar. 7, 2011.

[73] Brian Fung, *Blogs: The Switch, Targeted Ads Are About to Take Over Your TV*, Wash. Post (Jan. 31, 2014).

§ 6502(1). COPPA does not apply to information collected from adults about children under 13; it only applies to personal data collected *from* children themselves.

Personal Information. In 2013, the FTC clarified that "personal information" under COPPA includes a voice, audio, image file containing a child's voice and/or image; geolocation data that reveals a street name plus city, or equally revealing information; online contact information such as a screen name or user name, persistent identifiers that recognize users across time and sites or services, such as an IP address or device serial number. COPPA Final Rule, 78 Fed. Reg. 3971 (Jan. 17, 2013), 16 C.F.R. § 312.

Collection of Personal Information. The "collection" of personal information is defined broadly. It means "the gathering of any personal information from a child by any means, including but not limited to: (1) Requesting, prompting, or encouraging a child to submit personal information online; (2) Enabling a child to make personal information publicly available in identifiable form." 16 C.F.R. §312.2.

Notice. Children's websites must post privacy policies, describing "what information is collected from children by the operator, how the operator uses such information, and the operator's disclosure practices for such information." § 6502(b)(1)(A)(i).

Consent. Children's websites must "obtain verifiable parental consent for the collection, use or disclosure of personal information from children." § 6502(b)(1)(A)(ii). Websites cannot condition child's participation in a game or receipt of a prize on the disclosure of more personal information than is necessary to participate in that activity. § 6502(b)(1)(C). When information is not maintained in retrievable form, then consent is not required. § 6502(b)(2).

Right to Restrict Uses of Personal Information. If parent requests it, the operator must provide to the parent a description of the "specific types of personal information collected," the right to "refuse to permit the operator's further use or maintenance in retrievable form, or future online collection, of personal information from that child," and the right to "obtain any personal information collected from the child." § 6502(b)(1)(B).

Liability When Sites Operate in Connection with Third Parties. As of the 2013 rule change, both hosts of sites and third parties operating through sites are subject to enforcement under COPPA. Hosts regulated by COPPA are strictly liable for the activities of third parties operating on their site if the third party is an agent of the regulated service or the primary regulated service receives a benefit from a third party. The third party is liable if it has "actual knowledge" that the host site is directed to children. For example, a website using ads from an ad network is strictly liable for information collected by the ad network. The ad network would be liable if it has actual knowledge that the website is directed to children. *See* COPPA Final Rule, 16 § C.F.R. 312.

Enforcement. Violations of COPPA are "treated as a violation of a rule defining an unfair or deceptive act or practice" under 15 U.S.C. § 57a(a)(1)(B). Thus, the FTC enforces the law and can impose fines up to $16,000 per violation. The amount of the fine depends upon a number of factors including "the egregiousness of the violations, whether the operator has previously violated the Rule, the number of children involved, the amount and type of personal information collected, how the information was used, whether it was shared with third parties, and the size of the company."[74]

There is no private cause of action for violations of COPPA.

States can bring civil actions for violations of COPPA in the interests of its citizens to obtain injunctions and damages. § 6504.

Preemption. COPPA preempts state law. § 6502(d).

Safe Harbor. If an operator follows self-regulatory guidelines issued by marketing or online industry groups that are approved by the FTC, then the COPPA requirements will be deemed satisfied. § 6503.

Should COPPA be extended to apply to everyone, not just children? Should there be a private cause of action under COPPA? Note that COPPA only applies when a website has "actual knowledge" that a user is under 13 or operates a website specifically targeted to children. Is this too limiting? Would a rule dispensing with the "actual knowledge" requirement be feasible?[75]

UNITED STATES V. PATH, INC.

2012 WL 7006381 (N.D. Cal. 2012)

COMPLAINT

Plaintiff, the United States of America, acting upon notification and authorization to the Attorney General by the Federal Trade Commission ("FTC" or "Commission"), for its Complaint alleges:

1. Plaintiff brings this action under . . . the Children's Online Privacy Protection Act of 1998 ("COPPA") . . .

7. Defendant Path, Inc. ("Path") . . . develops, markets, distributes, or sells software applications for mobile devices to consumers throughout the U.S. and provides online services to users of its applications. From at least 2010, Defendant has operated a social networking online service that is accessible worldwide on the Internet through a website and mobile applications. . . .

---

[74] FTC, *Complying with COPPA: Frequently Asked Questions* (July 16, 2014), http://www.business.ftc.gov/documents/0493-Complying-with-COPPA-Frequently-Asked-Questions.

[75] For more information about COPPA, see Dorothy A. Hertzel, Note, *Don't Talk to Strangers: An Analysis of Government and Industry Efforts to Protect Child's Privacy Online*, 52 Fed. Comm. L.J. 429 (2000).

10. Defendant describes its social networking service as "the smart journal that helps you share life with the ones you love," and allows users to keep a journal about "moments" in the user's life and to share that journal with a network of up to 150 persons. Through the Path App, the user can upload, store and share photos, written "thoughts," the user's location, and the names of songs to which the user is listening. On the "About" page of its website, Defendant describes its "Values" and espouses that "Path should be private by default. Forever. You should always be in control of your information and experience."

11. At all times relevant to this Complaint, when a user registers for Defendant's social networking service, the user must provide an email address, a first name, and a last name. The user's email address serves as his or her login identity. At registration, the user is also invited to provide gender, phone number, and date of birth. The Path App for iOS has been downloaded and installed over 2.5 million times. . . .

20. In addition to its Path App for iOS, Defendant's social networking service is also accessible through a Path App for Google, Inc.'s Android operating system, and, until December 2011, through Defendant's website, path.com. The Path App for iOS, the Path App for Android, and the Defendant's website were all intended for a general audience, but also attracted a significant number of children.

21. As discussed in Paragraph 11, when a user registered for the Defendant's social networking service, whether through one of the Path Apps or through Defendant's website, the user was required to provide an email address, a first name, and a last name, and was invited to provide gender, phone number, and date of birth.

22. From November 14, 2010, through May 4, 2012, Defendant accepted registrations from users who entered a date of birth indicating that the user was under the age of 13. As a result, Defendant knowingly collected email address, first name, last name, date of birth, and if provided, gender and phone number, from approximately 3,000 children under age 13. Defendant, therefore, was an "operator" as defined in the Rule.

23. From November 29, 2011, through February 8, 2012, Defendant also knowingly collected from these children the following personal information for each contact in the child's mobile device address book, if available: first name, last name, address, phone numbers, email addresses, and date of birth.

24. A child who registered through the Path App or Defendant's website was able to create a journal and upload, store and share photos, written "thoughts," the child's precise location, and the names of songs to which the child was listening. In fact, each time a child uploaded a photo or posted a "thought," the Path App would invite the child to also share his or her location through the application's geo-location tracking feature and the names of any friends that were with the child when the photo was taken or the thought was posted. Likewise, if the child decided to share his or her location through the application's geo-location tracking feature, the Path App would invite the child to also share the names of friends that were with the child at that location, and prompt the child to add a "thought." The child could also comment on the posts of other users in the child's network.

25. Until May 4, 2012, Defendant knowingly collected children's personal information and enabled children to publicly disclose their personal information through the Defendant's social networking service.

26. Defendant's online notice of its information practices did not clearly, completely, or accurately disclose all of Defendant's information collection, use, and disclosure practices for children, as required by the Rule.

27. Defendant did not provide parents with a direct notice of its information practices prior to collecting, using, or disclosing children's personal information.

28. Defendant did not obtain verifiable consent from parents prior to collecting, using, or disclosing children's personal information.

29. In approximately 3,000 instances, Defendant knowingly collected, used, and/or disclosed personal information from children in violation of the Children's Online Privacy Protection Rule. . . .

34. In numerous instances, in connection with operating its Path App for iOS, its Path App for the Android operating system, and its website, path.com, Defendant collected, used, and/or disclosed, with actual knowledge, personal information online from children younger than age 13. Defendant failed to: (1) provide sufficient notice on its website or online services of the information it collects online from children, how it uses such information, and its disclosure practices, among other required content; (2) provide direct notice to parents of the information Defendant collects online from children, how it uses such information, and its disclosure practices for such information, among other required content; and (3) obtain verifiable parental consent before any collection, use, and/or disclosure of personal information from children. . . .

NOTES & QUESTIONS

1. *Settlement.* Path settled with the FTC, agreeing to destroy the data it had collected about children. Path also agreed to pay a civil payment of $800,000.
2. *Inadvertently Triggering COPPA.* Path's online service was not directed at children under 13; rather, it was for all users. It triggered COPPA because it collected birth dates, thus giving it actual knowledge that some users were under 13. Is it fair to punish Path for what might have been an inadvertent triggering of COPPA?
3. *Restricting Use to Users 13 Years or Older.* Some websites seek to avoid triggering COPPA by requiring users to be 13 years or older. For example, Facebook states:

> Facebook requires everyone to be at least 13 years old before they can create an account (in some jurisdictions, this age limit may be higher). Creating an account with false info is a violation of our terms. This includes accounts registered on the behalf of someone under 13

The result of COPPA thus means fewer sites that allow users under 13. Is this result desirable?

The reality is, however, that many children under 13 lie about their age in order to sign up for Facebook accounts. In June 2011, Consumer Reports found that "more than one-third of the 20 million minors who actively used

Facebook in the past year" were under 13.[76] This meant 7.5 million users of Facebook who were younger than 13. It stated: "Parents of kids 10 and younger on Facebook seem to be largely unconcerned." The magazine also warned, "Ten-year-olds need protection from . . . hazards that might lurk on the Internet, such as links that might infect their computer with malware and invitations from strangers, not to mention bullies."

To what extent should Facebook have an obligation to make it harder for children under 13 to sign up deceitfully? For all the children who do lie about their age, is Facebook just putting its head in the sand?

One possible solution is to remove the "actual knowledge" prong of COPPA and only apply the law to websites specifically directed at children. But would that be too limiting of COPPA and allow too much of an end-run around its protections?

4. ***FTC Enforcement Actions.*** The FTC has engaged in several enforcement actions pursuant to COPPA. These cases have resulted in settlements simultaneously with the filing of complaints. Heavy penalties have been assessed as part of some of the settlements. In 2011, the FTC received its largest civil settlement yet under COPPA. Playdom, an operator of online virtual worlds, agreed to pay $3 million to settle FTC charges that it had violated COPPA. The company was alleged to have illegally collected and disclosed personal information from hundreds of thousands of children under age 13 without their parents' prior consent.

In its complaint, the FTC stated that Playdom violated its stated privacy policy by collecting children's personal information and also enabled children to publicly disclose this information through their personal profile pages and in community forums at its websites. The company also did not take necessary steps "to provide parents with a direct notice of [its] information practices prior to collecting, using, or disclosing children's personal information" and to collect "verifiable consent from parents." The FTC tallied no fewer than 1.2 million instances of the company's collection, use, and/or disclosure of personal information in violation of COPPA.

As a further example, the FTC announced a settlement in 2006 with Xanga.com, which included a $1 million civil penalty. The complaint charges that Xanga.com, a social networking website, had actual knowledge of its collection of disclosure of children's personal information. The Xanga website stated that children under 13 could not join its social network, but it allowed visitors to create Xanga accounts even if they provided a birth date indicating that they were younger than that age. Moreover, Xanga did not provide parents with access to and control over their children's information, and did not notify the parents of children who joined the site of its information practices. Finally, the FTC found that Xanga had created 1.7 million accounts for users who submitted age information that indicated they were younger than 13 years old.

---

[76] *That Facebook Friend Might Be 10 Years Old, and Other Troubling News*, Consumer Reports (June 2011).

In 2011, in *United States v. W3 Innovations, LLC,* No. CV-11-03958-PSG (Aug. 12, 2011), the FTC settled an action against a developer of children's gaming apps for the iPhone and iPod. W3 Innovations (doing business as Broken Thumbs Apps) failed to have a privacy policy or to obtain parental consent before collecting and disclosing children's personal data. Under the settlement, W3 was fined $50,000 and ordered to delete all information collected in violation of COPPA.

5. *Is COPPA Too Paternalistic?* Consider the following critique of COPPA by Anita Allen:

> Not all parents welcome the veto power COPPA confers. New power has meant new responsibility. The statute forces parents who would otherwise be content to give their children free rein over their computers to get involved in children's use of Internet sites that are geared toward children and collect personal information. . . .
>
> Prohibiting voluntary disclosures by children lacking parental consent in situations in which they and their parents may be indifferent to privacy losses and resentful of government intervention, COPPA is among the most paternalistic and authoritarian of the federal privacy statutes thus far.[77]

More recently, Allen has wondered whether young adults might also need paternalistic laws.[78] At the same time, she concedes, "Sharing data is the way of the contemporary world. There is no chance the United States government will intervene in a strict censorship mode to curb radical forms of self-disclosure online." On a pessimistic note, Allen also notes:

> [COPPA] could be viewed as part of a nation's formative educational project: the young are to be taught the value of privacy by imposing privacy protection rules limiting their choices until they are old enough to choose responsibly. But it will be difficult for children to get the message that privacy is a duty of self-care if they closely observe the actual behavior of teens and young adults. Everyone under the age of forty seems to be freely sharing personal facts, ideas, fantasies, and revealing images of themselves all the time.

Is COPPA doomed by a decline of modesty about self-revelation on the Internet? What role, if any, should the law play in nudging or coercing people to protect their own privacy?

(b) The Electronic Communications Privacy Act

In several cases, plaintiffs have attempted to use the Electronic Communications Privacy Act (ECPA) to prevent certain kinds of information collection, use, and disclosure by commercial entities. Recall from Chapter 3 that EPCA consists of three acts: (1) the Wiretap Act, 18 U.S.C. §§ 2510–2522, which regulates the interception of communications; (2) the Stored Communications Act (SCA), 18 U.S.C. §§ 2701–2711, which regulates communications in storage and ISP subscriber records; and (3) the Pen Register Act, 18 U.S.C. §§ 3121–3127, which regulates the use of pen register and trap

---

[77] Anita L. Allen, *Minor Distractions: Children, Privacy and E-Commerce,* 38 Hous. L. Rev. 751, 752-53, 768-69, 775-76 (2001).

[78] Anita L. Allen, *Unpopular Privacy* 190-94 (2011).

and trace devices. The attempts to use ECPA to regulate commercial entities using personal information primarily seek to use the Wiretap Act or the SCA.

IN RE GOOGLE, INC. GMAIL LITIGATION

2013 WL 543918 (N.D. Cal. 2013)

KOH, J. In this consolidated multi-district litigation, Plaintiffs . . . allege that Defendant Google, Inc., has violated state and federal antiwiretapping laws in its operation of Gmail, an email service. Before the Court is Google's Motion to Dismiss Plaintiffs' Consolidated Complaint. . . .

Plaintiffs challenge Google's operation of Gmail under state and federal anti-wiretapping laws. The Consolidated Complaint seeks damages on behalf of a number of classes of Gmail users and non–Gmail users for Google's interception of emails over a period of several years. . . . Plaintiffs allege . . . that in all iterations of Google's email routing processes since 2008, Google has intercepted, read and acquired the content of emails that were sent or received by Gmail user while the emails were in transit. . . .

Plaintiffs further allege that Google used these . . . data to create user profiles and models. Google then allegedly used the emails, affiliated data, and user profiles to serve their profit interests that were unrelated to providing email services to particular users. . . .

Gmail implicates several different, but related, systems of email delivery, three of which are at issue here. The first is a free service, which allows any user to register for an account with Google to use Gmail. This system is supported by advertisements, though users can opt-out of such advertising or access Gmail accounts in ways that do not generate advertising, such as accessing email on a smartphone.

The second is Google's operation of email on behalf of Internet Service Providers ("ISPs"). Google, through its Google Apps Partner program, enters into contracts with ISPs, such as Cable One, to provide an email service branded by the ISP. The ISP's customers can register for email addresses from their ISP (such as "@mycableone.com"), but their email is nevertheless powered by Google through Gmail.

Third, Google operates Google Apps for Education, through which Google provides email on behalf of educational organizations for students, faculty, staff, and alumni. These users receive "@name.institution.edu" email addresses, but their accounts are also powered by Google using Gmail. *Id.* Universities that are part of Google Apps for Education require their students to use the Gmail–provided service.

Google Apps users, whether through the educational program or the partner program, do not receive content-based ads but can opt in to receiving such advertising. Google processes emails sent and received from all Gmail users, including Google Apps users, in the same way except that emails of users who do not receive advertisements are not processed through Google's advertising infrastructure, which attaches targeted advertisements to emails. . . . [E]mails to and from users who did not receive advertisements are nevertheless intercepted to create user profiles. . . .

The operation of the Gmail service implicates several legal agreements. Gmail users were required to agree to one of two sets of Terms of Service during the class periods. The first Terms of Service was in effect from April 16, 2007, to March 1, 2012, and the second has been in effect since March 1, 2012. The 2007 Terms of Service stated that:

> Google reserves the right (but shall have no obligation) to pre-screen, review, flag, filter, modify, refuse or remove any or all Content from any Service. For some Services, Google may provide tools to filter out explicit sexual content. These tools include the SafeSearch preference settings.... In addition, there are commercially available services and software to limit access to material that you may find objectionable.

A subsequent section of the 2007 Terms of Service provided that "[s]ome of the Services are supported by advertising revenue and may display advertisements and promotions" and that "[t]hese advertisements may be content-based to the content information stored on the Services, queries made through the Service or other information."

The 2012 Terms of Service deleted the above language and stated that users "give Google (and those [Google] work[s] with) a worldwide license to use . . . , create derivative works (such as those resulting from translations, adaptations or other changes we make so that your content works better with our Services), . . . and distribute such content."

Both Terms of Service reference Google's Privacy Policies, which have been amended three times thus far during the putative class periods. These Policies, which were largely similar, stated that Google could collect information that users provided to Google, cookies, log information, user communications to Google, information that users provide to affiliated sites, and the links that a user follows. The Policies listed Google's provision of "services to users, including the display of customized content and advertising" as one of the reasons for the collection of this information.

Google also had in place Legal Notices, which stated . . . that Google "will not use any of [users'] content for any purpose except to provide [users] with the service." . . .

Importantly, Plaintiffs who are not Gmail or Google Apps users are not subject to any of Google's express agreements. Because non-Gmail users exchange emails with Gmail users, however, their communications are nevertheless subject to the alleged interceptions at issue in this case.

Plaintiffs bring these cases alleging that Google, in the operation of its Gmail system, violated federal and state anti-wiretapping laws. . . .

The Wiretap Act, as amended by the ECPA, generally prohibits the interception of "wire, oral, or electronic communications." 18 U.S.C. § 2511(1); More specifically, the Wiretap Act provides a private right of action against any person who "intentionally intercepts, endeavors to intercept, or procures any other person to intercept or endeavor to intercept, any wire, oral, or electronic communication." 18 U.S.C. § 2511(1)(a); *see id.* § 2520 (providing a private right of action for violations of § 2511). The Act further defines "intercept" as "the aural or other acquisition of the contents of any wire, electronic, or oral communication through the use of any electronic, mechanical, or other device."

Plaintiffs contend that Google violated the Wiretap Act in its operation of the Gmail system by intentionally intercepting the content of emails that were in transit to create profiles of Gmail users and to provide targeted advertising. . . .

1. *"Ordinary Course of Business" Exception.* Google first contends that it did not engage in an interception because its reading of users' emails occurred in the ordinary course of its business. . . . The Court finds that the ordinary course of business exception is narrow. The exception offers protection from liability only where an electronic communication service provider's interception facilitates the transmission of the communication at issue or is incidental to the transmission of such communication. Specifically, the exception would apply here only if the alleged interceptions were an instrumental part of the transmission of email. Plaintiffs have alleged, however, that Google's interception is not an instrumental component of Google's operation of a functioning email system. In fact, Google's alleged interception of email content is primarily used to create user profiles and to provide targeted advertising— neither of which is related to the transmission of emails. The Court further finds that Plaintiffs' allegations that Google violated Google's own agreements and internal policies with regard to privacy also preclude application of the ordinary course of business exception. . . .

The narrow construction of "ordinary course of business" is most evident in section 2510(5)(a)(i) cases where an employer has listened in on employees' phone calls in the workplace. These cases suggest that an employer's eavesdropping on an employee's phone call is only permissible where the employer has given notice to the employee. Further, these cases have suggested that an employer may only listen to an employee's phone call for the narrow purpose of determining whether a call is for personal or business purposes. . . .

In light of the statutory text, case law, statutory scheme, and legislative history concerning the ordinary course of business exception, the Court finds that the section 2510(5)(a)(ii) exception is narrow and designed only to protect electronic communication service providers against a finding of liability under the Wiretap Act where the interception facilitated or was incidental to provision of the electronic communication service at issue. Plaintiffs have plausibly alleged that Google's reading of their emails was not within this narrow ordinary course of its business. Specifically, Plaintiffs allege that Google intercepts emails for the purposes of creating user profiles and delivering targeted advertising, which are not instrumental to Google's ability to transmit emails. . . . Plaintiffs support their assertion by suggesting that Google's interceptions of emails for targeting advertising and creating user profiles occurred independently from the rest of the email-delivery system. . . .

Accordingly, the Court denies Google's Motion to Dismiss based on the section 2510(5)(a)(ii) exception.

2. *Consent.* Google's second contention with respect to Plaintiffs' Wiretap Act claim is that all Plaintiffs consented to any interception of emails in question in the instant case. Specifically, Google contends that by agreeing to its Terms of Service and Privacy Policies, all Gmail users have consented to Google reading their emails Google further suggests that even though non–Gmail users have not

agreed to Google's Terms of Service or Privacy Policies, all non–Gmail users impliedly consent to Google's interception when non-Gmail users send an email to or receive an email from a Gmail user.

If either party to a communication consents to its interception, then there is no violation of the Wiretap Act. 18 U.S.C. § 2511(2)(d). Consent to an interception can be explicit or implied, but any consent must be actual. Courts have cautioned that implied consent applies only in a narrow set of cases. The critical question with respect to implied consent is whether the parties whose communications were intercepted had adequate notice of the interception. That the person communicating knows that the interceptor has the *capacity* to monitor the communication is insufficient to establish implied consent. Moreover, consent is not an all-or-nothing proposition. Rather, "[a] party may consent to the interception of only part of a communication or to the interception of only a subset of its communications." . . .

In its Motion to Dismiss, Google marshals both explicit and implied theories of consent. Google contends that by agreeing to Google's Terms of Service and Privacy Policies, Plaintiffs who are Gmail users expressly consented to the interception of their emails. Google further contends that because of the way that email operates, even non-Gmail users knew that their emails would be intercepted, and accordingly that non-Gmail users impliedly consented to the interception. Therefore, Google argues that in all communications, both parties— regardless of whether they are Gmail users—have consented to the reading of emails. The Court rejects Google's contentions with respect to both explicit and implied consent. Rather, the Court finds that it cannot conclude that any party— Gmail users or non-Gmail users—has consented to Google's reading of email for the purposes of creating user profiles or providing targeted advertising.

Google points to its Terms of Service and Privacy Policies, to which all Gmail and Google Apps users agreed, to contend that these users explicitly consented to the interceptions at issue. The Court finds, however, that those policies did not explicitly notify Plaintiffs that Google would intercept users' emails for the purposes of creating user profiles or providing targeted advertising.

Section 8 of the Terms of Service that were in effect from April 16, 2007, to March 1, 2012, stated that "Google reserves the right (but shall have no obligation) to pre-screen, review, flag, filter, modify, refuse or remove any or all Content from any Service." This sentence was followed by a description of steps users could take to avoid sexual and objectionable material. Later, section 17 of the Terms of Service stated that "advertisements may be targeted to the content of information stored on the Services, queries made through the Services or other information."

The Court finds that Gmail users' acceptance of these statements does not establish explicit consent. Section 8 of the Terms of Service suggests that content may be intercepted under a different set of circumstances for a different purpose—to exclude objectionable content, such as sexual material. This does not suggest to the user that Google would intercept emails for the purposes of creating user profiles or providing targeted advertising. Therefore, to the extent that section 8 of the Terms of Service establishes consent, it does so only for the purpose of interceptions to eliminate objectionable content. The Consolidated Complaint suggests, however, that Gmail's interceptions for the purposes of targeted advertising and creation of user profiles was separate from screening for any objectionable content. Because the two processes were allegedly separate, consent to one does not equate to consent to the other.

Section 17 of the Terms of Service—which states that Google's "advertisements may be targeted to the content of information stored on the Services, queries made through the Services or other information"—is defective in demonstrating consent for a different reason: it demonstrates only that Google has the *capacity* to intercept communications, not that it will. Moreover, the language suggests only that Google's advertisements were based on information "stored on the Services" or "queries made through the Services"—not information in transit via email. Plaintiffs here allege that Google violates the Wiretap Act, which explicitly protects communications in transit, as distinguished from communications that are stored. Furthermore, providing targeted advertising is only one of the alleged reasons for the interceptions at issue in this case. Plaintiffs also allege that Google intercepted emails for the purposes of creating user profiles. Section 17, to the extent that it suggests interceptions, only does so for the purposes of providing advertising, not creating user profiles. Accordingly, the Court finds that neither section of the Terms of Service establishes consent.

The Privacy Policies explicitly state that Google collects "user communications ... *to Google*." This could mislead users into believing that user communications to each other or to nonusers were not intercepted and used to target advertising or create user profiles. As such, these Privacy Policies do not demonstrate explicit consent, and in fact suggest the opposite.

After March 1, 2012, Google modified its Terms of Service and Privacy Policy. The new policies are no clearer than their predecessors in establishing consent. The relevant part of the new Terms of Service state that when users upload content to Google, they "give Google (and those [Google] work[s] with) a worldwide license to use . . . , create derivative works (such as those resulting from translations, adaptations or other changes we make so that your content works better with our Services), . . . and distribute such content."

The Terms of Service cite the new Privacy Policy, in which Google states to users that Google "may collect information about the services that you use and how you use them, like when you visit a website that uses our advertising services or you view and interact with our ads and content. This information include [device information, log information, location information, unique application numbers, local storage, cookies, and anonymous identifiers]. The Privacy Policy further states that Google "use[s] the information [it] collect[s] from all [its] services to provide, maintain, protect and improve them, to develop new ones, and to protect Google and [its] users. [Google] also use[s] this information to offer you tailored content—like giving you more relevant search results and ads." These new policies do not specifically mention the content of users' emails to each other or to or from non-users; these new policies are not broad enough to encompass such interceptions. Furthermore, the policies do not put users on notice that their emails are intercepted to create user profiles. The Court therefore finds that a reasonable Gmail user who read the Privacy Policies would not have necessarily understood that her emails were being intercepted to create user profiles or to provide targeted advertisements. Accordingly, the Court finds that it cannot conclude at this phase that the new policies demonstrate that Gmail user Plaintiffs consented to the interceptions.

Finally, Google contends that non-Gmail users—email users who do not have a Gmail account and who did not accept Gmail's Terms of Service or Privacy Policies—nevertheless impliedly consented to Google's interception of their emails to and from Gmail users, and to Google's use of such emails to create user profiles and to provide targeted advertising. Google's theory is that all email users understand and accept the fact that email is automatically processed. However, the cases Google cites for this far-reaching proposition hold only that the sender of an email consents to the intended recipients' recording of the email—not, as has been alleged here, interception by a third-party service provider. Google has cited no case that stands for the proposition that users who send emails impliedly consent to interceptions and use of their communications by third parties other than the intended recipient of the email. Nor has Google cited anything that suggests that by doing nothing more than receiving emails from a Gmail user, non–Gmail users have consented to the interception of those communications. Accepting Google's theory of implied consent—that by merely sending emails to or receiving emails from a Gmail user, a non–Gmail user has consented to Google's interception of such emails for any purposes—would eviscerate the rule against interception. The Court does not find that non-Gmail users who are not subject to Google's Privacy Policies or Terms of Service have impliedly consented to Google's interception of their emails to Gmail users.

Because Plaintiffs have adequately alleged that they have not explicitly or implicitly consented to Google's interceptions, the Court denies Google's Motion to Dismiss on the basis of consent. . . .

NOTES & QUESTIONS

1. *Gmail's Business Model.* Google offers Gmail for free to users and makes money from Gmail through targeted advertising. Google can fix its problems obtaining user consent by providing more explicit notice to Gmail account holders. But how should it deal with non-Gmail users who correspond with Gmail users? Does this problem make the business model unworkable? Is there a way to readily obtain the consent of non-Gmail users?

2. *The Scope of the Wiretap Act.* In *Joffe v. Google, Inc.,* 746 F.3d 920 (9th Cir. 2013), plaintiffs sued Google alleging that it violated the Wiretap Act by collecting data from unecrypted wi-fi networks. Google argued that data transmitted via wi-fi is a "radio communication" that is "readily accessible to the general public" and exempt from the Wiretap Act. The court rejected Google's argument.

3. *Does ECPA Prohibit Cookies?* When a person interacts with a website, the site can record certain information about the person, such as what parts of the website the user visited, what the user clicked on, and how long the user spent reading different parts of the website. This information is called "clickstream data."

Websites use "cookies" to identify particular users.[79] A cookie is a small text file that is downloaded into the user's computer when a user accesses a Web page. The text in a cookie, which is often encoded, usually includes an identification number and several other data elements, such as the website and the expiration date. The cookie lets a website know that a particular user has returned. The website can then access any information it collected about that individual on her previous visits to the website. Cookies can also be used to track users as they visit multiple websites.

In *In re Doubleclick Inc. Privacy Litigation*, 154 F. Supp. 2d 497 (S.D.N.Y. 2001), a group of plaintiffs challenged DoubleClick's use of cookies under the Stored Communications Act (SCA) and Wiretap Act. In 2001, DoubleClick was the leading company providing online advertising. DoubleClick helps advertisers distribute advertisements to websites based on information about specific web surfers. When a person visits a DoubleClick-affiliated website, DoubleClick places a cookie on that person's computer. As the person visits other sites that use DoubleClick, it builds a profile of that person's Web surfing activity. DoubleClick then can target ads to specific people based on their profile. For example, suppose a news website uses DoubleClick. A person visits the news website. The website checks with DoubleClick to see if DoubleClick recognizes the person. If the person's computer has a DoubleClick cookie, DoubleClick then looks up the profile associated with the cookie and sends the website advertisements tailored to that person's interests. Suppose Person A likes tennis and Person B likes golf. When Person A goes to the news website, a banner ad for tennis might appear. When Person B visits the same site, a banner ad for golf might appear.

The plaintiffs in the *DoubleClick* case raised an SCA claim and a Wiretap Act claim. Regarding the SCA claim, the Act provides:

> [W]hoever (1) intentionally accesses without authorization a facility through which an electronic information service is provided; or (2) intentionally exceeds an authorization to access that facility; and thereby obtains . . . access to a wire or electronic communication while it is in electronic storage in such system shall be punished. . . . 18 U.S.C. § 2701(a).

Although the court ultimately concluded that the SCA did not apply, its reasoning was very controversial. The court first held that an individual's computer, when connected to the Internet, was a "facility through which an electronic information service is provided." This means that when DoubleClick accessed cookies on people's computers, it was "intentionally access[ing] without authorization a facility through which an electronic information service is provided." However, the consent exception to this provision of the SCA is that "users" may authorize access "with respect to a communication of or intended for that user." § 2701(c). The individuals whose computers were accessed were obviously users, and they did not consent. But the websites that the users visited that used DoubleClick cookies

---

[79] For a discussion of the *DoubleClick* case, see Tal Zarsky, *Cookie Viewers and the Undermining of Data-Mining: A Critical Review of the DoubleClick Settlement*, 2002 Stan. Tech. L. Rev. 1.

were also "users" in the court's interpretation, and they consented. Only one party needs to consent for the SCA consent exception to apply.

Moreover, the court noted that the SCA only applies to "temporary, intermediate storage of a wire or electronic communication," § 2510(17), and that DoubleClick's cookies were not "temporary" because they exist on people's hard drives for a virtually infinite time period.

Commentators argue that the court's application of the SCA is wrong because a "facility" refers to an Internet Service Provider, not an individual computer. Consider Orin Kerr:

> [T]he Stored Communications Act regulates the privacy of Internet account holders at ISPs and other servers; the law was enacted to create by statute a set of Fourth Amendment-like set of rights in stored records held by ISPs. The theory of the *Doubleclick* plaintiffs turned this framework on its head, as it attempted to apply a law designed to give account holders privacy rights in information held at third-party ISPs to home PCs interacting with websites.[80]

In *In re Pharmatrak Inc. Privacy Litigation*, 220 F. Supp. 2d 4 (D. Mass. 2002), aff'd 392 F.3d 9 (1st Cir. 2003), the court interpreted the SCA as Kerr suggests, holding that an individual's personal computer was not a "facility" under the SCA.

Regarding the Wiretap Act claim, DoubleClick conceded, for the purposes of summary judgment, that it had "intercepted" electronic communications. Orin Kerr also takes issue with this concession:

> [T]he Wiretap Act prohibits a third-party from intercepting in real-time the contents of communications between two parties unless one of the two parties consents. This law had no applicability to Doubleclick's cookies, as the cookies did not intercept any contents and did not intercept anything in real-time. The cookies merely registered data sent to it from Doubleclick's servers.[81]

DoubleClick argued that even if it intercepted electronic communications, the consent exception applied, since one party (the websites using DoubleClick) consented. The court agreed. The consent exception, however, does not apply if even with consent the "communication is intercepted for the purpose of committing any criminal or tortious act." 18 U.S.C. § 2511(2)(d). The court concluded: "DoubleClick's purpose has plainly not been to perpetuate torts on millions of Internet users, but to make money by providing a valued service to commercial Web sites."

4. *Web Bugs.* Beyond cookies, another device for collecting people's data is called a "Web bug." As one court describes it, Web bugs (or "action tags") are very tiny pixels on a website that can record how a person navigates around the Internet. Unlike a cookie, which can be accepted or declined by a user, a Web bug is a very small graphic file that is secretly downloaded to the user's computer. Web bugs enable the website to monitor a person's

---

[80] Orin S. Kerr, *Lifting the "Fog" of Internet Surveillance: How a Suppression Remedy Would Change Computer Crime Law*, 54 Hastings L.J. 805, 831 (2003).

[81] *Id.* at 831.

keystrokes and cursor movement. Web bugs can also be placed in e-mail messages that use HTML, or HyperText Markup Language. E-mail using HTML enables users to see graphics in an e-mail. A Web bug in an e-mail message can detect whether the e-mail was read and to whom it was forwarded. According to computer security expert Richard M. Smith, a Web bug can gather the IP address of the computer that fetched the Web bug; the URL of the page that the Web bug is located on; the URL of the Web bug image; the time the Web bug was viewed; the type of browser that fetched the Web bug image; and a previously set cookie value. Is the use of a Web bug a violation of federal electronic surveillance law?

DYER V. NORTHWEST AIRLINES CORP.

334 F. Supp. 2d 1196 (D.N.D. 2004)

HOVLAND, C.J. . . . Following September 11, 2001, the National Aeronautical and Space Administration ("NASA") requested system-wide passenger data from Northwest Airlines for a three-month period in order to conduct research for use in airline security studies. Northwest Airlines complied and, unbeknownst to its customers, provided NASA with the names, addresses, credit card numbers, and travel itineraries of persons who had flown on Northwest Airlines between July and December 2001.

The discovery of Northwest Airlines' disclosure of its customers' personal information triggered a wave of litigation. Eight class actions — seven in Minnesota and one in Tennessee — were filed in federal court prior to March 19, 2004. The seven Minnesota actions were later consolidated into a master file.

[In this case, t]he complaint alleges that Northwest Airlines' unauthorized disclosure of customers' personal information constituted a violation of the Electronic Communications Privacy Act ("ECPA"), 18 U.S.C. §§ 2702(a)(1) and (a)(3). . . .

The Electronic Communications Privacy Act (ECPA) provides in relevant part that, with certain exceptions, a person or entity providing either an electronic communication service or remote computing service to the public shall not:

- knowingly divulge to any person or entity the contents of a communication while in electronic storage by that service (18 U.S.C. § 2702(a)(1)); and

- knowingly divulge a record or other information pertaining to a subscriber to or customer of such service . . . to any governmental entity (18 U.S.C. § 2702(a)(3)).

In its complaint, the Plaintiffs asserted claims under both 18 U.S.C. §§ 2702(a)(1) and (a)(3) of the ECPA. The plaintiffs have conceded no claim exists under 18 U.S.C. § 2702(a)(1). Consequently, the Court's focus will be directed at the Plaintiffs' ability to sustain a claim against Northwest Airlines under 18 U.S.C. § 2702(a)(3). To sustain a claim under 18 U.S.C. § 2702(a)(3), the Plaintiffs must establish that Northwest Airlines provides either electronic communication services or remote computing services. It is clear that Northwest Airlines provides neither.

The ECPA defines "electronic communication service" as "any service which provides the users thereof the ability to send or receive wire or electronic communications." 18 U.S.C. § 2510(15). In construing this definition, courts have distinguished those entities that sell access to the internet from those that sell goods or services on the internet. 18 U.S.C. § 2702(a)(3) prescribes the conduct only of a "provider of a remote computing service or electronic communication service to the public." A provider under the ECPA is commonly referred to as an internet service provider or ISP. There is no factual allegation that Northwest Airlines, an airline that sells airline tickets on its website, provides internet services.

Courts have concluded that "electronic communication service" encompasses internet service providers as well as telecommunications companies whose lines carry internet traffic, but does not encompass businesses selling traditional products or services online. See *In re DoubleClick Inc. Privacy Litig.*, 154 F. Supp. 2d 497 (S.D.N.Y. 2001). . . .

The distinction is critical in this case. Northwest Airlines is not an electronic communications service provider as contemplated by the ECPA. Instead, Northwest Airlines sells its products and services over the internet as opposed to access to the internet itself. The ECPA definition of "electronic communications service" clearly includes internet service providers such as America Online, as well as telecommunications companies whose cables and phone lines carry internet traffic. However, businesses offering their traditional products and services online through a website are not providing an "electronic communication service." As a result, Northwest Airlines falls outside the scope of 18 U.S.C. § 2702 and the ECPA claim fails as a matter of law. The facts as pled do not give rise to liability under the ECPA. 18 U.S.C. § 2702(a) does not prohibit or even address the dissemination of business records of passenger flights and information as described in the complaint. Instead, the focus of 18 U.S.C. § 2702(a) is on "communications" being stored by the communications service provider for the purpose of subsequent transmission or for backup purposes.

[The plaintiffs also raised a claim under the Minnesota Deceptive Trade Practices Act. The court held that the claim was barred by the federal Airline Deregulation Act, which preempts state regulation of "a price, route, or service of an airline carrier." 49 U.S.C. § 4173(b)(1).]

NOTES & QUESTIONS

1. *ISPs vs. Non-ISPs.* In this case, Northwest Airlines violated its privacy policy by disclosing its customer records to the government. Suppose Northwest Airlines had been an ISP like AOL or Earthlink. Would it have been liable under the Stored Communications Act?

2. *Other Remedies.* What other potential remedies might the plaintiffs have in this case? The plaintiffs brought an action for breach of contract, which was discussed earlier in this chapter in the section on privacy policies. Besides breach of contract, can you think of any other causes of action that might be brought?

(c) The Computer Fraud and Abuse Act

The Computer Fraud and Abuse Act (CFAA) of 1984, 18 U.S.C. § 1030, provides criminal and civil penalties for unauthorized access to computers. Originally passed in 1984, the statue was amended updated throughout the 1990s. Several states have similar statutes regarding the misuse of computers. As Orin Kerr notes:

> While no two statutes are identical, all share the common trigger of "access without authorization" or "unauthorized access" to computers, sometimes in tandem with its close cousin, "exceeding authorized access" to computers.[82]

Scope. The CFAA applies to all "protected computer[s]." A "protected computer" is any computer used in interstate commerce or communication. Whereas the Stored Communications Act of ECPA appears to apply only to ISPs, the CFAA applies to both ISPs and individual computers.

Criminal Penalties. The CFAA creates seven crimes. Among these, it imposes criminal penalties when a person or entity "intentionally accesses a computer without authorization or exceeds authorized access, and thereby obtains . . . information from any protected computer." § 1030(a)(2)(c). It criminalizes unauthorized access to "any nonpublic computer of a department or agency of the United States." § 1030(a)(3). The CFAA also criminalizes unauthorized access to computers "knowingly with intent to defraud" and the obtaining of "anything of value, unless the object of the fraud and the thing obtained consists only of the use of the computer and the value of such use is not more than $5,000 in any 1-year period." § 1030(a)(4). Yet another crime created by the CFAA prohibits knowingly transmitting "a program, information, code, or command" or "intentionally access[ing] a protected computer without authorization" that causes damage to a protected computer. § 1030(5)(A)(i). Punishments range from fines to imprisonment for up to 20 years depending upon the provision violated.

Damage. The term "damage" means "any impairment to the integrity or availability of data, a program, a system, or information." § 1030(e). In many provisions in the CFAA, the damage must exceed $5,000 in a one-year period.

Civil Remedies. "Any person who suffers damage or loss by reason of a violation of this section may maintain a civil action against the violator to obtain compensatory damages or injunctive relief or other equitable relief." § 1030(g). "Damage" must cause a "loss aggregating at least $5,000 in value during any 1-year period to one or more individuals." § 1030(e).

---

[82] Orin S. Kerr, *Cybercrime's Scope: Interpreting "Access" and "Authorization" in Computer Misuse Statutes*, 78 N.Y.U. L. Rev. 1596, 1615 (2003).

Exceeding Authorized Access. Many provisions in the CFAA can be violated not just by unauthorized access, but also when one "exceeds authorized access." To exceed authorized access means "to access a computer with authorization and to use such access to obtain or alter information in the computer that the accesser is not entitled so to obtain and alter." § 1030(e)(6).

CREATIVE COMPUTING V. GETLOADED.COM LLC

386 F.3d 930 (9th Cir. 2004)

KLEINFELD, J. Truck drivers and trucking companies try to avoid dead heading. "Dead heading" means having to drive a truck, ordinarily on a return trip, without a revenue-producing load. If the truck is moving, truck drivers and their companies want it to be carrying revenue-producing freight. In the past, truckers and shippers used blackboards to match up trips and loads. Eventually television screens were used instead of blackboards, but the matching was still inefficient. Better information on where the trucks and the loads are — and quick, easy access to that information — benefits shippers, carriers, and consumers.

Creative Computing developed a successful Internet site, truckstop.com, which it calls "The Internet Truckstop," to match loads with trucks. The site is very easy to use. It has a feature called "radius search" that lets a truck driver in, say, Middletown, Connecticut, with some space in his truck, find within seconds all available loads in whatever mileage radius he likes (and of course lets a shipper post a load so that a trucker with space can find it). The site was created so early in Internet history and worked so well that it came to dominate the load-board industry.

Getloaded decided to compete, but not honestly. After Getloaded set up a load-matching site, it wanted to get a bigger piece of Creative's market. Creative wanted to prevent that, so it prohibited access to its site by competing loadmatching services. The Getloaded officers thought trucking companies would probably use the same login names and passwords on truckstop.com as they did on getloaded.com. Getloaded's president, Patrick Hull, used the login name and password of a Getloaded subscriber, in effect impersonating the trucking company, to sneak into truckstop.com. Getloaded's vice-president, Ken Hammond, accomplished the same thing by registering a defunct company, RFT Trucking, as a truckstop.com subscriber. These tricks enabled them to see all of the information available to Creative's bona fide customers.

Getloaded's officers also hacked into the code Creative used to operate its website. Microsoft had distributed a patch to prevent a hack it had discovered, but Creative Computing had not yet installed the patch on truckstop.com. Getloaded's president and vice-president hacked into Creative Computing's website through the back door that this patch would have locked. Once in, they examined the source code for the tremendously valuable radius-search feature. . . .

Getloaded argues that no action could lie under the Computer Fraud and Abuse Act because it requires a $5,000 floor for damages from each unauthorized access, and that Creative Computing submitted no evidence that would enable a jury to find that the floor was reached on any single unauthorized access. . . .

The briefs dispute which version of the statute we should apply — the one in effect when Getloaded committed the wrongs, or the one in effect when the case went to trial (which is still in effect). The old version of the statute made an exception to the fraudulent access provision if "the value of such use [unauthorized access to a protected computer] is not more than $5,000 in any 1-year period."[83] The new version, in effect now and during trial, says "loss . . . during any 1-year period . . . aggregating at least $5,000 in value."[84] These provisions are materially identical.

The old version of the statute defined "damage" as "any impairment to the integrity or availability of data, a program, a system, or information" that caused the loss of at least $5,000. It had no separate definition of "loss." The new version defines "damage" the same way, but adds a definition of loss. "Loss" is defined in the new version as "any reasonable cost to any victim, including the cost of responding to an offense, conducting a damage assessment, and restoring the data . . . and any revenue lost, cost incurred, or other consequential damages incurred because of interruption of service."

For purposes of this case, we need not decide which version of the Act applies, because Getloaded loses either way. Neither version of the statute supports a construction that would require proof of $5,000 of damage or loss from a single unauthorized access. The syntax makes it clear that in both versions, the $5,000 floor applies to how much damage or loss there is to the victim over a one-year period, not from a particular intrusion. Getloaded argues that "impairment" is singular, so the floor has to be met by a single intrusion. The premise does not lead to the conclusion. The statute (both the earlier and the current versions) says "damage" means "any impairment to the integrity or availability of data [etc.] . . . that causes loss aggregating at least $5,000." Multiple intrusions can cause a single impairment, and multiple corruptions of data can be described as a single "impairment" to the data. The statute does not say that an "impairment" has to result from a single intrusion, or has to be a single corrupted byte. A court construing a statute attributes a rational purpose to Congress. Getloaded's construction would attribute obvious futility to Congress rather than rationality, because a hacker could evade the statute by setting up thousands of $4,999 (or millions of $4.99) intrusions. As the First Circuit pointed out in the analogous circumstance of physical impairment, so narrow a construction of the $5,000 impairment requirement would merely "reward sophisticated intruders." The damage floor in the Computer Fraud and Abuse Act contains no "single act" requirement.

---

[83] 18 U.S.C. § 1030(a)(4) (2001) ("[Whoever] knowingly and with intent to defraud, accesses a protected computer without authorization, or exceeds authorized access, and by means of such conduct furthers the intended fraud and obtains anything of value, unless the object of the fraud and the thing obtained consists only of the use of the computer and the value of such use is not more than $5,000 in any 1-year period.").

[84] 18 U.S.C. § 1030(a)(5)(B)(i) ("[Whoever caused] loss to 1 or more persons during any 1-year period (and, for purposes of an investigation, prosecution, or other proceeding brought by the United States only, loss resulting from a related course of conduct affecting 1 or more other protected computers) aggregating at least $5,000 in value.").

NOTES & QUESTIONS

1. ***The $5,000 Threshold.*** In *In re Doubleclick Inc. Privacy Litigation*, 154 F. Supp. 2d 497 (S.D.N.Y. 2001), the plaintiffs brought a CFAA claim and contended that collectively they suffered more than $5,000 in damages. But the court held that the plaintiffs could not add up their damages. Damages could only be combined "for a single act" against "a particular computer." Since the plaintiffs' CFAA claims concerned multiple acts against many different computers, they could not be aggregated to reach the $5,000 threshold.

2. ***Spyware.*** Spyware is a new kind of computer program that raises significant threats to privacy. Paul Schwartz distinguishes "spyware" from "adware" in terms of the notice provided to the user. He also explains how these programs come about through the linking of personal computers via the Internet: "Spyware draws on computer resources to create a network that can be used for numerous purposes, including collecting personal and nonpersonal information from computers and delivering adware or targeted advertisements to individuals surfing the Web. Adware is sometimes, but not always, delivered as part of spyware; the definitional line between the two depends on whether the computer user receives adequate notice of the program's installation."[85] Would the CFAA apply to a company that secretly installs spyware in a person's computer that transmits her personal data back to the company without her awareness? Would the Wiretap Act apply?

3. ***State Spyware Statutes.*** The state of Utah became the first state to pass legislation to regulate spyware. The original Spyware Control Act, Utah Code Ann. §§ 13-40-101 *et seq.*, prohibited the installation of spyware on another person's computer, limited the display of certain types of advertising, created a private right of action, and empowered the Utah Division of Consumer Protection to collect complaints. WhenU, an advertising network, challenged the Act in 2004, arguing that it violated the Commerce Clause of the U.S. Constitution, and it obtained a preliminary injunction against the statute. A revised bill was signed by the Utah governor on March 17, 2005. The revised Act defines "spyware" as "software on a computer of a user who resides in this state that . . . collects information about an Internet website at the time the Internet website is being viewed in this state, unless the Internet website is the Internet website of the person who provides the software; and . . . uses the information . . . contemporaneously to display pop-up advertising on the computer."

Following Utah's lead, California enacted a spyware bill, which was signed by Governor Arnold Schwarzenegger on September 28, 2004. The Consumer Protection Against Computer Spyware Act, SB 1426, prohibits a person from causing computer software to be installed on a computer and using the software to (1) take control of the computer; (2) modify certain settings relating to the computer's access to the Internet; (3) collect, through

---

[85] Paul M. Schwartz, *Property, Privacy, and Personal Data*, 117 Harv. L. Rev. 2055 (2004).

intentionally deceptive means, personally identifiable information; (4) prevent, without authorization, the authorized user's reasonable efforts to block the installation of or disable software; (5) intentionally misrepresent that the software will be uninstalled or disabled by the authorized user's action; or (6) through intentionally deceptive means, remove, disable, or render, inoperative security, anti-spyware, or antivirus software installed on the computer.

UNITED STATES V. DREW

259 F.R.D. 449 (C.D. Cal. 2009)

WU, J. This case raises the issue of whether (and/or when will) violations of an Internet website's terms of service constitute a crime under the Computer Fraud and Abuse Act ("CFAA"), 18 U.S.C. § 1030. . . .

In the Indictment, Drew was charged with one count of conspiracy in violation of 18 U.S.C. § 371 and three counts of violating a felony portion of the CFAA, *i.e.,* 18 U.S.C. §§ 1030(a)(2)(C) and 1030(c)(2)(B)(ii), which prohibit accessing a computer without authorization or in excess of authorization and obtaining information from a protected computer where the conduct involves an interstate or foreign communication and the offense is committed in furtherance of a crime or tortious act.

The Indictment included, *inter alia,* the following allegations (not all of which were established by the evidence at trial). Drew, a resident of O'Fallon, Missouri, entered into a conspiracy in which its members agreed to intentionally access a computer used in interstate commerce without (and/or in excess of) authorization in order to obtain information for the purpose of committing the tortious act of intentional infliction of emotional distress upon "M.T.M.," subsequently identified as Megan Meier ("Megan"). Megan was a 13 year old girl living in O'Fallon who had been a classmate of Drew's daughter Sarah. Pursuant to the conspiracy, on or about September 20, 2006, the conspirators registered and set up a profile for a fictitious 16 year old male juvenile named "Josh Evans" on the www. My Space. com website ("MySpace"), and posted a photograph of a boy without that boy's knowledge or consent. Such conduct violated My Space's terms of service. The conspirators contacted Megan through the MySpace network (on which she had her own profile) using the Josh Evans pseudonym and began to flirt with her over a number of days. On or about October 7, 2006, the conspirators had "Josh" inform Megan that he was moving away. On or about October 16, 2006, the conspirators had "Josh" tell Megan that he no longer liked her and that "the world would be a better place without her in it." Later on that same day, after learning that Megan had killed herself, Drew caused the Josh Evans MySpace account to be deleted.

At the trial, after consultation between counsel and the Court, the jury was instructed that, if they unanimously decided that they were not convinced beyond a reasonable doubt as to the Defendant's guilt as to the felony CFAA violations of 18 U.S.C. §§ 1030(a)(2)(C) and 1030(c)(2)(B)(ii), they could then consider whether the Defendant was guilty of the "lesser included" misdemeanor CFAA violation of 18 U.S.C. §§ 1030(a)(2)(C) and 1030(c)(2)(A). [The jury found

Drew not guilty of the felony CFAA violations and guilty of the misdemeanor CFAA violation. Drew made a motion for judgment of acquittal under Fed. R. Crim. P. 29(c).]

As Jae Sung (Vice President of Customer Care at MySpace) testified at trial, MySpace is a "social networking" website where members can create "profiles" and interact with other members. . . .

In 2006, to become a member, one had to go to the sign-up section of the MySpace website and register by filling in personal information (such as name, email address, date of birth, country/state/postal code, and gender) and creating a password. In addition, the individual had to check on the box indicating that "You agree to the MySpace Terms of Service and Privacy Policy." The terms of service did not appear on the same registration page that contained this "check box" for users to confirm their agreement to those provisions. . . . A person could become a MySpace member without ever reading or otherwise becoming aware of the provisions and conditions of the MySpace terms of service [MSTOS] by merely clicking on the "check box" and then the "Sign Up" button without first accessing the "Terms" section.

The MSTOS prohibited the posting of a wide range of content on the website including (but not limited to) material that: a) "is potentially offensive and promotes racism, bigotry, hatred or physical harm of any kind against any group or individual"; b) "harasses or advocates harassment of another person"; c) "solicits personal information from anyone under 18"; d) "provides information that you know is false or misleading or promotes illegal activities or conduct that is abusive, threatening, obscene, defamatory or libelous"; e) "includes a photograph of another person that you have posted without that person's consent"; f) "involves commercial activities and/or sales without our prior written consent"; g) "contains restricted or password only access pages or hidden pages or images"; or h) "provides any phone numbers, street addresses, last names, URLs or email addresses. . . ."

[In 2006, the CFAA (18 U.S.C. § 1030) punished a person who "intentionally accesses a computer without authorization or exceeds authorized access, and thereby obtains . . . information from any protected computer."]

As used in the CFAA, the term "computer" "includes any data storage facility or communication facility directly related to or operating in conjunction with such device. . . ." 18 U.S.C. § 1030(e)(1). The term "protected computer" "means a computer—(A) exclusively for the use of a financial institution or the United States Government . . . ; or (B) which is used in interstate or foreign commerce or communication. . . ." *Id.* § 1030(e)(2). The term "exceeds authorized access" means "to access a computer with authorization and to use such access to obtain or alter information in the computer that the accesser is not entitled so to obtain or alter . . . ." *Id.* § 1030(e)(6).

In addition to providing criminal penalties for computer fraud and abuse, the CFAA also states that "[A]ny person who suffers damage or loss by reason of a violation of this section may maintain a civil action against the violator to obtain compensatory damages and injunctive relief or other equitable relief." 18 U.S.C. § 1030(g). Because of the availability of civil remedies, much of the law as to the meaning and scope of the CFAA has been developed in the context of civil cases.

During the relevant time period herein, the misdemeanor 18 U.S.C. § 1030(a)(2)(C) crime consisted of the following three elements:

First, the defendant intentionally [accessed without authorization] [exceeded authorized access of] a computer;

Second, the defendant's access of the computer involved an interstate or foreign communication; and

Third, by [accessing without authorization] [exceeding authorized access to] a computer, the defendant obtained information from a computer . . . [used in interstate or foreign commerce or communication] . . . .

As to the term "without authorization," the courts that have considered the phrase have taken a number of different approaches in their analysis. . . . [W]here the relationship between the parties is contractual in nature or resembles such a relationship, access has been held to be unauthorized where there has been an ostensible breach of contract. . . .

Within the breach of contract approach, most courts that have considered the issue have held that a conscious violation of a website's terms of service/use will render the access unauthorized and/or cause it to exceed authorization. *See, e.g., Southwest Airlines Co. v. Farechase, Inc.,* 318 F. Supp. 2d 435, 439-40 (N.D. Tex. 2004); *Nat'l Health Care Disc., Inc.,* 174 F. Supp. 2d at 899; *Register.com, Inc. v. Verio, Inc.,* 126 F. Supp. 2d 238, 247-51 (S.D.N.Y. 2000), *aff'd,* 356 F.3d 393 (2d Cir. 2004); *Am. Online, Inc. v. LCGM, Inc.,* 46 F. Supp. 2d 444, 450 (E.D. Va. 1998); *see also EF Cultural Travel BV v. Zefer Corp.,* 318 F.3d 58, 62-63 (1st Cir. 2003) ("A lack of authorization could be established by an explicit statement on the website restricting access. . . . [W]e think that the public website provider can easily spell out explicitly what is forbidden. . . ."). . . .

In this particular case, as conceded by the Government, the only basis for finding that Drew intentionally accessed MySpace's computer/servers without authorization and/or in excess of authorization was her and/or her co-conspirator's violations of the MSTOS by deliberately creating the false Josh Evans profile, posting a photograph of a juvenile without his permission and pretending to be a sixteen year old O'Fallon resident for the purpose of communicating with Megan. Therefore, if conscious violations of the My Space terms of service were not sufficient to satisfy the first element of the CFAA misdemeanor violation as per 18 U.S.C. §§ 1030(a)(2)(C) and 1030(b)(2)(A), Drew's Rule 29(c) motion would have to be granted on that basis alone. However, this Court concludes that an intentional breach of the MSTOS can potentially constitute accessing the MySpace computer/server without authorization and/or in excess of authorization under the statute. . . .

Justice Holmes observed that, as to criminal statutes, there is a "fair warning" requirement. . . .

The void-for-vagueness doctrine has two prongs: 1) a definitional/notice sufficiency requirement and, more importantly, 2) a guideline setting element to govern law enforcement. In *Kolender v. Lawson,* 461 U.S. 352 (1983), the Court explained that:

> As generally stated, the void-for-vagueness doctrine requires that a penal statute define the criminal offense with sufficient definiteness that ordinary people can

understand what conduct is prohibited and in a manner that does not encourage arbitrary and discriminatory enforcement. . . .

To avoid contravening the void-for-vagueness doctrine, the criminal statute must contain "relatively clear guidelines as to prohibited conduct" and provide "objective criteria" to evaluate whether a crime has been committed. . . .

The pivotal issue herein is whether basing a CFAA misdemeanor violation as per 18 U.S.C. §§ 1030(a)(2)(C) and 1030(c)(2)(A) upon the conscious violation of a website's terms of service runs afoul of the void-for-vagueness doctrine. This Court concludes that it does primarily because of the absence of minimal guidelines to govern law enforcement, but also because of actual notice deficiencies. . . .

First, an initial inquiry is whether the statute, as it is written, provides sufficient notice. Here, the language of section 1030(a)(2)(C) does not explicitly state (nor does it implicitly suggest) that the CFAA has "criminalized breaches of contract" in the context of website terms of service. Normally, breaches of contract are not the subject of criminal prosecution. Thus, while "ordinary people" might expect to be exposed to civil liabilities for violating a contractual provision, they would not expect criminal penalties. . . .

Second, if a website's terms of service controls what is "authorized" and what is "exceeding authorization" — which in turn governs whether an individual's accessing information or services on the website is criminal or not, section 1030(a)(2)(C) would be unacceptably vague because it is unclear whether any or all violations of terms of service will render the access unauthorized, or whether only certain ones will. . . .

Third, by utilizing violations of the terms of service as the basis for the section 1030(a)(2)(C) crime, that approach makes the website owner — in essence — the party who ultimately defines the criminal conduct. This will lead to further vagueness problems. The owner's description of a term of service might itself be so vague as to make the visitor or member reasonably unsure of what the term of service covers. . . .

Fourth, because terms of service are essentially a contractual means for setting the scope of authorized access, a level of indefiniteness arises from the necessary application of contract law in general and/or other contractual requirements within the applicable terms of service to any criminal prosecution. . . .

Treating a violation of a website's terms of service, without more, to be sufficient to constitute "intentionally access[ing] a computer without authorization or exceed[ing] authorized access" would result in transforming section 1030(a)(2)(C) into an overwhelmingly overbroad enactment that would convert a multitude of otherwise innocent Internet users into misdemeanant criminals. . . .

One need only look to the MSTOS terms of service to see the expansive and elaborate scope of such provisions whose breach engenders the potential for criminal prosecution. Obvious examples of such breadth would include: 1) the lonely-heart who submits intentionally inaccurate data about his or her age, height and/or physical appearance, which contravenes the MSTOS prohibition against providing "information that you know is false or misleading"; 2) the student who posts candid photographs of classmates without their permission, which breaches the MSTOS provision covering "a photograph of another person that you have posted without that person's consent"; and/or 3) the exasperated parent who sends out a group message to neighborhood friends entreating them to purchase his or her daughter's girl scout cookies, which transgresses the MSTOS rule against "advertising to, or solicitation of, any Member to buy or sell any products or services through the Services." However, one need not consider hypotheticals to demonstrate the problem. In this case, Megan (who was then 13 years old) had her own profile on MySpace, which was in clear violation of the MSTOS which requires that users be "14 years of age or older." No one would seriously suggest that Megan's conduct was criminal or should be subject to criminal prosecution. . . .

In sum, if any conscious breach of a website's terms of service is held to be sufficient by itself to constitute intentionally accessing a computer without authorization or in excess of authorization, the result will be that section 1030(a)(2)(C) becomes a law "that affords too much discretion to the police and too little notice to citizens who wish to use the [Internet]."

NOTES & QUESTIONS

1. *The Implications of* **Drew.** Is the prosecutor's theory consistent with the CFAA's purpose? Suppose the court in *Drew* had reached the opposite conclusion. What effect would criminal liability for violating a website's terms of service have for people who use the Internet?

2. *Is the CFAA Unconstitutionally Vague?* The *Drew* court's holding is narrow, concluding only that the application of the CFAA to website terms of service violations would be unconstitutionally vague. More broadly, is the CFAA unconstitutionally vague on its face?

3. MARKETING

(a) The Telephone Consumer Protections Act

The Telephone Consumer Protections Act (TCPA) of 1991, Pub. L. No. 102-243, 47 U.S.C. § 227, requires the FCC to promulgate rules to "protect residential telephone subscribers' privacy rights and to avoid receiving telephone solicitations to which they object." § 227(c)(1). In addition, the FCC is authorized to require that a "single national database" be established of a "list of telephone numbers of residential subscribers who object to receiving telephone solicitations." § 227(c)(3).

Private Right of Action. The FCPA provides plaintiffs with a private right of action in small claims court against an entity for each call received after requesting to no longer receive calls from that entity. Plaintiffs can sue for an actual loss or up to $500 (whichever is greater). If telemarketer has acted "willfully or knowingly," then damages are trebled. § 227(c)(5).

Affirmative Defense. Telemarketers can offer as an affirmative defense that they established "reasonable practices and procedures to effectively prevent telephone solicitations in violation of the regulations prescribed under this subsection." § 227(c)(5).

Prohibition on Using Pre-Recorded Messages. The TCPA prohibits telemarketers from calling residences and using prerecorded messages without the consent of the called party. 47 U.S.C. § 227(b)(1)(B).

Fax Machines. The TCPA prohibits the use of a fax, computer, or other device to send an unsolicited advertisement to a fax machine. § 227(b)(1)(C).

State Enforcement. States may initiate actions against telemarketers "engaging in a pattern or practice of telephone calls or other transmissions to residents of that State" in violation of the TCPA. § 227(f)(1).

NOTES & QUESTIONS

1. *First Amendment Limitations?* In *Destination Ventures, Ltd. v. FCC,* 46 F.3d 54 (9th Cir. 1995), Destination Ventures challenged a provision of the TCPA banning unsolicited faxes that contained advertisements on First Amendment grounds. The court upheld the ban because it was designed to prevent shifting advertising costs to consumers, who would be forced to pay for the toner and paper to receive the ads.

2. *A Do Not Track List.* As a continuation of the "Do Not Call" list, a discussion is now emerging about "Do Not Track" (DNT) protection for the Internet. The idea of DNT turns on the use of an "opt-out header" in a Web browser.[86] The FTC has told Congress that it supports giving consumers a DNT option to give them a simple and easy way to control the fashion in which companies track them online.

   In contrast to "Do Not Call," considerable complexity exists around the concept of "tracking" on the Internet. The Center for Democracy and Technology (CDT) has defined tracking "as the collection and correlation of data about the Internet activities of a particular user, computer or device, over time and across non-commonly branded websites, for any purpose other than fraud prevention or compliance with law enforcement requests."[87] Thus, CDT considers behavioral advertising as "tracking."

   CDT also argues that any "actively shared" data, such as information that data users provide in social networking profiles and Web forums or by registering for various accounts, should not fall within Do Not Track prohibitions.

   Consider Omer Tene and Jules Polonetsky:

---

[86] For more on the technology behind this policy proposal, see *Do Not Track,* at http://www.donottrack.us/.

[87] CDT, *What Does "Do Not Track" Mean?* (Jan. 31, 2011). For an approach that is largely in agreement with the CDT, see Electronic Frontier Foundation, *What Does the "Track" in "Do Not Track" Mean?* (Feb. 19, 2011).

The FTC put forth the following criteria to assess industry responses: DNT should be universal, that is, a single opt-out should cover all would-be trackers; easy to find, understand, and use; persistent, meaning that opt-out choices do not "vanish"; effective and enforceable, covering all tracking technologies; and controlling not only use of data but also their collection.[88] As discussed, the FTC has not yet taken a position on whether any legislation or rulemaking is necessary for DNT. It is clear, however, that regardless of the regulatory approach chosen, industry collaboration will remain key since the system will only work if websites and ad intermediaries respect users' preferences. . . .

The debate raging around online behavioral tracking generally and DNT in particular is a smoke screen for a discussion that all parties hesitate to hold around deeper values and social norms. Which is more important — efficiency or privacy; law enforcement or individual rights; reputation or freedom of speech? Policymakers must engage with the underlying normative question: is online behavioral tracking a societal good, funding the virtue of the online economy and bringing users more relevant, personalized content and services; or is it an evil scheme for businesses to enrich themselves on account of ignorant users and for governments to create a foundation for pervasive surveillance? Policymakers cannot continue to sidestep these questions in the hope that "users will decide" for themselves.[89]

3. ***Revocation of Consent.*** In *Gager v. Dell Financial Services*, 727 F.3d 265 (3d Cir. 2013), the plaintiff applied for a credit line from Dell to purchase computer equipment. She listed her cell phone number. Dell began calling her cell phone using an automated telephone dialing system. The plaintiff wrote a letter to Dell requesting that it stop calling. Dell continued its calls, calling about 40 times over a three-week span. The plaintiff brought a TCPA action. Dell moved to dismiss claiming that the FTCPA did not provide a way for people to revoke prior consent. The court, however, concluded that "the absence of an express statutory authorization for revocation of prior express consent in the TCPA's provisions on autodialed calls to cellular phones does not tip the scales in favor of a position that no such right exists." The court reasoned that "the common law concept of consent shows that it is revocable" and that "in light of the TCPA's purpose, any silence in the statute as to the right of revocation should be construed in favor of consumers."

(b) The CAN-SPAM Act

In 2003, Congress enacted the Controlling the Assault of Non-Solicited Pornography and Marketing (CAN-SPAM) Act, Pub. L. No. 108-187, 15 U.S.C. §§ 7701 *et seq.*, to address the problem of spam. Spam is a term to describe unsolicited commercial e-mail sent to individuals to advertise products and

---

[88] Ed Felten, FTC Perspective, W3C Workshop on Web Tracking and User Privacy, Apr. 28-29, 2011, http://www.w3.org/2011/track-privacy/slides/Felten.pdf.

[89] Omer Tene & Jules Polonetsky, *To Track or "Do Not Track": Advancing Transparency and Individual Control in Online Behavioral Advertising*, available at http://www.futureofprivacy.org/tracking/.

services.[90] Companies that send unsolicited e-mail are referred to as spammers. Spam is often mailed out in bulk to large lists of e-mail addresses. A recent practice has been to insert hidden HTML tags (also known as "pixel tags" or "Web bugs") into spam. This enables the sender of the e-mail to detect whether the e-mail was opened. It can also inform the sender about whether the e-mail message was forwarded, to what e-mail address it was forwarded, and sometimes, even comments added by a user when forwarding the e-mail. This only works if the recipient has an HTML-enabled e-mail reader rather than a text-only reader. HTML e-mail is e-mail that contains pictures and images rather than simply plain text.

Applicability. The CAN-SPAM Act applies to commercial e-mail, which it defines as a "message with the primary purpose of which is the commercial advertisement or promotion of a commercial product or service."

Prohibitions. The Act prohibits the knowing sending of commercial messages with the intent to deceive or mislead recipients.

Opt Out. The CAN-SPAM Act also requires that a valid opt-out option be made available to e-mail recipients. To make opt out possible, the Act requires senders of commercial e-mail to contain a return address "clearly and conspicuously displayed." Finally, it creates civil and criminal penalties for violations of its provisions. For example, the law allows the DOJ to seek criminal penalties, including imprisonment, for commercial e-mailers who engage in activities such as using a computer to relay or retransmit multiple commercial e-mail messages to receive or mislead recipients or an Internet access service about the message's origin and falsifying header information in multiple e-mail messages and initiate the transmission of these messages.

Enforcement. The CAN-SPAM Act is enforced by governmental and private entities. The chief enforcement entities are the Department of Justice (DOJ), the Federal Trade Commission (FTC), state attorney generals, and "Internet access services" (IAS). Unlike similar laws in other countries, such as Canada's Anti-Spam Legislation (CASL), the CAN-SPAM Act lacks a general private right of action.

The DOJ is charged with enforcing the Act's criminal provisions. These prohibit the unlawful transmission of sexually oriented unsolicited commercial e-mail as well as certain methods of sending commercial e-mail, such as zombie drones, materially false header information, and obtaining IP addresses through fraudulent methods. The FTC and state attorney generals also have an enforcement role under the CAN-SPAM Act. The FTC has been involved both in litigation and settlement actions.

Finally, an IAS that has been adversely affected by violations of the CAN-SPAM Act has standing under the statute. The Act defines an IAS as "a service that enables users to access content, information, electronic mail, or other

---

[90] For more information on spam, see David E. Sorkin, *Technical and Legal Approaches to Unsolicited Electronic Mail*, 35 U.S.F. L. Rev. 325, 336 (2001).

services over the Internet. . ." 47 U.S.C. § 231(e)(4) . Courts have found Internet Service Providers, social networking websites, and email providers to be an IAS.

Assessing the Act. A year after enactment of CAN-SPAM, media accounts faulted the law as ineffective. Indeed, reports stressed the increase in spam during this time. According to one anti-spam vendor, 67 percent of all e-mail was spam in February 2004, and 75 percent in November 2004. Some spammers employed new tactics after the passage of the Act, such as using "zombie networks," which involve hijacking computers with Trojan horse programs. Anti-spam activists faulted CAN-SPAM for preempting tougher state laws, failing to provide a general private right of action, and providing an opt-out option instead of an opt in.[91]

State Anti-Spam Laws. At least 20 states have anti-spam statutes. For example, Cal. Bus. & Professions Code § 17538.4 mandates that senders of spam include in the text of their e-mails a way through which recipients can request to receive no further e-mails. The sender must remove the person from its list. A provider of an e-mail service located within the state of California can request that spammers stop sending spam through its equipment. If the spammer continues to send e-mail, it can be liable for $50 per message up to a maximum of $25,000 per day. *See* § 17538.45.

A Critique of Anti-Spam Legislation. Consumers don't always dislike marketing messages. As Eric Goldman reminds us, "consumers want marketing when it creates personal benefits for them, and marketing also can have spillover benefits that improve social welfare." Goldman is worried that current legal regulation will block the kinds of filters that will improve the ability of consumers to manage information and receive information that will advance their interests. He points to anti-adware laws in Utah and Alaska as especially problematic; these statutes "prohibit client-side software from displaying pop-up ads triggered by the consumer's use of a third party trademark or domain name — even if the consumer has fully consented to the software." For Goldman, these statutes are flawed because they try to "ban or restrict matchmaking technologies." The ideal filter would be a "mind-reading wonder" that "could costlessly — but accurately — read consumers' minds, infer their expressed and latent preferences without the consumer bearing any disclosure costs, and act on the inferred preferences to screen out unwanted content and proactively seek out wanted content." Goldman is confident that such filtering technology is not only possible, but "inevitable — perhaps imminently."[92] What kind of regulatory approach would encourage development and adoption of Goldman's favored filters while also blocking existing SPAM technology? Will surrendering more privacy help better target marketing and thus clear out our inboxes of unwanted spam?

---

[91] For a range of reform proposals, see David Lorentz, *Note: The Effectiveness of Litigation Under the CAN-SPAM Act*, 30 Rev. Litig. 559 (2011).

[92] Eric Goldman, *A Cosean Analysis of Marketing*, 2006 Wis. L. Rev. 1151, 1154-55, 1202, 1211-12.

Spam and Speech. Is spam a form of speech, protected by the First Amendment? In *Cyber Promotions, Inc. v. America Online, Inc.*, 948 F. Supp. 436 (E.D. Pa. 1996), Cyber Promotions, Inc. sought a declaratory judgment that America Online (AOL) was prohibited under the First Amendment from denying it the ability to send AOL customers unsolicited e-mail. The court rejected Cyber Promotion's argument because of a lack of state action: "AOL is a private online company that is not owned in whole or part by the government." Today, the Internet is increasingly becoming a major medium of communication. Prior to modern communications media, individuals could express their views in traditional "public fora" — parks and street corners. These public fora are no longer the central place for public discourse. Perhaps the Internet is the modern public forum, the place where individuals come to speak and express their views. If this is the case, is it preferable for access to the Internet to be controlled by private entities?

International Approaches. Unlike the CAN-SPAM in the United States, most other countries favor an opt-in approach as a legal response to commercial unsolicited emails. For example, CASL in Canada generally permits the sending of commercial email only when there is consent.[93] CASL provides for strong administrative penalties as well as a private right of action.

This preference for an opt-in regime is also found in Australia's Spam Act of 2003 and New Zealand's Unsolicited Electronic Messages Act of 2007. In the European Union, the E-Privacy Directive, first enacted in 2002 and amended in 2009, states that the use of "electronic mail for the purposes of direct marketing may be only allowed in respect of subscribers who have given their prior consent."[94]

Within the EU, Germany is the country that may have the strictest regulation of spam. Its main provision prohibiting spam is Article 7 of the Act against Unfair Competition (UWG). This clause prohibits the sending of advertising emails that constitute an "unconscionable pestering." Clause 7(2) no.3 of this statute contains the critical language; it forbids advertising through email without "prior express consent" of the recipient. In German law, prior express consent requires a process termed "double opt-in." For example, a consumer might agree to receive commercial emails by checking a box, confirming the selection, and then opt-in in again by clicking on a link contained in the first email that she received after enrollment.[95]

---

[93] Bill C-28, Fighting Internet and Wireless Spam Act, 3rd Session, 40th Parl., 2010.

[94] Directive 2002/58/EC of the European Parliament and of the Council of 12 July 2002 concerning the processing of personal data and the protection of privacy in the electronic communications sector (Directive on privacy and electronic communications), L201, 2002-07-31, pp. 37-47 (2002); Directive 2009/136/EC of the European Parliament and of the Council of 25. November 2009, L337, 2009-12-18, pp. 11-36 (2009).

[95] For German caselaw finding a requirement of double-opt in, see AG Düsseldorf, Decision of July 14, 2009 - 48 C 1911/09, BeckRS 2009, 25861; LG Essen, Decision of April 20, 2009 - 4 O 368/08, NJW-RR 2009, 1556; OLG Hamm, Decision of February 17, 2011 - I-4 U 174/10 (LG Dortmund) (rechtskräftig), MMR 2011, 539; OLG Jena, Decision of April 21, 2010 – 2 U 88/10, NJOZ 2011, 1164.

Would an opt-in system be preferable to the current U.S. approach? Would there be benefits for the U.S. switching to opt-in to make regulations in this area of law more uniform internationally?

G. FIRST AMENDMENT LIMITATIONS ON PRIVACY REGULATION

Although the First Amendment protects privacy, privacy restrictions can come into conflict with the First Amendment. In particular, many privacy statutes regulate the disclosure of true information. The cases in this section explore the extent to which the First Amendment limits the privacy statutes. Before turning to the cases, some background about basic First Amendment jurisprudence is necessary. The cases in this section often focus on commercial speech, and the Court analyzes commercial speech differently than other forms of expression.

First Amendment Protection of Commercial Speech. For a while, the Court considered commercial speech as a category of expression that is not accorded First Amendment protection. However, in *Virginia State Board of Pharmacy v. Virginia Citizens Consumer Council, Inc.,* 425 U.S. 748 (1976), the Court held that commercial speech deserves constitutional protection. However, the Court held that commercial speech has a lower value than regular categories of speech and therefore is entitled to a lesser protection. *Ohralik v. Ohio State Bar Ass'n,* 436 U.S. 447 (1978).

Defining Commercial Speech. What is "commercial speech"? The Court has defined it as speech that "proposes a commercial transaction," *Virginia State Board,* 425 U.S. 748 (1976), and as "expression related solely to the economic interests of the speaker and its audience." *Central Hudson Gas & Electric Corp. v. Public Service Comm'n of New York,* 447 U.S. 557 (1980). The Court later held that neither of these are necessary requirements to define commercial speech; both are factors to be considered in determining whether speech is commercial. *See Bolger v. Youngs Drug Products Corp.,* 463 U.S. 60 (1983).

The Central Hudson Test. In *Central Hudson,* 447 U.S. 557 (1980), the Court established a four-part test for analyzing the constitutionality of restrictions on commercial speech:

> At the outset, we must determine whether the expression is protected by the First Amendment. For commercial speech to come within that provision, it at least must concern lawful activity and not be misleading. Next, we ask whether the asserted governmental interest is substantial. If both inquiries yield positive answers, we must determine whether the regulation directly advances the governmental interest asserted, and whether it is not more extensive than is necessary to serve that interest.

In *Board of Trustees of State University of New York v. Fox*, 492 U.S. 469 (1989), the Court revised the last part of the *Central Hudson* test — that speech "not [be] more extensive than is necessary to serve [the governmental] interest" — to a requirement that there be a "fit between the legislature's ends and the means chosen to accomplish the ends, . . . a fit that is not necessarily perfect, but reasonable."

In *Cincinnati v. Discovery Network, Inc.,* 507 U.S. 410 (1993), the Court, applying the commercial speech test in *Central Hudson* and *Fox*, struck down an ordinance that banned news racks with "commercial handbills." The ordinance did not apply to news racks for newspapers. The Court concluded that the ban was not a "reasonable fit" with the city's interest in aesthetics. Moreover, the Court concluded that the ordinance was not content-neutral. The Court held that Cincinnati "has enacted a sweeping ban on the use of newsracks that distribute 'commercial handbills,' but not 'newspapers.' Under the city's newsrack policy, whether any particular newsrack falls within the ban is determined by the content of the publication resting inside that newsrack. Thus, by any commonsense understanding of the term, the ban in this case is 'content based.' . . . [B]ecause the ban is predicated on the content of the publications distributed by the subject newsracks, it is not a valid time, place, or manner restriction on protected speech."

ROWAN V. UNITED STATES POST OFFICE DEPARTMENT
397 U.S. 728 (1970)

[A federal statute permitted individuals to require that entities sending unwanted mailings remove the individuals' names from their mailing lists and cease to send future mailings. A group of organizations challenged the statute on First Amendment grounds.]

BURGER, C.J. . . . The essence of appellants' argument is that the statute violates their constitutional right to communicate. . . . Without doubt the public postal system is an indispensable adjunct of every civilized society and communication is imperative to a healthy social order. But the right of every person "to be let alone" must be placed in the scales with the right of others to communicate.

In today's complex society we are inescapably captive audiences for many purposes, but a sufficient measure of individual autonomy must survive to permit every householder to exercise control over unwanted mail. To make the householder the exclusive and final judge of what will cross his threshold undoubtedly has the effect of impeding the flow of ideas, information, and arguments that, ideally, he should receive and consider. Today's merchandising methods, the plethora of mass mailings subsidized by low postal rates, and the growth of the sale of large mailing lists as an industry in itself have changed the mailman from a carrier of primarily private communications, as he was in a more leisurely day, and have made him an adjunct of the mass mailer who sends unsolicited and often unwanted mail into every home. It places no strain on the doctrine of judicial notice to observe that whether measured by pieces or pounds, Everyman's mail today is made up overwhelmingly of material he did not seek from persons he does not know. And all too often it is matter he finds offensive. . . .

The Court has traditionally respected the right of a householder to bar, by order or notice, solicitors, hawkers, and peddlers from his property. In this case the mailer's right to communicate is circumscribed only by an affirmative act of the addressee giving notice that he wishes no further mailings from that mailer.

To hold less would tend to license a form of trespass and would make hardly more sense than to say that a radio or television viewer may not twist the dial to cut off an offensive or boring communication and thus bar its entering his home. Nothing in the Constitution compels us to listen to or view any unwanted communication, whatever its merit; we see no basis for according the printed word or pictures a different or more preferred status because they are sent by mail. The ancient concept that "a man's home is his castle" into which "not even the king may enter" has lost none of its vitality, and none of the recognized exceptions includes any right to communicate offensively with another. . . .

If this prohibition operates to impede the flow of even valid ideas, the answer is that no one has a right to press even "good" ideas on an unwilling recipient. That we are often "captives" outside the sanctuary of the home and subject to objectionable speech and other sound does not mean we must be captives everywhere. The asserted right of a mailer, we repeat, stops at the outer boundary of every person's domain. . . .

MAINSTREAM MARKETING SERVICES, INC. V. FEDERAL TRADE COMMISSION

358 F.3d 1228 (10th Cir. 2004)

EBEL, J. . . . In 2003, two federal agencies—the Federal Trade Commission (FTC) and the Federal Communications Commission (FCC) — promulgated rules that together created the national do-not-call registry *See* 16 C.F.R. § 310.4(b)(1)(iii)(B) (FTC rule); 47 C.F.R. § 64.1200(c)(2) (FCC rule). The national do-not-call registry is a list containing the personal telephone numbers of telephone subscribers who have voluntarily indicated that they do not wish to receive unsolicited calls from commercial telemarketers. Commercial telemarketers are generally prohibited from calling phone numbers that have been placed on the do-not-call registry, and they must pay an annual fee to access the numbers on the registry so that they can delete those numbers from their telephone solicitation lists. So far, consumers have registered more than 50 million phone numbers on the national do-not-call registry.

The national do-not-call registry's restrictions apply only to telemarketing calls made by or on behalf of sellers of goods or services, and not to charitable or political fundraising calls. Additionally, a seller may call consumers who have signed up for the national registry if it has an established business relationship with the consumer or if the consumer has given that seller express written permission to call. Telemarketers generally have three months from the date on which a consumer signs up for the registry to remove the consumer's phone number from their call lists. Consumer registrations remain valid for five years, and phone numbers that are disconnected or reassigned will be periodically removed from the registry.

The national do-not-call registry is the product of a regulatory effort dating back to 1991 aimed at protecting the privacy rights of consumers and curbing the risk of telemarketing abuse. In the Telephone Consumer Protection Act of 1991 ("TCPA") — under which the FCC enacted its do-not-call rules — Congress found that for many consumers telemarketing sales calls constitute an intrusive invasion of privacy. . . . The TCPA therefore authorized the FCC to establish a national database of consumers who object to receiving "telephone solicitations," which the act defined as commercial sales calls. . . .

The national do-not-call registry's telemarketing restrictions apply only to commercial speech. Like most commercial speech regulations, the do-not-call rules draw a line between commercial and non-commercial speech on the basis of content. In reviewing commercial speech regulations, we apply the *Central Hudson* test. *Central Hudson Gas & Elec. Corp. v. Pub. Serv. Comm'n of N.Y.*, 447 U.S. 557 (1980).

Central Hudson established a three-part test governing First Amendment challenges to regulations restricting non-misleading commercial speech that relates to lawful activity. First, the government must assert a substantial interest to be achieved by the regulation. Second, the regulation must directly advance that governmental interest, meaning that it must do more than provide "only ineffective or remote support for the government's purpose." Third, although the regulation need not be the least restrictive measure available, it must be narrowly tailored not to restrict more speech than necessary. Together, these final two factors require that there be a reasonable fit between the government's objectives and the means it chooses to accomplish those ends. . . .

The government asserts that the do-not-call regulations are justified by its interests in 1) protecting the privacy of individuals in their homes, and 2) protecting consumers against the risk of fraudulent and abusive solicitation. Both of these justifications are undisputedly substantial governmental interests.

In *Rowan v. United States Post Office Dep't,* the Supreme Court upheld the right of a homeowner to restrict material that could be mailed to his or her house. The Court emphasized the importance of individual privacy, particularly in the context of the home, stating that "the ancient concept that 'a man's home is his castle' into which 'not even the king may enter' has lost none of its vitality." In *Frisby v. Schultz,* the Court [held] . . .

> One important aspect of residential privacy is protection of the unwilling listener. . . . [A] special benefit of the privacy all citizens enjoy within their own walls, which the State may legislate to protect, is an ability to avoid intrusions. Thus, we have repeatedly held that individuals are not required to welcome unwanted speech into their own homes and that the government may protect this freedom.

A reasonable fit exists between the do-not-call rules and the government's privacy and consumer protection interests if the regulation directly advances those interests and is narrowly tailored. . . .

These criteria are plainly established in this case. The do-not-call registry directly advances the government's interests by effectively blocking a significant number of the calls that cause the problems the government sought to redress. It is narrowly tailored because its opt-in character ensures that it does not inhibit any speech directed at the home of a willing listener.

The telemarketers assert that the do-not-call registry is unconstitutionally underinclusive because it does not apply to charitable and political callers. First Amendment challenges based on underinclusiveness face an uphill battle in the commercial speech context. As a general rule, the First Amendment does not require that the government regulate all aspects of a problem before it can make progress on any front. . . . The underinclusiveness of a commercial speech regulation is relevant only if it renders the regulatory framework so irrational that it fails materially to advance the aims that it was purportedly designed to further. . .

As discussed above, the national do-not-call registry is designed to reduce intrusions into personal privacy and the risk of telemarketing fraud and abuse that accompany unwanted telephone solicitation. The registry directly advances those goals. So far, more than 50 million telephone numbers have been registered on the do-not-call list, and the do-not-call regulations protect these households from receiving most unwanted telemarketing calls. According to the telemarketers' own estimate, 2.64 telemarketing calls per week — or more than 137 calls annually — were directed at an average consumer before the do-not-call list came into effect. *Cf.* 68 Fed. Reg. at 44152 (discussing the five-fold increase in the total number of telemarketing calls between 1991 and 2003). Accordingly, absent the do-not-call registry, telemarketers would call those consumers who have already signed up for the registry an estimated total of 6.85 *billion* times each year.

To be sure, the do-not-call list will not block all of these calls. Nevertheless, it will prohibit a substantial number of them, making it difficult to fathom how the registry could be called an "ineffective" means of stopping invasive or abusive calls, or a regulation that "furnish[es] only speculative or marginal support" for the government's interests. . . .

Finally, the type of unsolicited calls that the do-not-call list does prohibit— commercial sales calls — is the type that Congress, the FTC and the FCC have all determined to be most to blame for the problems the government is seeking to redress. According to the legislative history accompanying the TCPA, "[c]omplaint statistics show that unwanted commercial calls are a far bigger problem than unsolicited calls from political or charitable organizations." H.R. Rep. No. 102-317, at 16 (1991). Additionally, the FTC has found that commercial callers are more likely than non-commercial callers to engage in deceptive and abusive practices. . . . The speech regulated by the do-not-call list is therefore the speech most likely to cause the problems the government sought to alleviate in enacting that list, further demonstrating that the regulation directly advances the government's interests. . . .

Although the least restrictive means test is not the test to be used in the commercial speech context, commercial speech regulations do at least have to be "narrowly tailored" and provide a "reasonable fit" between the problem and the solution. Whether or not there are "numerous and obvious less-burdensome alternatives" is a relevant consideration in our narrow tailoring analysis. . . . We hold that the national do-not-call registry is narrowly tailored because it does not over-regulate protected speech; rather, it restricts only calls that are targeted at unwilling recipients. . . .

The Supreme Court has repeatedly held that speech restrictions based on private choice (i.e., an opt-in feature) are less restrictive than laws that prohibit speech directly. In *Rowan,* for example, the Court approved a law under which an individual could require a mailer to stop all future mailings if he or she received advertisements that he or she believed to be erotically arousing or sexually provocative. Although it was the government that empowered individuals to avoid materials they considered provocative, the Court emphasized that the mailer's right to communicate was circumscribed only by an affirmative act of a householder. . . .

Like the do-not-mail regulation approved in *Rowan,* the national do-not-call registry does not itself prohibit any speech. Instead, it merely "permits a citizen to erect a wall . . . that no advertiser may penetrate without his acquiescence." *See Rowan,* 397 U.S. at 738. Almost by definition, the do-not-call regulations only block calls that would constitute unwanted intrusions into the privacy of consumers who have signed up for the list. . . .

NOTES & QUESTIONS

1. *The Do Not Call List and* **Rowan.** To what extent is this case controlled by *Rowan*? Does the Do Not Call (DNC) list go beyond the statute in *Rowan*?
2. *Charitable and Political Calls.* The DNC list permits calls based on charitable or political purposes. There is no way to block such calls. Suppose that Congress decided that all calls could be included. Would a charity or political group have a First Amendment ground to overturn the DNC list?

U.S. West, Inc. v. Federal Communications Commission

182 F.3d 1224 (10th Cir. 1999)

TACHA, J. . . . U.S. West, Inc. petitions for review of a Federal Communication Commission ("FCC") order restricting the use and disclosure of and access to customer proprietary network information ("CPNI"). *See* 63 Fed. Reg. 20,326 (1998) ("CPNI Order"). [U.S. West argues that FCC regulations, implementing 47 U.S.C. § 222, among other things, violate the First Amendment. These regulations require telecommunications companies to ask consumers for approval (to "opt-in") before they can use a customer's personal information for marketing purposes.] . . .

The dispute in this case involves regulations the FCC promulgated to implement provisions of 47 U.S.C. § 222, which was enacted as part of the Telecommunications Act of 1996. Section 222, entitled "Privacy of customer information," states generally that "[e]very telecommunications carrier has a duty to protect the confidentiality of proprietary information of, and relating to . . . customers." To effectuate that duty, § 222 places restrictions on the use, disclosure of, and access to certain customer information. At issue here are the

FCC's regulations clarifying the privacy requirements for CPNI. The central provision of § 222 dealing with CPNI is § 222(c)(1), which states:

> Except as required by law or with the approval of the customer, a telecommunications carrier that receives or obtains customer proprietary network information by virtue of its provision of a telecommunications service shall only use, disclose, or permit access to individually identifiable customer proprietary network information in its provision of (A) the telecommunication service from which such information is derived, or (B) services necessary to, or used in, the provision of such telecommunications service, including the publishing of directories.

Section 222(d) provides three additional exceptions to the CPNI privacy requirements. [These exceptions permit the companies to use and disclose CPNI for billing purposes, to prevent fraud, and to provide services to the consumer if the consumer approves of the use of such information to provide the service. Any other uses or disclosures of CPNI not specifically permitted by § 222 require the consumer's consent. The regulations adopted by the CPNI Order implementing § 222 divides telecommunications services into three categories: (1) local, (2) long-distance, and (3) mobile or cellular. A telecommunications carrier can use or disclose CPNI to market products within one of these service categories if the customer already subscribes to that category of service. Carriers can't use or disclose CPNI to market categories of service to which the customer does not subscribe unless first obtaining the customer's consent. The regulations also prohibit using CPNI without consent to market other services such as voice mail or Internet access, to track customers that call competitors, or to try to regain the business of customers that switch carriers.] . . .

The regulations also describe the means by which a carrier must obtain customer approval. Section 222(c)(1) did not elaborate as to what form that approval should take. The FCC decided to require an "opt-in" approach, in which a carrier must obtain prior express approval from a customer through written, oral, or electronic means before using the customer's CPNI. The government acknowledged that the means of approval could have taken numerous other forms, including an "opt-out" approach, in which approval would be inferred from the customer-carrier relationship unless the customer specifically requested that his or her CPNI be restricted. . . .

Petitioner argues that the CPNI regulations interpreting 47 U.S.C. § 222 violate the First Amendment. . . .

Because petitioner's targeted speech to its customers is for the purpose of soliciting those customers to purchase more or different telecommunications services, it "does no more than propose a commercial transaction." Consequently, the targeted speech in this case fits soundly within the definition of commercial speech. It is well established that nonmisleading commercial speech regarding a lawful activity is a form of protected speech under the First Amendment, although it is generally afforded less protection than noncommercial speech. The parties do not dispute that the commercial speech based on CPNI is truthful and nonmisleading. Therefore, the CPNI regulations implicate the First Amendment by restricting protected commercial speech. . . .

We analyze whether a government restriction on commercial speech violates the First Amendment under the four-part framework set forth in *Central Hudson* [*Gas & Elec. Corp. v. Public Serv. Comm'n of N.Y.*, 477 U.S. 557 (1980)]. First, we must conduct a threshold inquiry regarding whether the commercial speech concerns lawful activity and is not misleading. If these requirements are not met, the government may freely regulate the speech. If this threshold requirement is met, the government may restrict the speech only if it proves: "(1) it has a substantial state interest in regulating the speech, (2) the regulation directly and materially advances that interest, and (3) the regulation is no more extensive than necessary to serve the interest." As noted above, no one disputes that the commercial speech based on CPNI is truthful and nonmisleading. We therefore proceed directly to whether the government has satisfied its burden under the remaining three prongs of the *Central Hudson* test. . . .

The respondents argue that the FCC's CPNI regulations advance two substantial state interests: protecting customer privacy and promoting competition. While, in the abstract, these may constitute legitimate and substantial interests, we have concerns about the proffered justifications in the context of this case. . . .

. . . Although we agree that privacy may rise to the level of a substantial state interest, the government cannot satisfy the second prong of the *Central Hudson* test by merely asserting a broad interest in privacy. It must specify the particular notion of privacy and interest served. Moreover, privacy is not an absolute good because it imposes real costs on society. Therefore, the specific privacy interest must be substantial, demonstrating that the state has considered the proper balancing of the benefits and harms of privacy. In sum, privacy may only constitute a substantial state interest if the government specifically articulates and properly justifies it.

In the context of a speech restriction imposed to protect privacy by keeping certain information confidential, the government must show that the dissemination of the information desired to be kept private would inflict specific and significant harm on individuals, such as undue embarrassment or ridicule, intimidation or harassment, or misappropriation of sensitive personal information for the purposes of assuming another's identity. Although we may feel uncomfortable knowing that our personal information is circulating in the world, we live in an open society where information may usually pass freely. A general level of discomfort from knowing that people can readily access information about us does not necessarily rise to the level of a substantial state interest under *Central Hudson* for it is not based on an identified harm.

Neither Congress nor the FCC explicitly stated what "privacy" harm § 222 seeks to protect against. The CPNI Order notes that "CPNI includes information that is extremely personal to customers . . . such as to whom, where, and when a customer places a call, as well as the types of service offerings to which the customer subscribes," and it summarily finds "call destinations and other details about a call . . . may be equally or more sensitive [than the content of the calls]." The government never states it directly, but we infer from this thin justification that disclosure of CPNI information could prove embarrassing to some and that the government seeks to combat this potential harm. . . .

Under the next prong of *Central Hudson,* the government must "demonstrate that the harms it recites are real and that its restriction will in fact alleviate them to a material degree.". . . On the record before us, the government fails to meet its burden.

The government presents no evidence showing the harm to either privacy or competition is real. Instead, the government relies on speculation that harm to privacy and competition for new services will result if carriers use CPNI. . . . While protecting against disclosure of sensitive and potentially embarrassing personal information may be important in the abstract, we have no indication of how it may occur in reality with respect to CPNI. Indeed, we do not even have indication that the disclosure might actually occur. The government presents no evidence regarding how and to whom carriers would disclose CPNI. . . . [T]he government has not explained how or why a carrier would disclose CPNI to outside parties, especially when the government claims CPNI is information that would give one firm a competitive advantage over another. This leaves us unsure exactly who would potentially receive the sensitive information. . . .

In order for a regulation to satisfy this final *Central Hudson* prong, there must be a fit between the legislature's means and its desired objective. . . .

. . . [O]n this record, the FCC's failure to adequately consider an obvious and substantially less restrictive alternative, an opt-out strategy, indicates that it did not narrowly tailor the CPNI regulations regarding customer approval. . . .

The respondents merely speculate that there are a substantial number of individuals who feel strongly about their privacy, yet would not bother to opt-out if given notice and the opportunity to do so. Such speculation hardly reflects the careful calculation of costs and benefits that our commercial speech jurisprudence requires. . . .

In sum, even assuming that respondents met the prior two prongs of *Central Hudson,* we conclude that based on the record before us, the agency has failed to satisfy its burden of showing that the customer approval regulations restrict no more speech than necessary to serve the asserted state interests. Consequently, we find that the CPNI regulations interpreting the customer approval requirement of 47 U.S.C. § 222(c) violate the First Amendment.

BRISCOE, J. dissenting. . . . After reviewing the CPNI Order and the administrative record, I am convinced the FCC's interpretation of § 222, more specifically its selection of the opt-in method for obtaining customer approval, is entirely reasonable. Indeed, the CPNI Order makes a strong case that, of the two options seriously considered by the FCC, the opt-in method is the only one that legitimately forwards Congress' goal of ensuring that customers give informed consent for use of their individually identifiable CPNI. . . .

. . . U.S. West suggests the CPNI Order unduly limits its ability to engage in commercial speech with its existing customers regarding new products and services it may offer. . . .

The problem with U.S. West's arguments is they are more appropriately aimed at the restrictions and requirements outlined in § 222 rather than the approval method adopted in the CPNI Order. As outlined above, it is the statute, not the CPNI Order, that prohibits a carrier from using, disclosing, or permitting access to individually identifiable CPNI without first obtaining informed consent from its customers. Yet U.S. West has not challenged the constitutionality of § 222, and this is not the proper forum for addressing such a challenge even if it was raised. . . .

The majority, focusing at this point on the CPNI Order rather than the statute, concludes the FCC failed to adequately consider the opt-out method, which the majority characterizes as "an obvious and substantially less restrictive alternative" than the opt-in method. Notably, however, the majority fails to explain why, in its view, the opt-out method is substantially less restrictive. Presumably, the majority is relying on the fact that the opt-out method typically results in a higher "approval" rate than the opt-in method. Were mere "approval" percentages the only factor relevant to our discussion, the majority would perhaps be correct. As the FCC persuasively concluded in the CPNI Order, however, the opt-out method simply does not comply with § 222's requirement of informed consent. In particular, the opt-out method, unlike the opt-in method, does not guarantee that a customer will make an informed decision about usage of his or her individually identifiable CPNI. To the contrary, the opt-out method creates the very real possibility of "uninformed" customer approval. In the end, I reiterate my point that the opt-in method selected by the FCC is the only method of obtaining approval that serves the governmental interests at issue while simultaneously complying with the express requirement of the statute (i.e., obtaining informed customer consent). . . .

In conclusion, I view U.S. West's petition for review as little more than a run-of-the-mill attack on an agency order "clothed by ingenious argument in the garb" of First Amendment issues. . . .

NOTES & QUESTIONS

1. *The Aftermath of* U.S. West: *The FCC and the D.C. Circuit.* The FCC responded to the *U.S. West* decision at length in its 2007 CPNI Order and largely rejected its holdings. FCC Report and Order, 07-22 (April 2, 2007). The one change that it made was to modify its 1998 Order at issue in *U.S. West* so that opt-in consent would be required only with respect to a carrier's sharing of customer information with third-party marketers.

The FCC also declared that the Tenth Circuit in *U.S. West* had based its decision "on a different record than the one compiled here" and in particular on premises that were no longer valid. First, the FCC reasoned, there was now ample evidence of disclosure of CPNI and the adverse effects it could have on customers. Second, there was now substantial evidence that an opt-out strategy would not adequately protect customer privacy "because most customers either do not read or do not understand carriers' opt-out notices." The FCC also stated that requiring opt-in consent from customers before sharing CPNI with joint venture partners and independent contractors for marketing purposes would pass First Amendment scrutiny.

The D.C. Circuit upheld the FCC's 2007 Report and Order. *National Cable and Telecommunications Association*, 555 F.3d 996 (D.C. Cir. 2009). It found that the government had a "substantial" interest, under the *Central Hudson* test, in "protecting the privacy of consumer credit information." In its analysis of the second part of the *Central Hudson* test, the D.C. Circuit found that the Commission's 2007 Order "directly advances" the government's interest:

> [C]ommon sense supports the Commission's determination that the risk of unauthorized disclosure of customer information increases with the number of entities possessing it. The Commission therefore reasonably concluded that an opt-in consent requirement directly and materially advanced the interests in protecting customer privacy and in ensuring customer control over the information.

Finally, the court found that under *Central Hudson*'s final requirement the 2007 Report and Order easily met the standard of a regulation proportionate to the government's interest. The court reasoned that the difference between opt in and opt out is only a marginal one in the relative degree of burden on First Amendment interests. The D.C. Circuit found that the "Commission carefully considered the differences between the two regulatory approaches, and the evidence supports the Commission's decision to prefer opt-in consent."

If the *U.S. West* court were to examine the FCC's 2007 Report and Order, would it likely agree or disagree with the D.C. Circuit?

2. *Is Opt In Narrowly Tailored?* Is the opt-in system involved in *U.S. West* more restrictive than the do-not-mail list in *Rowan* or the DNC list in *Mainstream Marketing*? Is the privacy interest in *U.S. West* different than in *Rowan* and *Mainstream Marketing*?

3. *Personal Information: Property, Contract, and Speech.* Consider the following critique of *U.S. West* by Julie Cohen:

> The law affords numerous instances of regulation of the exchange of information as property or product. Securities markets, which operate entirely by means of information exchange, are subject to extensive regulation, and hardly anybody thinks that securities laws and regulations should be subjected to heightened or strict First Amendment scrutiny. Laws prohibiting patent, copyright, and trademark infringement, and forbidding the misappropriation of trade secrets, have as their fundamental purpose (and their undisputed effect) the restriction of information flows. The securities and intellectual property laws, moreover, are expressly content-based, and thus illustrate that (as several leading First Amendment scholars acknowledge) this characterization doesn't always matter. Finally, federal computer crime laws punish certain uses of information for reasons entirely unrelated to their communicative aspects. . . .
>
> The accumulation, use, and market exchange of personally-identified data don't fit neatly into any recognized category of "commercial speech" . . . because in the ways that matter, these activities aren't really "speech" at all. Although regulation directed at these acts may impose some indirect burden on direct-to-consumer communication, that isn't the primary objective of data privacy regulation. This suggests that, at most, data privacy regulation should be subject to the intermediate scrutiny applied to indirect speech regulation.[96]

---

[96] Julie E. Cohen, *Examined Lives: Informational Privacy and the Subject as Object*, 52 Stan. L. Rev. 1373, 1416-18, 1421 (2000).

4. *Is Opt In Too Expensive?* Michael Staten and Fred Cate have defended the *U.S. West* decision by noting the results of the testing of an opt-in system by U.S. West:

> In 1997, U.S. West (now Qwest Communications), one of the largest telecommunications companies in the United States, conducted one of the few affirmative consent trials for which results are publicly available. In that trial, the company sought permission from its customers to utilize information about their calling patterns (e.g., volume of calls, time and duration of calls, etc.) to market new services to them. The direct mail appeal for permission received a positive response rate between 5 and 11 percent for residential customers (depending upon the size of a companion incentive offered by the company). Residential customers opted in at a rate of 28 percent when called about the service.
>
> When U.S. West was actually communicating in person with the consumers, the positive response rate was three to six times higher than when it relied on consumers reading and responding to mail. But even with telemarketing, the task of reaching a customer is daunting. U.S. West determined that it required an average of 4.8 calls to each consumer household before they reached an adult who could grant consent. In one-third of households called, U.S. West never reached the customer, despite repeated attempts. In any case, many U.S. West customers received more calls than would have been the case in an opt-out system, and despite repeated contact attempts, one-third of their customers missed opportunities to receive new products and services. The approximately $20 cost per positive response in the telemarketing test and $29 to $34 cost per positive response in the direct mail test led the company to conclude that opt-in was not a viable business model because it was too costly, too difficult, and too time intensive.[97]

Robert Gellman, however, generally disputes the findings of industry studies about the costs of privacy protective measures. With regard to opt-in cost assessments, Gellman argues that industry studies often fail "to consider other ways [beyond direct mail and telemarketing] that business and charities can solicit individuals to replace any losses from opt-in requirements. Newspaper, Internet, radio, and television advertising may be effective substitutes for direct mail. There are other ways to approach individuals without the compilation of detailed personal dossiers. None of the alternatives is adequately considered."[98]

5. *Is Commercial Transaction Information Different from Other Speech?* Courts analyzing First Amendment challenges to regulation of data about commercial transactions have typically viewed the dissemination and use of such data as commercial speech, and they have applied the *Central Hudson* test. This test is less protective than regular First Amendment protection. Solveig Singleton contends that data about commercial transactions should be considered regular speech, not commercial speech:

---

[97] Michael E. Staten & Fred H. Cate, *The Impact of Opt-In Privacy Rules on Retail Credit Markets: A Case Study of MBNA*, 52 Duke L.J. 745, 767-68 (2003).

[98] Robert Gellman, *Privacy, Consumers, and Costs: How the Lack of Privacy Costs Consumers and Why Business Studies of Privacy Costs Are Biased and Incomplete* (Mar. 2002), at http://www.epic.org/reports/dmfprivacy.html.

Is commercial tracking essentially different from gossip? . . .

Gossip and other informal personal contacts serve an important function in advanced economies. In Nineteenth Century America, entrepreneurs would increase their sales by acquiring information about their customers. Customers relied on their neighborhood banker, whom they knew since childhood, to grant them credit. They would return again and again to the same stores for personalized service. . . .

[E]conomic actors must develop new mechanisms of relaying information to each other about fraud, trust, and behavior of potential customers. Towards the end of the Nineteenth Century and throughout the Twentieth Century, formal credit reporting began to evolve out of gossip networks. . . .

The equivalence of gossip and consumer databases suggests that there is no need to treat the evolution of databases as a crisis. Those who argue for a new legal regime for privacy, however, view new uses of information as having crossed an "invisible line" between permissible gossip and violative information collection. While the use of new technology to collect information may make people uneasy, is there any reason to suppose that any harm that might result will amount to greater harm than the harm that could come from being a victim of vicious gossip?[99]

Singleton goes on to contend that information collected by businesses in databases is less pernicious than gossip because few people have access to it and it is "likely to be much more accurate than gossip." Is the information in computer databases merely gossip on a more systemic scale? Compare how the First Amendment regulates gossip with how it regulates commercial speech.

6. *The Value of Privacy.* What is the value of protecting the privacy of consumer information maintained by telecommunications companies? Is it more important than the economic benefits that the telecommunications companies gain by using that information for marketing? How should policymakers go about answering such questions? Consider James Nehf:

The choice of utilitarian reasoning — often reduced to cost-benefit analysis ("CBA") in policy debates — fixes the outcome in favor of the side that can more easily quantify results. In privacy debates, this generally favors the side arguing for more data collection and sharing. Although CBA can mean different things in various contexts, the term here means a strategy for making choices in which quantifiable weights are given to competing alternatives. . . .

We should openly acknowledge that non-economic values are legitimate in privacy debates, just as they have been recognized in other areas of fundamental importance. Decisions about the societal acceptance of disabled citizens, the codification of collective bargaining rights for workers, and the adoption of fair trial procedures for the accused did not depend entirely, or even primarily, on CBA outcomes. Difficulties in quantifying costs and benefits do not present insurmountable obstacles when policymakers address matters of basic human dignity. The protection of personal data should be viewed in a similar way, and CBA should play a smaller role in privacy debates. . . .

---

[99] Solveig Singleton, *Privacy Versus the First Amendment: A Skeptical Approach*, 11 Fordham Intell. Prop. Media & Ent. L.J. 97, 126-32 (2000).

A similar phenomenon is at work in the formulation of public policy. Policymakers are often asked to compare incomparable alternatives. . . .

By converting all values to money, the incomparability problem is lessened, but only if we accept the legitimacy of money as the covering value. In the privacy debate, the legitimacy of monetizing individual privacy preferences is highly suspect. Benefits are often personal, emotional, intangible, and not readily quantifiable. Preferences on privacy matters are generally muddled, incoherent, and ill-informed. If privacy preferences are real but not sufficiently coherent to form a sound basis for valuation, any attempt to place a monetary value on them loses meaning. The choice of CBA as the model for justifying decisions fixes the end, because the chosen covering value will usually result in a decision favoring data proliferation over data protection. . . .

People make choices between seemingly incomparable things all the time, and they can do so rationally. A person is not acting irrationally by preferring a perceived notable value over an incomparable nominal value, even if she cannot state a normative theory to explain why the decision is right. A similar phenomenon may be seen in the formulation of public policy. Notable values may be preferred over nominal ones in the enactment of laws and the implementation of policies even if policymakers cannot explain why one alternative is better than the other. Moreover, by observing a number of such decisions over time, we may begin to see a pattern develop and covering values emerge that can serve as guides to later decisions that are closer to the margin.[100]

TRANS UNION CORP. V. FEDERAL TRADE COMMISSION

245 F.3d 809 (D.C. Cir. 2001)

TATEL, J. . . . Petitioner Trans Union sells two types of products. First, as a credit reporting agency, it compiles credit reports about individual consumers from credit information it collects from banks, credit card companies, and other lenders. It then sells these credit reports to lenders, employers, and insurance companies. Trans Union receives credit information from lenders in the form of "tradelines." A tradeline typically includes a customer's name, address, date of birth, telephone number, Social Security number, account type, opening date of account, credit limit, account status, and payment history. Trans Union receives 1.4 to 1.6 billion records per month. The company's credit database contains information on 190 million adults.

Trans Union's second set of products — those at issue in this case — are known as target marketing products. These consist of lists of names and addresses of individuals who meet specific criteria such as possession of an auto loan, a department store credit card, or two or more mortgages. Marketers purchase these lists, then contact the individuals by mail or telephone to offer them goods and services. To create its target marketing lists, Trans Union maintains a database known as MasterFile, a subset of its consumer credit database. MasterFile consists of information about every consumer in the

---

[100] James P. Nehf, *Incomparability and the Passive Virtues of Ad Hoc Privacy Policy*, 76 U. Colo. L. Rev. 1, 29-36, 42 (2005).

company's credit database who has (A) at least two tradelines with activity during the previous six months, or (B) one tradeline with activity during the previous six months plus an address confirmed by an outside source. The company compiles target marketing lists by extracting from MasterFile the names and addresses of individuals with characteristics chosen by list purchasers. For example, a department store might buy a list of all individuals in a particular area code who have both a mortgage and a credit card with a $10,000 limit. Although target marketing lists contain only names and addresses, purchasers know that every person on a list has the characteristics they requested because Trans Union uses those characteristics as criteria for culling individual files from its database. Purchasers also know that every individual on a target marketing list satisfies the criteria for inclusion in MasterFile.

The Fair Credit Reporting Act of 1970 ("FCRA"), 15 U.S.C. §§ 1681, 1681a-1681u, regulates consumer reporting agencies like Trans Union, imposing various obligations to protect the privacy and accuracy of credit information. The Federal Trade Commission, acting pursuant to its authority to enforce the FCRA, *see* 15 U.S.C. § 1681s(a), determined that Trans Union's target marketing lists were "consumer reports" subject to the Act's limitations. [The FTC concluded that targeted marketing was not an authorized use of consumer reports under the FCRA and ordered Trans Union to halt its sale of the lists.] . . .

. . . [Trans Union challenges the FTC's application of the FCRA as violative of the First Amendment.] Banning the sale of target marketing lists, the company says, amounts to a restriction on its speech subject to strict scrutiny. Again, Trans Union misunderstands our standard of review. In *Dun & Bradstreet, Inc. v. Greenmoss Builders, Inc.,* 472 U.S. 749 (1985), the Supreme Court held that a consumer reporting agency's credit report warranted reduced constitutional protection because it concerned "no public issue." "The protection to be accorded a particular credit report," the Court explained, "depends on whether the report's 'content, form, and context' indicate that it concerns a public matter." Like the credit report in *Dun & Bradstreet,* which the Supreme Court found "was speech solely in the interest of the speaker and its specific business audience," the information about individual consumers and their credit performance communicated by Trans Union target marketing lists is solely of interest to the company and its business customers and relates to no matter of public concern. Trans Union target marketing lists thus warrant "reduced constitutional protection."

We turn then to the specifics of Trans Union's First Amendment argument. The company first claims that neither the FCRA nor the Commission's Order advances a substantial government interest. The "Congressional findings and statement of purpose" at the beginning of the FCRA state: "There is a need to insure that consumer reporting agencies exercise their grave responsibilities with . . . respect for the consumer's right to privacy." 15 U.S.C. § 1681(a)(4). Contrary to the company's assertions, we have no doubt that this interest — protecting the privacy of consumer credit information — is substantial.

Trans Union next argues that Congress should have chosen a "less burdensome alternative," i.e., allowing consumer reporting agencies to sell credit information as long as they notify consumers and give them the ability to "opt out." Because the FCRA is not subject to strict First Amendment scrutiny, however, Congress had no obligation to choose the least restrictive means of accomplishing its goal.

Finally, Trans Union argues that the FCRA is underinclusive because it applies only to consumer reporting agencies and not to other companies that sell consumer information. But given consumer reporting agencies' unique "access to a broad range of continually-updated, detailed information about millions of consumers' personal credit histories," we think it not at all inappropriate for Congress to have singled out consumer reporting agencies for regulation. . . .

NOTES & QUESTIONS

1. **U.S. West *vs.* Trans Union.** Compare *U.S. West* with *Trans Union.* Are these cases consistent with each other? Which case's reasoning strikes you as more persuasive?

2. **Trans Union II.** In *Trans Union v. FTC*, 295 F.3d 42 (D.C. Cir. 2002) (*Trans Union II*), Trans Union sued to enjoin regulations promulgated pursuant to the Gramm-Leach-Bliley Act (GLBA), alleging, among other things, that they violated the First Amendment. Trans Union argued that these regulations would prevent it from selling credit headers, which consist of a consumer's name, address, Social Security number, and phone number. Trans Union contended that the sale of credit headers is commercial speech. The court concluded that Trans Union's First Amendment arguments were "foreclosed" by its earlier opinion in *Trans Union v. FTC,* which resolved that "the government interest in 'protecting the privacy of consumer credit information' 'is substantial.' "

3. ***Free Speech and the Fair Information Practices.*** Recall the discussion of the Fair Information Practices from Chapter 6. The Fair Information Practices provide certain limitations on the uses and disclosure of personal information. Eugene Volokh contends:

   I am especially worried about the normative power of the notion that the government has a compelling interest in creating "codes of fair information practices" restricting true statements made by nongovernmental speakers. The protection of free speech generally rests on an assumption that it's not for the government to decide which speech is "fair" and which isn't; the unfairnesses, excesses, and bad taste of speakers are something that current First Amendment principles generally require us to tolerate. Once people grow to accept and even like government restrictions on one kind of supposedly "unfair" communication of facts, it may become much easier for people to accept "codes of fair reporting," "codes of fair debate," "codes of fair filmmaking," "codes of fair political criticism," and the like. . . .[101]

   Consider Paul Schwartz, who contends that free discourse is promoted by the protection of privacy:

---

[101] Eugene Volokh, *Freedom of Speech and Information Privacy: The Troubling Implications of a Right to Stop People from Speaking About You,* 52 Stan. L. Rev. 1049, 1090 (2000).

When the government requires fair information practices for the private sector, has it created a right to stop people from speaking about you? As an initial point, I emphasize that the majority of the core fair information practices do not involve the government preventing disclosure of personal information. [The fair information practices generally require: (1) the creation of a statutory fabric that defines obligations with respect to the use of personal information; (2) the maintenance of processing systems that are understandable to the concerned individual (transparency); (3) the assignment of limited procedural and substantive rights to the individual; and (4) the establishment of effective oversight of data use, whether through individual litigation (self-help), a government role (external oversight), or some combination of these approaches.] . . . [F]air information practices one, two, and four regulate the business practices of private entities without silencing their speech. No prevention of speech about anyone takes place, for example, when the Fair Credit Reporting Act of 1970 requires that certain information be given to a consumer when an "investigative consumer report" is prepared about her.

These nonsilencing fair information practices are akin to a broad range of other measures that regulate information use in the private sector and do not abridge the freedom of speech under any interpretation of the First Amendment. The First Amendment does not prevent the government from requiring product labels on food products or the use of "plain English" by publicly traded companies in reports sent to their investors or Form 10-Ks filed with the Securities and Exchange Commission. Nor does the First Amendment forbid privacy laws such as the Children's Online Privacy Protection Act, which assigns parents a right of access to their children's online data profiles. The ultimate merit of these laws depends on their specific context and precise details, but such experimentation by the State should be viewed as noncontroversial on free speech grounds.

Nevertheless, one subset of fair information practices does correspond to Volokh's idea of information privacy as the right to stop people from speaking about you. . . . [S]o long as [laws protecting personal information disclosure] are viewpoint neutral, these laws are a necessary element of safeguarding free communication in our democratic society. . . .

. . . [A] democratic order depends on both an underlying personal capacity for self-governance and the participation of individuals in community and democratic self-rule. Privacy law thus has an important role in protecting individual self-determination and democratic deliberation. By providing access to one's personal data, information about how it will be processed, and other fair information practices, the law seeks to structure the terms on which individuals confront the information demands of the community, private bureaucratic entities, and the State. Attention to these issues by the legal order is essential to the health of a democracy, which ultimately depends on individual communicative competence.[102]

---

[102] Paul M. Schwartz, *Free Speech vs. Information Privacy: Eugene Volokh's First Amendment Jurisprudence*, 52 Stan. L. Rev. 1559 (2000).

SORRELL V. IMS HEALTH, INC.

131 S. Ct. 2653 (2011)

KENNEDY, J. Vermont law restricts the sale, disclosure, and use of pharmacy records that reveal the prescribing practices of individual doctors. Vt. Stat. Ann., Tit. 18, § 4631. Subject to certain exceptions, the information may not be sold, disclosed by pharmacies for marketing purposes, or used for marketing by pharmaceutical manufacturers. Vermont argues that its prohibitions safeguard medical privacy and diminish the likelihood that marketing will lead to prescription decisions not in the best interests of patients or the State. It can be assumed that these interests are significant. Speech in aid of pharmaceutical marketing, however, is a form of expression protected by the Free Speech Clause of the First Amendment. As a consequence, Vermont's statute must be subjected to heightened judicial scrutiny. The law cannot satisfy that standard. . . .

Pharmaceutical manufacturers promote their drugs to doctors through a process called "detailing." This often involves a scheduled visit to a doctor's office to persuade the doctor to prescribe a particular pharmaceutical. Detailers bring drug samples as well as medical studies that explain the "details" and potential advantages of various prescription drugs. Interested physicians listen, ask questions, and receive followup data. Salespersons can be more effective when they know the background and purchasing preferences of their clientele, and pharmaceutical salespersons are no exception. Knowledge of a physician's prescription practices—called "prescriber-identifying information"—enables a detailer better to ascertain which doctors are likely to be interested in a particular drug and how best to present a particular sales message. Detailing is an expensive undertaking, so pharmaceutical companies most often use it to promote high-profit brand-name drugs protected by patent. Once a brand-name drug's patent expires, less expensive bioequivalent generic alternatives are manufactured and sold.

Pharmacies, as a matter of business routine and federal law, receive prescriber-identifying information when processing prescriptions. Many pharmacies sell this information to "data miners," firms that analyze prescriber-identifying information and produce reports on prescriber behavior. Data miners lease these reports to pharmaceutical manufacturers subject to nondisclosure agreements. Detailers, who represent the manufacturers, then use the reports to refine their marketing tactics and increase sales.

In 2007, Vermont enacted the Prescription Confidentiality Law. The measure is also referred to as Act 80. It has several components. The central provision of the present case is § 4631(d).

"A health insurer, a self-insured employer, an electronic transmission intermediary, a pharmacy, or other similar entity shall not sell, license, or exchange for value regulated records containing prescriber-identifiable information, nor permit the use of regulated records containing prescriber-identifiable information for marketing or promoting a prescription drug, unless the prescriber consents . . . . Pharmaceutical manufacturers and pharmaceutical marketers shall not use prescriber-identifiable information for marketing or promoting a prescription drug unless the prescriber consents. . . ."

The quoted provision has three component parts. The provision begins by prohibiting pharmacies, health insurers, and similar entities from selling prescriber-identifying information, absent the prescriber's consent. . . . The provision then goes on to prohibit pharmacies, health insurers, and similar entities from allowing prescriber-identifying information to be used for marketing, unless the prescriber consents. This prohibition in effect bars pharmacies from disclosing the information for marketing purposes. Finally, the provision's second sentence bars pharmaceutical manufacturers and pharmaceutical marketers from using prescriber-identifying information for marketing, again absent the prescriber's consent. The Vermont attorney general may pursue civil remedies against violators. § 4631(f). . . .

On its face, Vermont's law enacts content- and speaker-based restrictions on the sale, disclosure, and use of prescriber-identifying information. The provision first forbids sale subject to exceptions based in large part on the content of a purchaser's speech. For example, those who wish to engage in certain "educational communications," § 4631(e)(4), may purchase the information. The measure then bars any disclosure when recipient speakers will use the information for marketing. Finally, the provision's second sentence prohibits pharmaceutical manufacturers from using the information for marketing. The statute thus disfavors marketing, that is, speech with a particular content. More than that, the statute disfavors specific speakers, namely pharmaceutical manufacturers. As a result of these content- and speaker-based rules, detailers cannot obtain prescriber-identifying information, even though the information may be purchased or acquired by other speakers with diverse purposes and viewpoints. . . . For example, it appears that Vermont could supply academic organizations with prescriber-identifying information to use in countering the messages of brand-name pharmaceutical manufacturers and in promoting the prescription of generic drugs. But § 4631(d) leaves detailers no means of purchasing, acquiring, or using prescriber-identifying information. The law on its face burdens disfavored speech by disfavored speakers. . . .

Act 80 is designed to impose a specific, content-based burden on protected expression. It follows that heightened judicial scrutiny is warranted. . . . Vermont's law does not simply have an effect on speech, but is directed at certain content and is aimed at particular speakers. The Constitution "does not enact Mr. Herbert Spencer's Social Statics." *Lochner v. New York*, 198 U.S. 45 (1905) (Holmes, J., dissenting). It does enact the First Amendment.

This Court has held that the creation and dissemination of information are speech within the meaning of the First Amendment. *See, e.g., Bartnicki* ("[I]f the acts of 'disclosing' and 'publishing' information do not constitute speech, it is hard to imagine what does fall within that category, as distinct from the category of expressive conduct"). Facts, after all, are the beginning point for much of the speech that is most essential to advance human knowledge and to conduct human affairs. There is thus a strong argument that prescriber-identifying information is speech for First Amendment purposes.

The State asks for an exception to the rule that information is speech, but there is no need to consider that request in this case. The State has imposed content- and speaker-based restrictions on the availability and use of prescriber-identifying information. So long as they do not engage in marketing, many speakers can obtain and use the information. But detailers cannot. Vermont's statute could be compared with a law prohibiting trade magazines from purchasing or using ink. As a consequence, this case can be resolved even assuming, as the State argues, that prescriber-identifying information is a mere commodity. . . .

The State's asserted justifications for § 4631(d) come under two general headings. First, the State contends that its law is necessary to protect medical privacy, including physician confidentiality, avoidance of harassment, and the integrity of the doctor-patient relationship. Second, the State argues that § 4631(d) is integral to the achievement of policy objectives—namely, improved public health and reduced healthcare costs. Neither justification withstands scrutiny.

Vermont argues that its physicians have a "reasonable expectation" that their prescriber-identifying information "will not be used for purposes other than . . . filling and processing" prescriptions. It may be assumed that, for many reasons, physicians have an interest in keeping their prescription decisions confidential. But § 4631(d) is not drawn to serve that interest. Under Vermont's law, pharmacies may share prescriber-identifying information with anyone for any reason save one: They must not allow the information to be used for marketing. . . .

Perhaps the State could have addressed physician confidentiality through "a more coherent policy." *Greater New Orleans Broadcasting*, [527 U.S. 173, 195 (1999)]. For instance, the State might have advanced its asserted privacy interest by allowing the information's sale or disclosure in only a few narrow and well-justified circumstances. *See, e.g.,* Health Insurance Portability and Accountability Act of 1996, 42 U.S.C. § 1320d–2; 45 CFR pts. 160 and 164. A statute of that type would present quite a different case than the one presented here. But the State did not enact a statute with that purpose or design. Instead, Vermont made prescriber-identifying information available to an almost limitless audience. The explicit structure of the statute allows the information to be studied and used by all but a narrow class of disfavored speakers. Given the information's widespread availability and many permissible uses, the State's asserted interest in physician confidentiality does not justify the burden that § 4631(d) places on protected expression.

. . . Section 4631(d) may offer a limited degree of privacy, but only on terms favorable to the speech the State prefers. Cf. *Rowan* (sustaining a law that allowed private parties to make "unfettered," "unlimited," and "unreviewable" choices regarding their own privacy). This is not to say that all privacy measures must avoid content-based rules. Here, however, the State has conditioned privacy on acceptance of a content-based rule that is not drawn to serve the State's asserted interest. To obtain the limited privacy allowed by § 4631(d), Vermont physicians are forced to acquiesce in the State's goal of burdening disfavored speech by disfavored speakers.

The State also contends that § 4631(d) protects doctors from "harassing sales behaviors." It is doubtful that concern for "a few" physicians who may have "felt coerced and harassed" by pharmaceutical marketers can sustain a broad content-based rule like § 4631(d). Many are those who must endure speech they do not like, but that is a necessary cost of freedom. In any event the State offers no explanation why remedies other than content-based rules would be inadequate. Physicians can, and often do, simply decline to meet with detailers, including detailers who use prescriber-identifying information. Doctors who wish to forgo detailing altogether are free to give "No Solicitation" or "No Detailing" instructions to their office managers or to receptionists at their places of work...

Vermont argues that detailers' use of prescriber-identifying information undermines the doctor-patient relationship by allowing detailers to influence treatment decisions. . . . But the State does not explain why detailers' use of prescriber-identifying information is more likely to prompt these objections than many other uses permitted by § 4631(d). In any event, this asserted interest is contrary to basic First Amendment principles. . . . If pharmaceutical marketing affects treatment decisions, it does so because doctors find it persuasive. Absent circumstances far from those presented here, the fear that speech might persuade provides no lawful basis for quieting it.

The State contends that § 4631(d) advances important public policy goals by lowering the costs of medical services and promoting public health. If prescriber-identifying information were available for use by detailers, the State contends, then detailing would be effective in promoting brand-name drugs that are more expensive and less safe than generic alternatives. . . . While Vermont's stated policy goals may be proper, § 4631(d) does not advance them in a permissible way. . . . The State seeks to achieve its policy objectives through the indirect means of restraining certain speech by certain speakers—that is, by diminishing detailers' ability to influence prescription decisions. Those who seek to censor or burden free expression often assert that disfavored speech has adverse effects. But the "fear that people would make bad decisions if given truthful information" cannot justify content-based burdens on speech. . . .

It is true that content-based restrictions on protected expression are sometimes permissible, and that principle applies to commercial speech. . . . Here, however, Vermont has not shown that its law has a neutral justification.

The State nowhere contends that detailing is false or misleading within the meaning of this Court's First Amendment precedents. Nor does the State argue that the provision challenged here will prevent false or misleading speech. The State's interest in burdening the speech of detailers instead turns on nothing more than a difference of opinion. . . .

The capacity of technology to find and publish personal information, including records required by the government, presents serious and unresolved issues with respect to personal privacy and the dignity it seeks to secure. In considering how to protect those interests, however, the State cannot engage in content-based discrimination to advance its own side of a debate.

If Vermont's statute provided that prescriber-identifying information could not be sold or disclosed except in narrow circumstances then the State might have a stronger position. Here, however, the State gives possessors of the information broad discretion and wide latitude in disclosing the information, while at the same time restricting the information's use by some speakers and for some purposes, even while the State itself can use the information to counter the speech it seeks to suppress. Privacy is a concept too integral to the person and a right too essential to freedom to allow its manipulation to support just those ideas the government prefers. . . .

The State has burdened a form of protected expression that it found too persuasive. At the same time, the State has left unburdened those speakers whose messages are in accord with its own views. This the State cannot do. . . .

BREYER, J., joined by GINSBURG, J. and KAGAN, J., dissenting. The Vermont statute before us adversely affects expression in one, and only one, way. It deprives pharmaceutical and data-mining companies of data, collected pursuant to the government's regulatory mandate, that could help pharmaceutical companies create better sales messages. In my view, this effect on expression is inextricably related to a lawful governmental effort to regulate a commercial enterprise. The First Amendment does not require courts to apply a special "heightened" standard of review when reviewing such an effort. And, in any event, the statute meets the First Amendment standard this Court has previously applied when the government seeks to regulate commercial speech. For any or all of these reasons, the Court should uphold the statute as constitutional. . . .

In this case I would ask whether Vermont's regulatory provisions work harm to First Amendment interests that is disproportionate to their furtherance of legitimate regulatory objectives. . . .

[O]ur cases make clear that the First Amendment offers considerably less protection to the maintenance of a free marketplace for goods and services. And they also reflect the democratic importance of permitting an elected government to implement through effective programs policy choices for which the people's elected representatives have voted. . . .

Vermont's statute neither forbids nor requires anyone to say anything, to engage in any form of symbolic speech, or to endorse any particular point of view, whether ideological or related to the sale of a product. . . . Further, the statute's requirements form part of a traditional, comprehensive regulatory regime. The pharmaceutical drug industry has been heavily regulated at least since 1906. Longstanding statutes and regulations require pharmaceutical companies to engage in complex drug testing to ensure that their drugs are both "safe" and "effective." 21 U.S.C. §§ 355(b)(1), 355(d). Only then can the drugs be marketed, at which point drug companies are subject to the FDA's exhaustive regulation of the content of drug labels and the manner in which drugs can be advertised and sold.

Finally, Vermont's statute is directed toward information that exists only by virtue of government regulation. Under federal law, certain drugs can be dispensed only by a pharmacist operating under the orders of a medical practitioner. 21 U.S.C. § 355(b). Vermont regulates the qualifications, the fitness, and the practices of pharmacists themselves, and requires pharmacies to maintain a "patient record system" that, among other things, tracks who prescribed which drugs. But for these regulations, pharmacies would have no way to know who had told customers to buy which drugs (as is the case when a doctor tells a patient to take a daily dose of aspirin).

Regulators will often find it necessary to create tailored restrictions on the use of information subject to their regulatory jurisdiction. A car dealership that obtains credit scores for customers who want car loans can be prohibited from using credit data to search for new customers. *See* 15 U.S.C. § 1681b; *cf. Trans Union Corp. v. FTC,* 245 F.3d 809, *reh'g denied,* 267 F.3d 1138 (D.C. Cir. 2001). Medical specialists who obtain medical records for their existing patients cannot purchase those records in order to identify new patients. *See* 45 CFR § 164.508(a)(3). Or, speaking hypothetically, a public utilities commission that directs local gas distributors to gather usage information for individual customers might permit the distributors to share the data with researchers (trying to lower energy costs) but forbid sales of the data to appliance manufacturers seeking to sell gas stoves. . . . Thus, it is not surprising that, until today, this Court has *never* found that the First Amendment prohibits the government from restricting the use of information gathered pursuant to a regulatory mandate—whether the information rests in government files or has remained in the hands of the private firms that gathered it.

In short, the case law in this area reflects the need to ensure that the First Amendment protects the "marketplace of ideas," thereby facilitating the democratic creation of sound government policies without improperly hampering the ability of government to introduce an agenda, to implement its policies, and to favor them to the exclusion of contrary policies. To apply "heightened" scrutiny when the regulation of commercial activities (which often involve speech) is at issue is unnecessarily to undercut the latter constitutional goal. The majority's view of this case presents that risk. . . .

Moreover, given the sheer quantity of regulatory initiatives that touch upon commercial messages, the Court's vision of its reviewing task threatens to return us to a happily bygone era when judges scrutinized legislation for its interference with economic liberty. History shows that the power was much abused and resulted in the constitutionalization of economic theories preferred by individual jurists. *See Lochner v. New York,* 198 U.S. 45 (1905) (Holmes, J., dissenting). . . .

The statute threatens only modest harm to commercial speech. I agree that it withholds from pharmaceutical companies information that would help those entities create a more effective selling message. But I cannot agree with the majority that the harm also involves unjustified discrimination in that it permits "pharmacies" to "share prescriber-identifying information with anyone for any reason" (but marketing). Whatever the First Amendment relevance of such discrimination, there is no evidence that it exists in Vermont. The record contains no evidence that prescriber-identifying data is widely disseminated. . . .

The legitimate state interests that the statute serves are "substantial." *Central Hudson,* 447 U.S., at 564. . . . The protection of public health falls within the traditional scope of a State's police powers. The fact that the Court normally exempts the regulation of "misleading" and "deceptive" information even from the rigors of its "intermediate" commercial speech scrutiny testifies to the importance of securing "unbiased information," as does the fact that the FDA sets forth as a federal regulatory goal the need to ensure a "fair balance" of information about marketed drugs. As major payers in the health care system, health care spending is also of crucial state interest. And this Court has affirmed the importance of maintaining "privacy" as an important public policy goal— even in respect to information already disclosed to the public for particular purposes (but not others). *See Department of Justice v. Reporters Comm. for*

Freedom of Press, 489 U.S. 749 (1989); *see also* Solove, *A Taxonomy of Privacy,* 154 U. Pa. L. Rev. 477, 520–522 (2006); *cf. NASA v. Nelson,* 131 S. Ct. 746 (2011) (discussing privacy interests in nondisclosure). . . .

The record also adequately supports the State's privacy objective. Regulatory rules in Vermont make clear that the confidentiality of an individual doctor's prescribing practices remains the norm. Exceptions to this norm are comparatively few.

. . . The prohibition against pharmaceutical firms using this prescriber-identifying information works no more than modest First Amendment harm; the prohibition is justified by the need to ensure unbiased sales presentations, prevent unnecessarily high drug costs, and protect the privacy of prescribing physicians. There is no obvious equally effective, more limited alternative. . . .

In sum, I believe that the statute before us satisfies the "intermediate" standards this Court has applied to restrictions on commercial speech. *A fortiori* it satisfies less demanding standards that are more appropriately applied in this kind of commercial regulatory case—a case where the government seeks typical regulatory ends (lower drug prices, more balanced sales messages) through the use of ordinary regulatory means (limiting the commercial use of data gathered pursuant to a regulatory mandate). The speech-related consequences here are indirect, incidental, and entirely commercial. . . .

Regardless, whether we apply an ordinary commercial speech standard or a less demanding standard, I believe Vermont's law is consistent with the First Amendment. And with respect, I dissent.

NOTES & QUESTIONS

1. ***The Impact of* Sorrell.** The Supreme Court takes an expansive view of commercial speech, which encompasses the sale and use of personal data. What kind of impact will this case likely have on other privacy laws regulating the trade of personal data? Does *Sorrell* affect *Mainstream Marketing Services, Inc. v. FTC* (excerpted above)? Does it affect the *Trans Union* cases (excerpted and discussed above)? What likely impact, if any, will it have?

2. ***Narrow vs. Broad Laws.*** Ironically, the Court's decision to strike down the law was based in part on how narrowly the law restricted the use or disclosure of personal data. How would you redraft the law to address the Court's concerns?

3. ***HIPAA.*** The *Sorrell* Court characterizes HIPAA as a law "allowing the information's sale or disclosure in only a few narrow and well-justified circumstances." Is this an accurate characterization of HIPAA? If HIPAA's restrictions pass muster, then can *Sorrell* be read as a narrow holding that applies only to laws that single out one particular use or one particular group of speakers?

4. ***Is Information Speech?*** Is the collection, use, and/or transfer of personal information a form of speech? Or is it merely trade in property?

Eugene Volokh contends that such information processing constitutes speech:

> Many . . . databases — for instance, credit history databases or criminal record databases — are used by people to help them decide whom it is safe to deal with and who is likely to cheat them. Other databases, which contain less incriminating information, such as a person's shopping patterns . . . [contain] data [that] is of direct daily life interest to its recipients, since it helps them find out with whom they should do business.[103]

Further, Volokh contends: "[I]t is no less speech when a credit bureau sends credit information to a business. The owners and managers of a credit bureau are communicating information to decisionmakers, such as loan officers, at the recipient business."[104]

Daniel Solove recognizes that some forms of database information transfer and use can constitute speech:

> There are no easy analytic distinctions as to what is or is not "speech." The "essence" of information is neither a good, nor is it speech, for information can be used in ways that make it akin to either one. It is the *use* of the information that determines what information is, not anything inherent in the information itself. If I sell you a book, I have engaged in a commercial transaction. I sold the book as a good. However, the book is also expressing something. Even though books are sold as goods, the government cannot pass a law restricting the topics of what books can be sold. . . .
>
> Volokh appears to view all information dissemination that is communicative as speech. Under Volokh's view, therefore, most forms of information dissemination would be entitled to equal First Amendment protection. . . .
>
> However, Volokh's view would lead to severe conflicts with much modern regulation. Full First Amendment protection would apply to statements about a company's earnings and other information regulated by the SEC, insider trading, quid pro quo sexual harassment, fraudulent statements, perjury, bribery, blackmail, extortion, conspiracy, and so on. One could neatly exclude these examples from the category of speech, eliminating the necessity for First Amendment analysis. Although this seems the easiest approach, it is conceptually sloppy or even dishonest absent a meaningful way to argue that these examples do not involve communication. I contend that these examples of highly regulated forms of communication have not received the full rigor of standard First Amendment analysis because of policy considerations. Categorizing them as nonspeech conceals these policy considerations under the façade of an analytical distinction that thus far has not been persuasively articulated. . . .
>
> I am not eschewing all attempts at categorization between speech and nonspeech. To do so would make the First Amendment applicable to virtually anything that is expressive or communicative. Still, the distinction as currently constituted hides its ideological character. . . .
>
> Dealing with privacy issues by categorizing personal information as nonspeech is undesirable because it cloaks the real normative reasons for why

---

[103] Volokh, *Freedom of Speech, supra,* at 1093-94.

[104] *Id.* at 1083-84.

society wants to permit greater regulation of certain communicative activity. Rather than focusing on distinguishing between speech and nonspeech, the determination about what forms of information to regulate should center on policy considerations. These policy considerations should turn on the uses of the information rather than on notions about the inherent nature of the information.[105]

Solove goes on to argue that although transfers of personal information may be speech, they are of lower value than other forms of free speech, such as political speech. He contends that whereas speech of public concern is of high value, speech of private concern is given a lower constitutional value, and hence less stringent scrutiny, as is commercial speech and other lower-value categories of speech.

Neil Richards, however, contends that "most privacy regulation that interrupts information flows in the context of an express or implied commercial relationship is neither 'speech' within the current meaning of the First Amendment, nor should it be viewed as such." He criticizes Schwartz and Solove because "they grant too much ground to the First Amendment critique, and may ultimately prove to be underprotective of privacy interests, particularly in the database context." Richards finds Solove's contextual balancing approach too messy to "provide meaningfully increased protection for privacy in the courts." Richards argues instead for a categorical solution and contends that much regulation of speech in the commercial context should be seen as falling entirely outside the scope of the heightened First Amendment scrutiny:

> This might be the case because the speech is threatening, obscene, or libelous, and thus part of the "established" categories of "unprotected speech." But it might also be the case because the speech is an insider trading tip, . . . an offer to create a monopoly in restraint of trade, or a breach of the attorney-client privilege. In either case, the speech would be outside the scope of the First Amendment and could be regulated as long as a rational basis existed for so doing. . . .
>
> [I]nformation disclosure rules that are the product of generally applicable laws fall outside the scope of the First Amendment. Where information is received by an entity in violation of some other legal rule — whether breach of contract, trespass, theft, or fraud — the First Amendment creates no barrier to the government's ability to prevent and punish disclosure. This is the case even if the information is newsworthy or otherwise of public concern. . . .
>
> From a First Amendment perspective, no such equivalently important social function [as dissemination of information by the press] . . . is played by database companies engaged in the trade of personal data. Indeed, a general law regulating the commercial trade in personal data by database, profiling, and marketing companies is far removed from the core speech protected by the First Amendment, and is much more like the "speech" outside the boundaries of heightened review.

---

[105] Daniel J. Solove, *The Virtues of Knowing Less: Justifying Privacy Protections Against Disclosure*, 53 Duke L.J. 967, 979-80 (2003).

Richards goes on to equate the First Amendment critique of privacy regulation to *Lochnerism*, where the Supreme Court in *Lochner v. New York*, 198 U.S. 45 (1905), struck down a statute regulating the hours bakers could work per week based on "freedom of contract." *Lochner* was, and remains, highly criticized for being an impediment to New Deal legislation by an activist ideological Court. Richards notes:

> [T]here are some fairly strong parallels between the traditional conception of *Lochner* and the First Amendment critique of data privacy legislation. Both theories are judicial responses to calls for legal regulation of the economic and social dislocations caused by rapid technological change. *Lochnerism* addressed a major socio-technological problem of the industrial age — the power differential between individuals and businesses in industrial working conditions, while the First Amendment critique is addressed to a major socio-technological problem of our information age — the power differential between individuals and businesses over information in the electronic environment. Both theories place a libertarian gloss upon the Constitution, interpreting it to mandate either "freedom of contract" or "freedom of information." Both theories seek to place certain forms of economic regulation beyond the power of legislatures to enact. And both theories are eagerly supported by business interests keen to immunize themselves from regulation under the aegis of Constitutional doctrine. To the extent that the First Amendment critique is similar to the traditional view of *Lochner*, then, its elevation of an economic right to first-order constitutional magnitude seems similarly dubious.[106]

---

[106] Neil Richards, *Reconciling Data Privacy and the First Amendment*, 52 UCLA L. Rev. 1149, 1169, 1180, 1172-73, 1206, 1212-13 (2005).

DATA SECURITY

CHAPTER OUTLINE

A. INTRODUCTION

Consumers at Risk. In testimony to Congress in 2014, Edith Ramirez, the Chairwoman of the Federal Trade Commissioner, bluntly stated, "Consumers' data is at risk."[1] She also noted the critical importance of data security to consumers: "If companies do not protect the personal information they collect and store, that information could fall into the wrong hands, resulting in fraud, identity theft, and other harm, along with a potential loss of consumer confidence in the marketplace." Data security is more crucial than ever before, but more data breaches are taking places. The leaks involve Social Security numbers, payment card data, account passwords, health data, information about children, and many other types of personal information.

A data breach involving Target made worldwide headlines in 2013 and 2014. According to subsequent investigations, hackers using credentials from a HVAC vendor of the retailer entered into Target's computer network.[2] Once inside, the hackers installed malware that allowed them to steal credit card numbers from cashier stations in Target stores. The stolen information was temporarily stored within Target servers then sent to a hijacked "staging point" in the United States and then onward to the hackers in Russia. Target was obliged to announce the

---

[1] Edith Ramirez, Prepared Statement of the Federal Trade Commission on Data Breach on the Rise: Protecting Personal Information from Harm, Before the Committee on Homeland Security and Governmental Affairs, U.S. Senate (Apr. 2, 2014).

[2] Michael Riley et al., *Missed Alarms and 40 Million Stolen Credit Card Numbers: How Target Blew It*, Business Week (Mar. 13, 2014).

breach at perhaps the worst point possible in its sales year: December 15. By this point, 40 million credit card numbers had been stolen from the retailer. In August 2014, Target announced that it expected $148 million in expenses related to the breach.[3]

The problem of data security goes far beyond Target, and the dimensions of the problem are staggering. According to a Pew Research Poll from 2014, 18 percent of all online Americans report having had personal information stolen.[4] Separate studies by the Javelin Strategy and Research Group and by LexisNexis estimate that one-fourth of records involved in data breaches are used for fraudulent purposes, such as identity theft.[5] For a snapshot of the extent of data breaches today, two state reports are highly useful. Both California and New York require reporting of data breach notifications to state officials in their respective jurisdictions. In 2013, the California Department of Justice (DOJ) published its first review of these reports.[6] In 2012, it received reports of 131 data breaches, which put more than 2.5 million Californians at risk. Had the data in question only been encrypted, more than 1.4 million Californians would not have been put at risk and 28 percent of the breaches would not have required notification. The industries that reported the most data breaches in the state were the retail industry, followed by finance and insurance. Finally, more than half of the breaches involved Social Security numbers, which, according to the California DOJ, "pose the greatest risk of the most serious types of identity theft."

While California only mandated the filing of notices with state officials in 2011 and received its first reports in 2012, New York has been receiving breach notification reports since 2006. Its 2014 report was therefore able to analyze eight years of data breach notifications.[7] Between 2006 and 2013, the number of reported data security breaches more than tripled. As the Attorney General (AG) of New York, observes: "Over 22 million personal records have been exposed since 2006, jeopardizing the financial health and well-being of countless New Yorkers and costing the public and private sectors in New York – and around the world – billions of dollars." The report estimates the cost of data breaches for 2013 alone at more than $1.37 billion. It also found that five of the ten largest breaches affecting New York residents occurred in the past three years. Moreover, "mega-breaches" were responsible for nearly 80 percent of the personal records exposed in the state. Specifically, the New York State AG found that 28 mega-breaches exposed approximately 18.2 million personal records of New Yorkers.

---

[3] Michael Calia, *Target Lowers Outlook on Retail Softness, Data Breach Expenses*, Wall St. J. (Aug. 5, 2014).

[4] Mary Madden, Pew Research Center, More online Americans say they've experienced a personal data breach (Apr. 14, 2014).

[5] Lexis-Nexis True Cost of Fraud Study, Merchants Struggle Against an Onslaught of High-Cost Identity Fraud and Online Fraud 6 (2013).

[6] California Department of Justice, Data Breach Report 2012 (2013).

[7] New York State Attorney General, Information Exposed: Historical Examination of Data Breaches in New York State (2014).

Fines, Settlements, and High Financial Stakes. The stakes for consumers in data breaches are high. This area is equally important for organizations. Writing in *Computer World*, Jay Cline has tallied up the overall enforcement actions and fines for data privacy violations.[8] His conclusion: "Over the last 15 years, security breaches were the most likely to draw a large fine. They accounted for some 35% of the sizable penalties in our database." The top government-imposed fines for security flaws are against ChoicePoint, a database company, for $15 million (2006); LifeLock, an identity theft protection company, for $12 million (2010); CVS Caremark, a pharmacy chain, for $2.25 million (2009). The ChoicePoint settlement was with the FTC; the CVS Caremark settlement was with the U.S. Department of Health of Health and Human Services and the FTC; the LifeLock settlement was with the FTC and a group of 35 state attorneys general. In a tally from FTC Chairwoman Ramirez, this agency alone has settled more than 50 cases with businesses that it charged with failing to provide reasonable protection for the personal information of consumers.

Another reason that data security is a high-risk area for organizations is the threat of class action lawsuits. Data breach class action lawsuits have led to massive financial settlements. For example, in 2014, Sony agreed to a $15 million settlement of a class action lawsuit for the 2011 hacking of its PlayStation Network. The overall cost of cleaning up the breach, which caused a shut-down of the PlayStation Network for several weeks, has been estimated at $171 million. A data breach lawsuit in Florida against Avmed, Inc, a health care company, led to a $3 million settlement in 2013. The Eleventh Circuit's opinion in this case, *Resnick v. Avmed*, is excerpted below. Once the appellate court denied Avmed's motion for summary judgment, the company quickly settled.

B. DATA SECURITY BREACH NOTIFICATION STATUTES

California was the first state to require companies that maintain personal information to notify individuals in the event of a security breach where personal information is leaked or improperly accessed. The California statute was enacted in 2003. Pursuant to SB 1386, codified at Cal. Civ. Code § 1798.82(a):

> Any person or business that conducts business in California, and that owns or licenses computerized data that includes personal information, shall disclose any breach of the security of the system following discovery or notification of the breach in the security of the data to any resident of California whose unencrypted personal information was, or is reasonably believed to have been, acquired by an unauthorized person. The disclosure shall be made in the most expedient time possible and without unreasonable delay, consistent with the legitimate needs of law enforcement. . . .

---

[8] Jay Cline, U.S. takes the gold in doling out privacy fines, Computer World (Feb. 17, 2014).

The California security breach notice provision received national attention after the ChoicePoint data security breach in 2005. At the time, California was the only state with such a law. The security breach occurred because an identity theft crime ring set up fake businesses and then signed up to receive ChoicePoint's data. As a result, personal information, including names, addresses, and Social Security numbers of over 145,000 people, were improperly accessed. Over 700 of these individuals were victimized by some form of identity theft.

The fraud was discovered in October 2004 by ChoicePoint, but victims were not notified until February 2005 to avoid impeding the law enforcement investigation. When news of the breach was announced, it sparked considerable public attention. After angry statements by many state attorneys general and a public outcry, ChoicePoint decided to voluntarily notify all individuals affected by the breach, not just Californians.

Today, 47 states and the District of Columbia have such laws. Alabama, New Mexico, and South Dakota are the remaining states without a breach notification law. Data breach notification statutes require governmental agencies and/or private companies to disclose security breaches involving personal information.[9] The resulting laws vary according to the following criteria: (1) the definition of covered information; (2) the trigger for notification; (3) any exceptions to the law's notification requirement; (4) a requirement of notification to a state agency or attorney general; (5) the presence or absence of a substantive requirement for data security; and (6) the presence or absence of a private right of action.[10]

Although the federal government has yet to enact a general federal data breach notification statute, in 2009, Congress enacted a data breach notification requirement for entities regulated by HIPAA as part of the HITECH Act.

The idea of data breach notification, born in California, has grown to achieve international popularity. The EU's ePrivacy Directive, as revised in 2009, requires telecommunication operators and Internet service providers to report "personal data breaches" to the respective national authority. When a breach is likely to adversely affect personal data, affected subscribers must be notified. More broadly, the Proposed General Data Protection Regulation of 2012 contains a requirement of notification of the supervisory authority within 24 hours of a breach. When a breach is likely to affect the privacy of an individual adversely, the data controller must inform this affected party without undue delay. Once enacted, the Data Protection Regulation will be immediately binding on all Member States and extend a breach notification requirement throughout the European Union.

Covered Information. The California data breach statute defines the underlying "notice-triggering information" as "first name or initial and last

---

[9] National Conference of State Legislatures, State Security Breach Notifications Laws, http://www.ncsl.org/programs/lis/cip/priv/breachlaws.htm (last visited July 16, 2008. For an analysis of data security breach laws, see Paul Schwartz & Edward Janger, *Notification of Data Security Breaches*, 105 Mich. L. Rev. 913, 924-25 (2007).

[10] For a chart examining these laws, state by state, see Daniel J. Solove & Paul M. Schwartz, *Privacy Law Fundamentals* 172-74 (2013).

name" and any of the following list of other data: Social Security number; driver's license number; financial account number plus a password. In a 2013 amendment to the statute, California became the first state to expand this definition to include user names or e-mail addresses in combination with a password or a security question and answer that would permit access to an online account. Florida, Georgia, and other states have followed this approach.

Like California, other states also define personal information as a party's name in conjunction with a list of other elements. For example, Maine has a data elements list that includes a broad savings clause to broaden the law beyond a person's name. Maine extends its data breach law to any of the listed data elements *without* a person's name "if the information if compromised would be sufficient to permit a person to fraudulently assume or attempt to assume the identity of the person whose information was compromised."

Trigger for Notification. Most states follow the California approach and rely on the "acquisition" standard for breach notification. These states generally require notification whenever there is a reasonable likelihood that an unauthorized party has "acquired" person information. A minority of states have adopted a higher standard. These states consider whether there is a reasonable likelihood of "misuse" of the information, or "material risk" of harm to the person. The idea is that a breach letter should not be sent to the affected public unless there is a more significant likelihood of harm.

Thus, California's breach notification law requires notification when "unencrypted personal information was, or is reasonably believed to have been, acquired by an unauthorized person." Cal. Civ. Code 17982(a). The California Office of Privacy Protection has issued a white paper with its recommendations regarding notification of security breaches.[11] In the white paper, it lists three factors to be considered, among others, in determining whether unencrypted notice-triggering information has been acquired:

1. Indications that the information is in the physical possession and control of an unauthorized person, such as a lost or stolen computer or other device ....

2. Indications that the information has been downloaded or copied.

3. Indications that the information was used by an unauthorized person, such as fraudulent accounts opened or instances of identity theft reported.

Other states have a stricter notification standard, that is, one that is further from the pro-notification side of the continuum than California. These states generally require notification only if "misuse" of a state resident's personal information has occurred or is reasonably likely to occur. States that use a misuse standard include Delaware and Kansas. Other states require a "risk of analysis" finding that misuse is *not* likely to occur. Such states include Maryland, Maine, and New Jersey. Which of these standards do you think is best?

---

[11] California Office of Privacy Protection, Recommended Practices on Notice of Security Breach Involving Personal Information (Jan. 2012).

Exceptions to Notification. Numerous states provide exceptions to the notification requirement if a risk of harm analysis shows that harm to a consumer will not result. Thus, Michigan does not require notification if the "person or agency determines that the security breach has not or is not likely to cause substantial loss or injury to, or result in identity theft with respect to, [one] or more residents." Me. Rev. Stat. tit. 10 § 1348(1)(B) (2014). North Carolina does not consider an acquisition of information a "security breach" if illegal use of the information did not occur or is not reasonably likely to occur, or does not "create[] a material risk of harm to a consumer." N.C. Gen. Stat. § 75-61(14) (2014). The New Jersey exception is for a business that establishes that "misuse of the information is not reasonably possible." N.J. Stat. § 56:8-163(a) (2014).

Florida has recently narrowed its risk analysis against possible misuse. Traditionally, it has not required notification if a data breach "has not and will not result in identity theft or other financial harm to the individual whose personal information has been acquired and accessed." Fla. Stat. § 817.5681(10)(a) (2013) (repealed 2014). However, the Florida Information Protection Act of 2014 (FIPA) requires "appropriate investigation and consultation with relevant federal, state, or local law enforcement agencies" before it can make a "no harm" determination, which it must provide to the Florida Department of Legal Affairs (FDLA). 2014 Fla. Laws ch. 189 § 3(4)(c). Moreover, the amendment requires notification to the FDLA of a breach affecting 500 or more individuals in Florida, without regard to likely harm. This notice is to include key details of the event, and the FDLA is authorized to request copies of the relevant police report, forensic report, and existing security policies of the affected entity.

Notification to State Agency or Attorney General. All the breach notification statutes require notification to the affected party. Writing in 2007, Paul Schwartz and Edward Janger argued that a critical need in the area of data security breaches was for a "coordinated response architecture," which would include a "coordinated response agent" (CRA) to help tailor notice content and supervise the decision whether to give notice.[12] The CRA was to help coordinate actions that companies take after a breach, tailor the content of the notification in light of the nature of the data breach, and help prepare comparative statistical information regarding data security events. Data breach notification laws that require notification to state entities are a strong step towards creation of such a "response architecture." Now states have information about the kinds of breaches that are occurring, whether notification has occurred, and indications of the kinds of potential harms to state residents. Notification also helps state entities decide whether to begin investigations and enforcement actions.

States that require notice to a state agency or attorney general include Alaska, California, Connecticut, Florida, Hawaii, Illinois, Indiana, Iowa, Maryland, Massachusetts, New York, North Carolina, South Carolina, Vermont, and

---

[12] Paul M. Schwartz & Edward J. Janger, *Notification of Data Security Breaches,* 105 Mich. L. Rev. 913, 962-63 (2007).

Virginia. As noted above, attorney generals in California and New York have drawn on the information received due to these notifications in preparing reports on data breaches in their respective states.

Substantive Data Security. Beyond data breach notification, a handful of states create a substantive duty to take reasonable steps to safeguard data. Typically, these statutes provide open-ended, general standards, such as California's requirement to provide "reasonable security procedures and practices appropriate to the nature of the information." Cal. Pub. Util. Code § 8381 (2014). Other states with such laws include Oregon and Nevada. The Massachusetts Standards for the Protection of Personal Information is considered to be the strictest state security law. It extends to any business, no matter where located, that processes personal information of a resident of Massachusetts. 201 Mass. Code Regs. 17.03 (2014). The statute requires the development of a "readily accessible . . . comprehensive information security program" that is "appropriate to (a) the size, scope, and type of business . . . (b) the amount of resources available to such person; (c) the amount of stored data; and (d) the need for security and confidentiality of both consumer and employee information."

Moreover, Massachusetts sets requirements beyond that of a security program. It calls for "the establishment and maintenance of a security system" that includes elements "to the extent technically feasible" including secure user authentication protocols, secure access control measures, and "encryption of all transmitted records and files containing personal information." An FAQ from the Office of Consumer Affairs and Business Regulation of Massachusetts warns that if it is not technically feasible to encrypt e-mail with personal information, the organization should "implement best practices by not sending unencrypted personal information in an email."[13]

Private Right of Action. Only a minority of the statutes provides a private right of action for individuals whose information has been breached. These states include Alaska, California, Maryland, Massachusetts, North Carolina, and Washington. In some states, the private right of action is found in the statute itself. In other states, the private right of action is located in the state's Unfair or Deceptive Trade Practices Act. State laws that do not have a private right of action generally assign their enforcement powers of the notification requirement to the attorney general.

---

[13] Commonwealth of Massachusetts, Office of Consumer Affairs and Business Regulation, Frequently Asked Questions Regarding 201 CMR 17.00 (Nov. 3, 2009).

C. CIVIL LIABILITY AND STANDING

PISCIOTTA V. OLD NATIONAL BANCORP
499 F.3d 629 (7th Cir. 2007)

RIPPLE, J. Plaintiffs Luciano Pisciotta and Daniel Mills brought this action on behalf of a putative class of customers and potential customers of Old National Bancorp ("ONB"). They alleged that, through its website, ONB had solicited personal information from applicants for banking services, but had failed to secure it adequately. As a result, a third-party computer "hacker" was able to obtain access to the confidential information of tens of thousands of ONB site users. The plaintiffs sought damages for the harm that they claim to have suffered because of the security breach; specifically, they requested compensation for past and future credit monitoring services that they have obtained in response to the compromise of their personal data through ONB's website. ONB answered the allegations and then moved for judgment on the pleadings under Rule 12(c). The district court granted ONB's motion and dismissed the case. The plaintiffs timely appeal. For the reasons set forth in this opinion, we affirm the judgment of the district court. . . .

ONB operates a marketing website on which individuals seeking banking services can complete online applications for accounts, loans and other ONB banking services. The applications differ depending on the service requested, but some forms require the customer or potential customer's name, address, social security number, driver's license number, date of birth, mother's maiden name and credit card or other financial account numbers. In 2002 and 2004, respectively, Mr. Pisciotta and Mr. Mills accessed this website and entered personal information in connection with their applications for ONB banking services.

In 2005, NCR, a hosting facility that maintains ONB's website, notified ONB of a security breach. ONB then sent written notice to its customers. The results of the investigation that followed have been filed under seal in this court; for present purposes, it will suffice to note that the scope and manner of access suggests that the intrusion was sophisticated, intentional and malicious.

Mr. Pisciotta and Mr. Mills, on behalf of a putative class of other ONB website users, brought this action in the United States District Court for the Southern District of Indiana. They named ONB and NCR as defendants and asserted negligence claims against both defendants as well as breach of implied contract claims by ONB and breach of contract by NCR. The plaintiffs alleged that:

> [b]y failing to adequately protect [their] personal confidential information, [ONB and NCR] caused Plaintiffs and other similarly situated past and present customers to suffer substantial potential economic damages and emotional distress and worry that third parties will use [the plaintiffs'] confidential

personal information to cause them economic harm, or sell their confidential information to others who will in turn cause them economic harm.

In pleading their damages, the plaintiffs stated that they and others in the putative class "have incurred expenses in order to prevent their confidential personal information from being used and will continue to incur expenses in the future." Significantly, the plaintiffs did not allege any *completed direct* financial loss to their accounts as a result of the breach. Nor did they claim that they or any other member of the putative class *already had been* the victim of identity theft as a result of the breach. The plaintiffs requested "[c]ompensation for all economic and emotional damages suffered as a result of the Defendants' acts which were negligent, in breach of implied contract or in breach of contract," and "[a]ny and all other legal and/or equitable relief to which Plaintiffs . . . are entitled, including establishing an economic monitoring procedure to insure [sic] prompt notice to Plaintiffs . . . of any attempt to use their confidential personal information stolen from the Defendants." . . .

As we have noted, in reaching the conclusion that dismissal was appropriate, the district court in this case relied on several cases from other district courts throughout the Country. Many of those cases have concluded that the federal courts lack jurisdiction because plaintiffs whose data has been compromised, but not yet misused, have not suffered an injury-in-fact sufficient to confer Article III standing. We are not persuaded by the reasoning of these cases. As many of our sister circuits have noted, the injury-in-fact requirement can be satisfied by a threat of future harm or by an act which harms the plaintiff only by increasing the risk of future harm that the plaintiff would have otherwise faced, absent the defendant's actions. We concur in this view. Once the plaintiffs' allegations establish at least this level of injury, the fact that the plaintiffs anticipate that some greater potential harm might follow the defendant's act does not affect the standing inquiry. . . .

The principal claims in this case are based on a negligence theory. The elements of a negligence claim under Indiana law are: "(1) a duty owed to plaintiff by defendant, (2) breach of duty by allowing conduct to fall below the applicable standard of care, and (3) a *compensable injury* proximately caused by defendant's breach of duty." The plaintiffs' complaint also alleges that ONB has breached an implied contract. Compensable damages are an element of a breach of contract cause of action as well.

As this case comes to us, both the negligence and the contractual issues can be resolved, and the judgment of the district court affirmed, *if* the district court was correct in its determination that Indiana law would not permit recovery for credit monitoring costs incurred by the plaintiffs. . . . We must determine whether Indiana would consider that the harm caused by identity information exposure, coupled with the attendant costs to guard against identity theft, constitutes an existing *compensable injury and consequent damages* required to state a claim for negligence or for breach of contract. Neither the parties' efforts nor our own have identified any Indiana precedent addressing this issue. Nor have we located the decision of any court (other than the district court in this case) that examines

Indiana law in this context. We are charged with predicting, nevertheless, how we think the Supreme Court of Indiana would decide this issue. . . .

We begin our inquiry with the Indiana authority most closely addressed to the issue before us. On March 21, 2006, the Indiana legislature enacted a statute that applies to certain database security breaches. Specifically, the statute creates certain duties when a database in which personal data, electronically stored by private entities or state agencies, potentially has been accessed by unauthorized third parties. I.C. § 24-4.9 *et seq.* The statute took effect on July 1, 2006, after the particular incident involved in this case; neither party contends that the statute is directly applicable to the present dispute. We nevertheless find this enactment by the Indiana legislature instructive in our evaluation of the probable approach of the Supreme Court of Indiana to the allegations in the present case.

The provisions of the statute applicable to private entities storing personal information require only that a database owner *disclose* a security breach to potentially affected consumers; they do not require the database owner to take any other affirmative act in the wake of a breach. If the database owner fails to comply with the only affirmative duty imposed by the statute — the duty to disclose — the statute provides for enforcement *only* by the Attorney General of Indiana. It creates no private right of action against the database owner by an affected customer. It imposes no duty to compensate affected individuals for inconvenience or potential harm to credit that may follow. . . .

The plaintiffs maintain that the statute is evidence that the Indiana legislature believes that an individual has suffered a compensable injury at the moment his personal information is exposed because of a security breach. We cannot accept this view. Had the Indiana legislature intended that a cause of action should be available against a database owner for failing to protect adequately personal information, we believe that it would have made some more definite statement of that intent. Moreover, given the novelty of the legal questions posed by information exposure and theft, it is unlikely that the legislature intended to sanction the development of common law tort remedies that would apply to the same factual circumstances addressed by the statute. The narrowness of the defined duties imposed, combined with state-enforced penalties as the exclusive remedy, strongly suggest that Indiana law would not recognize the costs of credit monitoring that the plaintiffs seek to recover in this case as compensable damages.

The plaintiffs further submit that cases decided by the Indiana courts in analogous areas of the law instruct that they suffered an immediate injury when their information was accessed by unauthorized third parties. Specifically, the plaintiffs claim that Indiana law acknowledges special duties on the part of banks to prevent the disclosure of the personal information of their customers; they further claim that Indiana courts have recognized explicitly the significant harm that may result from a failure to prevent such a loss. . . . [One of these cases concerned disclosure to law enforcement that a bank account had been "marked for repossession"; the other, a creditor who was told that the plaintiff's bank account had insufficient funds to cover checks written.]

Whatever these cases say about the relationship of banks and customers in Indiana, they are of marginal assistance to us in determining whether the present plaintiffs are entitled to the remedy they seek as a matter of Indiana law. The reputational injuries suffered by the plaintiffs in [the previous Indiana cases] were direct and immediate; the plaintiffs sought to be compensated for that harm, rather than to be reimbursed for their efforts to guard against some future, anticipated harm. We therefore do not believe that the factual circumstances of the cases relied on by the plaintiffs are sufficiently analogous to the circumstances that we confront in the present case to instruct us on the probable course that the Supreme Court of Indiana would take if faced with the present question.

Although not raised by the parties, we separately note that in the somewhat analogous context of toxic tort liability, the Supreme Court of Indiana has suggested that compensable damage requires more than an exposure to a future potential harm. Specifically, in *AlliedSignal, Inc. v. Ott*, 785 N.E.2d 1068 (Ind. 2003), the Supreme Court of Indiana held that no cause of action accrues, despite incremental physical changes following asbestos exposure, until a plaintiff reasonably could have been diagnosed with an actual exposure-related illness or disease. . . . [E]xposure alone does not give rise to a legally cognizable injury.

Although some courts have allowed medical monitoring damages to be recovered or have created a special cause of action for medical monitoring under similar circumstances, *see Badillo v. American Brands, Inc.*, 16 P.3d 435 (Nev. 2001) (citing cases interpreting the law of seventeen states to allow medical monitoring in some form), no authority from Indiana is among them. Indeed, its recent holding in *AlliedSignal* indicates a contrary approach. To the extent the decision of the Supreme Court of Indiana in that matter provides us with guidance on the likely approach that court would adopt with respect to the information exposure injury in this case, we think it supports the view that no cause of action for credit monitoring is available.

Finally, without Indiana guidance directly on point, we next examine the reasoning of other courts applying the law of other jurisdictions to the question posed by this case. *Allstate Ins. Co.*, 392 F.3d at 952. In this respect, several district courts, applying the laws of other jurisdictions, have rejected similar claims on their merits. In addition to those cases in which the district court held that the plaintiff lacked standing, a series of cases has rejected information security claims on their merits. Most have concluded that the plaintiffs have not been injured in a manner the governing substantive law will recognize.

Although some of these cases involve different types of information losses, all of the cases rely on the same basic premise: Without more than allegations of increased risk of future identity theft, the plaintiffs have not suffered a harm that the law is prepared to remedy. Plaintiffs have not come forward with a single case or statute, from any jurisdiction, authorizing the kind of action they now ask this federal court, sitting in diversity, to recognize as a valid theory of recovery under Indiana law. We decline to adopt a "substantive innovation" in state law, or "to invent what would be a truly novel tort claim" on behalf of the state, absent some authority to suggest that the approval of the Supreme Court of Indiana is forthcoming.

In sum, all of the interpretive tools of which we routinely make use in our attempt to determine the content of state law point us to the conclusion that the Supreme Court of Indiana would not allow the plaintiffs' claim to proceed.

REILLY V. CERIDIAN CORPORATION

664 F.3d 38 (3rd Cir. 2011)

ALDISERT, CJ. Kathy Reilly and Patricia Pluemacher, individually and on behalf of all others similarly situated, appeal from an order of the United States District Court for the District of New Jersey, which granted Ceridian Corporation's motion to dismiss for lack of standing, and alternatively, failure to state a claim. Appellants contend that (1) they have standing to bring their claims in federal court, and (2) they stated a claim that adequately alleged cognizable damage, injury, and ascertainable loss. We hold that Appellants lack standing and do not reach the merits of the substantive issue. We will therefore affirm.

Ceridian is a payroll processing firm with its principal place of business in Bloomington, Minnesota. To process its commercial business customers' payrolls, Ceridian collects information about its customers' employees. This information may include employees' names, addresses, social security numbers, dates of birth, and bank account information.

Reilly and Pluemacher were employees of the Brach Eichler law firm, a Ceridian customer, until September 2003. Ceridian entered into contracts with Appellants' employer and the employers of the proposed class members to provide payroll processing services.

On or about December 22, 2009, Ceridian suffered a security breach. An unknown hacker infiltrated Ceridian's Powerpay system and potentially gained access to personal and financial information belonging to Appellants and approximately 27,000 employees at 1,900 companies. It is not known whether the hacker read, copied, or understood the data.

Working with law enforcement and professional investigators, Ceridian determined what information the hacker may have accessed. On about January 29, 2010, Ceridian sent letters to the potential identity theft victims, informing them of the breach: "[S]ome of your personal information ... may have been illegally accessed by an unauthorized hacker.... [T]he information accessed included your first name, last name, social security number and, in several cases, birth date and/or the bank account that is used for direct deposit." Ceridian arranged to provide the potentially affected individuals with one year of free credit monitoring and identity theft protection. Individuals had until April 30, 2010, to enroll in the free program, and Ceridian included instructions on how to do so within its letter.

Appellants' allegations of hypothetical, future injury do not establish standing under Article III. For the following reasons we will therefore affirm the District Court's dismissal.

Article III limits our jurisdiction to actual "cases or controversies." U.S. Const. art. III, § 2. One element of this "bedrock requirement" is that plaintiffs "must establish that they have standing to sue." *Raines v. Byrd,* 521 U.S. 811 (1997). It is the plaintiffs' burden, at the pleading stage, to establish standing. *See Lujan v. Defenders of Wildlife,* 504 U.S. 555 (1992).

We conclude that Appellants' allegations of hypothetical, future injury are insufficient to establish standing. Appellants' contentions rely on speculation that the hacker: (1) read, copied, and understood their personal information; (2) intends to commit future criminal acts by misusing the information; and (3) is able to use such information to the detriment of Appellants by making unauthorized transactions in Appellants' names. Unless and until these conjectures come true, Appellants have not suffered any injury; there has been no misuse of the information, and thus, no harm.

The requirement that an injury be "certainly impending" is best illustrated by *City of Los Angeles v. Lyons,* 461 U.S. 95 (1983). There, the Court held that a plaintiff lacked standing to enjoin the Los Angeles Police Department from using a controversial chokehold technique on arrestees. Although the plaintiff had already once been subjected to this maneuver, the future harm he sought to enjoin depended on the police again arresting and choking him. Appellants in this case have yet to suffer any harm, and their alleged increased risk of future injury is nothing more than speculation. As such, the alleged injury is not "certainly impending." *Lujan.*

Our Court, too, has refused to confer standing when plaintiffs fail to allege an imminent injury-in-fact.

In this increasingly digitized world, a number of courts have had occasion to decide whether the "risk of future harm" posed by data security breaches confers standing on persons whose information *may* have been accessed. Most courts have held that such plaintiffs lack standing because the harm is too speculative. *See Amburgy v. Express Scripts, Inc.,* 671 F. Supp. 2d 1046 (E.D. Mo. 2009); *see also Key v. DSW Inc.,* 454 F. Supp. 2d 684 (S.D. Ohio 2006). We agree with the holdings in those cases. Here, no evidence suggests that the data has been—or will ever be—misused. The present test is actuality, not hypothetical speculations concerning the possibility of future injury. Appellants' allegations of an increased risk of identity theft resulting from a security breach are therefore insufficient to secure standing. . . .

[Regarding comparisons of data-security-breach situations to defective-medical-device, toxic-substance-exposure, or environmental-injury cases, the Third Circuit stated, "These analogies do not persuade us, because defective-medical-device and toxic-substance-exposure cases confer standing based on two important factors not present in data breach cases."]

First, in those cases, an injury has undoubtedly occurred. In medical-device cases, a defective device has been implanted into the human body with a quantifiable risk of failure. Similarly, exposure to a toxic substance causes injury; cells are damaged and a disease mechanism has been introduced. Hence, the damage has been done; we just cannot yet quantify how it will manifest itself.

In data breach cases where no misuse is alleged, however, there has been no injury—indeed, no change in the status quo. Here, Appellants' credit card statements are exactly the same today as they would have been had Ceridian's database never been hacked. Moreover, there is no quantifiable risk of damage in the future. Any damages that may occur here are entirely speculative and dependent on the skill and intent of the hacker.

Second, standing in medical-device and toxic-tort cases hinges on human health concerns. . . . The deceased, after all, have little use for compensation. This case implicates none of these concerns. The hacker did not change or injure Appellants' bodies; any harm that may occur—if all of Appellants' stated fears are actually realized—may be redressed in due time through money damages after the harm occurs with no fear that litigants will be dead or disabled from the onset of the injury.

An analogy to environmental injury cases fails as well. [S]tanding is unique in the environmental context because monetary compensation may not adequately return plaintiffs to their original position. In a data breach case, however, there is no reason to believe that monetary compensation will not return plaintiffs to their original position completely—*if* the hacked information is actually read, copied, understood, and misused to a plaintiff's detriment. To the contrary, unlike priceless "mountains majesty," the thing feared lost here is simple cash, which is easily and precisely compensable with a monetary award. We therefore decline to analogize this case to those cases in the medical device, toxic tort or environmental injury contexts.

Finally, we conclude that Appellants' alleged time and money expenditures to monitor their financial information do not establish standing, because costs incurred to watch for a speculative chain of future events based on hypothetical future criminal acts are no more "actual" injuries than the alleged "increased risk of injury" which forms the basis for Appellants' claims.

RESNICK V. AVMED

693 F.3d 1317 (11th Cir. 2012)

WILSON, CJ. Juana Curry and William Moore (collectively "Plaintiffs") appeal the district court's dismissal of their Second Amended Complaint ("Complaint") for failure to state a claim upon which relief may be granted. The district court held that among its other deficiencies, the Complaint failed to state a cognizable injury. We find that the complaint states a cognizable injury for the purposes of standing and as a necessary element of injury in Plaintiffs' Florida law claims. We also conclude that the Complaint sufficiently alleges the causation element of negligence, negligence *per se*, breach of contract, breach of implied contract, breach of the implied covenant of good faith and fair dealing, and breach of fiduciary duty . . . . The Complaint similarly alleges facts sufficient to withstand a motion to dismiss on the restitution/unjust enrichment claim. However, the Complaint fails to allege entitlement to relief under Florida law for the claims of negligence *per se* and breach of the implied covenant of good faith and fair dealing. We therefore reverse in part, affirm in part, and remand the case to the district court for further proceedings.

AvMed, Inc. is a Florida corporation that delivers health care services through health plans and government-sponsored managed-care plans. AvMed has a corporate office in Gainesville, Florida, and in December 2009, two laptop computers were stolen from that office. Those laptops contained AvMed customers' sensitive information, which included protected health information, Social Security numbers, names, addresses, and phone numbers. AvMed did not take care to secure these laptops, so when they were stolen the information was readily accessible. The laptops were sold to an individual with a history of dealing in stolen property. The unencrypted laptops contained the sensitive information of approximately 1.2 million current and former AvMed members.

The laptops contained personal information of Juana Curry and William Moore. Plaintiffs are careful in guarding their sensitive information and had never been victims of identity theft before the laptops were stolen. Curry guards physical documents that contain her sensitive information and avoids storing or sharing her sensitive information digitally. Similarly, Moore guards physical documents that contain his sensitive information and is careful in the digital transmission of this information.

Notwithstanding their care, Plaintiffs have both become victims of identity theft. Curry's sensitive information was used by an unknown third party in October 2010—ten months after the laptop theft. Bank of America accounts were opened in Curry's name, credit cards were activated, and the cards were used to make unauthorized purchases. Curry's home address was also changed with the U.S. Postal Service. Moore's sensitive information was used by an unknown third party in February 2011 — fourteen months after the laptop theft. At that time, an account was opened in Moore's name with E*Trade Financial, and in April 2011, Moore was notified that the account had been overdrawn.

Prior to making an adjudication on the merits, we must assure ourselves that we have jurisdiction to hear the case before us. Litigants must show that their claim presents the court with a case or controversy under the Constitution and meets the "irreducible constitutional minimum of standing." *Lujan,* 504 U.S. at 560. To fulfill this requirement, a plaintiff must show that:

> (1) it has suffered an "injury in fact" that is (a) concrete and particularized and (b) actual or imminent, not conjectural or hypothetical; (2) the injury is fairly traceable to the challenged action of the defendant; and (3) it is likely, as opposed to merely speculative, that the injury will be redressed by a favorable decision.

Friends of the Earth, Inc. v. Laidlaw Envtl. Servs. (TOC), Inc., 528 U.S. 167 (2000). "At the pleading stage, general factual allegations of injury resulting from the defendant's conduct may suffice" to establish standing. *Lujan.*

Whether a party claiming actual identity theft resulting from a data breach has standing to bring suit is an issue of first impression in this Circuit. Plaintiffs allege that they have become victims of identity theft and have suffered monetary damages as a result. This constitutes an injury in fact under the law.[1]

We must next determine whether Plaintiffs' injury is fairly traceable to AvMed's actions. A showing that an injury is "fairly traceable" requires less than a showing of "proximate cause." *Focus on the Family v. Pinellas Suncoast Transit Auth.,* 344 F.3d 1263 (11th Cir. 2003). Even a showing that a plaintiff's injury is indirectly caused by a defendant's actions satisfies the fairly traceable requirement. Plaintiffs allege that AvMed failed to secure their information on company laptops, and that those laptops were subsequently stolen. Despite

Plaintiffs' personal habits of securing their sensitive information, Plaintiffs became the victims of identity theft after the unencrypted laptops containing their sensitive information were stolen. For purposes of standing, these allegations are sufficient to "fairly trace" their injury to AvMed's failures.

Finally, Plaintiffs must show that a favorable resolution of the case in their favor could redress their alleged injuries. Plaintiffs allege a monetary injury and an award of compensatory damages would redress that injury. Plaintiffs have alleged sufficient facts to confer standing, and we now turn to the merits of their appeal. . . .

At the pleading stage, a complaint must contain a "short and plain statement of the claim showing that the pleader is entitled to relief." Fed. R. Civ. P. 8(a)(2). Plaintiffs must plead all facts establishing an entitlement to relief with more than "labels and conclusions" or "a formulaic recitation of the elements of a cause of action." *Twombly*, 550 U.S. at 555. The complaint must contain enough facts to make a claim for relief plausible on its face; a party must plead "factual content that allows the court to draw the reasonable inference that the defendant is liable for the misconduct alleged."

. . . Plaintiffs brought seven counts against AvMed, all under Florida law. Of the seven causes of action alleged, Florida law requires a plaintiff to show that the defendant's challenged action *caused* the plaintiff's harm in six of them: negligence, negligence *per se,* breach of fiduciary duty, breach of contract, breach of contract implied in fact, and breach of the implied covenant of good faith and fair dealing. A negligence claim requires a plaintiff to show that (1) defendants owe plaintiffs a duty, (2) defendants breached the duty, (3) defendants' breach injured plaintiffs, and "(4) [plaintiffs'] damage [was] *caused by* the injury to the plaintiff as a result of the defendant's breach of duty." Similarly, under Florida law, an action for negligence *per* se requires a plaintiff to show "violation of a statute which establishes a duty to take precautions to protect a particular class of persons from a particularly injury or type of injury." As part of this showing, plaintiffs must establish "that the violation of the statute *was the proximate cause* of [their] injury." The elements of a cause of action for breach of fiduciary duty in Florida include "damages *flowing from* the breach."

The contract claims also require a showing of causation. In Florida, a breach of contract claim requires a party to show that *damages resulted from* the breach. Florida courts use breach of contract analysis to evaluate claims of breach of contract implied in fact and breach of the covenant of good faith and fair dealing.

We now consider the well-pleaded factual allegations relating to causation. . . . The complaint alleges that, prior to the data breach, neither Curry nor Moore had ever had their identities stolen or their sensitive information "compromised in any way." It further alleges that "Curry took substantial precautions to protect herself from identity theft," including not transmitting sensitive information over the Internet or any unsecured source; not storing her sensitive information on a computer or media device; storing sensitive information in a "safe and secure physical location;" and destroying "documents she receives in the mail that may contain any of her sensitive information, or that contain any information that could otherwise be used to steal her identity, such as credit card offers." Similarly, Moore alleges in the complaint that he "took substantial precautions to protect himself from identity theft," including not transmitting unencrypted sensitive information over the internet or any other source, storing documents containing sensitive information "in a safe and secure physical location and destroy[ing] any documents he receives in the mail" that include either sensitive information or information that "could otherwise be used to steal his identity." Plaintiffs became victims of identity theft for the first time in their lives ten and fourteen months after the laptops containing their sensitive information were stolen. Curry's sensitive information was used to open a Bank of America account and change her address with the United States Post Office, and Moore's sensitive information was used to open an E*Trade Financial account in his name.

Our task is to determine whether the pleadings contain "sufficient factual matter, accepted as true, to 'state a claim to relief that is plausible on its face.' " A claim is facially plausible when the court can draw "the reasonable inference that the defendant is liable for the misconduct alleged" from the pled facts. Taken as true, these factual allegations are consistent with Plaintiffs' conclusion that AvMed's failure to secure Plaintiffs' information caused them to become victims of identity theft. After thorough consideration, we conclude that the allegations are sufficient to cross the line from merely possible to plausible.

Generally, to prove that a data breach caused identity theft, the pleadings must include allegations of a nexus between the two instances beyond allegations of time and sequence. . . . Here, Plaintiffs allege a nexus between the two events that includes more than a coincidence of time and sequence: they allege that the sensitive information on the stolen laptop was the same sensitive information used to steal Plaintiffs' identity. Plaintiffs explicitly make this connection when they allege that Curry's identity was stolen by changing her address and that Moore's identity was stolen by opening an E*Trade Financial account in his name because in both of those allegations, Plaintiffs state that the identity thief used Plaintiffs' sensitive information. We understand Plaintiffs to make a similar allegation regarding the bank accounts opened in Curry's name even though they do not plead precisely that Curry's sensitive information was used to open the Bank of America account. The Complaint states that Curry's sensitive information was on the unencrypted stolen laptop, that her identity was stolen, and that the *stolen identity* was used to open unauthorized accounts. Considering the Complaint as a whole and applying common sense to our understanding of this allegation, we find that Plaintiffs allege that the same sensitive information that was stored on the stolen laptops was used to open the Bank of America account. Thus, Plaintiffs' allegations that the data breach caused their identities to be stolen move from the realm of the possible into the plausible. Had Plaintiffs alleged fewer facts, we doubt whether the Complaint could have survived a motion to dismiss. However, Plaintiffs have sufficiently alleged a nexus between the data theft and the identity theft and therefore meet the federal pleading standards. Because their contention that the data breach caused the identity theft is plausible under the facts pled, Plaintiffs meet the pleading standards for their allegations on the counts of negligence, negligence *per se,* breach of fiduciary duty, breach of contract, breach of implied contract, and breach of the implied covenant of good faith and fair dealing. . . .

To establish a cause of action for unjust enrichment/restitution, a Plaintiff must show that "1) the plaintiff has conferred a benefit on the defendant; 2) the defendant has knowledge of the benefit; 3) the defendant has accepted or retained the benefit conferred; and 4) the circumstances are such that it would be inequitable for the defendant to retain the benefit without paying fair value for it." *Della Ratta v. Della Ratta*, 927 So. 2d 1055, 1059 (Fla. Dist. Ct. App. 2006).

Plaintiffs allege that they conferred a monetary benefit on AvMed in the form of monthly premiums, that AvMed "appreciates or has knowledge of such benefit," that AvMed uses the premiums to "pay for the administrative costs of data management and security," and that AvMed "should not be permitted to retain the money belonging to Plaintiffs ... because [AvMed] failed to implement the data management and security measures that are mandated by industry standards." Plaintiffs also allege that AvMed either failed to implement or inadequately implemented policies to secure sensitive information, as can be seen from the data breach. Accepting these allegations as true, we find that Plaintiffs alleged sufficient facts to allow this claim to survive a motion to dismiss. . . .

AvMed argues that we can affirm the district court because the Complaint fails to allege an entitlement to relief under Florida law on each count. On review, we find that two of the pled causes of action do not allow Plaintiffs to recover under Florida law. We address only the two claims that fail: negligence *per se,* and breach of the covenant of good faith and fair dealing. . . .

[The Eleventh Circuit found that the negligence *per se* failed because the statutory section that the plaintiffs argued was contained in a chapter regulating the licensure, development, establishment, and minimum standard enforcement of hospitals, ambulatory surgical centers, and mobile surgical facilities. Fla. Stat. § 395.001. It stated: "Because AvMed is an integrated managed-care organization and not a hospital, ambulatory surgical center, or mobile surgical facility, AvMed is not subject to this statute."

The Eleventh Circuit also found that there was no violation of the implied covenant of good faith and fair dealing under Florida law by Avmed. Florida requires a "conscious act" to frustrate the common purpose of a contract and the Plaintiffs failed to allege "AvMed's shortcomings were conscious acts to frustrate the common purpose of the agreement."]

In this digital age, our personal information is increasingly becoming susceptible to attack. People with nefarious interests are taking advantage of the plethora of opportunities to gain access to our private information and use it in ways that cause real harm. Even though the perpetrators of these crimes often remain unidentified and the victims are left to clean up the damage caused by these identity thieves, cases brought by these victims are subject to the same pleading standards as are plaintiffs in all civil suits. Here, Plaintiffs have pled a cognizable injury and have pled sufficient facts to allow for a plausible inference that AvMed's failures in securing their data resulted in their identities being stolen. They have shown a sufficient nexus between the data breach and the identity theft beyond allegations of time and sequence.

PRYOR, CJ., dissenting. I agree with the majority opinion that Curry and Moore have standing to sue, but Curry and Moore's complaint should be dismissed for failure to state a claim. Their complaint fails to allege a plausible basis for finding that AvMed caused them to suffer identity theft, and their claim of unjust enrichment fails as a matter of law. . . .

The parties do not dispute that laptops containing the sensitive information of Curry and Moore was stolen from AvMed, but Curry and Moore's second amended complaint fails to plead enough facts to allow a factfinder to draw a reasonable inference that the sensitive information identity thieves used to open the fraudulent accounts in the plaintiffs' names was obtained from AvMed. In an attempt to bridge this gap, Curry and Moore allege that they have both been *very* careful to protect their sensitive information. But the manner in which Curry and Moore care for the sensitive information they receive from third parties tells us nothing about how the third parties care for that sensitive information before or after they send it to Curry and Moore.

Regarding the cause of the identity theft that Curry and Moore suffered it is conceivable that the unknown identity thieves used the sensitive information stolen from AvMed to open the fraudulent accounts, but it is equally conceivable, in the light of the facts alleged in the complaint, that the unknown identity thieves obtained the information from third parties. Curry and Moore do not allege any facts that make it plausible that the unknown identity thieves who opened the fraudulent accounts obtained the sensitive information necessary to do so from AvMed. . . .

The complaint also fails to state a claim of unjust enrichment under Florida law. "Florida courts have held that a plaintiff cannot pursue a quasi-contract claim for unjust enrichment if an express contract exists concerning the same subject matter." The parties do not dispute that they entered into an enforceable contract; they dispute whether the contract has been breached. In that circumstance, a claim of unjust enrichment cannot be maintained.

I respectfully dissent.

NOTES & QUESTIONS

1. *Harm? No Harm?* The stakes in data security breach litigation are high. Plaintiffs want companies to guard their information more carefully and are concerned about identity theft. Companies face considerable financial exposure. Consider that after the Eleventh Circuit allowed the lawsuit in *Resnick* to continue, AvMed negotiated a $3 million settlement quickly with the attorneys for the plaintiffs. That is a high cost for leaving two laptops unsecured in a corporate office.

   This high stakes litigation is also accompanied by legal uncertainty regarding the nature of the harm to plaintiffs and whether standing is present. The three preceding cases, *Pisciotta*, *Reilly*, and *Resnick* evaluated a different range of claims and reached sometimes contrary results. Analogies were attempted with toxic torts, defective medical devices, and environmental injury. Do you find any of these areas closer or farther from the concerns in data security? In *Resnick*, the plaintiffs were actual victims of identity theft occurring after the theft of the AvMed laptops. Why does that fact make a difference for the Eleventh Circuit?

2. *Tort Negligence for Data Security Breaches.* In tort law, under a general negligence theory, litigants might sue a company after a data security incident and seek to collect damages. In contrast to *Resnick*, however, many class

action lawsuits following data breaches have been notably unsuccessful. Among other problems, claimants are facing trouble convincing courts that the data processing entities owe a duty to the individuals whose data are leaked, or that damages can be inferred from the simple fact of a data breach. For example, a South Carolina court declared in 2003 that "[t]he relationship, if any, between credit card issuers and potential victims of identity theft is far too attenuated to rise to the level of a duty between them." *Huggins v. Citibank*, 585 S.E.2d 275 (S.C. 2003).

3. ***Proving Harm from Data Security Breaches.*** Suppose a person has been notified that her personal information has been improperly accessed, but she has not yet suffered from identity theft. Should she be entitled to any form of compensation? Has she suffered an injury? One might argue that being made more vulnerable to future harm has made her worse off than before. The individual might live with greater unease knowing that she is less secure. On the other hand, no identity theft has occurred, and it may never occur. How should the law address this situation? Recognize a harm? If so, how should damages be assessed?

For data security breaches, plaintiffs have generally advanced one or more of the following theories of harm: (1) The exposure of their data has caused them emotional distress; (2) The exposure of their data has subjected them to an increased risk of harm from identity theft, fraud, or other injury; or (3) The exposure of their data has resulted in their having to expend time and money to prevent future fraud, such as signing up for credit monitoring, contacting credit reporting agencies and placing fraud alerts on their accounts, and so on.

Courts have generally dismissed these arguments. According to Daniel Solove, courts take a "visceral and vested approach" approach to harm: "Harms must be *visceral* — they must involve some dimension of palpable physical injury or financial loss. And harms must be *vested* — they must have already occurred." Solove observes:

> For harms that involve emotional distress, courts are skeptical because people can too easily say they suffered emotional distress. It can be hard to prove or disprove statements that one suffered emotional distress, and these difficulties make courts very uneasy.
>
> For the future risk of harm, courts generally want to see harm that has actually manifested rather than harm that is incubating. Suppose you're exposed to a virus that silently waits in your bloodstream for 10 years and then suddenly might kill you. Most courts would send you away and tell you to come back after you've dropped dead, because then we would know for sure you're injured. But then, sadly, the statute of limitations will have run out, so it's too late to sue. Tough luck, the courts will say.
>
> For harms that involve time and money you spend to protect yourself, that's on your own dime. If you want to collect damages for being harmed, then leave yourself exposed, wait until you're harmed, and hope that it happens within the statute f limitations. . . .
>
> Occasionally, a court recognizes a harm under one of the above theories, but for the most part, the cases are losers. One theory that has gained a small bit of traction is if plaintiffs can prove that they paid fees based on promises of security that were broken. But this is in line with visceral and vested approach

because it focuses on money spent. And many people can't prove that they read the privacy policy or relied on the often vague and general statements made in that policy.[14]

For example, in *Forbes v. Wells Fargo Bank, N.A.*, 420 F. Supp. 2d 1018 (D. Minn. 2006), a contractor for Wells Fargo Bank had computers stolen containing unencrypted data about customers, such as names, addresses, Social Security numbers, and account numbers. A group of customers sued for breach of contract, breach of fiduciary duty, and negligence. The court, however, dismissed the case:

> Plaintiffs allege that Wells Fargo negligently allowed Regulus to keep customers' private information without adequate security. To establish a negligence claim, a plaintiff must prove that (1) the defendant owed plaintiff a duty of care, (2) the defendant breached that duty, (3) the plaintiff sustained damage and (4) the breach of the duty proximately caused the damage. A plaintiff may recover damages for an increased risk of harm in the future if such risk results from a present injury and indicates a reasonably certain future harm. Alone, however, "the threat of future harm, not yet realized, will not satisfy the damage requirement."
>
> Plaintiffs contend that the time and money they have spent monitoring their credit suffices to establish damages. However, a plaintiff can only recover for loss of time in terms of earning capacity or wages. Plaintiffs have failed to cite any Minnesota authority to the contrary. Moreover, they overlook the fact that their expenditure of time and money was not the result of any present injury, but rather the anticipation of future injury that has not materialized. In other words, the plaintiffs' injuries are solely the result of a perceived risk of future harm. Plaintiffs have shown no present injury or reasonably certain future injury to support damages for any alleged increased risk of harm. For these reasons, plaintiffs have failed to establish the essential element of damages. Therefore, summary judgment in favor of defendant on plaintiffs' negligence claim is warranted.
>
> Plaintiffs also bring a claim for breach of contract against Wells Fargo. To establish their claim, plaintiffs must show that they were damaged by the alleged breach. *See Jensen v. Duluth Area YMCA*, 688 N.W.2d 574, 578-79 (Minn. App. 2004). For all of the reasons discussed above, plaintiffs have failed to establish damages. Therefore, summary judgment in favor of defendant on plaintiffs' breach of contract claim is warranted.

Another rejected claim was for a failure to receive the "benefit of the bargain" of a premium membership. *In re LinkedIn User Privacy Litigation*, 932 F. Supp. 1089 (N.D. Cal. 2013). The plaintiffs in the case argued that in consideration of their payment for a premium membership, LinkedIn promised to secure their personal information "with industry standard protocols and technology." The district court rejected this argument for a number of reasons, including the "User Agreement and Privacy Policy" at

---

[14] Daniel J. Solove, *Privacy and Data Security Violations: What's the Harm?* LinkedIn (June 25, 2014), https://www.linkedin.com/today/post/article/20140625045136-2259773-privacy-and-data-security-violations-what-s-the-harm.

LinkedIn being identical for the nonpaying basic membership and the premium membership. As a result, "when a member purchases a premium account upgrade, the bargain is not for a particular level of security, but actually for the advanced networking tools and capabilities to facilitate enhanced usage of LinkedIn's services."

Also consider *In re Hannaford Bros. Co. Customer Data Security Breach Litigation*, 4 A.3d 492 (Me. 2010). Customers of a store whose payment data was stolen sued, claiming "that time and effort expended to avoid or remediate harm from fraudulent charges was a cognizable loss." The court disagreed:

> Our case law . . . does not recognize the expenditure of time and effort alone as a harm. The plaintiffs contend that because their time and effort represented reasonable efforts to avoid reasonably foreseeable harm, it is compensable. However, we do not attach such significance to mitigation efforts. . . . Unless the plaintiffs' loss of time reflects a corresponding loss of earnings or earning opportunities, it is not a cognizable injury under Maine law of negligence.

Why aren't expenditures to reduce risks of future harm created by another recoverable? Suppose a company leaks a toxic chemical, causing a person to have an increased risk of cancer. The person sees a doctor and gets a prescription for a drug that will reduce the likelihood that the chemical will cause cancer. Would the expenses of seeing the doctor and purchasing the drug be recoverable? Is this hypothetical analogous to a data security breach?

Although most courts conclude that data security breaches that do not lead to an incident of identity theft or fraud do not give rise to cognizable injuries sufficient for standing, a few courts have departed from this trend. *Pisciotta* and *Resnick* are two of these cases. Although the plaintiffs ultimately lost, the court concluded that the plaintiff at least had standing because "the injury-in-fact requirement can be satisfied by a threat of future harm or by an act which harms the plaintiff only by increasing the risk of future harm that the plaintiff would have otherwise faced, absent the defendant's actions." In *Resnick*, the plaintiffs suffered identity fraud several months after the breach and the Eleventh Circuit concluded that their allegations were sufficient to "fairly trace" their injury to AvMed's information security failures.

Likewise, in *Krottner v. Starbucks Corp.*, 628 F.3d 1139 (9th Cir. 2010), the court concluded that increased vulnerability to identity theft could give rise to standing:

> If a plaintiff faces "a credible threat of harm," and that harm is "both real and immediate, not conjectural or hypothetical," the plaintiff has met the injury-in-fact requirement for standing under Article III. Here, Plaintiffs–Appellants have alleged a credible threat of real and immediate harm stemming from the theft of a laptop containing their unencrypted personal data. Were Plaintiffs–Appellants' allegations more conjectural or hypothetical—for example, if no laptop had been stolen, and Plaintiffs had sued based on the risk that it would be stolen at some point in the future—we would find the threat far less

credible. On these facts, however, Plaintiffs–Appellants have sufficiently alleged an injury-in-fact for purposes of Article III standing.

4. *The Nature of Data Security Harms.* Ryan Calo has proposed a theory for how privacy harms should be understood:

> [T]he vast majority of privacy harms fall into just two categories — one subjective, the other objective. The subjective category of privacy harm is the perception of unwanted observation. This category describes unwelcome mental states — anxiety, for instance, or embarrassment — that accompany the belief that one is or will be watched or monitored. . . .
>
> The objective category of privacy harm is the unanticipated or coerced use of information concerning a person against that person. These are negative, external actions justified by reference to personal information. Examples include the unanticipated sale of a user's contact information that results in spam and the leaking of classified information that exposes an undercover intelligence agent.

How does Calo's theory apply to data security breaches? Consider his analysis:

> As an initial matter, data breaches register as subjective privacy harms. When a consumer receives a notice in the mail telling her that her personal information has leaked out into the open, she experiences the exact sort of apprehension and feeling of vulnerability the first category of privacy harm is concerned about. That is, she believes that there has been or could be unwanted sensing of her private information. The same is true, to a lesser degree, when any of us read about a data breach — we feel less secure in our privacy overall.
>
> But what if there is a data breach or other increased risk of adverse consequence and the "victim" never knows about it? Then there has been neither subjective nor objective privacy harm, unless or until the information is used. Worse still, it would appear on this analysis that breach notification is a net evil in that it creates (subjective) privacy harm where there would be none.
>
> Here I disagree with this premise. A risk of privacy harm is no more a privacy harm than a chance of a burn is a burn. They are conceptually distinct: one is the thing itself, the other the likelihood of that thing. A feeling of greater vulnerability can constitute privacy harm, just as the apprehension of battery can constitute a distinct tort. But there is no assault or battery without the elements of apprehension or unwanted contact. . . .
>
> Similarly, it does not disparage the seriousness of a data breach, nor the inconvenience of having to protect against identity theft, to deny that any objective privacy harm has yet occurred. If anything, clarifying the nature of the harm at risk should help us protect against that harm actually occurring by selecting the appropriate remedy. The goal of some rules is to deter specific harms, for instance; others exist to empower the vulnerable or hinder the powerful in an effort to make harm less likely. Data breach notification laws

fulfill both functions, even if they are technically the "but for" cause of one category of privacy harm.[15]

Daniel Solove examines why courts often fail to recognize harm in data breach cases:

> One of the challenges with data harms is that they are often created by the aggregation of many dispersed actors over a long period of time. They are akin to a form of pollution where each particular infraction might, in and of itself, not cause much harm, but collectively, the infractions do create harm....
>
> The flip side of collective harm is what I call the "multiplier problem," which affects the companies that cause privacy and data security problems. A company might lose personal data, and these days, even a small company can have data on tens of millions of people. Judges are reluctant to recognize harm because it might mean bankrupting a company just to give each person a very tiny amount of compensation.
>
> Today, organizations have data on so many people that when there's a leak, millions could be affected, and even a small amount of damages for each person might add up to insanely high liability.
>
> Generally, we make those who cause wide-scale harm pay for it. If a company builds a dam and it bursts and floods a town, that company must pay. But with a data leak, courts are saying that companies should be off the hook. In essence, they get to use data on millions of people without having to worry about the harm they might cause. This seems quite unfair.
>
> It takes a big entity to build a dam, but a person in a garage can create an app that gathers data on vast numbers of people. Do we want to put a company out of business for a data breach that only causes people a minor harm? When each case is viewed in isolation, it seems quite harsh to annihilate a company for causing tiny harms to many people. . . . But that still leaves the collective harm problem. If we let it go all the time, then we have death by a thousand bee stings. . . .[16]

5. **Class Actions.** Many of the lawsuits in the wake of data security breaches are class actions. Although many have been dismissed because courts do not recognize a harm from a mere data leak without more direct proof of injuries to plaintiffs, others have ended in multi-million dollar settlements. Defendants may choose to settle, among other reasons, due to the high expense of litigation.

Do these class actions serving a valuable purpose? The attorneys receive a large award for attorney's fees, and class members rarely get significant benefits from the settlement. One might view class actions for data security breaches as a kind of opportunistic extortion of settlement money. On the other hand, class actions provide a strong incentive for companies to be careful with personal data and take measures to avoid data security breaches. The attorney's fees serve as an incentive for spurring lawyers to bring and litigate the case — a reward for serving as a kind of "private attorney

---

[15] M. Ryan Calo, The Boundaries of Privacy Harm, 86 Ind. L.J. 1131, 1133, 1256-57 (2011).

[16] Daniel J. Solove, Why the Law Often Doesn't Recognize Privacy and Data Security Harms, LinkedIn (July 2, 2014), https://www.linkedin.com/today/post/article/20140702054230-2259773-why-the-law-often-doesn-t-recognize-privacy-and-data-security-harms.

general." If not class action litigation, is there a more appropriate mechanism to deter data security breaches?

6. ***Strict Liability for Data Security Breaches?*** Danielle Citron argues for strict liability for harms caused by data breaches. Computer databases of personal information, Citron contends, are akin to the water reservoirs of the early Industrial Age:

> The dynamics of the early Industrial Age, a time of great potential and peril, parallel those at the advent of the Information Age. Then, as now, technological change brought enormous wealth and comfort to society. Industry thrived as a result of machines powered by water reservoirs. But when the dams holding those reservoirs failed, the escaping water caused massive property and personal damage different from the interpersonal harms of the previous century. *Rylands v. Fletcher* provided the Industrial Age's strict-liability response to the accidents caused by the valuable reservoirs' escaping water. The history of *Rylands*'s reception in Britain and the United States reflects the tension between that era's desire for economic growth and its concern for security from industrial hazards.
>
> Computer databases are this century's reservoirs. . . . Much as water reservoirs drove the Industrial Age, computer databases fuel the Internet economy of our Information Age.

Citron argues that a strict liability regime is preferable to negligence tort liability:

> The rapidly changing nature of information technologies may create uncertainty as to what a negligence regime entails. . . .
>
> Due to the rapidly changing threats to information security, database operators will likely be uncertain as to what constitutes optimal care. Cyber-intruders employ increasingly innovative techniques to bypass security measures and steal personal data, thereby requiring an ever-changing information-security response to new threats, vulnerabilities, and technologies. . . .
>
> A negligence regime will fail to address the significant leaks that will occur despite database operators' exercise of due care over personal data. Security breaches are an inevitable byproduct of collecting sensitive personal information in computer databases. No amount of due care will prevent significant amounts of sensitive data from escaping into the hands of cyber-criminals. Such data leaks constitute the predictable residual risks of information reservoirs.
>
> Consequently, negligence will not efficiently manage the residual risks of hazardous databases. Negligence would neither induce database operators to change their activity level nor discourage marginal actors from collecting sensitive information because such operators need not pay for the accident costs of their residual risk. . . .
>
> Classifying database collection as an ultrahazardous activity is a logical extension of Posner's analysis. Just as no clear safety standard governing the building and maintenance of water reservoirs had emerged in the 1850s, a stable set of information-security practices has not yet materialized today. . . .

In this analysis, strict liability has the potential to encourage a change in activity level respecting the storage of sensitive personal information, unless and until more information allows operators to better assess optimal precaution levels and to respond to the persistent problem of residual risk. Because strict liability would force database operators to internalize the full costs of their activities, marginally productive database operators might refrain from maintaining cyber-reservoirs of personal data. Strict liability also may decrease the collection of ultrasensitive data among those who are at greatest risk of security breaches. Moreover, as insurance markets develop in this emerging area, database operators that continue collecting sensitive information will be better positioned to assess the cost of residual risk and the extent to which they can spread the cost of such risk onto consumers.[17]

Are you convinced by the analogy between the database industry and reservoirs? Will strict liability lead to the correct level of investment in security by companies? Could it lead to over-investment in data security?

7. *Assessing the Federal Approach to Data Security.* As discussed above, after the ChoicePoint data security breach in 2005 — along with the numerous other breaches that followed — a majority of states have now passed data security breach legislation. Despite several proposed bills, the federal government has yet to pass a comprehensive data security law. However, some existing federal privacy laws protect data security in the context of particular industries. Consider Andrea Matwyshyn:

> The current approach to information security, exemplified by statutes such as COPPA, HIPAA, and GLBA, attempts to regulate information security by creating legal "clusters" of entities based on the type of business they transact, the types of data they control, and that data's permitted and nonpermitted uses. In other words, the current regulatory approach has singled out a few points in the system for the creation of information security enclaves. . . .
>
> The current approach ignores the fundamental tenet of security that a system is only as strong as its weakest links, not its strongest points. . . . It will not prove adequate to only ensure that a few points or clusters in the system are particularly well-secured. . . .
>
> The biggest economic losses arise not out of illegal leveraging of these protected categories of data; rather, losses arise out of stolen personally identifiable information, such as credit card data and social security numbers, which are warehoused frequently by entities that are not regulated by COPPA, HIPAA or GLBA. Therefore, creating enclaves of superior data security for data related to children online, some financial information, and some health data will not alleviate the weak information security in other parts of the system and will not substantially diminish information crime. . . . [18]

---

[17] Danielle Keats Citron, Reservoirs of Danger: The Evolution of Public and Private Law at the Dawn of the Information Age, 80 S. Cal. L. Rev. 241, 243-44, 263-67 (2007).

[18] Andrea M. Matwyshyn, Material Vulnerabilities: Data Privacy, Corporate Information Security, and Securities Regulation, 3 Berkeley Bus. L.J. 129, 169-70 (2005).

D. FTC REGULATION

The Federal Trade Commission (FTC) has acted on numerous occasions to penalize companies that fail to take reasonable measures to protect customer data. There are several sources of authority that the FTC uses to regulate data security.

Section 5 of the FTC Act. Since the late 1990s, the FTC has concluded in more than 50 enforcement actions that companies with inadequate data security are engaging in "unfair or deceptive acts or practices" in violation of Section 5 of the FTC Act, 15 U.S.C. § 45(a). Section 5 covers a very wide array of industries, but there are a few carve outs where other statutes govern, specifically with certain types of financial institutions, airlines, and telecommunications carriers. Non-profit institutions are generally not covered by the FTC Act.

The FTC's initial enforcement actions for data security involved companies that failed to live up to promises made about data security in their privacy policies. The FTC has deemed the failure to follow statements made in a privacy policy to be a deceptive act or practice. A deceptive act or practice is a material "representation, omission or practice that is likely to mislead the consumer acting reasonably in the circumstances, to the consumer's detriment."[19]

— deceptive act

The FTC later started finding certain data security practices to be "unfair" regardless of what was promised in the privacy policy. Under the FTC Act, a practice is unfair if it "causes or is likely to cause substantial injury to consumers which is not reasonably avoidable by consumers themselves and is not outweighed by countervailing benefits to consumers or competition." 15 U.S.C. § 45(n).

— unfair act

In many cases, the FTC charges that a company's practices are both deceptive and unfair.

Under Section 5, the FTC lacks the authority to issue fines. When a company violates a consent decree previously entered into for a Section 5 violation, then the FTC can issue fines. Although the FTC cannot issue fines under Section 5, when it has authority under other statutes to regulate data security, some of these laws grant the FTC the ability to seek monetary penalties. Under Section 5, though, the FTC can still obtain injunctive relief. There is no private right of action for violations of Section 5 — only the FTC can enforce.

The FTC does not have specific rulemaking authority under Section 5, but it can make rules according to Magnuson-Moss rulemaking authority. This method of making rules is so burdensome that the FTC has barely used it. Instead, the FTC has focused its Section 5 efforts on enforcement.

Gramm-Leach-Bliley Act. The FTC can also act pursuant to its specific authority, under statutes and rules, to oversee how businesses protect consumer data. For example, the FTC's has issued the Safeguards Rule pursuant to its

---

[19] Letter from James C. Miller III, Chairman, FTC, to Hon. John D. Dingell, Chairman, House Comm. on Energy & Commerce (Oct. 14, 1983).

authority under the Gramm-Leach-Bliley Act (GLBA). The Safeguards Rule mandates data security requirements for non-bank financial institutions.

Children's Online Privacy Protection Act. The Children's Online Privacy Protection Act (COPPA) requires reasonable security for children's information collected online, and the FTC has issued a rule specifying the kinds of security provisions that companies should develop. These security obligations extend to service parties and third parties that a company uses in processing the personal information of children.

Fair Credit Reporting Act. Inadequate data security can also lead to data being disclosed impermissibly under the Fair Credit Reporting Act (FCRA). The FTC used to have primary enforcement responsibility of the FCRA, but now the enforcement is shared with the Consumer Financial Protection Bureau (CFPB), which has primary enforcement power. Fines can be issued under FCRA.

One of the most dramatic of the FTC enforcement actions for data security involved ChoicePoint. In settling the FTC charges for violating FCRA and Section 5 of the FTC Act, ChoicePoint agreed in January 2006 to pay $10 million in civil penalties and $5 million into a consumer redress fund. ChoicePoint also promised changes to its business and improvements to its security practices.

The stipulated final judgment bars the company from furnishing consumer reports to customers without a permissible purpose and requires it to establish reasonable procedures to ensure that it will provide consumer reports only to those with a permissible purpose. One requirement placed on ChoicePoint is to verify the identity of businesses that apply to receive consumer reports by auditing subscribers' use of consumer reports and by making site visits to certain of its customers.

Finally, the settlement obligated ChoicePoint to establish and maintain a comprehensive information security program and to submit this program for two decades to outside independent audits. It agreed to "establish and implement, and thereafter maintain, a comprehensive information security program that is reasonably designed to protect the security, confidentiality, and integrity of personal information collected from or about consumers." In maintaining this "comprehensive information security program," ChoicePoint promised to engage in risk assessments and to design and implement regular testing of the effectiveness of its security program's key controls, systems, and procedures. It also agreed to obtain an initial and then biennial outside assessment of its data security safeguards from an independent third-party professional.

For nearly two decades, FTC Section 5 data security cases settled. But finally, a company challenged the FTC. Wyndham Worldwide Corporation, a hotel company, argued that the FTC lacked authority under Section 5 to regulate data security and could only do so pursuant to a specific statute. Consider the case below, where the court rules on the issue.

FTC v. Wyndham Worldwide Corporation

2014 WL 1349019 (D.N.J. 2014)

SALAS, J. The Federal Trade Commission (the "FTC") brought this action under Section 5(a) of the Federal Trade Commission Act (the "FTC Act"), 15 U.S.C. § 45(a), against Wyndham Worldwide Corporation. . . . The FTC alleges that Wyndham violated Section 5(a)'s prohibition of "acts or practices in or affecting commerce" that are "unfair" or "deceptive."

Specifically, the FTC alleges that Defendants violated both the deception and unfairness prongs of Section 5(a) "in connection with Defendants' failure to maintain reasonable and appropriate data security for consumers' sensitive personal information." [Wyndham made a motion to dismiss.] . . . .

Wyndham Worldwide is in the hospitality business. "At all relevant times," Wyndham Worldwide controlled the acts and practices of the following subsidiaries: Hotel Group, Hotels and Resorts, and Hotel Management. Through these three subsidiaries, Wyndham Worldwide "franchises and manages hotels and sells timeshares."

More specifically, "Hotel Group is a wholly-owned subsidiary of Wyndham Worldwide." Both Hotels and Resorts and Hotel Management, in turn, are wholly-owned subsidiaries of Hotel Group. Hotels and Resorts licensed the "Wyndham" name to approximately seventy-five independently-owned hotels under franchise agreements. Similarly, Hotel Management licensed the "Wyndham" name to approximately fifteen independently-owned hotels under management agreements.

Under these agreements, Hotels and Resorts and Hotel Management require each Wyndham-branded hotel to purchase—and "configure to their specifications"—a designated computer system that, among other things, handles reservations and payment card transactions. This system, known as a "property management system," stores consumers' personal information, "including names, addresses, email addresses, telephone numbers, payment card account numbers, expiration dates, and security codes."

The property management systems for all Wyndham-branded hotels "are part of Hotels and Resorts' computer network" and "are linked to its corporate network." Indeed, Hotels and Resorts' computer network "includes its central reservation system" that "coordinates reservations across the Wyndham brand" and, using Hotels and Resorts' website, "consumers. . . .

The FTC alleges that, since at least April 2008, Wyndham "failed to provide reasonable and appropriate security for the personal information collected and maintained by Hotels and Resorts, Hotel Management, and the Wyndham-branded hotels." The FTC alleges that Wyndham did this "by engaging in a number of practices that, taken together, unreasonably and unnecessarily exposed consumers' personal data to unauthorized access and theft."

As a result of these failures, between April 2008 and January 2010, intruders gained unauthorized access—on three separate occasions—to Hotels and Resorts' computer network, including the Wyndham-branded hotels' property management systems. . . . And, after discovering the first two breaches, Wyndham "failed to take appropriate steps in a reasonable time frame to prevent the further compromise of Hotels and Resorts' network."

Wyndham's "failure to implement reasonable and appropriate security measures exposed consumers' personal information to unauthorized access, collection, and use" that "has caused and is likely to cause substantial consumer injury, including financial injury, to consumers and businesses." Defendants' failure "to implement reasonable and appropriate security measures" caused, for example, the following:

> [T]he three data breaches described above, the compromise of more than 619,000 consumer payment card account numbers, the exportation of many of those account numbers to a domain registered in Russia, fraudulent charges on many consumers' accounts, and more than $10.6 million in fraud loss. Consumers and businesses suffered financial injury, including, but not limited to, unreimbursed fraudulent charges, increased costs, and lost access to funds or credit. Consumers and businesses also expended time and money resolving fraudulent charges and mitigating subsequent harm.

Given these allegations, the FTC brought this action, seeking a permanent injunction to prevent future violations of the FTC Act, as well as certain other relief. . . .

"When reviewing a motion to dismiss, '[a]ll allegations in the complaint must be accepted as true, and the plaintiff must be given the benefit of every favorable inference to be drawn therefrom.' " . . .

Hotels and Resorts first challenges the FTC's unfairness claim. Under this claim, the FTC alleges that "Defendants have failed to employ reasonable and appropriate measures to protect personal information against unauthorized access." The FTC alleges that "Defendants' actions caused or are likely to cause substantial injury to consumers that consumers cannot reasonably avoid themselves and that is not outweighed by countervailing benefits to consumers or competition" and, therefore, "Defendants' acts and practices . . . constitute unfair acts or practices" under Section 5 of the FTC Act. . . .

Hotels and Resorts analogizes this action to *Brown & Williamson*, arguing that the FTC's unfairness authority does not cover data security. . . .[20]

Specifically, Hotels and Resorts identifies several statutes that purportedly authorize "particular federal agencies to establish minimum data-security standards in narrow sectors of the economy," including: the Fair Credit Reporting Act ("FCRA"); the Gramm-Leach-Bliley Act ("GLBA"); the Children's Online Privacy Protection Act ("COPPA"); and the Health Insurance Portability and Accountability Act of 1996 ("HIPPA"). . . .

---

[20] Editors' Note: In FDA v. Brown & Williamson Tobacco Corp, 529 U.S. 120 (2000), the Supreme Court declared that an administrative agency's scope of authority is determined by its "organic statute." This term refers to the statute that creates the agency and defines its powers and responsibilities. The Supreme Court found in Brown & Williamson that the FDA lacked statutory authority to enact and enforce its contested regulations over the tobacco industry. In reaction, Congress in 2009 enacted the Family Smoking Prevention and Tobacco Control Act, which explicitly gave the FDA the power it sought.

The FTC argues that, in actuality, Hotels and Resorts cites statutes that supplement the FTC's Section 5 authority for three reasons: (1) those statutes do not have the "consumer injury" requirement that Section 5 has; (2) they grant the FTC additional powers that it otherwise lacks; and (3) they "affirmatively compel (rather than merely authorize) the FTC to use its consumer-protection authority in specified ways." Indeed, the FTC avers that Congress purposely gave it broad power under Section 5 of the FTC Act and that its decision to enforce the FTC Act in the data-security context is entitled to deference. . . .

The Court rejects Hotels and Resorts' invitation to carve out a data-security exception to the FTC's unfairness authority because this case is different from *Brown & Williamson*. In *Brown & Williamson*, the Supreme Court determined that, "[c]onsidering the [Food, Drug, and Cosmetic Act ("FDCA")] as a whole, it is clear that Congress intended to exclude tobacco products from the FDA's jurisdiction." It reasoned that "if tobacco products were within the FDA's jurisdiction, the Act would require the FDA to remove them from the market entirely. But, the Court determined that this "would contradict Congress'[s] clear intent as expressed in its more recent, tobacco-specific legislation" in which it "foreclosed the removal of tobacco products from the market." The Supreme Court explained that "Congress, for better or for worse, has created a distinct regulatory scheme for tobacco products, squarely rejected proposals to give the FDA jurisdiction over tobacco, and repeatedly acted to preclude any agency from exercising significant policymaking authority in the area."

no contradiction
- of policy

But no such dilemma exists here. Hotels and Resorts fails to explain how the FTC's unfairness authority over data security would lead to a result that is incompatible with more recent legislation and thus would "plainly contradict congressional policy." Instead, Hotels and Resorts unequivocally recognizes that "the FCRA, GLBA, and COPPA all contain detailed provisions granting the FTC substantive authority over data-security practices." . . . .

Specifically, the FTC Act defines "unfair acts or practices" as those that "cause[] or [are] likely to cause substantial injury to consumers which [are] not reasonably avoidable by consumers themselves and not outweighed by countervailing benefits to consumers or to competition." 15 U.S.C. § 45(n). And Hotels and Resorts identifies statutes, such as the FCRA, GLBA, and COPPA, that each set forth different standards for injury in certain delineated circumstances, granting the FTC additional enforcement tools.

Thus, unlike the FDA's regulation over tobacco, the FTC's unfairness authority over data security can coexist with the existing data-security regulatory scheme. . . .

Hotels and Resorts argues that, even if Section 5 gives the FTC sufficient authority, "it would violate basic principles of fair notice and due process to hold [Hotels and Resorts] liable. . . .

Hotels and Resorts further asserts that, generally, agencies cannot rely on enforcement actions to make new rules and concurrently hold a party liable for violating the new rule. Indeed, Hotels and Resorts avers that, to do so, the agency must have previously set forth with ascertainable certainty the standards it

fair notice

expects private parties to obey—but that the FTC's mere reasonableness standard provides no such guidance "in the highly complex and sophisticated world of data security." . . .

In response, the FTC argues that, in the data-security context, "reasonableness is the touchstone" and that "unreasonable data security practices are unfair."

"A fundamental principle in our legal system is that laws which regulate persons or entities must give fair notice of conduct that is forbidden or required."

"[W]here an agency . . . is given an option to proceed by rulemaking or by individual adjudication the choice is one that lies in the informed discretion of the administrative agency." . . .

. . . [T]he Court is unpersuaded that regulations are the only means of providing sufficient fair notice. Indeed, Section 5 codifies a three-part test that proscribes whether an act is "unfair." And, notably, Hotels and Resorts' only response to the FTC's analogy to tort liability—where liability is routinely found for unreasonable conduct without the need for particularized prohibitions—is the following: "While the negligence standard has long been a cornerstone of tort law, no Article III court has ever—not once—articulated the data-security standards that Section 5 of the FTC Act supposedly imposes on regulated parties." The Court is not persuaded by this argument that essentially amounts to: since no court has, no court can—especially since Hotels and Resorts itself recognizes how "quickly" the digital age and data-security world is moving. . . .

And, Hotels and Resorts invites this Court to dismiss the FTC's complaint on fair notice grounds despite the FTC's many public complaints and consent agreements, as well as its public statements and business guidance brochure— and despite Hotels and Resorts' own references to "industry standard practices" and "commercially reasonable efforts" in its privacy policy.

The Court declines to do so. Indeed, "the rulings, interpretations and opinions of the Administrator under this Act, while not controlling upon the courts by reason of their authority, do constitute a body of experience and informed judgment to which courts and litigants may properly resort for guidance." . . . Hotels and Resorts' argument that consent orders do not carry the force of law, therefore, misses the mark. . . .

Hotels and Resorts proclaims that an unfair practice must, by statute, cause or be likely to cause "substantial injury to consumers which is not reasonably avoidable by consumers themselves"—but that consumer injury from theft of payment card data is never substantial and always avoidable.

More specifically, Hotels and Resorts contends that federal law places a $50 limit on consumer liability for unauthorized use of a payment card and that all major credit card brands waive liability for even this small amount. And Hotels and Resorts contends that consumers can have their issuer rescind any unauthorized charges. Hotels and Resorts argues that consumers, therefore, cannot suffer any "substantial injury" from the breaches that were not reasonably avoidable. Hotels and Resorts adds that any "incidental injuries that consumers suffered," such as monitoring financial information, is insufficient. . . .

In opposition, the FTC argues that its complaint pleads sufficient facts to support an unfairness claim involving data-security practices as follows: (1) that substantial injury resulted from Hotels and Resorts' unreasonable data-security practices; (2) this injury was not reasonably avoidable by consumers; (3) Hotels and Resorts' practices caused this injury; and (4) Hotels and Resorts' practices were unreasonable and there were no countervailing benefits to Hotels and Resorts' failure to address its data-security flaws. (FTC's Opp. Br. at 3-4).

First, the FTC adequately pleads "substantial injury to consumers" and that Hotels and Resorts' practices caused this injury. It pleads, in relevant part, that:

> [E]xposure of consumers' personal information has caused and is likely to cause substantial consumer injury, including financial injury, to consumers and businesses. For example, Defendants' failure to implement reasonable and appropriate security measures resulted in the three data breaches . . . the compromise of more than 619,000 consumer payment card account numbers, the exportation of many of those account numbers to a domain registered in Russia, fraudulent charges on many consumers' accounts, and more than $10.6 million in fraud loss. Consumers and businesses suffered financial injury, including, but not limited to, unreimbursed fraudulent charges, increased costs, and lost access to funds or credit. Consumers and businesses also expended time and money resolving fraudulent charges and mitigating subsequent harm.

Indeed, the FTC here alleges that at least some consumers suffered financial injury that included "unreimbursed financial injury" and, drawing inferences in favor of the FTC, the alleged injury to consumers is substantial. . . .

The parties contest whether non-monetary injuries are cognizable under Section 5 of the FTC Act. Although the Court is not convinced that non-monetary harm is, as a matter of law, unsustainable under Section 5 of the FTC Act, the Court need not reach this issue given the analysis of the substantial harm element above. . . .

The FTC's allegations also permit the Court to reasonably infer that Hotels and Resorts' data-security practices caused theft of personal data, which ultimately caused substantial injury to consumers. The FTC alleges "a number of practices that, taken together, unreasonably and unnecessarily exposed consumers' personal data to unauthorized access and theft." And, making reasonable inferences in favor of the FTC, these practices correspond to the allegations involving how intruders perpetrated three data breaches, which ultimately resulted in the alleged substantial injury. . . .

For instance, the FTC alleges that Defendants "failed to employ commonly-used methods to require user IDs and passwords that are difficult for hackers to guess" and "did not require the use of complex passwords for access to the Wyndham-branded hotels' property management systems and allowed the use of easily guessed passwords." Correspondingly, the FTC alleges that "intruders attempted to compromise an administrator account on the Hotels and Resorts' network by guessing multiple user IDs and passwords—known as a brute force attack." . . . .

Similarly, the FTC alleges that Defendants "failed to adequately inventory computers connected to Hotels and Resorts' network so that Defendants could appropriately manage the devices on its network." And the FTC correspondingly alleges that, since "Defendants did not have an adequate inventory of the Wyndham-branded hotels' computers connected to its network . . . they were unable to physically locate those computers" and, therefore, "Defendants did not determine that Hotels and Resorts' network had been compromised until almost four months later."

Likewise, the FTC alleges that Defendants failed to "use readily available security measures to limit access between and among the Wyndham-branded hotels' property management systems," such as firewalls. And this aligns with the FTC's allegation that intruders "were able to gain unfettered access to the property management systems servers of a number of hotels" because "Defendants did not appropriately limit access between and among the Wyndham-branded hotels' property management systems, Hotels and Resorts' own corporate network, and the Internet—such as through the use of firewalls."

Finally, the FTC alleges that this "failure to implement reasonable and appropriate security measures exposed consumers' personal information to unauthorized access, collection, and use" and "has caused and is likely to cause substantial consumer injury, including financial injury, to consumers and businesses." Drawing inferences in favor of the FTC, the identified failures caused the breaches, resulting in the alleged substantial injury. . . .

Second, the FTC adequately pleads that the alleged substantial injury was not reasonably avoidable. Hotels and Resorts argues that "[c]onsumers can . . . always 'reasonably avoid' any financial injury stemming from the theft of payment card data simply by having their issuer rescind any unauthorized charges." . . .

But the Court cannot make such a far-reaching conclusion regarding an issue that seems fact-dependent. . . .

NOTES & QUESTIONS

1. *A Lack of Fair Notice?* One of Wyndham's arguments was that the FTC's method of enforcing data security — in a case-by-case fashion rather than a rulemaking—led to companies not being put on sufficient notice about the specific data security practices that were deemed inadequate.

   Daniel Solove and Woodrow Hartzog contend that the FTC's body of consent decrees constitutes a body of law similar to the common law with lawyers analyzing the settlements akin to the way they look at judicial decisions.[21]

   In contrast, Berin Szoka and Geoffrey Manne argue that "neither this 'common law of consent decrees' nor the FTC's privacy reports constitute

---

[21] Daniel J. Solove & Woodrow Hartzog, *The FTC and the New Common Law of Privacy*, 114 Colum. L. Rev. 583 (2014).

actual law. It's a flexible approach, but only in the worst sense: made by disposing of any legal constraints or due process."[22]

Gerard Stegmaier and Wendell Bartnick argue that a "standard based on 'reasonableness' grounded solely in settlements raises its own questions of whether constitutionally adequate fair notice was provided. Such a standard seems unfair and problematic to those tasked with assisting entities in avoiding unfair and deceptive trade practices."[23]

Hartzog and Solove contend:

> Many critics seem to want a "check list" of data security practices that will, in essence, provide a safe harbor in all contexts. Yet data security changes too quickly and is far too dependent upon context to be reduced to a one-size-fits-all checklist. Instead, the FTC has opted to defer to industry to set the appropriate standards for good data security practices by utilizing a "reasonableness" standard. . . .[24]

Hartzog and Solove point to many laws that require a reasonableness standard for data security. They further argue:

> In a common law system — or any system where matters are decided case-by-case and there is an attempt at maintaining consistency across decisions, any reasonableness standard will evolve into something more akin to a rule with specifics over time. Indeed, any broad standard will follow this evolutionary trajectory. Such a developmental pattern is inevitable if prior decisions have any kind of precedential effect or the functional equivalent of precedent. The standard will start out rather broadly, but each new case will bring a new application of that standard to a concrete situation. From these collected specific applications, the details start to accumulate around the standard's skeletal frame.[25]

2. ***Overlapping Regulatory Authority.*** After Wyndham brought its challenge, another company, LabMD, raised a similar objection to FTC authority. One of LabMD's contentions was that it is regulated by HIPAA and under the authority of the Department of Health and Human Services (HHS). Although HHS did not bring an action to enforce the HIPAA Security Rule, the FTC brought an action under Section 5 for inadequate data security. LabMD contended that because it was regulated by HIPAA, it should not fall under the FTC's Section 5 authority for data security. Assess the strength of LabMD's argument.

3. ***FTC Data Security Enforcement Under Section 5.*** Since it began enforcing Section 5 against companies for data security problems, the FTC has pursued more than 50 enforcement actions against companies for failure to provide

---

[22] Berin Szoka & Geoffrey Manne, *Now in Its 100th year, the FTC Has Become the Federal Technology Commission*, TechFreedom (Sept. 26, 2013), http://techfreedom.org/post/62344465210/now-in-its-100th-year-the-ftc-has-become-the-federal.

[23] Gerard M. Stegmaier & Wendell Bartnick, *Psychics, Russian Roulette, and Data Security: The FTC's Hidden Data-Security Requirements*, 20 Geo. Mason L. Rev. 673 (2013).

[24] Woodrow Hartzog & Daniel J. Solove, *The Scope and Potential of FTC Data Protection*, 83 Geo. Wash. L. Rev. ___ (forthcoming 2015), http://ssrn.com/abstract=2461096.

[25] *Id.*

reasonable security practices. Consider the following Congressional testimony by Woodrow Hartzog in 2014:

> The Privacy Rights Clearinghouse has reported that since 2005 there have been over 4300 data breaches made public with a total of over 868 million records breached. Yet the FTC has filed only 55 total data security-related complaints, averaging around five complaints a year since 2008.[26]

Is the number of actions sufficient? Should the FTC be more aggressively enforcing Section 5? Should a different approach be taken? Or is the FTC pursuing an appropriate amount of cases?

For example, these actions have led to settlements against Twitter, charged with bad password management practices (settlement in 2011); HTC America, charged with failure to take reasonable steps to secure tablet and phone software (settlement in 2013); and Fandago, charged with misrepresentation of its mobile applications (settlement in 2014). Consider the FTC's settlement in *Trendnet*, which involved a security camera that lacked security:

IN THE MATTER OF TRENDNET

(F.T.C. 2014)

[TRENDnet, Inc. sold a range of home networking devices. It has approximately 80 employees and $62 million in total revenue in 2012.

One of its products was a video camera that generated a live audio and video feed that users could view over an Internet connection. According to the FTC's Complaint, TRENDnet advertised the camera, named "SecurView," as a device to help consumers and small businesses monitor "babies at home, patients in the hospital, offices and banks, and more." The camera came with software that created a Web interface where the user could enter login credentials to view the live feed. The interface included an option to disable authentication, making the feed open to the public. TRENDnet also distributed Android apps that allowed users to access feeds from mobile devices.

TRENDnet had a software flaw that caused SecurView feeds to be publicly viewable even if the user had not disabled the access protections. According to the FTC Complaint, "[h]ackers could and did exploit" the vulnerability of the software. Specifically, a hacker on January 10, 2012 was able to access live feeds at Trendnet's website "without entering login credentials" and gain access to live feeds that were not intended to be public. This initial hacker posted information about the breach online and then other hackers posted links to live feeds for nearly 700 IP Cameras. The compromised live feeds allowed anyone to watch "unauthorized surveillance of infants sleeping in their cribs, young children playing, and adults engaging in typical daily activities." News stories published images from the feeds alongside photos of the locations from which the feeds were broadcast (based on geolocation of the feeds' IP addresses). Researchers

---

[26] Woodrow Hartzog, *Prepared Testimony and Statement for the Record*, U.S. House of Representatives, Committee on Oversight and Government Reform (July 24, 2014).

discovered other security vulnerabilities, including the transmission of unencrypted passwords. TRENDnet also had failed to perform ordinary security testing.

The FTC filed a complaint against TRENDnet on January 16, 2013, alleging that TRENDnet's claims of security constituted false or misleading representations because TRENDnet failed to provide reasonable security to prevent unauthorized access to the live feeds from its cameras. As the FTC's press release accompanying the settlement of January 17, 2014 stated, "This is the agency's first action against a marketer of an everyday product with interconnectivity to the Internet and other mobile devices—commonly referred to as the 'Internet of Things.' "]

AGREEMENT CONTAINING CONSENT ORDER

The respondent, its attorney, and counsel for the Commission having executed an Agreement Containing Consent Order ("Consent Agreement"), which includes: a statement by respondent that it neither admits nor denies any of the allegations in the draft complaint, except as specifically stated in the Consent Agreement, and, only for purposes of this action, admits the facts necessary to establish jurisdiction; and waivers and other provisions as required by the Commission's Rules. . . . .

IT IS ORDERED that respondent and its officers, agents, representatives, and employees, directly or through any corporation, subsidiary, division, website, other device, or an affiliate owned or controlled by respondent, in or affecting commerce, shall not misrepresent in any manner, expressly or by implication:

A. The extent to which respondent or its products or services maintain and protect:

1. The security of Covered Device Functionality;

2. The security, privacy, confidentiality, or integrity of any Covered Information; and

B. The extent to which a consumer can control the security of any Covered Information input into, stored on, captured with, accessed, or transmitted by a Covered Device. . . .

IT IS FURTHER ORDERED that respondent shall, no later than the date of service of this Order, establish and implement, and thereafter maintain, a comprehensive security program that is reasonably designed to (1) address security risks that could result in unauthorized access to or use of Covered Device Functionality, and (2) protect the security, confidentiality, and integrity of Covered Information, whether collected by respondent, or input into, stored on, captured with, accessed, or transmitted through a Covered Device. Such program, the content and implementation of which must be fully documented in writing, shall contain administrative, technical, and physical safeguards appropriate to respondent's size and complexity, the nature and scope of respondent's activities, and the sensitivity of the Covered Device Functionality or Covered Information, including:

A. The designation of an employee or employees to coordinate and be accountable for the security program;

B. The identification of material internal and external risks to the security of Covered Devices that could result in unauthorized access to or use of Covered Device Functionality, and assessment of the sufficiency of any safeguards in place to control these risks;

C. The identification of material internal and external risks to the security, confidentiality, and integrity of Covered Information that could result in the unauthorized disclosure, misuse, loss, alteration, destruction, or other compromise of such information, whether such information is in respondent's possession or is input into, stored on, captured with, accessed, or transmitted through a Covered Device, and assessment of the sufficiency of any safeguards in place to control these risks;

D. At a minimum, the risk assessments required by Subparts B and C should include consideration of risks in each area of relevant operation, including, but not limited to: (1) employee training and management; (2) product design, development, and research; (3) secure software design, development, and testing; and (4) review, assessment, and response to third-party security vulnerability reports;

E. The design and implementation of reasonable safeguards to control the risks identified through the risk assessments, including but not limited to reasonable and appropriate software security testing techniques, such as: (1) vulnerability and penetration testing; (2) security architecture reviews; (3) code reviews; and (4) other reasonable and appropriate assessments, audits, reviews, or other tests to identify potential security failures and verify that access to Covered Information is restricted consistent with a user's security settings;

F. Regular testing or monitoring of the effectiveness of the safeguards' key controls, systems, and procedures;

G. The development and use of reasonable steps to select and retain service providers capable of maintaining security practices consistent with this Order, and requiring service providers, by contract, to establish and implement, and thereafter maintain, appropriate safeguards consistent with this Order; and

H. The evaluation and adjustment of the security program in light of the results of the testing and monitoring required by Subpart F, any material changes to the respondent's operations or business arrangements, or any other circumstances that respondent knows or has reason to know may have a material impact on the effectiveness of its security program.

IT IS FURTHER ORDERED that, in connection with its compliance with Part II of this Order, respondent shall obtain initial and biennial assessments and reports ("Assessments") from a qualified, objective, independent third-party professional, who uses procedures and standards generally accepted in the profession. The reporting period for the Assessments shall cover: (1) the first one hundred eighty (180) days after service of the Order for the initial Assessment; and (2) each two (2) year period thereafter for twenty (20) years after service of the Order for the biennial Assessments.

IT IS FURTHER ORDERED that respondent shall:

A. Notify Affected Consumers, clearly and prominently, that their Cameras had a flaw that allowed third parties to access their Live Feed Information without inputting authentication credentials, despite their security setting choices; and provide instructions on how to remove this flaw. . . .

This Order will terminate on January 16, 2034, or [in] twenty (20) years. . . .

NOTES & QUESTIONS

1. *The Terms of Settlement.* This settlement illustrates the FTC's classic approach in its data security settlements of imposing long-term requirements for an information security program. Do you think that the settlement terms in *Trendnet* are appropriate? Does the FTC strike the correct balance in providing some flexibility to the companies in deciding the content of a reasonable security program? Is a 20-year enforcement period too long?

2. *The Internet of Things.* Trendnet is the FTC's first security case involving the "Internet of Things." This term refers to Web-enabled devices that generate data, some of which can be linked to specific individuals. Cisco has already predicted 50 billion connected devices by 2020. Are there special legal challenges in regulating the privacy issues of the Internet of Things?

   A white paper by the Future of Privacy Forum (FPF), released in November 2013, argued that current implementations of Fair Information Practice Principles (FIPPs) were outdated in the new frontier of connected devices. In particular, Christopher Wolf and Jules Polonetsky, co-chairs of the FPF, point to difficulties in providing meaningful notice on devices that lack meaningful screens or user interfaces. They also question FIPPs that limit future usage of data as roadblocks to socially valuable uses of information discoverable only once data is collected. The paper proposes these new principles: (1) use anonymized data when practical; (2) respect the context in which personally identifiable information is collected; (3) be transparent about data use; (4) automate accountability mechanisms; (5) develop codes of conduct; and (6) provide individuals with reasonable access to personally identifiable information.

   Has the FPF developed principles that serve progress in information use? Or do you consider these concepts a watering-down of FIPPs?

3. *M&A and Privacy.* In a complaint against Reed Elsevier and its Seisint subsidiary, the FTC alleged that Reed Elsevier and Seisint failed to provide "reasonable and appropriate security to prevent authorized access" to sensitive consumer information. It argued, "In particular, respondents failed to establish or implement reasonable policies and procedures governing the creation and authentication of user credentials for authorized customers. . . ." Among other flawed practices, the FTC pointed to the companies' failure to establish or enforce rules that would make it difficult to guess user credentials. It permitted their customers to use the same word as both password and user ID. In addition, it allowed the sharing of user credentials among multiple users at a single customer firm, which lowered the likely detection of unauthorized services. Seisint also failed to mandate periodic changes of user credentials and did not implement simple, readily available defenses against common network attacks.

   Reed Elsevier had acquired Seisint in September 2004 and operated it as a wholly owned subsidiary within LexisNexis, more widely known for providing legal information. The FTC privacy settlement followed in 2008. The timing of this enforcement action raises questions about merger and acquisitions for companies with possible privacy and security liability issues. What kinds of checklists should lawyers work with when advising companies that wish to merge or acquire new companies? Where do you think the greatest areas of liability are located in the privacy and security areas?

4. *Data Leaks:* **Eli Lilly.** In *FTC v. Eli Lilly*, No. 012-3214, the FTC charged Eli Lilly, a pharmaceutical company, with disclosing people's health data that it collected through its Prozac.com website. Prozac is a drug used for treating depression. Lilly offered customers an e-mail service that would send them e-mail messages to remind them to take or refill their medication. In June 2001, the company sent e-mail messages to all 669 users of the reminder service announcing that the service was terminated. However, this message contained the e-mail addresses of all subscribers in the "To" line of the message. The FTC alleged that the company's privacy policy promising confidentiality was deceptive because the company failed to establish adequate security protections for its consumers' data. Specifically, the FTC complaint alleged that Eli Lilly failed to

> provide appropriate training for its employees regarding consumer privacy and information security; provide appropriate oversight and assistance for the employee who sent out the e-mail, who had no prior experience in creating, testing, or implementing the computer program used; and implement appropriate checks and controls on the process, such as reviewing the computer program with experienced personnel and pretesting the program internally before sending out the e-mail.

In January 2002, Eli Lilly settled. The settlement required Eli Lilly to establish a new security program. It was compelled to designate personnel to oversee the program, identify and address various security risks, and conduct an annual review of the security program. FTC Commissioners voted 5–0 to approve the settlement.

Consider the settlements in this case and the ones described above. Do you think that these settlements are adequate to redress the rights of the individuals affected?

5. **Microsoft Passport** *and* **Guess***: Proactive FTC Enforcement?* Microsoft launched Microsoft.NET Passport, an online authentication service. Passport allowed consumers to use a single username and password to access multiple websites. The goal of Passport was to serve as a universal sign-on service, eliminating the need to sign on to each website separately. A related service, Wallet, permitted users to submit credit card and billing information in order to make purchases at multiple websites without having to reenter the information on each site.

The FTC initiated an investigation of the Passport services following a July 2001 complaint from a coalition of consumer groups. In the petition to the FTC, the privacy groups raised questions about the collection, use, and disclosure of personal information that Passport would make possible, and asserted that Microsoft's representations about the security of the system were both unfair and deceptive. In its privacy policy, Microsoft promised that ".NET Passport is protected by powerful online security technology and a strict privacy policy." Further, Microsoft stated: "Your .NET Passport information is stored on secure .NET Passport servers that are protected in controlled facilities."

On August 8, 2002, the FTC found that Microsoft had violated § 5 of the FTC Act and announced a proposed settlement with the company. *See In the Matter of Microsoft Corp.,* No. 012-3240. The Commission found that Microsoft falsely represented that (1) it employs reasonable and appropriate measures under the circumstances to maintain and protect the privacy and confidentiality of consumers' personal information collected through its Passport and Wallet services; (2) purchases made with Passport Wallet are generally safer or more secure than purchases made at the same site without Passport Wallet when, in fact, most consumers received identical security at those sites regardless of whether they used Passport Wallet to complete their transactions; (3) Passport did not collect any personally identifiable information other than that described in its privacy policy when, in fact, Passport collected and held, for a limited time, a personally identifiable sign-in history for each user; and (4) the Kids Passport program provided parents control over what information participating websites could collect from their children.

Under the terms of the proposed consent order, Microsoft may not make any misrepresentations, expressly or by implication, of any of its information practices. Microsoft is further obligated to establish a "comprehensive information security program," and conduct an annual audit to assess the security practices. Microsoft is also required to make available to the FTC for a period of five years all documents relating to security practices as well as compliance with the orders. The order remains in place for 20 years.

The FTC took a similar approach in *In re Guess.com, Inc.,* No. 022-3260 (July 30, 2003). Guess, a clothing company, had promised that all personal information "including . . . credit card information and sign-in password, are stored in an unreadable, encrypted format at all times." This assertion of company policy was false, and the FTC initiated an action even before data was leaked or improperly accessed. The case was eventually settled.

In both *Microsoft* and *Guess*, the FTC brought an action before any data security breach had occurred. Is this a form of proactive enforcement? Suppose a company merely makes a general promise to "keep customer data secure." The FTC believes that the company is not providing adequate security and brings an action. How should the adequacy of a company's security practices be evaluated, especially in cases in which privacy policies are vague about the precise security measures taken?

6. ***The Gramm-Leach-Bliley Act and the FTC.*** Consider the following observation by Daniel Solove:

[O]ne problem with the FTC's jurisdiction is that it is triggered when a company breaches its own privacy policy. But what if a company doesn't make explicit promises about security? One hopeful development is the Gramm-Leach-Bliley (GLB) Act. The GLB Act requires a number of agencies that regulate financial institutions to promulgate "administrative, technical, and physical safeguards for personal information." In other words, financial institutions must adopt a security system for their data, and the minimum specifications of this system are to be defined by government agencies. . . .[27]

Solove argues that the security practices of many financial institutions are quite lax, as such institutions often provide access to accounts if a person merely supplies her Social Security number. Based on the GLB Act, could the FTC use its enforcement powers to curtail such practices?

7. *Cybersecurity and the Security and Exchange Commission (SEC).* A new frontier for data security concerns disclosures within the context of federal security laws. A company subject to SEC requirements faces the issue of how much information to provide investors to allow them to understand the security risks that the enterprise faces. As an article by three experts in securities litigation advises: "Ultimately, the question is not whether a publicly held company should provide cybersecurity disclosures, but how it should do so effectively."[28]

Currently, there is no specific new federal disclosure standard or requirement from the SEC concerning cybersecurity disclosures. The most important policy document currently is an October 2011 Guidance from the SEC's Division of Corporation Finance. This staff guidance finds that there is no existing rule or regulation from the SEC that explicitly refers to cybersecurity risks, but a number of existing disclosure requirements may impose an obligation on SEC registrants to disclose risks and incidents. For example, in the filing of periodical reports with the SEC, such as the SEC's Regulation S-K, a registrant "should disclose the risk of cyber incidents if these issues are among the most significant factors that make an investment in the company speculative or risky."[29]

---

[27] Daniel J. Solove, The Digital Person: Technology and Privacy in the Information Age 107-08 (2004).

[28] Howard M. Privette et al., Practice Tips, Los Angeles Lawyer (forthcoming Sept. 2014).

[29] Division of Corporate Finance, SEC, CF Disclosure Guidance: Topic No: 2, Cybersecurity (Oct. 13, 2011).

INDEX